Building the Great Society

JOSHUA ZEITZ

Building the Great Society

Inside Lyndon Johnson's White House

VIKING

VIKING
An imprint of Penguin Random House LLC

375 Hudson Street
New York, New York 10014
penguin.com

ISBN 9780525428787 (hardcover)
ISBN 9780698191594 (ebook)

Printed in the United States of America
1   3   5   7   9   10   8   6   4   2

Set in Parkinson Electra Pro
Designed by Francesca Belanger

For Angela, Lillian, and Naomi

CONTENTS

PREFACE

November 22, 1963

Why don't you pack a bag and fly with me to Fort Worth tonight?" Lyndon Johnson suggested to his friend Jack Valenti. The date was November 21, 1963, and Valenti, who ran a successful advertising and public relations firm in Houston, could scarcely foretell the lasting effect that the invitation would have on his life.

The two men first met five years earlier at a luncheon that Johnson hosted for young, up-and-coming businessmen in Texas. Valenti subsequently volunteered as a floor aide at the 1960 Democratic National Convention in Los Angeles, where LBJ vied unsuccessfully for his party's presidential nomination, and that fall directed the Kennedy-Johnson ticket's advertising in Texas. "I knew few people in the Johnson entourage," he later admitted, "though I was a Johnson man and though I supported him vigorously and wholeheartedly and without reservation. I literally was on the darker edges of the last ring of the peripheral circle."

Texas had long been a sturdy brick in the Democratic Party's firewall. It remained critical to JFK's reelection prospects, but its electorate was drifting steadily rightward. Hoping to repair a widening breach between the state organization's liberal and conservative factions, Kennedy and Johnson scheduled a multiday political and fund-raising swing that would carry them from Houston to Fort Worth, to Dallas and then Austin, and finally to the LBJ Ranch deep in the Texas Hill Country, where the first and second families would break bread together over a weekend replete with political and symbolic importance. For Johnson, the stakes were high. He had never been especially close to the Kennedy clan, and in recent years his relationship with Attorney General Robert Kennedy—the president's brother and closest political adviser—had grown sharply discordant. Quietly beleaguered by a series of slow-percolating scandals involving his personal finances, and seemingly powerless to forge a truce between liberal and conservative Democrats in his own backyard, LBJ was no longer a certain asset to the president, either nationally or in Texas. He had legitimate reason to fear persistent, low whispers that Kennedy intended to drop him from the ticket the following year.

Facing these trials, the vice president called on trusted friends from Texas to ensure a successful presidential visit. Valenti had been charged with organizing a critical leg of the journey—a dinner in honor of Representative Albert Thomas in Houston on November 21. Despite widespread concern that the city's conservative citizens would shun the president, over 350,000 cheering local residents lined the city streets to greet JFK and his wife, who had arrived at 4:23 p.m. in "the lateness of a blue-skied day," Valenti later recalled, on "the sleek, silver-bellied Boeing 707, Air Force One." Riding in the official motorcade, he noticed that his seatmate, Kenneth O'Donnell, a principal White House aide, was "dour, unsmiling," and "visibly nervous." Only when he saw the crowds—"three, four, and five deep"—did O'Donnell relax. "They're here, aren't they?" he muttered with satisfaction. "They damn sure are," Valenti replied. Privately, he was equally relieved, and even more so when over 3,000 local business and civic leaders packed the Sam Houston Coliseum for the evening's dinner reception.

Short in stature but hard to miss in a crowd—"his dress was natty," recalled one of his contemporaries, and he was "imaginative, quick-thinking and fast-talking . . . a lively, friendly, sentimental human being"—Valenti was swept up in the moment. When LBJ pulled him backstage to meet the president, Kennedy warmly shook his hand and thanked him for producing so stellar a turnout.

He very much *wanted* to join the flight to the next stop, Fort Worth, and then on to Dallas and Austin the following day, but his wife, Mary Margaret—a former secretary in Johnson's Senate and vice presidential offices—had given birth to their first child just three weeks earlier. "Is this trip necessary?" she muttered with disapproval, even as she obligingly packed an overnight valise for Jack, complete with two changes of clothing.

After the president and the vice president finished their remarks at the Houston dinner, Valenti boarded the vice president's Boeing 707—a near, but not exact, replica of Air Force One—for the journey to Fort Worth. The next morning, November 22, he flew with LBJ's entourage to Dallas, where Kennedy and Johnson were scheduled to address a luncheon at the city's Trade Mart. At Love Field, around 12:00 p.m., Valenti stepped into a van with other vice presidential and White House aides, including Evelyn Lincoln, the president's private secretary.

"The motorcade went through Dallas," Valenti would remember, "and . . . we were all remarking about how marvelous the reception was. . . . It was about as big as it was in Houston. There were no hostile faces, not even a hostile sign, which was amazing." At the head of the official column led an unmarked police car, flanked by uniformed officers on motorcycles. Next in line was the deep-blue presidential limousine, which carried John and Jacqueline Kennedy and Governor John Connally and his wife, Nellie. They were followed in turn by a heavily fortified, open-topped limousine—reporters called it the "Queen Mary"—packed with eight Secret Service agents: four in the passenger seats and four others on running boards to either side, with O'Donnell and his fellow White House aide David Powers installed in the jump seats. LBJ's gray limousine—a rental—was next in line, trailing the Queen Mary at a distance of seventy-five feet. Behind LBJ traveled the vice presidential follow car, then a vehicle carrying three members of the press pool, a transport for other members of the news media, and vans and buses conveying news photographers, video men, and local elected officials. Valenti later estimated that his van was roughly twelfth in the motorcade. As the convoy turned onto Main Street, then right onto Houston Street and left onto Elm, he witnessed the impressive multitude of office workers who cheered from the windows of tall downtown buildings and saw the crowds—five and more deep—hoisting homemade signs in the bright afternoon sun and waving with admiration at the procession. "It was a beautiful day, beautiful weather," noted a reporter who was present that afternoon.

Too far back in line to hear the piercing crack of a rifle shot, followed by two more in close succession, Valenti first sensed trouble shortly after 12:30 p.m. when "all of a sudden the motorcade began without reason to speed up, tripling the speed, maybe quadrupling it. We attempted to keep up. And we knew something was wrong because all of a sudden we got separated from the cars." Uncertain what to do, his driver steered a direct course to the Trade Mart.

. . . . .

Around the time that Valenti was marveling at the warm embrace that the citizens of Dallas had extended to the president, Pierre Salinger, Kennedy's White House press secretary, was traveling aboard SAM 86972—the tail number of a Boeing 707 jet identical to the vice president's plane—en route to an economic forum in Tokyo. Also on the flight were half of the president's cabinet, including the secretaries of the Departments of State, Treasury, Commerce, Labor, Agriculture, and Interior, and the chairman of the president's Council of Economic Advisers (CEA). Flying at an altitude of thirty-five thousand feet, with nothing but blue sky around them, the men and their wives were already nine hundred miles west of Honolulu. Salinger quietly leafed through a dense briefing book on Japanese economics, while inside the plane's cramped communications shack two news tickers—one for the Associated Press (AP), another for United Press International (UPI)—rested silent.

He was deep in study when, shortly after 12:34 p.m. central time, a disconcerting bulletin crossed the UPI wire: "Three shots were fired at President Kennedy's motorcade in downtown Dallas." From inside the communications shack, Salinger placed a call to the White House Situation Room. After a delay of several minutes, operators were able to establish a patch with the navy commander Oliver Hallett. "All available information on President follows," Hallett began, before drawing a deep breath. "[The president] and Governor Connally of Texas have been hit in the car in which they were riding. We do not know how serious the situation is. We have no information. . . . We are getting our information over the tickers. Over."

Moments later, Hallett dictated a new AP dispatch: "Kennedy apparently shot in head. He fell face down in back seat of his car. Blood was on his head. Mrs. Kennedy cried, 'Oh no,' and tried to hold up his head. Connally remained half-seated, slumped to the left. There was blood on his face and forehead. The President and the Governor were rushed to Parkland Hospital near the Dallas Trade Mart where Kennedy was to have made a speech. Over."

Salinger moved between the communications shack and the main cabin, relaying updates on the president's status. At 1:10 p.m., just forty minutes after Kennedy was struck by the assassin's bullet, the Situation Room relayed instructions from Malcolm Kilduff—the deputy press secretary who was on the ground in Dallas and unaware that SAM 86972 was already speeding a course back to Hawaii—that the cabinet return to American soil. Soon thereafter, Hallett confirmed the cabinet members' worst fear. "Ah, this is [the] Situation Room following to WAYSIDE," he began in a slow and halting voice. "We have report quoting Mr. Kilduff that the President is dead. . . . Do you have that? Over."

Salinger repeated the dispatch in a hurried tone. "The President is dead. Is that correct?"

"That is correct," Hallett confirmed haltingly. "That is correct. New subject. Front office desires plane return [to] Washington, with no stop [in] Dallas. Over."

Horace Busby first intuited trouble when he heard the UPI news ticker in his office sound four staccato-like bells. This was a rare signal on Teletypes, but Busby, a former wire service reporter who now ran a private business consultancy based in Washington, D.C., knew what it meant: "a 'flash,' a terse, one-line report of a major news development. Only matters of earthshaking moment received the priority of a flash." A native Texan and longtime friend and associate of Lyndon Johnson's, Busby was deeply familiar with the political climate in Dallas and had feared that no good could come of the presidential visit. After pausing to read the initial UPI report, he placed an urgent call to his former colleague George Reedy, who was a member of LBJ's vice presidential staff. "Quick," Busby instructed. "Read your ticker—Kennedy's shot." Jolted, Reedy dropped the phone back on its hook without responding.

Busby's next call was to the Elms, the Johnson family's stately residence in northwest Washington, D.C., where his wife, Mary, was culling through photographs and memorabilia to fashion a montage as a Christmas present for her friend Lady Bird. Such was the relationship between the two families that Mary enjoyed access to the house, even when the Johnsons were out of town. "Don't hang up," her husband instructed. "If it hasn't already started yet, everybody will be trying to call . . . and we'll never get through to you again." As they spoke, a swarm of Secret Service agents descended upon the building and grounds. "Then came the telephone men," Busby recalled, "hurrying to install the communications required for a president, not required for a vice president."

As Mary remained at her post, waiting for Lady Bird to return, Busby listened in horror to radio news reports relating the details of LBJ's swearing-in ceremony aboard Air Force One and imminent return to Washington. Shortly after 6:00 p.m., the new president telephoned from his office suite in the Old Executive Office Building and instructed Busby to meet him at the Elms. "When I arrived," Busby remembered, "a large crowd already had formed around the gate, but they were being held back by the police." Busby drove up to the entrance and rolled down his window to identify himself to the Secret Service agents posted around the perimeter. As they waved him in, he heard a reporter call out to the guard, "Who's this one? What's his name? What does he do?"

Upon reaching the Trade Mart, Jack Valenti ascertained that the motorcade had proceeded directly to Parkland Memorial Hospital. He flagged down a deputy sheriff, explained that his party included the president's secretary, and secured an escort. When he arrived, the scene outside the emergency room doors was pure chaos: cars were parked at all angles, abandoned by their drivers. Uniformed and plainclothes officers stood around the perimeter of the building. Unbeknownst to the bystanders, moments earlier the Secret Service had whisked LBJ out a side door to his limousine. The new president was en route to Air Force One.

Valenti delicately handed off Evelyn Lincoln to a policeman and talked his way inside the building, where he spied the Texas congressmen Jack Brooks, Henry Gonzalez, and Homer Thornberry out of the corner of his eye. Though at the time he did not realize it, he was standing outside the doors to the operating room where John F. Kennedy had expired just moments before. Entering an empty stairwell, Valenti encountered Cliff Carter, a longtime political aide to LBJ. "The President is dead," Carter began, "and the Vice President has me looking for you. He wants you to come out to Love Field and get aboard the airplane." The two men walked at a brisk pace to the holding room that Johnson had departed only moments earlier. From there, a Secret Service agent, Lem Johns, escorted them to a waiting police car. "The vice president wants you aboard the plane now," the agent confirmed with tight, clipped speech.

. . . . .

"Am I going to shoot this in color or black and white?" Cecil Stoughton wondered silently. Unlike Jack Valenti, Stoughton did hear the three rifle shots that rang out from the Texas School Book Depository. A captain in the U.S. Army Signal Corps who since 1961 had served as the official White House photographer, he would now capture the transfer of power from John Kennedy to Lyndon Johnson. Knowing that the wire services could not process Kodacolor or Ektachrome, Stoughton loaded the magazine of his new Hasselblad camera, and that of an older 35-millimeter job, with black-and-white Tri-X film and strapped both devices around his neck. Inside Air Force One, all the window shades were drawn shut by order of the Secret Service. The main cabin was dim and growing warmer by the minute, because the plane's air-conditioning unit only functioned when its engines operated in flight. In addition to the original Kennedy staff contingent, on board were LBJ and his wife; three Texas congressmen whom Johnson had summoned to his side; Valenti, who was "not quite sure precisely why I was even here in the first place"; Bill Moyers, a former Johnson aide who, upon learning of JFK's death, chartered a flight from Austin, where he was advancing the next leg of the trip, to make certain that he was among the president's party; and a multitude of Secret Service agents, military advisers, valets, and secretaries. In later years, Kennedy and Johnson partisans would revisit any number of slights and rebuffs—both real and imagined—exchanged by both sides during that tense hour on the tarmac. Asked about his personal recollection of the occasion, Valenti admitted that he "never saw any of the so-called friction. . . . If it was there, I was not aware of it. Of course, you must understand that I didn't know the names and faces of the players."

Stoughton considered how to stage the scene. The Boeing airliner was narrowly constructed, leaving him little means to capture the principals—"the judge holding the Bible, and Mrs. Kennedy, and Mrs. Johnson, and the President, all things being equal"—in one frame. Fortunate to be carrying a wide-angle lens, he leaned back against the wall of the compartment and "just sort of sprayed the room with my 35, so that I got pictures of everybody in there."

The fruit of Stoughton's labor was an iconic photograph displaying Lyndon B. Johnson's formal assumption of the presidency. To the far left of the frame,

Valenti can be seen pushed up against one of the plane's windows in a half-crouched position, his eyes fixed in a bewildered stare. The memory of that flight back to Washington, and of the helicopter ride from Andrews Air Force Base to the White House, would forever remain etched in his mind.

Later that evening, Valenti found himself seated on the edge of a straight-backed chair in the president's bedroom at the Elms as LBJ—clad in pajamas and perched upright in his bed—fired off a seemingly endless line of directives. Also seated around him were Moyers and Cliff Carter. Horace Busby had only just departed. Johnson's aides were wearing the same suits they had climbed into that morning. The television set remained on, casting a dim glow across the room as it broadcast an endless loop of the day's tragedy.

The new president was famously addicted to the telephone and had already placed scores of calls to congressional leaders, cabinet members, foreign heads of state, and corporate chieftains. Working out of his office in the Executive Office Building, he had been briefed by his economic and military advisers. Now, as Valenti recalled, "he was surrounded by men whom he trusted, and in whose persons he fully knew reposed love and respect and enduring loyalty to him."

"You know, when I went into that office tonight and they came in and started briefing me on what I have to do," he told his aides, "do you realize that every issue that is on my desk tonight was on my desk when I came to Congress in 1937?" Civil rights. Health insurance for the elderly and the poor. Federal aid to primary and secondary education. Support for higher education. Anti-poverty and nutritional programs. It was there in LBJ's bedroom at the Elms, twelve hours after Johnson assumed the awesome powers of the presidency, that the first cornerstone was laid for the Great Society.

Building the
Great Society

Introduction

Boundless in his appetite for power and recognition, extreme in his personal habits and style, Lyndon Johnson was both a towering historical figure and a bundle of jarring contradictions. He was a crass political operator and liberal idealist, an unbridled opportunist and steadfast champion of the poor, a southern temporizer and civil rights trailblazer, a progressive hero and bête noire of the antiwar Left. "He was cruel and kind," John Connally observed, "generous and greedy, sensitive and insensitive, crafty and naive, ruthless and thoughtful, simple in many ways and yet extremely complex, caring and totally not caring; . . . he knew how to use people in politics in the way nobody else could that I know of."

There is no shortage of literature on LBJ or his presidency, but the vast body of writing and criticism focuses on how one individual—Lyndon Johnson—plied his mastery of the political process to push an ambitious slate of liberal legislation through Congress in 1964 and 1965. But not even so dynamic a leader as LBJ could do it alone. Who helped him along the way? And what came next?

It was no small accomplishment to secure passage of the Civil Rights Act of 1964 and the Voting Rights Act of 1965. It was another matter entirely to have it mean something—to leverage the full weight of the federal government to desegregate public and private institutions peacefully throughout one-third of the United States. Persuading Congress to enact a steady profusion of liberal initiatives was a crowning achievement. Equally remarkable was the Johnson administration's success in building programs like Medicare and Medicaid from the ground up, transforming the manner in which American elementary and secondary education was funded, providing food security to tens of millions of impoverished children and adults, inventing public television and radio, and restructuring the federal government's relationship with ordinary citizens on a scale unseen since Franklin Roosevelt's tenure in office—all in the space of five years, even as the Vietnam War increasingly strained the administration's credibility and means to advance its domestic agenda.

One man could not and did not go it alone. LBJ assembled a talented and energetic group of advisers who made his vision a reality. Some of his aides, like Jack Valenti, found themselves accidentally in the right place at the right time. Others, like Bill Moyers, made sure to put themselves there. Most, like Joe Califano, were relatively young men in their thirties and early forties, though LBJ, who deliberately aspired to match and then exceed FDR's achievements, turned regularly for counsel to a small cadre of New Deal veterans whom he had known intimately since his early days in Congress. The core of LBJ's staff claimed a Texas pedigree: Walter Jenkins, Bill Moyers, and Jack Valenti; Horace Busby, Johnson's in-house intellectual of long standing; Harry McPherson and Marvin Watson, who came aboard in 1965. Yet most were men of broad learning and experience, and it sometimes astonished jaded political observers how fluidly they worked with the "best and brightest" of the Ivy League set who had come to Washington to join John Kennedy's New Frontier, only to make history in Lyndon Johnson's Great Society.

Though different in temperament and background, each staff member believed that government should play an affirmative role in creating economic opportunity for its citizens and smoothing out the rougher edges of liberal capitalism. Each was also, in his own way, as pragmatic as Johnson himself— attuned to the workings of political power, skilled in the art of throwing a sharp elbow or building an administrative empire, and hungry for position and prominence.

Richard Goodwin, a former Kennedy aide who later joined LBJ's staff as chief speechwriter, coined the term "Great Society." Often invoked interchangeably with the "War on Poverty"—a term that Johnson introduced in his first State of the Union address in 1964—the Great Society included antipoverty programs, but it aspired more broadly to complete America's patchwork safety net and maximize the individual citizen's ability to realize his or her fullest potential. In effect, the War on Poverty was just one part of the puzzle. Conservatives then and later decried the Great Society as an engine of economic redistribution that led millions of Americans into a state of permanent dependency on the government, but in truth LBJ and his aides never seriously contemplated policies that would enforce equality of income, wealth, or condition. They did not broadly support quantitative measures like cash transfers or a guaranteed minimum income but, rather, believed that qualitative measures like education, workforce training, access to health care and food security, and full political empowerment would ensure each individual a level playing field and equal opportunity to share in the nation's prosperity.

This commitment to qualitative, rather than quantitative, liberalism cannot be understood outside the context of postwar American political culture, with its prevailing spirit of confidence and triumphalism. It was little wonder that citizens living in that age exhibited great hubris. In recent memory, the United States had weathered the Great Depression and defeated fascism in both Europe and the Pacific, and in the two decades that followed, Americans benefited from seemingly boundless economic growth that vastly expanded the ranks of the middle class. Looking back on the early postwar years, the columnist Robert J. Samuelson remembered that "you were constantly treated to the marvels of the time. At school, you were vaccinated against polio. . . . At home, you watched television. Every so often, you looked up into the sky and saw the white vapor trails of a new jet. . . . There was an endless array of new gadgets and machines. No problem seemed to be beyond solution. . . . You took prosperity for granted, and so, increasingly, did other Americans."

John Kennedy captured this can-do ethos when he challenged his fellow citizens to "explore the stars, conquer the deserts, eradicate disease, tap the ocean depths . . . encourage the arts and commerce [and] heed in all corners of the earth the command of Isaiah—to 'undo the heavy burdens . . . and to let the oppressed go free.'" Echoing his predecessor's outsized ambition, LBJ called on the nation to defeat "ignorance, illiteracy, ill health and disease." Liberal economists in this era were equally ebullient. They assumed that through close management of fiscal and monetary policy, the government could sustain economic growth indefinitely. For the architects of the Great Society, it was an unspoken article of faith that the means to a more just and equal society was not cutting the pie into smaller slices so that everyone would enjoy his or her fair share but baking a larger pie. The idea that the economy might someday stop growing rarely factored seriously into liberal thinking.

Predicated as it was on qualitative measures conceived to unlock individual opportunity, the Great Society would later draw sharp criticism for what it did not do. It did not eliminate poverty. It did not effect wide-scale cash transfers or establish a minimum family income. It did not extend quality medical care and educational opportunity to all Americans. It did not save urban America from blight or depressed rural areas from further decline. Essentially, it disappointed liberal aspirations and only confirmed the worst of conservative fears. George Reedy, who served as Johnson's White House press secretary and special assistant, later surmised that the sweeping promises associated with the Great Society "may have had a negative impact on the willingness of Americans to trust such efforts." When those measures did not meet the grandiose expectations that liberals established in the heady days of 1964, many Americans came to agree with LBJ's conservative critics that government itself was the cancer, not the cure. In a scorching address delivered some two decades later, Ronald Reagan gave voice to conservative criticism of the Great Society as a bundle of expensive and failed initiatives that contributed to, rather than alleviated, poverty. LBJ's legacy reinforced the "central political error of our time," the flawed notion that "government and bureaucracy" were the "primary vehicle for social change."

Yet if Johnson and his aides overpromised, they also outperformed. Few presidents have left in place so sweeping a list of positive domestic accomplishments. Fifty years after the fact, it is all but impossible to imagine the United States without Medicare, public television, integrated hotels and restaurants, federal aid to primary and secondary schools, or federally guaranteed college loans—all measures that continue to enjoy wide support. Moreover, if LBJ's Great Society failed in its ambition to eliminate poverty, it took a sizable bite out of it. The government normally measures poverty on the basis of pretax cash income, but when economists factor in noncash assistance including food stamps, Medicaid, and housing subsidies (all products of the Great Society) and tax adjustments like the earned income tax credit (a product of the Nixon administration), the poverty rate fell by 26 percent between 1960 and 2010, with two-thirds of the decline occurring before 1980. Some groups, like African Americans and the elderly, experienced a precipitous drop in poverty. Others, including children, did not. LBJ's domestic programs assumed that economic output and wages would continue to grow in perpetuity; they were

not designed to combat trends that neither the president nor his staff anticipated, including the rise of single-parent households, stagflation, supply
shocks, globalization, and—most important—stagnant wages in the 1970s and
beyond.

Equally underappreciated is the political capital that Johnson and his aides
readily spent down in the cause of laying Jim Crow in his grave. Excepting
Abraham Lincoln's government, no administration then or since pulled the
levers of government with such unwavering resolve to disrupt the economic,
political, and social privilege that many white Americans had long assumed
was their birthright. Desegregation was not a solitary building block of the
Great Society; it was a central theme that ran throughout most of its key initiatives, from health care and education to voting rights and urban renewal.
Moreover, Johnson's White House knowingly took the fight beyond the South
and challenged much of the hidden privilege that white northerners had grown
to expect—privilege that came in the form of the "de facto," or seemingly accidental, segregation in residential neighborhoods, schools, and workplaces.
With great valor came great risk. By numbers alone, far more white Americans
than black Americans benefited from the Great Society, but the administration's full-throated support for racial equality led many white voters to identify
Johnson's domestic programs as a minority handout. The Democratic Party
paid—and continues to pay—a heavy political price for its support of civil rights.

Several weeks after Johnson became president, Bill Moyers met with him in the
Yellow Oval Room on the second floor of the White House residence. Used by
most presidents from Lincoln through FDR as a private library or study, the
room now functioned as a formal living room and parlor. There, Moyers found
the president scrawling out columns and dates on a yellow legal pad:

> *November 22, 1963, to January 19, 1965.*
> *January 20, 1965, to January 19, 1969.*
> *January 20, 1969, to January 19, 1973.*

Alongside these columns he wrote, "1964, win. 1965, P&P"—propose and
pass. "And then for 1967," Moyers recalled, "it said 'hold gains.'" Johnson

looked up from his notepad and explained, "Bill, I've just been figuring out how much time we would have to do what we want to do. I really intend to finish Franklin Roosevelt's revolution.... In an ideal world ... we would have about 110 months to his 144 months.... I'll never make it that far of course, so let's assume we have to do it all in 1965 and 1966, and probably in 1966 we'll lose our big margin in the Congress. That means in 1967 and 1968 there will be a hell of a fight."

It was a moment of striking clairvoyance. The fight came when expected, but Johnson could not then have anticipated its source: the conflict in Vietnam. The war did much to undermine LBJ's credibility and standing with the American public. More fundamentally, it catalyzed economic and social trends that would erode the very intellectual foundation of the Great Society. When it became clear by 1967 that the country could not afford guns *and* butter—that permanent growth without inflation was in fact an elusive dream and that equal opportunity often fails to deliver equal results—Johnson's project fell into disrepute. For some fifty years, he would be known, at best, as a "flawed giant" who, in his own words, "left the woman I love—the Great Society—in order to fight that bitch of a war." At worst, he was the exemplar of runaway liberalism.

But history has a way of restoring focus. Far from the master legislator and failed executive of popular lore, LBJ was a skilled chief executive who assembled one of the finest White House staffs in modern history and exhibited as much success in establishing and administering programs as he did in securing their passage. Regarded as a poor and bumbling country cousin when compared with his intellectually dashing predecessor, in fact he drew more abundantly on the talent and expertise that resided in America's university campuses and think tanks. A product of the New Deal era, when the country's best minds gravitated to Washington to labor in agencies whose obscure names masked their true significance, Johnson appreciated both the power and limitations of the federal bureaucracy and taught his aides how to make it work like a finely tuned machine. A man of vast personal ambition, he deliberately drew down his political well in advance of causes that he knew to be controversial in their own time, and he encouraged his young staff to appreciate that power is only as meaningful as how—and for what purpose—one uses it.

"He felt entitled to every available lever, to help from every person, every branch of government, every business and labor leader," recalled Joe Califano, one of the brightest of the bright young men who brought LBJ's domestic agenda to life. "After all, as he often reminded us, he was the only President we had."

PART I

CHAPTER 1

Put the Ball Through the Hoop

Seated behind his desk in the Oval Office, Lyndon Johnson appeared pensive and subdued when, on the evening of Thursday, November 28, 1963, he delivered brief remarks to the nation. It was 6:15, and LBJ was only in the sixth full day of his presidency. "Tonight, on this Thanksgiving, I come before you to ask your help, to ask your strength, to ask your prayers that God may guard this Republic and guide my every labor," he began. "All of us have lived through 7 days that none of us will ever forget. We are not given the divine wisdom to answer why this has been, but we are given the human duty of determining what is to be, what is to be for America, for the world, for the cause we lead, for all the hopes that live in our hearts." Reading with deliberate care from a prepared text, the president acknowledged what was surely on every American's mind: "A great leader is dead; a great Nation must move on. Yesterday is not ours to recover, but tomorrow is ours to win or to lose."

The day before, LBJ had delivered his first speech before a joint session of Congress—a solemn and widely acclaimed address in which the new president pledged to pick up the mantle from John F. Kennedy and secure passage of the New Frontier's sweeping but stalled policy agenda, including a major tax cut that Kennedy's advisers believed would stimulate the economy; aid to primary and secondary education; and hospital care for seniors. Dozens of LBJ's former colleagues from Dixie sat in stone-cold silence as Johnson affirmed to stirring applause that "no memorial oration or eulogy could more eloquently honor President Kennedy's memory than the earliest possible passage of the civil rights bill for which he fought so long. We have talked long enough in this country about equal rights. We have talked for one hundred years or more. It is time now to write the next chapter, and to write it in the books of law."

Now, on Thanksgiving, Johnson doubled down, asking his countrymen to join him in prayer "for His divine wisdom in banishing from our land any injustice or intolerance or oppression to any of our fellow Americans whatever their opinion, whatever the color of their skins—for God made all of us, not some of us, in His image. All of us, not just some of us, are His children."

For most Americans, Thanksgiving week marked the start of the holiday season. For Lyndon Johnson, it signaled the beginning of an intense, yearlong sprint to prove that *he* could break the logjam, achieve the New Frontier, and surpass it beyond even the wildest expectations of John Kennedy's supporters. It would be no easy lift.

"I think the Congress looks more powerful sitting here than it did when I was there in the Congress," Kennedy remarked roughly a year before his death. For well over two decades, a coalition of conservative southern Democrats and northern Republicans had stymied the expansion of domestic policies first established during the New Deal era. In the Senate, an institution that the journalist William White once dubbed "the South's unending revenge upon the North for Gettysburg," conservatives made frequent use of the filibuster to prevent social welfare and civil rights legislation from coming to a vote, while in the House powerful southerners kept such measures forever bottled up in committee. Now, in a sharp rebuke to Kennedy's promise of dynamic action and national rejuvenation, the conservative coalition had all but ground the government to a halt. Not only did the House and the Senate refuse to take up key New Frontier measures. They *also* refused to pass eight of twelve routine appropriations bills, thus leaving whole parts of the government unfunded and operating on a continuing resolution that set spending at the previous year's levels.

Congressional Quarterly deemed the state of affairs "unprecedented," while Walter Lippmann, the dean of American journalism, bemoaned the "scandal of drift and inefficiency" that had beset Washington. "This Congress has gone further than any other within memory to replace debate and decision by delay and stultification. This is one of those moments when there is reason to wonder whether the congressional system as it now operates is not a grave danger to the Republic." Yet as Harry Truman famously asserted, the buck stopped with the president. A week before Kennedy's assassination, the columnist James Reston noted "a vague feeling of doubt and disappointment about

President Kennedy's first term.... He has touched the intellect of the country, but not its heart. He has informed but not inspired the nation. He is the most popular figure, but he has been lucky in his competition.... [H]is problem is probably not how to get elected but how to govern."

Such was the state of affairs when Lyndon Johnson entered the White House.

LBJ first came to Washington as a young congressional staff member in the early 1930s before returning to Texas in 1935 to serve as state director of the National Youth Administration (NYA), a marquee New Deal jobs project. Two years later, and against all odds, he won a special election to Congress at age twenty-eight. An ardent supporter of Franklin Roosevelt, Johnson established a more liberal voting record than most southern Democrats with whom he served in the House. Though he consistently opposed legislation to abolish the poll tax and to make lynching a federal crime, he joined northern Democrats in supporting expanded rights for organized labor, greater administrative oversight of business and industry, and funding for public works. Notably, he continued to do so long after most of his southern Democratic colleagues forged an informal alliance with northern Republicans to oppose the Roosevelt administration. On the strength of his New Deal credentials, FDR strongly backed Johnson in a special election to fill an unexpired Senate seat in 1941. LBJ most likely won the primary (in Texas, as throughout the South, the only vote that mattered), but party rivals stole it from him in a brazen display of election-night ballot fraud. Though in the coming years he aligned himself more closely with his state's oil and gas interests, when he ran a second time for the Senate in 1948, Johnson was once again recognized as the liberal option. After achieving a razor-thin primary victory over the conservative former governor Coke Stevenson—this time, it was likely LBJ's allies who stole the election—Johnson drifted rightward during his two terms in the Senate, in part out of recognition that Texas was moving strongly in that direction and in part to curry favor with the chamber's powerful southern chairmen, most notably Richard Brevard Russell of Georgia. Johnson delivered his maiden floor speech in opposition to civil rights, turned against former New Deal allies who now stood accused of communist loyalty, and, in his time as Democratic leader after 1953, cooperated closely with the Eisenhower administration. Many of the liberals in his caucus came to despise LBJ, particularly after he neutered their civil rights bill in 1957. They correctly perceived that he wanted to pass a weak bill in order to make his prospective presidential candidacy in 1960 palatable to northern Democrats but unobjectionable to his fellow southerners. On the day that he assumed office, very few people knew what to make of Lyndon Johnson. Was he simply a pragmatist who, deep in his heart, remained an ardent New Dealer? Or was he a southern conservative who would betray John Kennedy's unfinished legacy?

If Johnson's belief system was a matter of wide speculation, few observers doubted his keen understanding of Congress. LBJ knew that conservative Democrats, in loose cooperation with Republicans, had willfully manufactured a bottleneck of important legislation to form a bulwark against Kennedy's civil rights bill. Only when liberals capitulated and withdrew the Civil Rights Act would southern Democrats consent to bring Kennedy's tax stimulus to a vote and fund the many government initiatives—including bridges, highways, post offices, and defense projects—that their more liberal and moderate colleagues hoped to deliver to hometown constituents. Johnson knew the playbook because, as a freshman senator, he had helped to write it. As long as conservatives could hold the government hostage, much as they had in 1949, when they successfully fought back Harry Truman's civil rights agenda, they could forestall consideration of Kennedy's New Frontier agenda, including civil rights legislation that lay dying on the Hill.

It took LBJ less than a day to spring into action. In a series of phone calls before and after Thanksgiving 1963, the new president highlighted the imperative of using his political capital to clear the logjam; then, and only then, would members of Congress feel at liberty to bring civil rights and other New Frontier measures to a vote. In the meantime, however, he would keep up the pressure. On Saturday, November 30—just over a week after assuming the presidency—LBJ asked the former Treasury secretary Robert Anderson, a Republican and outspoken fiscal conservative, to intervene with Howard Smith, the chairman of the Rules Committee, which had broad authority to prevent legislation from proceeding to the House floor. Johnson reminded Anderson that "this country is not in any condition to take that kind of stuff . . . and that's going to hurt our people. And it's going to hurt the conservatives." Anderson agreed to speak with Smith and to convey the president's willingness to support a seldom-used measure—a discharge petition—to bypass Smith's committee altogether and bring the legislation directly to the full House.

Playing the other side just as artfully, Johnson placed a call to Dave McDonald, the president of the United Steelworkers of America (USWA) and a member in good standing of the liberal coalition. "They've got to petition it out," the president instructed. "That means we got to get 219. We'll start at about 150 Democrats; that means we got to get 60, 70 Republicans." The president spoke with the passion of a true believer ("we've been talking about this for 100 years. And they won't give us a hearing on this thing, so we got to do something about it") and implored McDonald to fire up his union's formidable lobbying operation—not only to support the discharge petition in the House, but also to move the tax and appropriations bills through committee.

Before and after the Thanksgiving holiday, Johnson repeated these conversations time and again, at once lining up support for a discharge petition in the House while affirming the need to clear the logjam of tax and spending bills *before* making a final push on civil rights in the Senate. Among those who understood the president's strategy was Senator George Smathers, a conservative Democrat from Florida who ultimately opposed the Civil Rights Act of 1964 but who represented a faction of the southern caucus that was disinclined to grind all government to a halt indefinitely over civil rights. The "sooner we can get a civil rights bill over with," he told Johnson, "get that part of it ended and out of the way, the better off the South's going to be, and the better off the North's going to be, and the better off everybody's going to be. And they wouldn't hide behind the tax bill—and hide behind a lot of other bills, just on the pretense of being against them when the real fact is they're against the civil rights bill."

Without prompting—and without the knowledge that LBJ had been making a similar case to his economic advisers for several days—Smathers suggested that the president make a concerted effort to woo Harry F. Byrd, the deeply conservative chairman of the Senate Finance Committee. If Johnson were willing to indulge Byrd's obsession with fiscal discipline and bring the 1964–1965 federal budget under $100 billion, then the chairman *might* allow the tax cut to clear through his committee. "Wish you'd feel Byrd out," LBJ agreed, "and give me a pretty good, full report." Unknowingly, George

Smathers would help set in motion a chain of events whose consequences would be far reaching.

The strategy that Lyndon Johnson developed in the first week of his presidency had a profound but highly calculated effect. The pressure that his supporters placed on Howard Smith—and the chairman's realization that a discharge petition, if successful, would permanently undermine his authority— persuaded the cantankerous Virginian to allow the Civil Rights Act to reach the House floor. Beginning with outreach from Smathers, LBJ simultaneously courted Harry Byrd until the patrician senator effectively agreed to swap budget cuts for a tax stimulus. With major economic legislation now cleared through Congress, the president had paved the way for passage of long-awaited civil rights legislation.

Just before the Thanksgiving holiday, some of Johnson's advisers cautioned him that presidents should not spend valuable capital on hopeless causes. "Well," he purportedly replied, "what the hell's the presidency for?"

LBJ ultimately brought his budget under $100 billion, pushed Kennedy's tax cut through Congress, and secured passage of the Civil Rights Act—all by late June 1964. He accomplished these measures while also declaring an "unconditional war on poverty" and creating the blueprint for the Great Society— the most ambitious domestic agenda since the New Deal. Though LBJ's early success owed in part to his mastery of legislative strategy, equally fundamental were efforts by advocacy groups—religious and lay alike—on behalf of civil rights and social justice legislation. Above all, Johnson benefited from a deep well of public support in the wake of Kennedy's assassination. The president's approval ratings, which fluctuated between 70 percent and 77 percent throughout the spring, owed at least as much to the country's determination to lock arms with its new leader as to LBJ's policy and political triumphs.

Unlike most of his predecessors, LBJ did not enjoy the benefit of a transition period to build the team that would help him, in turn, build his vision. Instead, he had little choice but to improvise on the spot—to pull a trusted friend like Jack Valenti along with him to the White House or entreat old hands from his House and Senate days to join him on a new and unfamiliar journey. These handicaps notwithstanding, in that first year of seemingly unrestrained activity and accomplishment—from the time of Kennedy's death to his own election to the presidency in late 1964—Johnson assembled an ad hoc staff that defied the expectations of even the most cynical Washington hands. They were a "coalition government" of Kennedy and Johnson men—a "strange amalgam of Austin and Boston, of cool, brainy Easterners and shrewd, folksy Texans, of men who had always been fiercely loyal to him and men who had fought and belittled him before the 1960 Los Angeles Democratic convention," according to Charles Roberts, who covered the White House for *Newsweek*. "It is some kind of tribute to Isaiah and the LBJ Way that the transition went as smoothly as it did."

"We are like a basketball team," Bill Moyers remarked during his tenure in Lyndon Johnson's White House. "To the spectator in the stands, what goes on down on the floor may look haphazard, with men moving back and forth in all directions. But each player on the court knows how to handle the ball, and what he's doing, and what the others are doing. There's no quarterback on the field to call signals. All our orders come from the coach—the President."

Having cut his political teeth as a congressional aide and, later, as Texas state director of the National Youth Administration, Lyndon Johnson had long appreciated the value of staff. During his two terms in the Senate, and especially during his six years as majority leader, he assembled what was arguably the most talented bench of speechwriters, policy experts, and legislative draftsmen in the institution's history. But in the same way that the vice presidency had deprived him of most trappings of power, during his years as John F. Kennedy's understudy LBJ had been obliged to make do with a skeletal organization. Gone were the legions of lawyers, idea men, secretaries, and political operatives who once filled the disparate office space that Johnson commandeered across far-flung corridors of the U.S. Capitol and Senate Office Building. Consigned to a three-room suite at the Old Executive Office Building and another in the Capitol, Johnson's small coterie reflected his diminished standing as vice president, a position that Daniel Webster once partially declined to seek on the grounds that "I do not propose to be buried until I am dead."

Now, as president, LBJ would command a White House staff numbering 250 political, policy, and clerical workers, in addition to 1,350 members of the Executive Office of the President, an administrative umbrella that included the Bureau of the Budget, the National Security Council, the Council of

Economic Advisers, and the Office of Emergency Planning. In addition, there were myriad cabinet departments and their affiliate agencies whose combined workforce numbered in the hundreds of thousands. The question was not *whether* Johnson would command the necessary resources to perform the responsibilities of president but *whom* he would tap to work by his side.

A White House staff member, Pierre Salinger later observed, "must be completely devoted to the man who is President. He must be willing to spend all his waking hours working for the President. He must sympathize with and support his general goals but be willing to argue with the President on specific policy decisions." Above all, he "can have only one loyalty—to the President himself." In all of these matters, there was little question that one man, above all, would serve as major-domo of Johnson's White House. Walter Jenkins was not just "*the key* staff member for at least twenty-five years," a senior Johnson aide once remarked, but "almost integral to his life."

Forty-five years old, Jenkins had been born into a struggling farm family in Jolly, Texas. After two years at Wichita Falls Junior College, he attended the University of Texas at Austin until 1939, when he could no longer afford the tuition. He managed somehow to earn an interview with Lyndon Johnson, who helped him secure a patronage position as a Capitol police officer. From there, Jenkins joined LBJ's congressional staff, rising quickly from clerk to de facto chief of staff. George Reedy, another longtime aide, viewed Jenkins as the "stabilizing force" in Johnson's congressional office, where LBJ demanded "loyalty," "real loyalty. I want someone who will kiss my ass in Macy's window and stand up and say, 'Boy, wasn't that sweet!'" Years later, a fellow congressman recalled joining LBJ for a drink in his hideaway office at the Capitol. Johnson buzzed for Jenkins, "the door opened, and there was this guy—shirt rumpled, tie askew, face pale, standing in the door holding a yellow legal pad waiting for orders—like a slave." And Jenkins took it for over two decades, interrupting his association with Johnson only twice—during World War II, when he served in the Quartermaster Corps in Africa and Italy, and in 1951, when he ran unsuccessfully for a congressional seat in Texas. Over the years, LBJ came to rely on Jenkins to oversee both his political and his personal affairs—a wide-ranging assignment that required him to file the Johnson family's taxes, intercede in their thriving radio and television business, collect and disperse political contributions on behalf of Senate Democrats, and manage the offices of the Senate majority leader and—later—vice president. He exhibited "brains, ability and political savvy," one observer noted. He was "the senior staff man," his fellow White House aides later insisted, and the only one who could truly claim "total rapport" with the new president. Yet in a city where most men would have reveled freely in their physical proximity to the Oval Office, Jenkins was "self-effacing" to a fault, a newspaperman observed, and quietly "satirized as the man who works best in the dark because he flatly denies interviews."

"Above all, Walter Jenkins was the man who was close to the President," recalled the historian Eric Goldman, who joined LBJ's presidential staff in early 1964. "The relationship was never confused. One was the boss, the other the employee. But the men and their families were like Johnson City neighbors, the one having done better in the world but each understanding and moving easily with the other." Their daughters Luci Johnson and Beth Jenkins were best friends. The very day the First Family moved into the White House, Lyndon and Lady Bird dined as guests at the home of Walter and Margie Jenkins. "It is difficult for a man in the presidency to find people who will say no," a Johnson White House staff member later observed. "And Walter did have that capability, because he was such a close confidant." James Rowe, a prominent Washington attorney who had known LBJ since the New Deal era, "always felt talking to Walter was like talking to Johnson."

Jenkins's authority sprang not only from his nearness to Johnson but also from his calm and steadying demeanor. "With no expression of liberal doctrine—a product of roughhouse Texas politics," Goldman observed, "he simply did not think in terms of liberalism or conservatism—he had a straightforward conviction that America is different, and that this special land, with all its talent and wealth, should create opportunities for ordinary people, like those from Jolly, Texas, to have better housing and food, a chance to finish college and higher odds on being able to enjoy the sunnier aspects of living."

Jenkins had been lunching at the Congressional Hotel on November 22 when he first heard of Kennedy's assassination. "I had a very sick feeling at the pit of my stomach," he remembered years later. Not long after returning to the vice president's suite, Jenkins received a summons from the West Wing. Requisitioning a vacant staff office, he monitored events by television until, soon enough, White House operators patched through a barrage of calls from the new president, who by years of habit began assigning him a multitude of responsibilities, large and small. "He called me once to get the wording of the oath," Jenkins recalled. "He called me once to ask me whether I had any feeling as to whether he should be immediately sworn in or not." In a city where proximity is power, Jenkins now found himself in a startling and altogether new dynamic. Kennedy aides who an hour earlier gave little consideration to what the staff members at EOB 274 thought about anything now turned to Jenkins to ask, "What do we do about this, you're making the decisions?" It was "very hard for me," he confided to an interviewer some years after the fact. "I didn't want [the responsibility]."

Johnson informed him that Air Force One was carrying a large contingent back to Washington and requested that marine helicopters be on hand at Andrews Air Force Base to convey the passengers to the White House. Walter Jenkins, putatively the chief counselor to the president of the United States, had no idea whom to call. "I didn't know anything about how you accomplished those things," he admitted. Just weeks later, he "sat in his big office in the West Wing," Goldman remembered, "suit baggy, his middle collecting fat, his dark hair graying and his face turning the more florid the wearier he became, endlessly doing a sweeping variety of tasks."

While the "self-effacing" Jenkins would serve as LBJ's untitled chief of staff, he was "not an idea or program initiator in the sense that Clark Clifford, Sherman Adams and Ted Sorensen were," explained Carroll Kilpatrick, the *Washington Post*'s chief White House correspondent. For those needs, the president turned instinctively to Horace Busby, a former member of his House and Senate staff who remained his in-house intellectual and speechwriter even after departing his direct employ. "Buzz," as friends affectionately called him, was the son of a Church of Christ preacher in Fort Worth. Freckled and wavy-haired in his youth and "seeming every inch the all-American boy," he enrolled at the University of Texas, where he became editor of the student newspaper. When the oil barons who controlled the university's board of trustees fired President Homer P. Rainey, a strong-minded reformer and champion of academic freedom, he turned out a chain of scorching editorials that earned him an exaggerated but enduring reputation for radicalism.

In fact, since the age of eight, when he sat rapturously in front of his parents' wireless to hear FDR accept the Democratic Party's presidential nomination, Busby had identified as a staunch but conventional New Dealer. "I'm going to go to Washington. I'm going to live in Washington and see presidents someday," he informed his parents. "I meant to. I mean, I meant to be a correspondent, eventually when I understood about newspapers." While his classmates followed baseball box scores and movie stars, Buzz flipped the pages of *Time* and *Life* and avidly read syndicated political columns chronicling affairs of state in the heady days of the New Deal. "You had Washington at one level, and you had the European situation, the war coming on at another," he remembered. "I was just juiced up above my eyebrows on this stuff before I was a junior in high school." Busby was employed as a statehouse reporter in Austin for the International News Service when, in 1948, Johnson plucked the young man—then just twenty-five years old—for his congressional office. At first, Buzz resisted Johnson's overtures. The staff job would occasion a sharp pay cut and, more important, would obligate him to subordinate his intellectual autonomy to the famously high-handed congressman. "There was no way in the world I was going to work for Lyndon Johnson," he thought to himself. But as Busby and others would learn, when Lyndon Johnson set his hooks in, there was no escape. At LBJ's prodding, Lieutenant Governor Allan Shivers implored him to accept the job—"You'll learn more from Lyndon in a year than you'd learn from all of us around here in ten years," he insisted. Buzz acquiesced but did not intend to linger long. At the very least, he could realize his boyhood ambition to work and live in Washington and perhaps even attend the Democratic National Convention in Philadelphia. After a year on staff, he might pole-vault his way to a reporting job with one of the New York dailies.

But life took another course. LBJ and Busby developed an almost instant affinity. A political animal himself, Johnson admired Buzz for his encyclopedic knowledge of Washington in the 1930s. "I knew those kinds of nuances, I knew the slogans, I knew the minor characters on the New Deal stage here," Busby reflected. "These things that I knew from my unusual and freakish . . . close study of the period, this was the stuff of Lyndon Johnson's life. . . . Well, this was rapport. Here was somebody he could [communicate with]. Here was this little fellow from the corner in his office that he could sit with and he could just re-live all this. Whether I was in his office or I was in a car with him or I was on a trip with him, it was that. He wasn't just talking to me about history, he was talking about what we had to do in this country. That's what he talked with me specifically about the night that I first met him."

In Johnson's House and Senate offices, Busby served as a minister without portfolio. His principal mandate was to generate ideas. The most successful politicians, LBJ told Busby, "'have some little fellow in their office who sits back in a corner. He doesn't have to have any personality, doesn't have to know how to dress, usually they don't have their tie tied right, a button off their shirt'—typical Johnson, running on at this—'nicotine stains on their fingers, no coat, all like that. But they sit back in the corner, they don't meet any of the people that come in the office. They read and they think and they come up with new ideas, and they make the fellow smart. I've never had one of those, and I want one.'" Off and on, for the better part of two decades, Buzz would play that role for Johnson. A White House reporter noted that their long association was marked by "several angry separations and friendly reconciliations," because Buzz consistently demonstrated less alacrity than his colleagues in surrendering to LBJ's unmannerly treatment.

After parting from LBJ's staff in 1951, Buzz returned to Austin and founded the *Texas Businessman*, a subscription newsletter whose tone and tenor increasingly sounded more in harmony with the state's right-wing professional class than with the New Dealers he lionized as a child. He soon aligned himself with the conservative faction of the state Democratic Party, led by Shivers, who acceded to the governorship in 1949, and Price Daniel, the state's other U.S. senator. Though both men were engaged in a bitter power struggle with moderate and liberal Democrats led by Lyndon Johnson, Busby's relationship with his onetime mentor did not appear to suffer for it. Buzz returned briefly to LBJ's employ in 1957 to assist in the Senate's "Sputnik investigation" and author the Space Act and later served as an unpaid aide during Johnson's unsuccessful presidential campaign in 1960. In between, he moved his family back to Washington, founded a successful consultancy, the American International Business Research Corporation, and rechristened his increasingly profitable newsletter the *American Businessman*. He also accompanied Johnson, who was now vice president, on a series of overseas trips.

Within official political circles, Busby fast acquired the "reputation of having become a standpatter," explained Goldman. "His newsletters had a businessman's ring and occasionally talked of liberals with asperity," and on the topic of John Kennedy's New Frontier he was especially cutting. "Kennedy's 'thinkers'—despite academic credentials—haven't innovated," he grumbled in a typical display of pragmatic derision for intellectuals who opined about, but could not achieve, lasting reform. "They are tinkerers, mechanics. Thus far, they've wrought very little of moment." But his was not a simple case of political apostasy. Busby "remained open and freewheeling, his conversation roamed left and right, his humaneness was undiminished."

In his capacity as a private adviser to the vice president, in 1963 he urged LBJ to accept an invitation to speak at Gettysburg National Cemetery on Memorial Day. Later that year, Americans would commemorate the centenary of Abraham Lincoln's dedication speech, and now, over a long, poolside conversation at the Elms, Buzz took a mental recording of Johnson's spontaneous and heartfelt sentiment about the meaning of that occasion. He returned home and typed out a short address that he believed captured the spirit of their discussion and thought nothing more about it until the *Washington Post* ran the text in its entirety on the front page. "One hundred years ago, the slave was freed," Johnson intoned. "One hundred years later, the Negro remains in bondage to the color of his skin. The Negro today asks justice. We do not answer him—we do not answer those who lie beneath this soil—when we reply to the Negro by asking, 'Patience.'" In a speech that excoriated the stall tactics that Johnson's Senate colleagues had deployed to block civil rights legislation, the vice president insisted that "our nation found its soul in honor on these fields of Gettysburg one hundred years ago. We must not lose that soul in dishonor now on the fields of hate."

Though some observers worried that Busby would pull Lyndon Johnson to the political right, on balance he would exert a strong and decidedly liberal— if not always crusading—influence on the new president.

Within a matter of weeks, Buzz—whom one colleague assessed as "one hell of a nice guy," "a genial man, just turned forty, stocky, soft-mannered and rarely without a good-humored word for everyone"—sold his interest in the American International Business Research Corporation and for the second time in his life took a steep cut in salary to work for Lyndon Johnson. Installing himself first in a palatial suite of rooms in the East Wing, and later in a small office just three doors from the Oval, he gradually assumed the responsibilities of senior speechwriter and cabinet secretary—the chief liaison between the White House and the various executive agencies that would administer LBJ's Great Society programs.

Rounding out LBJ's new "Texas mafia" was Bill Don Moyers, who rushed to Johnson's side on November 22 and swiftly became the president's indispensable man. He was, according to the new president, "about the most unusual 29-year-old I ever saw."

The son of a struggling truck driver and candy salesman, Moyers grew up in Marshall, Texas, where he excelled in high school and subsequently matriculated at North Texas State College in Denton. After his sophomore year, Bill—an ambitious, earnest sort who had been voted both class president and "most outstanding" boy on campus—wrote an ingratiating letter to the state's senior senator, Lyndon Johnson, seeking summer employment. He was deliberating on his major, he explained, and a tour in Washington might help him decide between government, journalism, and education. After checking his credentials with a local newspaper editor, LBJ offered the young man a temporary position in his Washington office. In a matter of weeks, Moyers graduated from addressing form letters by the thousand with a rickety foot-pedal machine to managing LBJ's personal correspondence. Impressed by his drive and acuity, Johnson helped him secure a transfer to the state's flagship public university at Austin and offered him a "part-time" job at the Johnson family's television affiliate, KTBC, where he ultimately worked fifty-hour weeks reporting news and traffic. The job not only secured his relationship with Johnson and paid his tuition; it also enabled him to marry his college sweetheart.

After graduating from UT, Moyers won a Rotary International Fellowship to the University of Edinburgh. There, his wife, Judy, taught school in a nearby coal town while Bill studied the interplay between church and state in Western civilization and developed a keen passion for Greek literature. (His White House colleagues later fell squarely into two camps: those who smiled in knowing approval and those who privately rolled their eyes when, as he was wont to do, he described the president's health policy adviser as exhibiting honor "that would have led Diogenes to extinguish his lamp.") Returning to Texas, Moyers spent a year at Southwestern Baptist Theological Seminary, became an ordained minister, and considered accepting a faculty position at Baylor University. But "there was something about being called 'reverend' that I couldn't endure and my wife couldn't either," he explained. Bill joined LBJ's presidential campaign and, despite his youth and inexperience, emerged as a trusted aide and able tactician. "John Connally is a really tough man," another aide observed of LBJ's longtime staff assistant and the future Texas governor, "but he couldn't organize him. But that Moyers, who was just a kid, could organize him. He could get him to do things he should do when none of the rest of us could. I suppose it was Moyers' gentle patience that did it."

He remained on staff through the fall campaign and carefully cultivated relationships with key advisers to the Kennedy family. Though Johnson asked him to join his vice presidential office, Moyers had something different in mind. Possessed of an evangelical reform spirit, but also attuned to where real power would lie in the new administration, he secured an introduction to Sargent Shriver, a Kennedy brother-in-law who had been designated to lead the Peace Corps—the New Frontier's signature initiative—and eventually rose to become the agency's director of public affairs. Through his close association with Shriver and his deliberate cultivation of younger, low-level and mid-level Kennedy aides, Moyers, more than anyone else on LBJ's White House staff, could credibly claim to be both "an authentic Johnson man and an authentic New Frontiersman," as Tom Wicker of the *New York Times* argued. He was a "useful linchpin holding Kennedy and Johnson men together."

Charles Roberts sized up Moyers as "a slight, bespectacled, scholarly-looking, 160-pound six footer" who looked "more like Clark Kent than Superman." But he was formidable. From his perch at the Peace Corps, and "in imitation of his mentor, LBJ," observed Goldman, "he began building an empire. He started binding to himself—by camaraderie, by favors given and favors hinted, by a general air of pushing ahead together—a number of younger men throughout the federal government." Given his religious piety and association with the Peace Corps, he soon gained recognition—deserved or not—as the social conscience of LBJ's White House. (For a time, the new president encouraged this notion: not long before he delivered the speech that heralded his Great Society program, Johnson instructed Moyers to "get your Bible . . . and get us some good quotations on equality, and we're all of God's children . . . you mark yourself a lot of good quotations on it, and then get a central theme and a good lead.") Jack Valenti later ventured that the robe "tended to lull people into a false sense of security, I mean, give them the idea that this was a nice young man. . . . But Bill was a technician in the use of power."

Well-known and equally well regarded within staff circles, Moyers settled easily into his new presidential staff role, even before he formally left the Peace Corps. Two days after Kennedy's assassination, Johnson spoke by phone with the civil rights leader Whitney Young, who explained that he and Roy Wilkins, the executive director of the National Association for the Advancement of Colored People (NAACP), had not managed to secure tickets to the funeral. The president used Moyers as a back channel to Shriver, who promptly made arrangements. "All right," Johnson told Young. "Now if you don't [receive the tickets], you call Bill Moyer [*sic*] through the White House switchboard."

"Bill Moyer?" Young asked in confirmation.

"Yeah. M-O-Y-E-R [*sic*]. He's my assistant," Johnson responded.

"Yes, I know him."

It took little time before *everyone* knew Bill D. Moyers. "As molder of the President's legislative program—the man to whom task forces, Cabinet officers and speechwriters submitted their ideas—he is more nearly the architect of the Great Society than any other man save the President himself," Roberts informed readers in early 1965. "He is involved in more policy decisions in more areas of government than any other Presidential aide. . . . He is the *primus inter pares* (first among equals). . . . He is, according to one LBJ friend, the President's 'good angel, representing his conscience when there's a conflict between conscience and expediency.'"

Exhibiting the same calculated earnestness that drove his critics to distraction, Moyers insisted that he was not an "exciting, interesting, mysterious person behind the scenes. I'm just here helping a friend, and when that ends I'll drift away and never be heard of again."

When Horace Busby first left LBJ's employ in 1951, the man whom he recommended as his replacement was George Reedy, an erudite newspaperman who graduated from the University of Chicago and served as an intelligence officer in the Pacific during World War II before moving to Washington to cover

Congress for UPI. "Six feet two inches tall, the loose body barely concealed in sagging suits, ponderous in walk and speech, Reedy had a swift, powerful mind, a delight in books and talking about them," recalled Goldman. He had "an instinct for philosophical quandrums, and a quiet, subtle religious faith."

During Johnson's tenure as majority leader, Reedy served as policy director, press secretary, and liberal alter ego. He was a shrewd counselor, and his outsized personality matched his expansive frame. "George lived a life that only a political junkie could live," Harry McPherson recalled. He would arrive at the office late in the morning, hours after most staff members had begun work. By routine, around 6:30 p.m. he made his way to an Italian restaurant near Eastern Market, where, in the company of reporters and labor leaders, he would inhale "an enormous number of martinis" before returning to the office at 11:30 p.m. to turn out another policy or political memorandum for LBJ.

Jim Rowe would later maintain that "George was a mirror of [Johnson's] thinking. I had trouble deciding which was which.... George had been around him so much he knew exactly how he thought, and knew how he would react." Yet as was so often the case in his interaction with staff members, LBJ's relationship with Reedy was rife with contradiction. Johnson regarded Reedy as a genuine intellectual and political asset, but he could also prove unfailingly cruel. A prodigious drinker, smoker, and eater, Reedy fluctuated in weight from as little as two hundred pounds to almost three hundred pounds and suffered from chronic hammertoes and hypertension. "I remember one time standing with Johnson on the [Senate] floor and George came heavily almost like Willy Loman down the halls and off to the chamber," McPherson told an interviewer, "perspiration coming down his face, face white, painfully coming across the floor, Johnson was saying, 'Look at George moving his fat ass across the floor.' I mean it was said with real contempt for this guy who was just busting his tail in every way for Lyndon Johnson and who adored him, who thought he was the greatest of all men." Such abuse was typical of LBJ, who routinely showered invective on his most loyal retainers—even those, like Reedy, for whom he felt genuine affection. When Reedy's obesity began to pose a real health threat in 1964, the president phoned George's physician, arranged for hospitalization and a weight-loss regimen, and offered to cover the bills. On another occasion, LBJ administered a "terrific tongue lashing" to Reedy but subsequently bought him a car—not at all out of character for Johnson, who lavished expensive gifts on his staff members.

Reedy, who had "grey hair *en brosse* and puffs at a pipe" while lecturing his audience on all manner of topics, impressed one veteran reporter as a "large, rumpled man whose ponderous approach sometimes obscures a well-stocked and active mind." There was a limit to LBJ's patience for his longtime aide; he sometimes preferred reading his memorandums to speaking with him in person. But there was little doubting LBJ's trust in his intellect and instinct. "You ask him what that tree is over there, and he'll tell you who first brought it to this country and talk half an hour before he tells you what you wanted to know in the first place," the president complained. "But he knows what he's talking about."

On the afternoon of Kennedy's assassination, Reedy had been working out of his office on the Senate side of the U.S. Capitol, where vice presidents traditionally based their small staffs. He first learned of the news when Busby telephoned him. Jenkins called him later in the afternoon and asked that he come directly to the White House. Though he was one of the president's longest-serving aides, Reedy shared his colleague's hesitation to overstep his place. "Both Walter and I took the position that we didn't want to be issuing orders or making determinations at that particular point," he later explained. "All we really knew, and our information was extremely sketchy . . . was what was on the ticker." On the helicopter to Andrews Air Force Base, Reedy sat beside Ted Sorensen, one of JFK's most trusted advisers, with whom he had been acquainted since their days as Senate staff members. He escorted the new president back to the Executive Office Building, where, the next morning, he reported directly for work. Weeks later, he installed himself in the White House; for the time being he would serve as a general utility player, hammering out policy and political memorandums and turning his years of service to good use in helping Johnson channel his inner liberal.

From the start, Johnson was determined to keep Kennedy's core White House aides in place. He understood that his Texans were untried and untested and that his early success was contingent on the appearance of continuity with JFK's New Frontier—a sentiment that he expressed in the most memorable line of his address to Congress on November 27: "Let us continue." In his first moments as president, aboard Air Force One as it sat on the runway at Love Field, Johnson huddled with Kenneth O'Donnell and Larry O'Brien, two of Kennedy's closest and most trusted aides, and pleaded with them to remain at their posts. "I need your help," he implored. "I need it badly. There is no one for me to turn to with as much experience as you have. I need you now more than President Kennedy needed you." It had been less than two hours since JFK died, and both men were still profoundly in shock. "We can talk about all that later, or some other time," O'Brien muttered. O'Donnell was equally "noncommittal," by his own account.

Among Kennedy's senior staff, O'Brien, who directed congressional outreach for the White House, was first to commit to the new president. The son of an Irish tavern keeper in Springfield, Massachusetts, O'Brien was a skilled and widely respected political operative who became acquainted with the Kennedys in 1952, when he agreed to work on Jack's first Senate race. He was a key architect of JFK's blowout reelection campaign in 1958 and engineered pivotal victories in the Wisconsin and West Virginia primaries in 1960. After directing political activities in the general election campaign, O'Brien staked his claim on the White House office of legislative liaison, only to learn that Jack and Bobby Kennedy felt it was a poor fit for someone with negligible experience on Capitol Hill. When he threatened to pack his bags and return to Springfield, the Kennedys relented, in part because they did not want to anger O'Brien's many supporters among the party's leadership ranks, but also because they envisioned little movement on domestic legislation in JFK's first term and regarded the legislative function as less important.

Because O'Brien was a long-standing member of Kennedy's "Irish mafia," a triad of senior advisers that also included O'Donnell and David Powers, LBJ might have assumed that he was loath to remain at his post. Certainly he pulled out all the stops in his courtship. In early December, he invited O'Brien and his wife to a private dinner at the Elms and plied them with gifts, including a bottle of perfume for Elva O'Brien and a sports shirt emblazed with the initials "LBJ" for Larry. Such gestures first left him uncomfortable, though by Christmas, when Johnson gave him an engraved wristwatch, O'Brien came to appreciate the president's solicitousness. Unlike the Kennedys, the Johnson family routinely invited aides to the White House residence for cocktails or dinner. "He would be interested in your wife and that she was included. Elva got to really love Lady Bird, and she was very much involved, which was not the case with Jackie. The situation was considerably different."

Johnson was a careful student of other people and quickly sized up his opportunity. Unlike many of his colleagues in the Kennedy White House, O'Brien was not a scion of Harvard or Yale, or a veteran combat officer, but a working-class graduate of Western New England University who had been drafted into the army as an enlisted man and, because of poor eyesight, never saw combat. He regarded himself as a trusted political associate of the Kennedys but not a "social friend." Conscious that he lacked the "Harvard style," he soon developed a more natural rapport with LBJ, who "ran an elevator and then . . . worked in a congressional office." LBJ encouraged him to make this connection. "I had gone to night law school, I was not part of the Eastern Establishment, I had worked for a congressman as a young guy, I had struggled in the boondocks of politics, in the nuts and bolts of politics. I had worked arduously and I had made a contribution to the legislative program, and it was high time that the record recognize me by title. That was really his whole pitch, and I think he really felt that way, that he and I did have a lot in common, and we did. . . . He wasn't the son of immigrant parents, but his years as a youth and the economic struggle and all was very much comparable to mine." Like Johnson, he regarded himself as "very much a New Dealer" in spirit. "I could equate with Lyndon Johnson's view of social problems, because as a kid my family and relatives and friends had many of the same experiences that Johnson's associates had when he was a young fellow. And we shared a strong, strong feeling about the Roosevelt era and what it meant. I think it had political connotations because it made us even prouder to be Democrats."

From the earliest days of his presidency, Johnson relied on the informal counsel of three friends whom he had known since the New Deal era: Jim Rowe and Clark Clifford—the architects of Harry Truman's improbable, come-from-behind electoral strategy in 1948—and Abe Fortas, a title partner in the powerful law firm of Arnold, Fortas & Porter.

Rowe was a native of Butte, Montana, who moved east at the age of eighteen to attend Harvard University. After remaining in Cambridge to earn his law degree, in 1934 he relocated to Washington, D.C., where he served as clerk to Oliver Wendell Holmes Jr., who—like many other retired Supreme Court justices—still maintained chambers. After Holmes's death, Rowe cycled between high-level posts at a number of New Deal agencies, including the Reconstruction Finance Corporation, the Public Works Administration, the Securities and Exchange Commission, and the Labor Department, where he helped launch Aid for Dependent Children (later renamed Aid to Families with Dependent Children). By the late 1930s, he was assigned to the White House, where he served as Franklin Roosevelt's chief administrative assistant, a role in which he enjoyed considerable influence. It was roughly around this time that the freshman congressman Lyndon Johnson befriended him. LBJ relied on Rowe and his wife, Elizabeth, for introductions to the city's leading New Deal staff members. The Johnsons soon enjoyed regular invitations to dinner parties at the Rowes' home, where Lyndon would suck the air out of the room and engage the other guests in long—often amusing—monologues until, eventually, "people would drift off and start having their own conversations. When he saw he had lost his audience, he would just go to sleep, just sit there [at the table] and go to sleep." The friendship was genuine, though each man benefited from his association with the other. When LBJ ran unsuccessfully for an unexpired Senate seat in 1941, Rowe, at FDR's direction, aggressively funneled federal projects through Texas to benefit the young, New Deal congressman. When the navy rejected Rowe in 1943 because of his poor eyesight, Johnson intervened to secure him a commission.

As deputy attorney general, adviser to the Nuremberg war crimes tribunal, campaign manager for Adlai Stevenson in 1952, and a partner in one of Washington's most prestigious law firms, Rowe built a distinguished career in parallel to Johnson. He was one of very few individuals whom Johnson regarded as an equal, though LBJ being LBJ, there was always a caveat. After suffering a near-fatal heart attack in 1955, he beseeched Rowe to take leave from his practice and join his Senate office. "I can't afford it," Rowe repeatedly demurred. "I'll lose clients." His real concern was that he would suffer the same abuse that Lyndon imposed on all of his beleaguered staff members. But Johnson was relentless. "People I knew were coming up to me on the street—on the *street*," Rowe later remembered, "and saying, 'Why aren't you helping Lyndon? Don't you know how sick he is? How can you let him down when he needs you?'" LBJ managed to enlist Rowe's law partner, Tom "the Cork" Corcoran, the legendary New Deal wunderkind and Washington, D.C., fixer. "You can't just do this to Lyndon Johnson!" Corcoran implored. "Never mind the clients. I'll hold down the law firm." He even conscripted Elizabeth Rowe, who asked her husband, "Why are you doing this to poor Lyndon?" Rowe took a leave of absence and, as he suspected, endured daily abuse from his temporary boss, the Senate majority leader. After a single session of Congress, he returned to his law practice.

In 1960, Rowe managed LBJ's unsuccessful bid for the Democratic presidential nomination. The two friends feuded bitterly over the campaign's direction, culminating in a vituperative exchange of accusations and insults. After that episode, they "more or less drifted apart," as Rowe later recalled. He would occasionally brush shoulders with LBJ and could not help but note the shabby way in which Robert Kennedy and other New Frontiersmen treated the vice president, but until November 1963 he kept a distance. Three days after taking the oath of office at Love Field, Johnson personally reached out to his onetime friend and—in a rare display of contrition—apologized for his role in breaching their friendship. It was an emotional conversation for both men. "My God, Mr. President, it wasn't your fault," Rowe said, with tears in his eyes. "Yes, it was," Johnson replied. "Don't argue with me. Just be content to be the first man to whom the 36th President of the United States has offered his apologies."

Rowe later concluded that Johnson was "touching all his old bases as soon as he became president.... He was seeing all his old friends that he had known from the beginning of the New Deal. Not so much he wanted their help, which he did want, but it's almost like a superstition, coming back and touching all these things."

Johnson offered Rowe various government appointments, including the post of budget director, a job that the president knew his friend had very much wanted ten years earlier, had Adlai Stevenson won the presidency. But Rowe was content to remain a close adviser, of but not in the White House.

Clark Clifford was a young attorney and navy reservist when in the spring of 1945 a local acquaintance from his hometown of St. Louis, Commander

James Vardaman, arranged his appointment as a military aide to fellow Missourian Harry Truman, who acceded to the presidency after FDR's death in April. Tall, wavy haired, and endowed with strong, chiseled features, Clifford looked the part. Despite his political inexperience, by 1946 he earned appointment as special counsel to the president, a senior role recently occupied by Roosevelt's indispensable legislative draftsman and political adviser, Sam Rosenman. In November 1947, Clifford and Rowe presented Truman with a forty-seven-page memorandum that laid out the elaborate strategy behind his improbable victory the following year, a coup for which they remained famous almost two decades later.

When Jim Rowe served as the top staff man to FDR, Johnson enjoyed essentially unfettered access to the Oval Office. He enjoyed no such preexisting relationship with "this curly-haired fellow, Clifford," who "doesn't want the President to be around southerners and political types," LBJ groused to Horace Busby in 1948. In fact, Truman had initially been friendly enough to Johnson, inviting him several times to sail on the presidential yacht and to meet with him at the White House. But after 1947, when Johnson joined other southern conservatives in voting to override the president's veto of the Taft-Hartley Act—a law that sharply curtailed the right of workers to join unions and bargain collectively—the president locked LBJ out.

In the years after he left government service and launched a successful law practice in Washington, D.C., Clifford would encounter LBJ every few months, usually on the cocktail circuit, though he was "a friend who was available to him as a consultant and as an advisor" and sometimes offered his assistance to the Senate majority leader or vice president. But their relationship, if cordial, "was not a real close one." That dynamic changed in November 1963. The day after JFK's assassination, Johnson summoned Clifford to the Elms, where the two men conferred from early afternoon until late evening, interrupted or joined by a flurry of aides and advisers who cycled through the temporary presidential residence. "From then on the relationship . . . really achieved an entirely different image and purpose and function," Clifford later recalled. "He had this mean job . . . and I had served as a presidential adviser for some four or five years before." He functioned thereafter as one of LBJ's wise men—an informal, outside adviser until 1968, when he agreed to join the cabinet.

. . . . .

Abe Fortas and Lyndon Johnson first made each other's acquaintance in 1938. Fortas—a Yale Law School graduate who came to Washington at the invitation of his mentor, the SEC chairman and future justice William O. Douglas—and LBJ, who was then serving his first term in Congress, belonged to a tight social network of upcoming New Dealers who shared a common ambition and liberal affinity. The group included LBJ and his wife, Lady Bird; Rowe, who was then serving as FDR's executive assistant; Clifford and Virginia Durr, who would later earn a place in history as friends and advocates of the civil rights pioneer Rosa Parks; and Justice Hugo Black and his wife, Josephine. The bonds that they forged over cocktail parties at the Johnsons' small apartment on Connecticut Avenue or back-garden cookouts at the Black family's more stately home on Seminary Hill would, with some strains and exceptions, last a lifetime.

After serving in a string of powerful New Deal posts, Fortas entered into private practice and swiftly emerged as one of Washington's highest-paid attorneys. By happy coincidence, he was on business in Dallas in late 1948, precisely when LBJ needed help in a last-ditch effort to overturn a federal court ruling that would have removed his name from the general election ballot pending resolution of a hotly contested U.S. Senate primary. Fortas devised a complicated, risky, and ultimately successful strategy that involved deliberately losing an appeal at the circuit court level in order to kick the case to Hugo Black, who enjoyed jurisdiction over the Fifth Circuit. The rest was history.

Even as he built a lucrative practice representing clients in the private sector, Fortas remained a committed advocate of liberal reform. He and his law partners, Thurman Arnold and Paul Porter, were among a handful of prominent attorneys who represented government employees before anticommunist loyalty boards in the late 1940s. "Everybody, I assume, now knows that in the thirties and part of the forties, thousands of fine, thoroughly non-Communist people contributed to Spanish relief organizations, attended anti-Fascist meetings, participated in rallies against Hitler, joined in organizations to promote friendship with the Soviet Union when it was our wartime ally," he explained. Now such past activities threatened to derail the careers of longtime civil servants and even result in criminal trials or public shaming before House and

Senate committees. Fortas and his partners handled most such cases at cost; their defense of Owen Lattimore, a leading Near East expert whom Joseph McCarthy publicly accused of spying for Russia, racked up $2.5 million in shadow billings. "We of course take his and all other cases for nothing and, if necessary, put up expenses," he told a reporter. They did so, he later explained, because "we were 'liberals.' We were New Dealers." If they lost corporate business because of their full-throated defense of McCarthy's victims, it was an outcome that the partners were willing to tolerate. "There are some things you have to do in order to live with yourself," he told a reporter.

Most famously, in 1963 Fortas provided pro bono representation for Clarence Gideon, a Florida man who had been convicted of a pool hall burglary two years earlier. Appearing before the U.S. Supreme Court, at whose request he agreed to serve as counsel, Fortas argued that the State of Florida had denied Gideon—who had been too poor to afford a lawyer at his original trial—due process rights. The resulting opinion in *Gideon v. Wainwright* established the fundamental right to counsel. Fortas never actually spoke with his client. "Why the hell would I want to meet a son of a bitch like that?" he told one of his cousins. "He's no good." He was motivated solely by the opportunity to establish a key civil liberty. That the Court had invited his participation was itself a justification for taking the case. It was "like a Presidential invitation to dine. Few are turned down." Eight months later, he would receive just such an invitation when his old friend Lyndon Johnson moved into the White House.

Over the years, Fortas had served LBJ informally as a legal and political adviser. That relationship intensified after Johnson became president. Days after Kennedy's assassination, Fortas found himself in LBJ's bedroom at the Elms until 2:30 a.m. helping to finish the draft of Johnson's speech before Congress.

Johnson repeatedly pressed him to accept a staff position in the White House; after Robert Kennedy left the cabinet, the president urged him to serve as attorney general. Fortas, who enjoyed his growing law practice and the comfortable lifestyle it afforded him, resisted at every turn. "I am desperately trying to avoid a government post," he told a friend. But even in private practice, his time and talent inevitably shifted to matters of state and politics. Another lawyer in his firm recalled that by early 1964 Fortas seemed to spend more time in the Oval Office with the president than attending to business. No sooner would he return to his desk and begin leafing through a mounting pile of draft briefs and phone messages than the "President would call and that was the end of it." When Paul Porter told LBJ that Fortas simply did not have enough hours in the day to practice law and serve as an on-call counselor to the president, Johnson replied tartly that he could "get up a little earlier in the morning."

Days after Kennedy's assassination, LBJ telephoned Larry O'Brien, unaware that Kenny O'Donnell was also in his office. "Needless to tell you, I'm most anxious for you to continue just like you have been, because I need you a lot more than he did," LBJ opened. O'Brien let out an audible sigh. "Mr. President," he began, "did you—Ken is here with me. Did you—do you have any immediate problem?"

A close intimate of the Kennedy family, O'Donnell had roomed with Bobby at Harvard and, after service in the U.S. Army Air Force during World War II, worked as campaign scheduler and political fixer on both of Jack's Senate races, as well as the 1960 presidential campaign. Possessed of sinewy features, a tightly wound demeanor, and a "grim, cryptic wit," O'Donnell was a tough and formidable operator. As White House appointments secretary, he exerted wide-ranging influence on the administration's agenda by controlling access to the Oval Office. "I found him to be one of the most candid and direct men I had ever met," noted Pierre Salinger, the White House press secretary. "He would never use five words if one would do, and that word was very often a flat 'no.'"

For days after the funeral, overcome by grief, he simply stopped coming to the office until Johnson, acting out of both personal concern and genuine need, instructed Jenkins to track him down. "He was bleary-eyed and unshaven" when Jenkins finally saw him. At first demurring, he ultimately pledged, "If I can, I'll be here Monday morning. I'll be ready to work, and I'll do everything I can. If I find I can't, I'll tell you so and know you'll understand." As Jenkins later recounted, O'Donnell resurfaced on "Monday morning and went to work, shaven and ready to go, and did, I think, a good job."

LBJ was equally determined to keep Salinger on staff. A rotund and expressive former investigative reporter, Salinger had transformed Kennedy into

America's first television president, first as director of press relations on the 1960 campaign and later in his role as White House press secretary. Johnson, who lacked JFK's native appeal with reporters, would need his skill set. In his first weeks with the new president, Salinger exhibited a strong determination to fit in, but in so doing, he unwittingly made his own life a living hell. As Arthur Schlesinger acidly observed in his private diary, "There is nothing more dangerous, so far as I can see, than being accepted by Johnson as one of his own." LBJ proved "meticulously polite" to Kennedy staffers, but "when he starts regarding them as Johnson men, their day is over. He begins to treat them like Johnson men, which means like servants. . . . Of all the Kennedy people, [Salinger] seemed to make the transition most easily—which meant that LBJ began shouting at him, ordering him around and humiliating him just as if he were Jenkins or Valenti."

Like many other liberal intellectuals, Schlesinger, a Pulitzer Prize–winning historian who took leave from Harvard to join the White House staff, had long held Johnson in disdain. But he was not entirely wrong: after a smooth several weeks in which the president and his press secretary seemed to become fast friends, LBJ began tormenting Salinger in ways large and small, compelling him at one point to don a cowboy suit that was anything but flattering to his heavy frame. "For all his striped shirts and big cigars, Salinger is a literate and subtle man, and not disposed toward cornball humor and a folksy approach," a reporter noted. "When I saw Lyndon having fun with Salinger and putting ten-gallon hats on him and so on, I just had a feeling Salinger wasn't going to wear that hat very long." He stuck by Johnson through early spring before departing the White House to run for the U.S. Senate in California.

Unsurprisingly, Schlesinger—whose East Wing office location spoke to his subordinate standing in the Kennedy administration—had little interest in staying on. He "declared war, I guess, the day that John F. Kennedy went into the ground," a fellow Kennedy aide said. Schlesinger privately mourned that it was "almost unbearable to watch that graceful witty, incandescent personality" replaced by the boorish image of Lyndon Johnson. By late January, he had resigned his position.

Gone, too, was Ted Sorensen. Johnson lobbied hard to retain Kennedy's longtime ghostwriter and most trusted of aides, out of both genuine respect for his talents and a pragmatic desire to maintain continuity with the New

Frontier. In the days immediately following JFK's assassination, the new president demonstrated extraordinary patience with Sorensen, who, when asked to draft LBJ's first address to Congress, included the line "I who cannot fill his shoes must occupy his desk." Most of the speech, though not that sentence, survived, but Sorensen deeply resented edits by Valenti, Abe Fortas, and Hubert Humphrey that ultimately worked their way into the text. Riding in the presidential limousine to the Capitol, Johnson gently tried to soothe his bruised ego. "You've got 80 percent of your stuff in there," he insisted. Days later, Katharine Graham, the publisher of the *Washington Post*, advised LBJ to show Sorensen "a little love." He was "marvelous," she insisted, but also "very hurt. I encountered him and I know the mood he was in, and I don't forgive him for it, but . . . we all have to just imagine how he feels, in that he is a man who [instead] of crying did this really naughty trick of being cantankerous and hurt." Despite Johnson's genuine efforts, Sorensen's heart was no longer in it. In late February, he submitted his formal resignation, which LBJ reluctantly accepted.

Hardened observers of national politics were genuinely surprised that "the mingling of Boston Brahmins and Texas Longhorns" proved as harmonious as it did. Joseph Alsop, a syndicated columnist who enjoyed wide influence, was impressed by the "continuity of the Johnson White House with the Kennedy White House," calling it "one of those very rare political events that are distinguished from the common run by the credible roles played by everyone concerned. Shabbiness and pettiness are generally to be found somewhere in every political process; but for once they have been absent." The Texas mafia—Jenkins, Moyers, Valenti, and Reedy—"miraculously but quite pointedly refrained from throwing their weight around," while the Kennedy partisans "have seen that they had a duty left to perform, not least to the lost president." In later years, the mounting feud between LBJ and Robert Kennedy would feed the perception that Johnson and Kennedy staff members were locked in unremitting struggle. The assumption was patently incorrect.

Bill Moyers, who likened the White House staff to a basketball team (and whose colleagues, in future years, would accuse him of hogging the ball), fairly summed up the role as such: "We all have one common goal—to put the ball through the hoop."

CHAPTER 2

Participation in Prosperity

W alter Heller, the chairman of the Council of Economic Advisers, would later recall the prevailing sense of unease and apprehension after SAM 86972 abandoned its original course for Tokyo and landed in Honolulu on the afternoon of November 22. Military officials posted armed soldiers with fixed bayonets around the plane's perimeter and instructed the cabinet members to remain inside the aircraft while it refueled. After receiving a briefing from the commander in chief of the Pacific forces, the officials took flight for Washington. Heller huddled in the back of the cabin with the cabinet secretaries Orville Freeman (agriculture), Luther Hodges (commerce), Stewart Udall (interior), and William Wirtz (labor). "The five of us had a long, long seminar, so to speak, on Lyndon Johnson," Heller would relate, "everybody tossing in his impressions. We went back to the events of 1960, going back to the relationships they had had one way or another over the years, what kind of man was this, and so forth."

They all agreed that there was little doubting LBJ's intelligence, but they were divided in their assessment of his political worldview. Some envisaged a deeply conservative Johnson presidency: LBJ was, after all, a former member in good standing of the Senate's "southern caucus" and had racked up a checkered legislative history that gave cold comfort to liberals. Others wondered if he were not more of a southwestern populist, remembering the young, New Deal congressman who might now move the country in a liberal direction. All agreed that he would likely be an impossible man for whom to work. "He'll just suck the guts out of you," one of the cabinet members warned.

Of all aboard the plane, Heller was arguably the most liberal and thus the most heavily invested in knowing what made Johnson tick. His father, a civil engineer in Milwaukee, had lost his job in the Great Depression, and had it not been for FDR's Works Progress Administration, the family would have been left penniless and without recourse. After earning his bachelor's degree from Oberlin College, Heller pursued graduate work at the University of Wisconsin, where a grant from the National Youth Administration—the same New Deal agency that LBJ administered in Texas—supported his doctoral research on state income taxes. During World War II, he helped engineer the federal government's income tax withholding system and later served as an adviser to General Lucius Clay, the military governor of Germany. He then spent the better part of fifteen years as an economics professor at the University of Minnesota, but in 1961 he traded the comfort and clubby environment of academic life for JFK's New Frontier.

As the key architect of JFK's tax cut—the very same measure that LBJ ultimately secured in 1964—Heller had struggled for several months to obtain Kennedy's support for a comprehensive federal initiative to combat poverty. Just three days before the assassination, he met with the president in the Oval Office to issue yet another plea for dedicated planning and resources. At last, he appeared to achieve a breakthrough. "Yes, Walter," the president assured him, "I am definitely going to have something in the line of an attack on poverty in my program. I don't know what yet. But, yes, keep your boys at work, and come back to me in a couple of weeks." Now, with Kennedy gone and an ostensibly more conservative president holding the reins of government, it was not altogether clear that his initiative would survive. Even *with* the new president's support, success was uncertain, given the state of Congress.

When Heller visited Johnson at the Executive Office Building early on Saturday evening, he raised the question of the poverty program and seemed to get a promising response. As the meeting appeared to wrap up and Heller—pleasantly surprised by Johnson's zeal in the antipoverty cause—stood to leave the office, "the President gently pushed [the door] shut and drew me back in." Leaning in close, LBJ unleashed his full powers of persuasion. "Now, I want to say something about all this talk that I'm a conservative who is likely to go back to the Eisenhower ways or give in to the economy bloc in Congress," he began. "It's not so, and I want you to tell your friends—Arthur Schlesinger, Galbraith and other liberals—that it is not so. . . . If you looked at my record, you would know that I am a Roosevelt New Dealer. As a matter of fact, to tell you the truth, John F. Kennedy was a little too conservative to suit my taste." As he later recalled, Johnson ended the meeting by affirming that the antipoverty initiative was "my kind of program. I'll find money for it one way or another."

The conversation was an iconic display of performance art, LBJ-style, designed in large part to earn the good grace of liberals who instinctively distrusted the president. But Johnson proved good to his word. On January 8, in his first State of the Union address before Congress, he boldly declared an "unconditional war on poverty." The "chief weapons" in this attack would include "better schools, and better health, and better homes, and better training, and better job opportunities to help more Americans, especially young Americans, escape from squalor and misery and unemployment rolls where other citizens help to carry them."

It was a lofty and even audacious proclamation—one that later critics would condemn for its seemingly impossible promise. But in that time and place, and for that president living in that moment, it made all the sense in the world.

Lyndon Johnson and his aides assumed that they could do it all because they lived in a wondrous age almost without parallel in American history. In the quarter century following World War II, the United States experienced an economic boom unprecedented in scope and size. Median family income grew by a stunning 30 percent in the 1950s, driving the typical American's transition from renter to homeowner, from blue-collar to white-collar worker, and from a culture of Depression-era scarcity and wartime rationing to postwar consumer abundance. Between 1950 and 1960, the average American family experienced a 330 percent hike in purchasing power, reflecting an amazing 55 percent increase in the gross national product over roughly the same period. These trends continued unabated into the next decade.

Affluence cannot be counted by numbers alone. By the late 1960s, most families enjoyed access to a broad range of consumer luxuries that were not even imaginable at the end of World War II, including Polaroid cameras; hi-fi stereo systems; long-playing records; electric refrigerators and freezers; cars with automatic transmissions, tubeless tires, and power steering; shopping malls; fast-food restaurants; and electricity, which almost one-fifth of households still lacked as recently as 1945. In 1950, only 3 percent of farm families owned televisions; ten years later, that figure rose to 80 percent, while almost all suburban and urban homes had at least one set. Americans also started drinking diet soda, cooking on nonstick pans, reading by halogen lamps, listening to audio cassettes, and wearing permanent-press clothing and soft contact lenses.

Abundance radically transformed the way that American policy makers thought about their country. In the bleakest days of the Great Depression, most liberal intellectuals and elected officials had agreed in some form or another that capitalism was foundationally broken. FDR's chief aide, Harry Hopkins, foresaw permanently high levels of unemployment "even in future 'prosperity' periods," while Alvin Hansen, a prominent economist who taught at Harvard University, warned in his presidential address to the American Economic Association in 1938 of a future marked by "sick recoveries which die in their infancy and depressions which feed on themselves and leave a hard and seemingly immovable core of unemployment." Against so gloomy a backdrop, many reformers assumed that government could mitigate the human toll of permanent economic contraction only by making broad and even radical changes to capitalism's underlying structure—changes as wide-ranging and sometimes inconsistent as public ownership of utilities and factories, a guaranteed family income, a breakup of monopolies and trusts or, conversely, industrial cartels invested with sweeping power to set uniform wages and prices. But the experience of World War II, in which the United States emerged as the world's "arsenal of democracy," forced a swift reappraisal of these reformist and, in many ways, radical assumptions. The federal government built ships, airplanes, and tanks by the thousands. It raised, supplied, and deployed a military force of sixteen million men. It defeated fascism in Europe and the Pacific and took a leading hand in establishing postwar economic order around the globe. In so doing, the government lifted the country out of the Depression and proved that through skilled planning and economic management policy makers could provide, as the labor leader Walter Reuther described it, "full production, full employment and full distribution in a society which has achieved economic democracy within the framework of political democracy." American capitalism "works," the economist John Kenneth Galbraith marveled a decade later, "and in the years since World War II, quite brilliantly." Thinking back on the New Deal era, Chester Bowles, who led the Office of

Price Administration during the war, recalled that "many frustrated economists told us that there was little more that we could do" to fix the country's underlying economic problems. "We must learn to live with a certain amount of scarcity in the midst of plenty," they had insisted. But now America was growing, and its "population isn't going to stop growing, technology isn't going to stand still, and all these new plants and machines . . . will steadily increase our ability to produce."

The growth of the federal state during the New Deal and World War II pushed the boundaries of how actively the federal government could manage the nation's economy by pulling the fiscal and monetary levers available to the executive branch. Many postwar liberals came to believe as an article of faith that through careful application of Keynesian economics expert bodies like the Council of Economic Advisers—created in 1946—could calibrate government spending to ensure sustained growth. Unlike the Roosevelt administration's halting embrace of countercyclical spending in 1935 and 1936—followed by its return to budget consciousness in 1937, which produced the "Roosevelt Recession"—postwar Keynesians did not view deficits just as temporary instruments to fight economic down cycles. Instead, they believed that such measures should be employed even in relatively flush times to drive the economy to full capacity. In this belief, they rejected as arbitrary and unscientific the idea that balancing the budget in a specific calendar year should outweigh the more farsighted work of creating full employment and output. Once the economy operated at peak capacity, tax revenues would erase whatever temporary deficits were incurred to secure growth.

Liberals needed little convincing that through expert management of the economy they could achieve full employment and low inflation. Signs of prosperity were seemingly in rich abundance everywhere. Richard Hofstadter, an influential historian and public intellectual, spoke for many on the center left when he observed that "a large part of the New Deal public, the jobless, distracted, and bewildered men of 1933, have in the course of the years found substantial places in society for themselves, have become homeowners, suburbanites, and solid citizens." Over 7.8 million Americans availed themselves of the G.I. Bill of Rights to attend college and vocational schools, and millions more benefited from G.I. housing loans that propelled them into suburban splendor. It was a decade when bulldozers and cement mixers swiftly transformed vast reaches of American farms and forests into so many streets and cul-de-sacs, each lined by rows of brand-new white Cape Cod homes, and when increasing numbers of middle-class and working-class employees enjoyed previously unimaginable benefits like annual cost-of-living adjustments to their wages and salaries, employer-based health insurance, paid vacations, and private pensions. Capitalism, which in recent memory seemed to have run its full course, was now functioning with great efficiency. This point, in turn, led many Democrats to rethink some of their long-standing ideas about policy and politics.

During the Depression, many liberals had advanced radical reforms to break up banking and industrial interests and reallocate resources; now they envisioned a consensus culture that was essentially classless in nature. Unbounded growth extended the promise of unlimited prosperity. If in the 1930s many liberals cheered mass strikes and demonstrations as necessary instruments to spur a redistribution of wealth, by the 1950s they regarded mass politics warily, particularly when it took the form of radical anticommunism, which seemed eerily parallel to European fascism of very recent memory. The sociologists David Riesman and Nathan Glazer captured this paradox neatly when they observed that many intellectuals felt a closer kinship with Wall Street, which was more tolerant of "civil rights and civil liberties"—two postwar liberal priorities—than with their "former allies"—"the farmers and lower classes of the city."

Firm in their belief that America had solved the twin problems of poverty and economic stability, liberal writers in the 1950s muted their criticism of capitalism and, in an ironic twist, fixed much of their criticism on *how* members of the once-impoverished working class—now comfortably ensconced in middle-class suburbs, leading happy middle-class lives—chose to spend their money. They deplored the "techno-burbs," with their "haggard men" all catching the same train each morning, each wearing the same gray flannel suit as the other, coming home to his "tense and anxious" wife and "gimme kids." Prosperity, wrote the critic Dwight Macdonald, had overwhelmed high culture and reduced the United States to an ugly amalgam of "Masscult and Midcult": the former embodied by the intellectually flimsy output of Disneyland, dime-store fiction, and commercial television; the latter, by faux intellectualism of the sort on display in the pages of the *Saturday Evening Post* or Book of the Month Club selections (offensive because it "pretends to respect the standards of High Culture while in fact it waters them down and vulgarizes them"). In a representative demonstration of liberal derision, a writer for the *Nation* sneered that the typical Middle American "buys the right car, keeps his lawn like his neighbor's, eats crunchy breakfast cereal, and votes Republican." Other critics fretted that affluence and suburban banality had stripped people of their personal agency, thus generating "alienation," a mass "identity crisis," an "age of anxiety," a "lonely crowd" composed of formerly autonomous, "inner-directed" individuals who had been reduced to "out-directed" conformists. Whereas liberals in the age of Franklin Roosevelt celebrated the ordinary worker and endeavored to secure for him or her a modicum of economic security, twenty years later they tended to worry more about the spiritual and cultural impoverishment that accompanied affluence.

This shift in outlook strongly influenced the development of the liberal agenda in the lead-up to the 1960s. The economist John Kenneth Galbraith represented the emerging liberal consensus when he argued that America should no longer direct resources to an ever-greater output of consumer goods to drive growth. In his award-winning and influential book, *The Affluent Society*, he argued that the economy had grown sufficiently that its surplus should be redirected away from crass commercial trappings to investments in education, infrastructure, and research and development. The political journalist Richard Rovere echoed this thinking when he observed that the country gained little from the "production, distribution, and consumption of trashy things, the creation of trashy houses and landscapes, the dissemination of trashy education and ideas."

In the 1950s, liberal intellectuals and policy makers pressed successfully for the expansion of Social Security, which until mid-decade excluded people who worked in domestic service, hotels and laundries, agriculture, or local government service. They also championed legacy components of Harry Truman's Fair Deal platform, including federal aid to education, public health insurance, and civil rights protections for African Americans. But many now also took up Galbraith's call to arms. Frank Church, a Democratic senator from Idaho, worried that America might soon become "a kind of modern Babylon of private plenty in the midst of public poverty." The country, lamented his colleague Mike Mansfield, was like a massive ocean liner "frozen in a dangerous course and with a hull in pressing need of repair." In effect, the United States was squandering its riches on frivolous things, at the expense of the public interest. Going forward, American liberalism would concern itself with the spiritual as well as the material well-being of its citizens.

It is little wonder that the image of the supermarket—that most iconic symbol of postwar plenty—haunted the liberal mind. "With the supermarket as our temple, and the singing commercial as our litany, are we likely to fire the world with an irresistible vision of America's exalted purposes and inspiring way of life?" Adlai Stevenson lamented in the pages of *Time* magazine in 1960. (Ironically, the table of contents that teased his article was sandwiched between advertisements for shiny new refrigerators stocked with a surfeit of food.) Writing just months later for *Esquire*, Norman Mailer conceded that "not all the roots of American life are uprooted, but almost all, and the spirit of the supermarket, that homogeneous extension of stainless surfaces and psychoanalyzed people, packaged commodities and ranch homes, interchangeable, geographically unrecognizable, that essence of a new postwar SuperAmerica," represented the hollowness of contemporary life in the United States. Mailer's essay—"Superman Comes to the Supermart"—tapped into a popular metaphor, for as *Life* magazine observed more favorably, the spirit of America was best captured by an image of suburban shopping carts, "cornucopias filled with abundance that no other country in the world has ever known."

In his poem "Superman," John Updike embraced abundance for what it was—all present and all consuming. His narrator, the archetypal middle-class American, drove each day to the "supermarket," parked in a "superlot," and bought "Super Suds." Most self-aware contemporaries would readily have appreciated the wry social commentary.

The liberal worldview assumed that a rising economic tide could and should lift all boats. Indeed, most critics and reformers agreed that America was an economic powerhouse; if only it were possessed of a more public-minded spirit, it could accomplish great things. Armed with this faith that the economy would grow in perpetuity under expert guidance—yet predisposed to believe that Americans were directing their energy and resources in the wrong direction—liberal intellectuals and policy experts in the early 1960s could conceivably believe they were armed with the tools to fight and win an "unconditional war on poverty." All they needed was to be shown that it still existed.

"People are poverty stricken when their income, even if adequate for survival, falls radically behind that of the community," Galbraith wrote in his influential book. This idea—that in an affluent society, most poor people had enough to get by and were thereby "poor" only by comparison to their more fortunate neighbors—interested the Democratic senator Paul Douglas of Illinois, a former economics professor who suspected that Galbraith understated the magnitude of the problem. Despite the fundamental strength of the American economy, he worried that many people still lived below an objective poverty line. As co-chairman of the Joint Economic Committee, Douglas hired Robert Lampman, a young economist at the University of Wisconsin, to dive deeper into the subject. The result, a report titled "The Low Income Population and Economic Growth," found that poverty remained a persistent challenge and that wealth and income distribution had grown more unequal in recent years. The study resonated with policy-minded liberals. In 1961, Heller invited the author—whom he knew casually from academic circles—to join the staff of the Council of Economic Advisers. For two years, Lampman worked primarily on other issues, but in early 1963 he and Heller saw an opening. The year before, the writer and socialist organizer Michael Harrington published an arresting volume on American poverty. Titled *The Other America*, it argued that upwards of fifty million people—over a quarter of the population—lived in a "system designed to be impervious to hope." The "other America" was "populated by the failures, by those driven from the land and bewildered by the city, by old people suddenly confronted with the torments of loneliness and poverty, and by minorities facing a wall of prejudice." Largely "invisible" to members of the prosperous middle class, other Americans were trapped in a national "ghetto, a modern poor farm for the rejects of society and of the economy."

Very few politicians or their staff members actually read Harrington's book, but many, including JFK, absorbed Dwight Macdonald's long and engaging review, which appeared in the *New Yorker* in January 1963. It shocked the liberal conscience to learn that even by the government's tight definition thirty-four million Americans—more than one out of six—lived beneath the poverty line and that three-quarters of these individuals were children and senior citizens. Many influential policy makers, including the president, also read a series of gut-wrenching articles in the *New York Times* by the veteran reporter Homer Bigart, who chronicled widespread destitution and social wreckage in West Virginia. Others were equally stirred by *Night Comes to the Cumberlands*, Harry Caudill's stark volume on economic want in the Appalachians.

Though critics would later identify the Great Society's antipoverty programs as a handout to black residents of urban ghettos, in the early 1960s policy makers and journalists still tended to associate the poverty with white families in areas of the Appalachians and Midwest that had been stripped clean of coal, or where automation had rendered human labor obsolete. Such families, whether in desolate hamlets in Kentucky or squalid white ghettos in Cincinnati or Detroit, were the public face of American poverty.

Perceiving an opening, Heller secured JFK's consent to develop the seeds of a comprehensive program. Beginning in May, he and Lampman convened brown-bag lunches each Saturday afternoon at the Executive Office Building, where a revolving-door cast from the CEA, the Budget Bureau, and the Departments of Health, Education, and Welfare (HEW), Agriculture, Labor, and Justice ruminated on the problem and how to eradicate it. Many of those present were former university professors, and their meetings often resembled graduate seminars. "Some people would say poverty obviously means lack of money income," Lampman told an interviewer. "That had the great merit of being something we had some numbers on. . . . But other people said that's really not what poverty means. . . . It's a spiritual concept; or it's a participation-in-government concept; or it's a lack of some kind of self-esteem, sort of a psychological or image problem that people had. . . . Still others would say it really has to do with lack of opportunity. It has to do with lack of public facilities like schools and so on. That's what makes people really poor."

While some participants, particularly those representing the Department of Labor, argued that what poor people needed most was income, which the government could provide in the form of public-sector relief jobs as it did during the Great Depression, the thrust of the conversation that summer identified such broad-based themes as a "culture of poverty" and lack of "opportunity" as the primary causes and drivers of poverty. Such thinking made sense in the context of 1963. The economy, after all, was robust, and most Americans enjoyed the material, if not the spiritual and cultural, benefits of prosperity. Those who had been left behind only needed to be equipped with the means to claim their fair share of an ever-growing pie. This outlook provided a ready answer to those citizens who sought reassurance that government would maintain "full employment at a time when automation is replacing men," as Kennedy framed the issue. The year he was elected, Gallup found that more Americans feared being displaced by machines than feared the Soviet Union. Opportunity theory promised every worker a chance to retrain and retool in a fast-changing workforce.

Soon after Lampman returned to Wisconsin in late summer, the brown-bag lunches evolved into an informal interagency task force. Heller and Kermit Gordon, the director of the Bureau of the Budget, solicited feedback from cabinet departments on three broad topics: how to prevent people from slipping into poverty, how to pull them out of it, and how to improve the lives of those living in its grip. The resulting input was "a lot of junk," recalled one of Heller's aides, "warmed-over revisions of proposals that had been around for a long time, coming up out of the bureaucracy, programs that had been already rejected by the Congress." Only when Heller sat down with David Hackett and Richard Boone did he hear something truly imaginative.

Hackett had been a close friend of Bobby Kennedy's during their days at Milton Academy, an elite boarding school in Massachusetts. As an Irish Catholic at what was "basically an Anglo-Saxon, WASP school," and as a relative latecomer who transferred in during his junior year, Kennedy was something of a "misfit," according to Hackett, who was the academy's golden boy: fair-haired and handsome, a stellar athlete, and armed with a natural charm, he was later the model for the character Phineas in the novelist John Knowles's adolescent classic, A Separate Peace. Though in his post-school days Hackett led an undistinguished professional life, Bobby involved him in his brother's 1960 presidential campaign and then hired him at the Justice Department, where he served as staff director for the President's Committee on Juvenile Delinquency (PCJD). Widely disparaged as a lightweight by the Ivy-educated lawyers who formed the attorney general's inner circle, Hackett worked hard to immerse himself in academic and field literature on juvenile crime. Though some Kennedy intimates joked that the former college hockey champion had been hit in the head with too many pucks, an economist at the CEA remembered him as "a very hard-driving, effective, caring person" who managed in a short space of time to master his adopted field.

Hackett spoke with representatives of the Ford Foundation, which for several years had been funding an initiative it called the Gray Areas project—a series of demonstration trials in such cities as New Haven and New York, where local organizations worked to improve conditions and create opportunities in the urban ghetto. Through the Ford Foundation, Hackett met Lloyd Ohlin and Richard Cloward, professors at Columbia University's School of Social Work who spearheaded Mobilization for Youth, a Gray Areas project centered on Manhattan's Lower East Side. In 1960, Ohlin and Cloward co-authored an academic book, *Delinquency and Opportunity*, which argued that juvenile delinquency was not an expression of personal pathology but rather a natural and rational response to the absence of opportunity in distressed urban areas. "The good society," Ohlin argued, "is one in which access to opportunities and the organization of facilities and resources are so designed as to maximize each individual's chance to grow and achieve his greatest potential for constructive contribution to the cultural life of the social order." He convinced Hackett that the key to reducing juvenile delinquency was to build local community organizations that operated from the ground up, identify gaps in social services and infrastructure in consultation with local residents, and provide tools that would create opportunity. Ohlin was working as a consultant to the PCJD in 1963 when he and Richard Boone, a veteran of the Ford Foundation who was then Hackett's deputy, received a summons to brief Walter Heller on the committee's "community action" projects. Their meeting was intended to last thirty minutes but instead ran over two hours.

"Community action appealed to me immediately," Heller later reflected. "The *moment* I heard about it, it became part of my thinking." Before leaving Washington, Robert Lampman cautioned his boss to "avoid completely any use of the term 'inequality' or the term '*redistribution* of income or wealth.'" His advice was both politically astute and in keeping with the spirit of growth liberalism, which assumed that no radical changes to the fundamental structure of the American economy were necessary to eradicate poverty. Not everyone agreed. When Heller approached some of his cabinet colleagues in late 1963 with the general concept of community action, William Wirtz, the secretary of labor and a longtime friend, was skeptical. "An attack on ignorance, on slums—fine," he told Heller. "But on poverty? That's too diffuse." Wirtz took a simpler view of the problem. The poor, he believed, were poor because they needed money. To make money, they needed jobs, and for a multitude of reasons there were pockets of the country where jobs were not to be had. "Without question," he implored his colleagues, "the biggest single immediate change which the poverty program could bring about in the lives of most of the poor would be to provide the family head with a regular, decently paid job." Wilbur Cohen, the assistant secretary of health, education, and welfare and a longtime Washington hand who had helped build the Social Security program in the 1930s, agreed in part. Community action would "not do enough for children, broken families where the women have to support the family, minority groups, and special problem areas like alcoholics, delinquents, and the mentally ill." What poor people needed was money, not opportunity. Cohen seemed skeptical that even a New Deal–style program of mass public employment would reduce poverty, given how ill-equipped many poor people were to avail themselves of the country's astounding economic growth.

Others agreed, including an ad hoc committee of left-wing intellectuals that drew such prominent names as Gunnar Myrdal, a Swedish economist and author of a famous exposé of American race relations; Michael Harrington; Todd Gitlin and Tom Hayden, founders of Students for a Democratic Society; Irving Howe, the founder of *Dissent* magazine; and Stewart Meacham of the American Friends Service Committee. Committee members endorsed an "incomes policy" that would furnish "every family with an adequate income as a matter of right." It was the only way, they believed, by which "the quarter of the nation now dispossessed and soon-to-be dispossessed by lack of employment can be brought within the abundant society."

But income redistribution was neither politically expedient nor inside the boundaries of contemporary liberal thought. It would be costly—as much as $11 billion annually—and would "leave the roots of poverty untouched and deal only with its symptoms," Heller believed. As the veteran columnist Walter Lippmann concurred, "A generation ago it would have been taken for granted that a war on poverty meant taking money away from the haves and turning it over to the have nots. . . . But in this generation a revolutionary idea has taken hold. The size of the pie can be increased by intention, by organized fiscal policy and then a whole society, not just one part of it, will grow richer."

It was this thinking that informed a memorandum that Heller and Gordon sent the president on December 20. They argued strongly in favor of an anti-poverty initiative heavy on "community action" programming and light by comparison on jobs creation. Assuming that the president was able to ram the Kennedy tax cut through Congress, and further assuming that the tax cut would accelerate economic growth—a hypothesis of which Heller, the tax cut's architect and most committed proponent, was certain—then community action was the key to helping poor people benefit from national wealth. At the start, Johnson was skeptical. His formative experience predisposed him to think of antipoverty measures through the lens of the New Deal: bulldozers and youth camps, large-scale public works programs, jobs initiatives that would secure the instant endorsement of congressmen, governors, and local elected officials. In effect, the president was closer to Wirtz's point of view than to that of the interagency task force. Days after Christmas, he strolled over to the modest green guesthouse at the LBJ Ranch, where Heller, Gordon, Moyers, and Valenti were huddled around a small kitchen table "littered with papers, coffee cups, and one ashtray brimming over with cigarettes and torn strips of paper." Mere yards away from the house and visible through the window, several Hereford cows grazed "placidly and a little noisily." Johnson was amused to see his budget director clad in an oversized khaki shirt and ill-fitting "city trousers." It was "an incongruous setting for Gordon and Heller, those two urbane scholars. I sat down at the table to talk about the poverty program they were preparing." LBJ told his advisers that he wanted to see "hard, bedrock content" behind their plan. Also on hand at the ranch was Horace Busby, who had not yet formally joined Johnson's staff. Instantly skeptical of community action, if not the blanket promise to eradicate so thorny and ever present a problem as poverty, Buzz spent the evening of December 30 clapping out a memo to the president. "There is no workable program yet conceived," he warned. He counseled broader initiatives that would benefit "the American in the middle" and that, non-coincidentally, would also help many poor citizens. "People know instinctively these are your kind of folks," he argued. "He pays most of the taxes, carries most of the credit, makes or breaks the consumer goods market, is the home-buyer, car-buyer," and "his consent is vital—his dissent fatal—to our social progress vis Negro rights."

"The politics of the extremes is what the typical American expects you to break away from," Busby advised. "If you can do so, you can broaden the Democratic party base as it has not been broadened in two decades." Busby worried that a program specifically tailored to the poor, rather than initiatives designed to lift the floor for all citizens—education, health care for the elderly—would create a political backlash. "America's real majority is suffering a minority complex of neglect," he presciently observed. "They have become the real foe of Negro rights, foreign aid, etc., because as much as anything, they feel forgotten, at the second table behind the tightly organized, smaller groups at either end of the U.S. spectrum."

Busby's warning—that liberalism grounded in identity group politics would be the undoing of the Democratic majority—was several years ahead of its time. But his was not the only voice to urge caution. Elizabeth Wickenden, a social worker and reformer whom LBJ had known since his days as Texas state administrator for the NYA, was also unconvinced. She privately told Sorensen that the "problems of poverty are only in limited instances localized in character. They are for the most part widely distributed, related to economic and social factors that operate nationwide, and would require more than local action for solution."

Ultimately, the economists prevailed—in no small part, thought Horace Busby, because community action began life as a Kennedy program. LBJ feared that if he rejected it out of hand, the "forces of learning and light" would have declared that LBJ was "just a Southern racist."

Ted Sorensen, who helped draft Johnson's first State of the Union address, later denied ownership of the term "War on Poverty." It did not "sound like something President Kennedy would have been comfortable saying, or that I would have been comfortable writing," he told an interviewer many years after the fact, and in any event so many staff members took a hand in writing the speech—Sorensen, Valenti, and Moyers, among others—that its provenance was lost to history. In fact, JFK first introduced the phrase in 1960 during a campaign speech at Hyde Park, New York, and, in his inaugural address, declared that if "the free society cannot help the many who are poor, it cannot save the few who are rich." Now, in January 1964, LBJ affirmed that "very often a lack of jobs and money is not the cause of poverty, but the symptom. The cause may lie deeper in our failure to give our fellow citizens a fair chance to develop their own capacities, in a lack of education and training, in a lack of medical care and housing, in a lack of decent communities in which to live and bring up their children." It was an extraordinary moment in American political history. Until 1964, the term "poverty" had been entirely absent from both the *Congressional Record*'s index and the *Public Papers of the Presidents*. Now it was like polio—a scourge that the federal government would marshal great resources to eradicate.

Two weeks after the president's State of the Union address, the administration submitted its first economic report to Congress. It found that between thirty-three million and thirty-five million Americans—almost one-fifth of the country—lived at or below the poverty line, which the government pegged at $3,000 in annual income for a family of four. That figure broke down to $800 each year for housing; $5 per week, per individual, for food; and less than $25 per week, per family, for everything else: medical care, school supplies, clothing, transportation, insurance, and household goods. "Obviously," the report declared, "it does not exaggerate the problem of poverty to regard $3000 as the boundary."

Notably, the Council of Economic Advisers cited hard facts and figures that established a positive correlation between both lack of education and discrimination—by which it meant *racial* discrimination—and income. Though the vast majority of poor families were white, the poverty *rate* among nonwhites was much higher. Roughly 40 percent of all farm families—and 80 percent of nonwhite farm families—were poor. But more poor people lived in cities. Though only one-quarter of poor families were headed by single mothers, among female-headed households the poverty rate was 50 percent. Buried in these statistics were several land mines that the Johnson administration did not perceive and later tripped. Most of the beneficiaries of the Great Society were white, but because its programs disproportionately aided nonwhites—and because conservative critics associated antipoverty initiatives with civil rights—backlash politicians were easily able to harness racial fears and resentments to scale back LBJ's legacy. Equally, though patterns of family dissolution had long been in evidence among rural white communities, the administration's focus on black poverty led many white Americans to assume that the rise of single-parent households and welfare dependency was unique to the black urban ghetto. These political complications lay in the distant future when Johnson launched his assault on poverty. "The poor inhabit a world scarcely recognizable, and rarely recognized, by the majority of fellow Americans," the CEA reported. "It is a world where Americans are literally concerned with day-to-day survival—a roof over their heads, where the next meal is coming from. It is a world where a minor illness is a major tragedy, where pride and privacy must be sacrificed to get help, where honesty can become a luxury and ambition a myth. Worst of all—the poverty of fathers is visited upon the children." No presidential administration, with the exception of Franklin Roosevelt's, had shone so bright a spotlight on economic want, and none had done so in an era of widely shared prosperity.

Though critics then and later would come to associate the War on Poverty with a narrow scope of initiatives, and particularly with community action, which would soon prove a magnet for controversy, in 1964 LBJ used the term as a wrapper for many of the qualitative measures that in later months he designated the "Great Society." Some of these measures—like federal aid to primary and secondary education and hospital insurance for the aged—had been part of liberalism's unfinished agenda since Harry Truman's tenure as president. (Kennedy tried, but failed, to earn congressional approval of both items.) Others, like food stamps and school nutrition programs, began as small-scale pilot initiatives under JFK's administration. Still others were altogether new and innovative: community action, early childhood education for disadvantaged youth, a job corps for young men in rural and urban areas, and free legal aid for the poor. What joined these disparate programs into a coherent approach was the underlying assumption that the poor principally needed basic protection against severe hardship and coordinated help in unlocking their fair share of national wealth—not government-guaranteed income. For that reason, Hubert Humphrey, who served as LBJ's vice president from 1965 through 1969, preferred "a better phrase than the 'War on Poverty'"—perhaps something along the lines of "an adventure in opportunity" or "an opportunity crusade."

As Heller originally pitched the idea to Johnson, the goal was "widening participation in prosperity." From the vantage point of the early 1960s, it hardly seemed worth the time to wonder what might happen in an age of economic retrenchment and austerity. The first task was maximizing economic output to support the antipoverty initiative: if the logic underpinning the War on Poverty was that all Americans should be equipped with the tools they needed to harvest a share of the growing economy, achieving full capacity and growth was key. Though the United States was a prosperous country, since the "Eisenhower Recession" of 1958 the pace of growth had slowed; GNP was rising at a clip of 2.5 percent annually, rather than a target rate of 3.5 percent, and unemployment stubbornly hovered between 5 percent and 6 percent. Heller convinced JFK, and later LBJ, that the economy was underperforming by $30 billion annually. A tax cut—even one that increased the deficit temporarily—would stimulate growth, close the gap between economic potential and performance, and achieve full employment.

Ironically, though the measure was born of liberal faith in the ability of experts to grow and manage the economy through the careful application of Keynesian measures, some of its sharpest critics were liberal economists. Leon Keyserling, who served as chairman of the Council of Economic Advisers under Harry Truman, thought that the tax bill constituted a misdirection of Keynesian theory. While he agreed that it would stimulate the economy, he calculated that the wealthiest 12 percent of Americans would reap almost half of its savings, an outcome that was both unjust and unsound, because so small a portion of the population could not consume enough goods and services to stimulate meaningful economic growth. John Kenneth Galbraith argued that tax cuts were the wrong Keynesian lever. If the government threw the budget out of balance through spending, it would stimulate the economy while also making core investments in public-sector infrastructure that would, in turn, generate more opportunity and growth. Tax cuts would merely feed the cycle of conspicuous middle-class consumption. "Needless to say," he told Kennedy shortly before his death, "the addition of more and better depilatories has nothing to do with national health and vigor." Michael Harrington, whose work on the hidden scourge of poverty had done so much to inspire the liberal imagination, was more scathing in his assessment. He scored the tax cut as "reactionary Keynesianism." Rather than cut taxes, the government could simply provide poor people with cash, thus eliminating poverty and priming the economic pump all at once. But such thinking was more in line with prevailing liberal wisdom of the 1930s, not the new consensus of the 1960s.

Indeed, for a time the tax cut appeared to accomplish what its framers intended. Within weeks of taking office, Johnson used both carrot and stick to bring his first budget in at $97.9 billion—under the $100 billion threshold needed to satisfy Harry Byrd—and in so doing eased the way for Heller's tax cut. In late February, the president signed into law the Revenue Act of 1964, which sharply reduced individual income tax rates. The results were almost instantaneous. In 1965, GNP exceeded even the CEA's optimistic forecast by a whopping $9 billion, and the official unemployment rate dropped to 4.1 percent—almost the textbook definition of full employment. "Though I cannot and do not suggest that we now have test-tube evidence of the success of the tax cut," Heller informed the president, "it is hard to explain the continued strong advance to date—and the budget prospects ahead—except in terms of fresh confidence, the expanded purchasing power, and the new incentives created by the Revenue Act of 1964." Outside observers were less tentative in their appraisal. "Tax relief, in massive doses, appears to have achieved something like magic," marveled U.S. News & World Report.

A critical building block of the Great Society—between 1961 and 1967, federal revenue increased from $94 billion to $150 billion, creating the wherewithal to adopt new government programs—the tax cut created more than growth. It fueled a sense of liberal ebullience and invincibility and established the intellectual foundation for the Johnson administration's domestic program. If government truly could create full employment and power the economy at full capacity, surely it could empower all of its citizens to enjoy access to their share of the pie. Even as LBJ and his aides set about securing the other components of his agenda for 1964—namely, passage of civil rights and antipoverty legislation—they began to debate the core role of government in an age of seemingly boundless, endless, and widely shared prosperity.

CHAPTER 3

Second Day

Serving in Lyndon Johnson's White House meant working seven days each week—or, fourteen days per week, given the president's unusual habit of keeping a "two-shift" day. LBJ would awaken each morning around 6:00 or 6:30 and read through a large stack of newspapers. By routine, Jack Valenti would be on hand—joined later in the morning by Walter Jenkins and Bill Moyers—to receive a thick stack of memos from Johnson's "night reading." Valenti would thumb through the stack "rapidly, reading some all the way through and only glancing at others." Sitting upright in bed, still clad in his pajamas, Johnson would begin placing phone calls, barking orders, and considering the day's calendar. So famous—and often lampooned—was Valenti's steadfastness that on his forty-third birthday reporters immediately got the joke when LBJ quipped that "he is one day older today and shows it. He was late this morning for the first time. He got in when the sun had been up and had to go pull the curtain with the sun shining in my eyes. He is usually there early." Busby later observed that his boss "never fully appreciated why people were oftentimes so sour when he woke them up at six with a phone call." (He was one of the lucky ones. Johnson "rarely called me . . . early in the morning," he clarified. "He called me at midnight.")

After working from bed for several hours, Johnson would arrive in the Oval Office at about 9:00 a.m. to begin meetings. In the early days of his presidency, the room still bore Jackie Kennedy's aesthetic touch: a new red carpet and white drapes, which she had ordered installed as a surprise for her husband upon his return from Texas. Only later would he make the room, with its stark white walls, three-inch-thick windows, and handsome French doors, his own. Around 2:00 p.m., the president routinely went for a swim in the White House pool, which was then located in the indoor area that today houses the press room. By habit, Johnson swam au naturel and expected that when his aides joined him—a frequent occurrence, given his predisposition to insist—they did as well. After a sparse lunch, he retired to his bedroom, changed into pajamas, and napped for an hour; he then showered, changed into fresh clothes, and resumed his schedule around 4:00 p.m.—the "second shift," as his aides called it. "It's like starting a new day," LBJ offered in a rare moment of introspection, "but at 5 in the afternoon I sometimes feel sorry for the poor Cabinet officers and other people I call in here who have been tied to their desks all day." When the president finished afternoon meetings at about 8:00 p.m., he retired to the residence for dinner, often with friends and family, and by 10:00 settled into bed for his "night reading"—stacks upon stacks of memos from his staff members, many of them requiring feedback ("OK/LBJ," or "Have him see me," or a simple check mark next to the words "Yes" and "No"). Valenti, who assembled the night reading and thereby enjoyed wide latitude in determining which voices the president heard, later estimated that LBJ pored over 200,000 words each week—which of course meant that Valenti read *more* than 200,000 words of policy and political memorandums weekly.

As he thumbed his way through the pages, Johnson would invariably pick up the phone and dial his staff members. For convenience—*his* convenience—each of the chauffeured black sedans assigned to presidential assistants was outfitted with a two-way radio that enabled Johnson to call them back from home or dinner, and each of their homes had been equipped with a direct line to phone consoles in LBJ's residence and office, thus eliminating the need to wait for an operator or the White House signal office to track down the right number. Some aides pined for the days when they might once again enjoy "freedom from the white telephone of President Johnson."

"It's real Orwellian," one bemused staff member admitted. "You can't escape him." Even in his Senate days, Johnson had been known as a tough boss, but it took little time before the country understood that he demanded absolute commitment from his advisers. "Where do they get the stories that I'm a slave driver?" he once whined. "I tell people to go home. But when there's a job to be done, they *want* to stay and work." (Perhaps from the cartoonist Herblock, who lampooned Johnson's staff as "fear-bent sharecroppers tugging their forelocks in cringing fealty as the master strode by with a coiled whip," as Merriman Smith of UPI described the rendering.)

Eric Goldman likened Johnson's attitude toward staff to that of "the head

of the duchy with all rights thereto appertaining." It was a near-feudal relationship: "When he did not like the length of a Special Assistant's hair, he told him
to go to a barbershop; he ordered a secretary to enroll in charm school." Yet as
a reporter for the *New York Times* aptly noted, despite the "heavy demands"
that he placed on his closest aides, Johnson inspired unusual loyalty. The flip
side of requiring their complete availability was that LBJ "made his assistants
his close personal and social companions. He likes them, trusts them; and
partly because he is addicted to shop talk, he likes to have them around for an
evening drink, a late dinner or a lazy weekend." The affection that Johnson
regularly showered on Valenti's daughter, who as a toddler would tumble down
the corridors of the West Wing and leap into the arms of "Prez!" spoke to his
genuine affection for his team, however abusive he might be in turn. A mid-
level holdover from the Kennedy administration begrudgingly acknowledged,
"Frankly, the people around Kennedy saw none of his faults, though he had
them. The people around Johnson see his faults, but think he has tremendous
attributes that more than counterbalance them." Shortly after the First Family
moved into the White House, they invited staff members to the private residence for a cocktail party. The wife of a former Kennedy aide confided to Lillian Reedy, George's wife, that she had never seen the inside of the living
quarters before. That small gesture made a considerable impression.

The relationship between Johnson and his staff posed one dynamic, the
relationship *among* the staff, another. Douglass Cater, a domestic policy specialist who joined the ranks of the senior staff in 1964, lauded the absence of
"prima donnas," but by the start of Johnson's full term conflicts began to surface. As George Reedy noted, "Court politics in the White House"—any
White House—"are always very severe. It's no place for a man of any real sensitivity whatsoever." No administration, Valenti surmised, was absent the "interplay of egos and clashings of ambitions, all sort of like satellites circling the
sun." Yet relatively speaking, LBJ's White House functioned with minimal
public spectacle or rancor, particularly in the first two years of his presidency.
This degree of harmony was all the more remarkable in light of the almost
complete lack of hierarchy and structure governing the president's staff. While
at different times certain staff men stood out as first among equals—Jenkins in
1963 and 1964, Moyers in 1965 and 1966, Califano in 1967 and 1968—
Johnson preferred a flat organizational structure and, compared with

Kennedy, kept an open door. "Neither Kennedy nor Johnson had a chief of staff," Valenti observed, "which any political pundit will tell you is quite surprising.... So how on earth did the West Wing function without one? Simply put: very, very well." Unlike in later administrations, most staff members did not generally confine themselves to narrow portfolios. This dynamic led to duplication of effort, Cater observed, particularly when the president grew impatient and assigned the same task to multiple actors. But it rarely resulted in discord. Though some old hands in government regarded LBJ's approach to staffing as "deliberately chaotic, governed by impulse and generally hit-or-miss," it worked.

Kenneth O'Donnell retained the title of appointments secretary until late in 1964, but in reality, Valenti—who first claimed a desk in the secretarial room outside the Oval and subsequently shared O'Donnell's office, two doors removed from the president's—gradually assumed the responsibilities of guarding LBJ's schedule. (O'Donnell's concentration, in turn, shifted to managing LBJ's 1964 campaign.) The function of appointments secretary, seemingly bureaucratic in nature, was at the time widely regarded as a senior role; the person filling it enjoyed broad leeway to set the president's agenda and to determine which voices he would hear—and, by extension, which he would not. Though Valenti and Busby acquired an early reputation as Texas conservatives, in fact both were conventional New Deal Democrats, and Valenti, in particular, was determined to ensure that access to Johnson was as unencumbered as possible. As LBJ liked to remind visitors, "Jack is really an intellectual. People would admit it if he didn't come from the wrong side of the Mason-Dixon line." Valenti was a voracious consumer of books—so much so that he installed a machine in his bathroom that enabled him to read while in the shower. Goldman, the Princeton University historian whom others on the White House staff sometimes derided as insufferably haughty and self-important, was impressed by the manner in which Valenti protected the president's time and focus without walling him off from the wider world. "[He] believed it important for the President to be brought into contact with a wide variety of people and ideas," Goldman remarked. "In his own way, Valenti was a friend in the White House of the offbeat, or at least of the new." This view was widely held. A veteran White House reporter credited Valenti with making Lyndon Johnson "the most accessible President in modern history."

In person, LBJ tended to dominate almost every conversation in which he took part. But through the memorandums they submitted for night reading, his staff members were able to engage him in a meaningful, written dialogue. They were also able to argue with and against each other. Because Jack Valenti ran an open process, the president could weigh markedly different ideas about the direction in which he might take the country.

In February 1964, Johnson summoned Bill Moyers and Richard Goodwin to the White House swimming pool and—as was his wont—obliged them to strip on the spot and join him for a dip. Goodwin, who had "been raising the eyebrows and blood pressure of conservatives" since the day that he "checked in" to Washington in 1958, was a celebrity in staff circles. The son of Jewish immigrants, he sailed through Tufts University and Harvard Law School, clerked for the Supreme Court justice Felix Frankfurter (making him perhaps the last of the "Little Frankfurters"—young aides whom the justice scouted on behalf of Democratic presidents and congressmen), and served as an investigator for the House Subcommittee on Legislative Oversight, in which role he was instrumental in exposing the common practice by which network television studios rigged popular game shows. After working as a speechwriter and Latin American policy aide on Kennedy's presidential campaign, he joined the White House staff as assistant special counsel under Ted Sorensen. He was, by one colleague's estimation, "dark, disheveled, brilliant and sardonic." Though a "Kennedyite of the Kennedyites," Goodwin—"connoisseur of the latest in literature and art who at the age of thirty-two, last week's soup stain on his suit, puffing his cigar and twirling his gold chain enigmatically, talked of power and policy with a faintly weary smile"—agreed to remain on Johnson's staff. Moyers was in awe of his establishment credentials and political savvy; Goodwin, in turn, had no other entrée into Johnson's inner circle but Moyers. The two men became fast friends and allies.

For weeks, LBJ had been grasping for a watchword that would describe his far-reaching but still inchoate agenda. Some of its pieces were holdovers from Kennedy's unfinished presidency: a tax cut to unlock economic growth and full employment, a civil rights bill that would at long last afford equal opportunity to African Americans, a sweeping initiative to eradicate poverty. Others were long-standing articles on the liberal wish list, including federal aid to schools and universities and hospital insurance for the elderly. Missing was an organizing thesis to join these policy items together. Theodore Roosevelt had promised a Square Deal, FDR a New Deal, Harry Truman a Fair Deal. What turn of phrase would Johnson deploy to articulate his vision? Bobbing about in the White House pool ("It's like going swimming with a polar bear," Moyers whispered), he instructed Goodwin and Moyers to help him introduce a "Johnson program, different in tone, fighting and aggressive"—more visionary even than John Kennedy's New Frontier.

His mandate in hand, Goodwin conferred with Goldman, who had already advised Johnson to "place his Administration in the perspective of the long-running American experience." Rather than recite the same tired trope that liberals had exhausted over several decades, he should arrange his program "not only to the quantity but to the quality of American living." Whether knowingly or not—and in all likelihood, the choice was deliberate—Goldman echoed Arthur Schlesinger, who in 1955 published a widely acclaimed article that challenged readers to reimagine the meaning of liberalism "in an age of abundance." "Instead of the quantitative liberalism of the 1930s, rightly dedicated to the struggle to secure the economic basis of life, we need now a 'qualitative liberalism' dedicated to bettering the quality of people's lives." Like many of his countrymen, Schlesinger took it for granted that economists and planners could, through a careful application of Keynesian measures, underwrite unlimited growth and prosperity. It was no longer necessary to speak as though "the necessities of living—a job, a square meal, a suit of clothes, and a roof—were at stake" but rather to "move on to the more subtle and complicated problem of fighting for individual dignity, identity, and fulfillment in a mass society." In conveying similar wisdom to both the president and his speechwriter, Goldman implicitly argued for a message *and* a program that would transcend partisan divisions and draw together as wide a coalition as possible behind essential policies like propping up the nation's education system and securing rights for African Americans. The phrase that he suggested, "the Good Society," owed its origins to Walter Lippmann's book of the same title. Goodwin preferred "the Great Society," though he might have been unaware that its provenance lay with a volume by Graham Wallas, a prominent socialist and professor at the London School of Economics in the early twentieth century. At first, Jack Valenti enthusiastically embraced the Great Society tag. "Why not enlarge the theme," he suggested to Johnson, "coupling the phrase with a new outline of what the president felt would be his philosophy, his précis of his move to the future, his aims and objectives for this country here at home." While the White House tested the phrase at least seventeen times in early 1964—along with close cousins like "greater society" and "glorious kind of society"—it was agreed that Johnson would unveil his platform in a commencement speech on May 22 at the University of Michigan.

Against advice to focus the president's remarks on a narrow list of bills expanding the New Deal, Goodwin went big. "My objective—my mandate—as I understood it—was not to produce a catalogue of specific projects, but a concept, an assertion of purpose, a vision . . . that went beyond the liberal tradition of the New Deal." In preparation for the assignment, he pored over the most current primary literature emanating from identity-conscious activists, including Betty Friedan's *Feminine Mystique*, Martin Luther King Jr.'s "Letter from Birmingham Jail," and the Port Huron Statement—the cri de coeur of the New Left. When Goodwin shared his draft, Valenti, Reedy, and Busby were unconvinced. Aside from perfectly acceptable rallying cries for classroom construction and teacher training, and a resounding call to eradicate racial discrimination, the speech—in their minds—was laden with woolly observations about how the loss of such values as "community with neighbors and communion with nature" bred "loneliness and boredom and indifference." What could the government possibly do, they wondered, to ensure that (as the draft proposed) the "meaning of our lives matches the marvelous products of our labor"? How could it build a country "where men are more concerned with the quality of their goals than the quantity of their goods"? It was challenge enough to keep inflation and growth in balance and to move pragmatic, liberal legislation through Congress. To promise utopia, or to suggest that LBJ's administration should be associated with that promise, seemed an overreach.

In the twilight days of Johnson's presidency, Reedy would confide to Juanita Roberts, the president's longtime senior secretary and confidante, that "the phrase bothered me because it seemed pompous and had many overtones of Marxist-style planning." Busby, for his part, prepared an alternative draft that envisioned the Great Society as the product of our "next scientific and technological capabilities." Almost futuristic in its anticipation of humankind's eventual ability to "fly oceans in an hour—see as well as hear over telephones—employ computers as everyday appliances in our homes—and find nothing novel in journeys to the moon or beyond," he framed the Great Society as a collection of lofty but concrete technological aspirations: new methods of desalination and irrigation, advances in chemistry and plant science to increase the food supply for a burgeoning world population—ambitions that would unlock the full promise of prosperity and in which government could undoubtedly serve as a catalyst and organizing force. Busby nevertheless hit the right liberal chords when he heralded a "society which knows no poverty, which knows no hunger, which knows no illiteracy—a society without slums in the cities or shame on the farms—a society in which leisure time is not wasted but the most useful time of our lives."

Moyers rejected Busby's draft as "adequate" but a "far cry from the original—in both quality and tone." In a tart memo to Valenti (who had collaborated in the Busby draft), he defended Goodwin's copy as "a provocative appeal to the mind of modern America." Perhaps it "sounded literate, too essay-like, but it was directed to the university audience—and beyond to the thinking people of our society." Moyers and Goodwin also fired off an ardent memo to Johnson—a document that Valenti could certainly have weeded out of the night reading but instead placed before the president. "This is a political year, but the President is not just thinking of the next election—*he is thinking of the next generation,*" they implored. "He believes there is danger that the *primacy of politics* this year will prevent the Nation from looking at the longer pull—hence *his deliberate decision to cast the spotlight on certain issues which ought to be imbedded in the Nation's consciousness.*" Appealing to LBJ's determination to equal the esteem in which liberal columnists and intellectuals held John Kennedy, they urged him to accept a draft "designed to make people like Reston and Lippmann, Pusey and Goheen, sit up and say: 'This President is *really* thinking about the *future problems of America.*'"

LBJ ultimately delivered Goodwin's draft (with embellishments by Moyers), and to great fanfare. Riding back to Washington on Air Force One, Charles Roberts witnessed "the president in his manic phase . . . he was absolutely euphoric . . . he was sweating and exuberant. He violated his old rule and had himself a drink, a Scotch highball, and came back to our press pool." When Roberts complimented the president on his performance, noting that the audience had interrupted him twenty-seven times with applause, LBJ excitedly called Jack Valenti over to display an annotated copy of the text. "No, no," Johnson insisted, "there were twenty-nine." Roberts grasped the import of the moment. "That was his unveiling of the Great Society, his own program, the program he was going to run on the next fall."

Years later, in a rare interview about his tenure in the White House, Moyers conceded that Johnson "never really liked the term Great Society. It didn't come easily to him." Like Busby, Valenti, and Reedy, he equated liberalism with "fulfilling FDR's mission." "I'm going to be President for nine years and so many days," he habitually reminded Moyers, "almost as long as FDR or second only to FDR." Yet "fulfilling FDR's mission" was by no means a cut-and-dried mission, because the New Deal itself had been a loose idea. Some of its components, like the National Industrial Recovery Act, sought to restructure American capitalism along the lines of European-style syndicates; others sought to break up monopolies. It was composed of temporary relief and infrastructure programs like the Works Progress Administration, the Public Works Administration, and the National Youth Administration and of lasting measures like old age insurance, unemployment insurance, and mortgage insurance, all of which removed some of the basic risks associated with everyday life. The New Deal was not in most respects redistributionist, though it did tilt the scales in favor of workers' rights by providing for collective bargaining, maximum hours, and a minimum wage. In effect, it was a malleable idea. "The country needs and, unless I mistake its temper, the country demands bold, persistent experimentation," Roosevelt famously argued. "It is common sense to take a method and try it: If it fails, admit it frankly and try another. But above all, try something." When they urged the president to pattern his agenda along the lines of the New Deal, Busby and Valenti were not arguing against the concrete action items that the president had prioritized for 1964—civil rights, an antipoverty measure, a tax cut to stimulate the economy. Neither were they opposed to promises that would follow in 1965—aid to schools and universities, environmental legislation, health care for the elderly. They wanted, rather, to identify his administration with concrete and attainable goals around which LBJ could build national consensus, and they recoiled from grandiose promises that the president might not be able to keep. George

Reedy, who later had a serious ax to grind with Bill Moyers, identified a divide between younger staff members of the 1960s generation and older advisers who had come of age in the days of the Roosevelt and Truman administrations. Others perceived the emergence of rival camps: "liberals" like Moyers and Richard Goodwin, on the one hand, and "conservatives" like Busby and Valenti, on the other. The debate was about what liberalism meant, not whether it should inform domestic policy.

Busby, who had served off and on since 1948 as LBJ's "ideas man," was now in direct conflict with Bill Moyers, whose "militant conscience," according to an admiring journalist—"not zealot, not fanatic, just that of a young man responding with a wish for action to inner knowledge of what is right"—made him the resident White House moralist. Widely hailed as the administration's bridge to the Kennedys, Moyers appeared to be the very antithesis of Busby, a pro-business Texan more than ten years his senior (though as one astute columnist observed, "Mr. Busby would not seem conservative in Congress or in most state capitals"). Some of the distance between the two men was simply personal. They "clashed very early," Valenti would explain. "Buzz had been with the President the longest, his oldest and trusted aide, and probably next to Goodwin the best writer I ever saw. Buzz is a philosophical man; he's not happy in the corridors of raw naked power. He'd rather philosophize than brutalize. He thought a good deal, and while this is very useful to a President, it doesn't help you if you get in open conflict with some colleague who has shored up all the sides of the circle." An ardent student of politics from his early days as an elementary school student, Busby—who once told a colleague, "I am not the praying type myself"—seemed galled to find himself politically outmaneuvered at every step by a Baptist preacher.

But their friction was also philosophical in nature. Where Moyers and Goodwin would refashion LBJ in the image of a prophet, Busby feared that displays of "evangelistic fervor" would play poorly with "the vast middle majority of America—particularly beyond the Eastern seaboard." Ordinary voters would support tangible programs that benefited a broad swath of the citizenry. They would not be moved by gauzy promises of a better world or more meaningful human existence. By contrast, Moyers invoked the memory of Theodore Roosevelt when he urged Johnson to regard the White House as "a bully good pulpit." The president, he believed, "must use it to exert the moral leadership *without which none of these issues can capture the public attention or concern.*"

However much they differed in their temperamental and rhetorical approach to presidential leadership, Johnson's aides shared prevailing liberal orthodoxy that the United States was a rich nation and advised the president that "we are enjoying abundance, we have statistically and actually the best life any people have ever known. But we are putting proportionately less of that wealth and abundance back into the *renewal* of our society than at any time since the pre-depression era." Buzz agreed with his younger colleagues that "while comfort has come to us abundantly, abundance itself has brought us little comfort. Our age is eventful and exciting—but many lives are afflicted with boredom and dullness." Moreover, all of Johnson's aides—Busby, Valenti, and Reedy; Moyers and Goodwin—concurred that the "Great Society rests on abundance and liberty for all. It demands an end to poverty and racial injustice, to which we are totally committed in our time." They shared a commitment to build schools and make financial investments in urban renewal. If Moyers and Goodwin fundamentally envisioned the Great Society as proof that "our material progress is only the foundation on which we will build a richer life of mind and spirit," for Buzz it was something far more concrete. Having built a successful private-sector research consultancy, he envisioned the Great Society in brick-and-mortar terms: investments in science ("perhaps the most universally intriguing field of the present period"), mental health services, transportation and infrastructure (including 150-mile-per-hour trains that would connect metropolitan areas), library construction, and small businesses. And—a theme to which he would return time and again—a sweeping overhaul of government at all levels, to bring the full advantages of modern business management to the public sector. His vision was by no means as grandiose as that which Moyers and Goodwin urged on the president, but it reflected the spirit of growth liberalism in its faith that government could unlock opportunity by making broad investments that benefited all of its citizens.

In later years, Johnson's disparagers would argue that the administration raised public expectations with elaborate promises to remedy problems that government simply could not solve. Reedy would claim that this had always been his criticism of the Great Society's sales pitch. But the real divide among

Johnson's aides was not whether the agenda should be narrow or expansive. Even the relative moderates among them aspired to complete Roosevelt's New Deal by enacting and administering comprehensive education and health-care programs, enhancing the safety net for the most vulnerable Americans, and integrating schools, hospitals, and places of public accommodation. It was rather a gulf between conventional liberals like Reedy, Valenti, and Busby, who championed tangible measures that would materially benefit as many Americans as possible, and younger liberals like Moyers and Goodwin, who believed that government should also address more nebulous, qualitative challenges to the public spirit. There was a good deal of common ground. Douglass Cater, who did not fall neatly in either camp, suggested to the president that just as the Council of Economic Advisers delivered an annual report to Congress on the nation's "economic well-being," the administration ought to initiate an annual report "examining the 'quality' of life in the Great Society." Most of the benchmarks that he proposed reflected long-standing liberal programs: achieving benchmarks for life expectancy, infant mortality, the eradication of disease, school completion, and crime prevention. But he distinguished between the "'quality' [and] the 'quantity' of life in America. This cannot be stated solely with an economic yardstick."

All of Johnson's aides spoke the common vernacular of growth liberalism, with its faith in quantitative measures to unlock individual opportunity. Some also echoed liberal economic and social critics like Dwight Macdonald and John Kenneth Galbraith who regarded the country's misuse of its wealth and power as a missed opportunity. Others, like Busby, Valenti, and Reedy, preferred to keep the administration's feet firmly on the ground. The promise of good schools and access to medical care was lofty enough without faraway promises to fix humankind's broken spirit.

It was not simply that Busby remained unconvinced that Goodwin's prose would work for Johnson. He doubted that it had worked for Kennedy. Early in 1964, Buzz carefully analyzed the Kennedy administration's poll numbers and concluded that for all of JFK's dash and youthful appeal—and however intensely the illuminati in official Washington circles might have worshipped him—the New Frontier had racked up precious few domestic achievements. On the eve of his death, JFK was personally popular, but his agenda remained bottled up in Congress, and his administration's approval ratings were plummeting.

As late as May 19—just three days before LBJ's speech in Ann Arbor—Busby urged the president to tell reporters that he was "rejecting efforts to label his Administration's program, such as FDR's 'New Deal,' Truman's 'Fair Deal,' Kennedy's 'New Frontier.'" He would ultimately reconcile himself to the term, though not to Bill Moyers's and Dick Goodwin's understanding of what it meant.

No component of the Great Society was more critical than the civil rights bill before Congress. In his first hours as president, Johnson signaled to friend and foe alike that its passage would be a central feature of his agenda in 1964. "Dick, I love you," he told his mentor Richard Brevard Russell, the senior senator from Georgia and acknowledged leader of the chamber's southern bloc. "I owe you. But I'm going to run over you if you challenge me or get in my way. I aim to pass the civil rights bill, only this time, Dick, there will be no caviling, no compromise, no falling back. This bill is going to pass." During his tenure in the House, Johnson had been a reliable vote against civil rights legislation, including measures that would have made lynching a federal crime, outlawed the poll tax, and established a permanent fair employment practices committee. In the Senate, he devoted his maiden speech to a ringing defense of southern traditions and repeatedly frustrated liberals by forestalling consideration of civil rights legislation. Only in 1957, with one eye cast on the White House, did he concede the necessity of mollifying his liberal critics by moving a bill through the Senate, but he stripped that measure down so severely that it was little better than a token measure.

In later years, George Reedy, whose relationship with Johnson ended on bad terms, was unsparing in his criticism of his longtime boss. Yet he would go to the grave firm in the conviction that LBJ was "one of the least prejudiced or biased or intolerant or bigoted men I have ever met. He has many shortcomings and he has many failings, but I don't believe there is any racial prejudice in him whatsoever; and this is the thing that became very, very apparent to most of the Negro leaders when they had a chance to know him personally." As a young man in Texas in the early 1930s, Johnson taught at an elementary school populated by impoverished Mexican children. His commitment to his students was so ardent that even his most critical biographers acknowledge it as a genuine reflection of his character. Those few observers who bothered to take note of LBJ during his years in JFK's shadow saw a new and unanticipated persuasion emerge as though from nowhere. He delivered stirring remarks in favor of civil rights at Detroit's Wayne State University in January 1963 and again at Gettysburg in May. He signaled his strong support for Kennedy's civil rights bill but voiced legitimate concern that the administration had no viable plan to navigate the complicated roadblocks that southern lawmakers would inevitably stand up in both houses of Congress. When in the spring of 1963 JFK hosted a sequence of meetings with civic, religious, and business leaders to build support for the legislation, LBJ confounded liberal activists by emerging as the strongest voice for action. "Kennedy had made an intellectual appeal for the lawyers' duty and so forth," remembered one prominent civil rights leader. "There was no passion in any of it until LBJ took the podium. And he gave an impassioned speech about what kind of a country is this that a man can go die in a foxhole and can't get a hamburger in a public restaurant. I would say he was by far the most effective fellow there. I was impressed by him."

In 1957, Senate majority leader Johnson had twisted arms, deployed obscure parliamentary procedure, and doled out rewards and punishments to neuter an otherwise strong civil rights measure. Now, as president, Johnson threw the weight of his office behind the fight to pass a bill that would outlaw segregation in public accommodations and provide for remedies to combat racial discrimination in the workplace. He urged union leaders like Dave McDonald of the United Steelworkers to apply lobbying muscle on Capitol Hill. He implored friends like Katharine Graham, publisher of the *Washington Post*, to turn up the heat on recalcitrant members of Congress. He actively encouraged the bill's managers to whip up support for a discharge petition in the House and might have played a decisive role in persuading House Republicans to threaten to join with liberal Democrats in a bipartisan takeover of the Rules Committee. ("If I were you, Charlie," LBJ told the House GOP leader, Charles Halleck of Indiana, "I wouldn't dare go out and try to make a Lincoln Birthday speech" without committing to the bill. "They'll laugh you right out of the goddamned park when Howard Smith's got his foot on Lincoln's neck." For good measure, he held out the possibility of building a NASA science center in Halleck's district.) Faced with the real likelihood that he would lose his gavel, Smith relented. "I've been around a long time, and I recognize the facts of life," he conceded, "and one of the facts of life is that this bill is going to the floor, and that it is going soon." After several days of debate, on February 10 the House passed the bill by a vote of 290 in favor to 130 opposed.

It took four months before Senate liberals were able to break a southern filibuster and send the Civil Rights Act to Johnson's desk. The president and his aides—particularly Larry O'Brien and his legislative affairs team—were deeply involved in driving strategy, but contrary to popular lore the president did not play a decisive role in securing cloture. He persuaded just one senator, Carl Hayden of Arizona, to absent himself from the chamber rather than vote to sustain the filibuster. While he attempted to move several southerners, including Al Gore Sr. of Tennessee, William Fulbright of Arkansas, and Robert Byrd of West Virginia ("You're with me!" he pleaded with Byrd. "You've got to be with me"), all three opposed the bill to the bitter end—none more forcefully than Byrd, who personally filibustered it for over fourteen uninterrupted hours. Johnson wheedled the Senate Republican leader, Everett Dirksen, spoke strongly in favor of equal rights during his "Poverty Tour"—a series of speeches in favor of the administration's War on Poverty that April—and signaled that he was willing to sacrifice other legislative priorities. If the Senate accomplished nothing else, he insisted, it must pass the civil rights bill.

By throwing the full moral weight of the presidency behind the bill, LBJ did more for civil rights than any president since Lincoln. His outspoken support established a sense of purpose and urgency. But it was grassroots activists, religious and lay, who won the votes. Richard Russell later confided to a friend that the southern bloc "had been able to hold the line until all the churches joined the civil rights lobby in 1964." Under the leadership of national organizations—and with coordination from Victor Reuther, an official with the United Auto Workers who also worked with the National Council of Churches—Catholic, Protestant, and Jewish clergy mounted an unrelenting and politically sophisticated campaign to win over strategically identified members of Congress. If organized labor held little sway with Republicans, ministers did. A loose confederation of clergymen activated a network of thousands of lay and religious community leaders who in turn spurred congregants to inundate key congressmen with telegrams and office visits. Congressional staff members soon became accustomed to the heavy volume of mail that poured in on Tuesdays and Wednesdays, inspired by synagogue and church sermons the weekend before. Joe Rauh, a prominent labor attorney and liberal leader who helped whip for the bill, remembered that in the Capitol complex that spring, "You couldn't turn around where there wasn't a clerical collar next to you."

Johnson was delivering a speech at the College of the Holy Cross in Worcester, Massachusetts, on June 9 when an aide stepped quietly to his side to whisper the news. He reacted immediately. "We are going ahead in our country to bring an end to poverty and racial injustice," he told the assembled audience. "In the last ten minutes we made progress. The Senate voted 71 to 29 for cloture." The crowd roared. On July 2, at a White House ceremony, the president signed the Civil Rights Act of 1964 into law.

The new law mandated the integration of all facilities that received federal funds and—more jarring to many white southerners—places of public accommodation. From hotels, buses, and rest stops to golf courses, restaurants, and swimming pools, Jim Crow was now a violation of federal law. "Desegregation was absolutely incomprehensible to the average southerner," said an attorney from Greensboro, "absolutely unbelievable." "How can I destroy the lingering faces of Stepin Fetchit, Amos & Andy, Buckwheat and all the others?" wondered a college student from North Carolina. "[My] world view is still strongly rooted in . . . a rural, agrarian, black-belt county, which is, in many ways, the same way as it was in 1900." For southerners like Margaret Jones Bolsterli, who grew up on a cotton plantation in Arkansas, "racism permeated every aspect of our lives, from little black Sambo . . . in the first stories read to us, to the warning that drinking coffee before the age of sixteen would turn us black. It was part of the air everyone breathed."

Observing the scene outside Montgomery's Jefferson Davis Hotel a year later, Jimmy Breslin, the irascible New York City newspaperman, wrote, "You have not lived, in this time when everything is changing, until you see an old black woman with mud on her shoes stand on the street of a Southern city and sing '. . . we are not afraid . . .' and then turn and look at the face of a cop near her and see the puzzlement, and the terrible fear in his eyes. Because he knows, and everybody who has ever seen it knows, that it is over." "This thing here is a revolution," a businessman from Montgomery confided to Breslin. "And some of us know it. The world's passed all of us by . . . unless we start to live with it." The bill's passage promised a definitive end to the brutal and comprehensive system of de jure segregation that existed in the South since the turn of the century: "white" and "colored" water fountains, schools, and medical facilities; whites-only swimming pools, movie theaters, and restaurants; legally permissible discrimination in the workplace. For white southerners, the year 1964 portended the end of life as they knew it, if the government proved serious about enforcing the law.

Some people proved able to reconcile themselves to the changes around them. In Birmingham, Ollie McClung, owner of a popular barbecue shack, mounted a legal challenge to the Civil Rights Act, claiming that the federal government had no jurisdiction over intrastate commerce. When the Supreme Court ruled against him in December 1964, finding that his restaurant was engaged in meaningful interstate commerce (much of its pork and beef was purchased from out-of-state vendors), McClung opened his doors to black diners. "As law-abiding Americans we feel we must bow to the edict of the Supreme Court," he grudgingly announced. On December 16, five black diners came to Ollie's to feast on his legendary ribs and chicken. To everyone's surprise—McClung's included—nothing happened. "Everything was lovely," said one of the black customers. "Lovely. Not a single incident. We sure enjoyed Ollie's good barbecue." Others proved less flexible. In Greenwood, Mississippi, the local government drained and shuttered a municipal pool rather than open it to black citizens. In Atlanta, Lester Maddox, a prominent cafeteria owner, chased black diners out of his establishment with a gun and an ax handle, then defiantly closed his restaurant rather than integrate it. In 1966, he was elected governor of Georgia, indicating the limits of white accommodation.

Yet among private businesses, the "general picture" was "one of large-scale compliance," the U.S. Justice Department concluded shortly after the civil rights bill became law. Church, business, and civic leaders throughout the country had combined forces even before July to smooth the way for compliance. Julius Manger, a wealthy hotel mogul and "one of the unsung heroes of the civil rights era," personally traveled the South that spring and summer to plead with other hospitality executives to effect a swift and peaceful integration of their facilities. Where his company owned a significant concentration of properties, he recalled, "I was able to say to other hotel and motel owners that I was not just asking them to do something and then going to walk away, but that we actually had a bigger investment to lose than they did."

Notwithstanding their signature accomplishments, civic, business, and religious leaders could only move the needle so far. By late 1964, thousands of southern schools, hospitals, and nursing homes remained strictly segregated, and in Deep South states like Mississippi only 10 percent of eligible black citizens were registered to vote. Cracking decades of state-enforced segregation and political disenfranchisement was beyond the means of private individuals and organizations. Compliance with the law would require the full force of the federal government. Ironically, southern congressmen had concentrated their fire on the bill's public accommodations provision rather than on Title VI, which stipulated that no public funds could support racially exclusive or segregated programs. It would ultimately prove easier to persuade restaurants and hotels to open their doors to African Americans than to compel public schools to mingle students and faculty, or health-care facilities to place black and white patients side by side. Even before the legislation cleared Congress, one of LBJ's top domestic policy advisers was readying federal departments to issue sweeping rules that would fundamentally reorder southern society. Securing a bill was a monumental achievement. Breathing life into it would carry far greater political risk.

As the day of the bill signing—July 2—faded into night, Bill Moyers found Johnson in a glum mood. "I think we just delivered the South to the Republican Party for a long time to come," Johnson told his aide.

CHAPTER 4

Revolutionary Activity

To spirit his antipoverty initiative to life, Lyndon Johnson turned to the one member of the extended Kennedy family who had ever shown him a moment's consideration: Sargent Shriver, the handsome, Yale-educated attorney whom JFK tapped to run the Peace Corps—arguably the most successful and popular of the New Frontier's domestic initiatives. Born to a prominent Catholic family in Maryland, Shriver fought in the Battle of Guadalcanal before returning to the United States. He moved to Chicago, where he managed Joseph P. Kennedy's Merchandise Mart out of the red and swiftly established himself as one of the emerging pillars of the city's business community. Along the way, he met and married Kennedy's daughter Eunice and became chairman of both the Chicago Board of Education and the Catholic Interracial Council. Devoted to the social justice wing of the Roman Catholic Church, he fused a tradition of faith and service to an impressive private-sector career. In 1960, he had been widely touted as a possible candidate for governor of Illinois, but he deferred to the wishes of his wife's brothers, who were determined that only one member of the Kennedy family should appear on the ballot in that election season. Among his responsibilities on JFK's presidential campaign was co-coordination of civil rights policy. When officials in Georgia arrested Martin Luther King Jr. on dubious charges that fall, it was Shriver who famously prodded the candidate to place a phone call to Coretta Scott King—a small gesture that later became central to Camelot lore. ("What the hell," his brother-in-law JFK responded. "That's a decent thing to do.") "He was just enormously impressive," recalled a reporter. "All the clichés fit: tall, dark, handsome. Fit as a college athlete at forty-five. He was warm and friendly and funny—was interested in everything, full of anecdotes. He knew as much about sports as he did about politics and as much about the civil rights movement as he did about theology." "Shriver had the kind of charisma that makes men charge the barricades," a Peace Corps staff member later said.

Johnson's principal tie to Shriver was Bill Moyers, who in the weeks after JFK's assassination had technically been on loan to the White House from his role as associate director of the Peace Corps. From their first meeting in late 1960, Shriver had been deeply impressed by Moyers, particularly by his almost singular ability to tolerate the famous LBJ "treatment." "Johnson would just come in and stand over you and try to overpower you with his physical presence," Shriver would explain. "And he'd do that to Moyers. And Moyers was just a kid, maybe less than 125 pounds. Johnson would yell at him, tell him what to do. And then I'd see Moyers stick his head back, and his jaw would clench and he'd grit his teeth and say, 'No.'" So close were Moyers and Johnson that when Shriver first angled to hire him, Kenny O'Donnell tried to block the appointment. "He's the only one on Johnson's staff we trust," he barked at Harris Wofford, a close associate of Shriver's. "The president's going to tell him to stay there, and you can tell Sarge to keep his cotton-picking hands off Moyers." Kennedy ultimately agreed to release Moyers to the Peace Corps, and in the months that followed, he became Shriver's indispensable right hand. The two men spent weeks lobbying skeptical legislators to secure passage of the Peace Corps bill. Though only twenty-seven years old, Moyers was by far a more experienced hand in the ways of congressional politics. "Bill Moyers and I have been living on the Hill," Shriver reported to the president at one critical moment. When Congress finally authorized the program, Moyers was recognized as the most influential among the legion of young, idealistic staffers who gathered each weekend at the Shrivers' rambling country estate, Timberlawn, for hours of Peace Corps meetings, family barbecues, and raucous outdoor sporting competitions.

After the assassination, Shriver managed the details of JFK's funeral while also serving as a conduit between LBJ and the Kennedy family. He even went so far as to present the new president with a brief memorandum, "What Bobby Thinks," outlining the psychology behind his brother-in-law's seemingly intractable hatred of Lyndon Johnson. Moyers also let it slip to reporters that Shriver was under consideration for vice president in the 1964 election, as indeed he was for a time. Johnson was under intense pressure to show solidarity with the

Kennedys, and as a member of the clan—but not quite a Kennedy himself—
Shriver provided Johnson with insulation against Bobby's ambitions. Moyers
and LBJ well understood that Shriver was in, but not of, RFK's orbit. Bobby
often derided Shriver as the resident "Boy Scout" and "house Communist"—
too soft to be a real Kennedy. "Believe me," recounted one of Bobby's longtime
aides, "Sarge was no close pal brother-in-law and he wasn't giving Robert Kennedy any extra breaks." With Moyers on loan to the White House and his own
brand rising in value, Shriver staked his future with LBJ. But even he was surprised when the president asked him to lead his new "War on Poverty."

Shriver returned to Washington on Friday, January 31, 1964, after a
monthlong international tour for the Peace Corps. Reporting to the Oval Office to brief the president on his travels, he thought little of it when Johnson
remarked, "You know, we're getting this war against poverty started. I'd like
you to think about that, because I'd like you to run that program for us." Shriver
would later admit that he was "totally unfamiliar with the whole project, having been in Asia when he announced the proposal. All I knew was a little item
I read in a Bangkok newspaper." The next afternoon, Johnson reached him by
phone at Timberlawn, where the director was spending a quiet day with his
wife and children, of whom he had seen precious little in the prior months,
given his punishing travel schedule. LBJ explained that in a matter of hours he
intended to announce Shriver's appointment to lead the War on Poverty. He
could retain ownership of the Peace Corps or hand that job off to a subordinate, but his primary responsibility going forward would be domestic policy.
Shriver protested repeatedly, but Johnson leaned in with his classic "treatment."

He enjoyed his work at the Peace Corps. ("You can write your ticket on
anything you want to do there," the president assured him.)

He knew nothing about poverty. ("Let me make it clear. Let me say that I
have asked you to study this.")

He would need help. ("If you want Bill to help you, I'll let him do that.")

He worried that "Bill Moyers and Sarge Shriver really to 99 percent of the
people abroad" were the face of the Peace Corps. With both of them deployed
elsewhere, the staff and volunteers might lose faith. ("Well, don't you think
that they're not damn glad that both of them have taken over the White
House?" the president asked.)

Could Moyers come back to the Peace Corps to help relieve him of administrative duties while he concentrated on poverty? ("I need him more than anybody in the world right here. And you need him here too. He's good for Shriver here.")

Could he not make Moyers acting director of the Peace Corps? ("Not and run the White House, too. And that's what he's doing now . . . now don't go raiding the White House! Go on and get your own damn talent.")

In the end, it came down, as it always did with Johnson, to a crude test of will. "Hell, it'll be a promotion!" he insisted. "You've got your identification with the Peace Corps. You've got everything you ever had there plus this. . . . Unless you've got some women that you think you won't have enough time to spend with them."

Shriver, a devout Catholic who since his college days had celebrated High Mass each day, laughed nervously.

"You've got the responsibility. You've got the authority. You've got the power. You've got the money. Now you may not have the glands."

"The glands?" Shriver replied incredulously.

"Yes."

"I got plenty of glands."

With that conversation, Sargent Shriver agreed reluctantly to lead the president's war to eradicate poverty.

Shriver's first move was to build his own group of trusted confidants to help fashion a legislative proposal. Chief among his advisers was Frank Mankiewicz, who headed the Peace Corps in Peru but happened to be in Washington, where he was slated to appear before the House Foreign Relations Committee. On Sunday afternoon, as he prepared his testimony, Mankiewicz found himself summoned to Shriver's office at the Peace Corps to participate in the first planning session. He would remain in Washington for six weeks, on loan from the job that he truly loved. "Through all of this period Shriver was perfectly willing to let us do anything in a sense, come up with all kinds of suggestions, and these would all go into a pot and people would talk about them," Mankiewicz would remark. "We'd discuss it. It was rather informal. We spent a lot of time at Shriver's house. We would stay up late because it was the best time to get work done because there were no phones ringing."

The working group brought together in one room several of the country's most capable minds: Daniel Patrick Moynihan, a working-class New Yorker and onetime longshoreman who earned a Ph.D. in international relations at Tufts University and was now serving as assistant secretary of labor, a post in which he functioned as the department's house intellectual; Harris Wofford, a white Peace Corps official with close ties to Martin Luther King Jr.; Wilbur Cohen of HEW, whom John Kennedy called "Mr. Social Security," in respectful acknowledgment of his role as a young New Dealer in establishing the Social Security Board and lifting the program off the ground; Dick Goodwin, who was already at work with Moyers in fashioning the organizing thesis of LBJ's Great Society; Michael Harrington, whose book *The Other America* had been instrumental in animating liberal passion around the blight of poverty; Dave Hackett and Dick Boone; Charles Schultze, the assistant budget director; Louis Martin; and Adam Yarmolinsky, the intense, fiery-eyed special assistant to Secretary of Defense Robert McNamara—a sober-minded tactician who wore a tight-cropped crew cut and perpetually looked "like he's got a bomb in his back pocket, ready to throw," by one colleague's estimation. A graduate of Harvard University and Yale Law School, Yarmolinsky clerked for the Supreme Court justice Stanley Reed before launching a successful legal career. As one of McNamara's bright young men, he earned the lasting enmity of southern congressmen when he cajoled the Defense Department into barring all servicemen from visiting or patronizing segregated facilities—a proviso that infuriated businessmen who operated stores and restaurants outside southern military installations.

Because all of the principals held day jobs at the highest echelons of the federal government, meetings were scheduled on weekends or weekday evenings. The planning committee had neither a budget (Shriver relied on a small appropriation from Johnson's presidential contingency fund) nor adequate offices. Initially housed in the Court of Claims building—an abandoned structure that predated the Civil War—the small support staff was forced to relocate when a large portion of its plaster ceiling caved in and engineers declared the entire edifice unsafe. From there, they claimed space in the basement of a decrepit hospital and a floor of a derelict hotel that in its glory days had functioned as a "second-class whorehouse." Each time they moved, secretaries and task force members were assigned new telephone extensions, contributing to almost constant logistical confusion. Badly under-resourced, they pilfered office supplies from other federal agencies. Despite these deficiencies, Shriver's makeshift operation soon became a center of gravity in Washington. There was an "excellent esprit de corps," remembered one of the participants. Johnson would later salute the "contagious" enthusiasm behind the antipoverty working group. "They went at it with a fervor and created a ferment unknown since the days of the New Deal," he wrote, "when lights burned through the night as men worked to restructure society."

James L. Sundquist, an official on loan from the Department of Agriculture, observed that "Shriver's own temperament and method of operation was extremely open and fluid. He doesn't like fixed organizations anyway, so he was perfectly in his milieu on this one." Yet even though Shriver cast a "dragnet out for new ideas and additional ideas," the departments offered precious few new ideas—except for community action. When Heller's group first met with Shriver, they imparted their shared conviction that the larger initiative should focus on unlocking opportunity through an attack on the "root causes" of poverty, rather than redistributing wealth or income. Community action programs (CAPs) of the variety pioneered by the Ford Foundation and the juvenile delinquency commission, Schultze advised, should be the driving force behind the administration's program. Shriver was initially skeptical. "It'll never fly," he told Yarmolinsky. Both men soon came around and agreed that community action should constitute an important part of the antipoverty plan, if not its entirety. For one, the governing ethos behind community action—that local communities should be equipped with the means to build sustainable, homegrown institutions—was not altogether different from what the Peace Corps was attempting outside the United States. Mankiewicz believed "the notion of organizing people around their grievances to accomplish a single thing, whether it was to set up a co-op or clinic or soccer team or to get the playground open at night or whatever it might have been, was . . . in a sense revolutionary since the idea of it was to create alternate situations of power in a country where most people were powerless." Moreover, as Yarmolinsky observed, it was clear from the start that funds would be limited—at least in the first year. "One of the choices we had to make was whether to concentrate on preparing jobs for people or preparing people for jobs. We decided for the latter, partly because we thought that the president's tax cuts would in effect be job-creating, partly because we thought it takes more time to prepare people for jobs than jobs for people." Firm in the shared conviction that economic planners could manufacture permanent growth—the very purpose of the Kennedy/Johnson tax cuts—Shriver's group assumed prima facie that antipoverty policy need not concern itself with redistributing resources in the form of make-work programs or income floors.

Shriver's freewheeling approach carried genuine benefits and drew many admirers. No proposal was too impractical to consider. Experts were flown in from universities and think tanks at the eleventh hour. There were countless salon-style dinners at Timberlawn, where "doctors, theologians . . . psychologists . . . all manner of people" debated long into the night. A friend remarked that Sarge was "crazy about these ideas, and many of these ideas were, in fact, crazy." But the hurried pace and emphasis on bold experimentation and immediate results—qualities that many observers so admired about the Peace Corps—sometimes translated poorly to the War on Poverty. In a rush to introduce a program before Congress, Shriver's committee never reached consensus on the meaning of its central premise: "community action."

Some participants did not believe that community action required "any radical shift of authority to the poor." Rather, they assumed that "the appointment of poor people or their representatives to program governing bodies or advisory committees" was essentially "more symbolic than substantive." On the other side of the spectrum, Mankiewicz and some of the younger members of the task force assumed that community action was "an essentially revolutionary activity"—a way to equip the poor with resources to challenge local institutions, both in the public sector and in the private sector, in the pursuit of greater opportunity. They regarded municipal and county governments, school districts, and old-line social service agencies as entrenched interests that were fundamentally hostile to the aspirations of poor people.

Among the skeptics was Lyndon Johnson, who told Bill Moyers in August, "You—all, you boys got together and wrote this stuff, and I thought we were just going to have [another] NYA [National Youth Administration]. . . . I thought that we'd say to a high school boy that was about to drop out, 'We'll let you work for the library or sweep the floors or work in the shrubs or pick the rocks, and we'll pay you enough,' so he can stay in school."

"We've got that," Moyers responded, referring to the bill's inclusion of a Job Corps program for impoverished youth.

"I thought we were going to have community action, where a city or county or a school district or some governmental agency could sponsor a project. I never heard of liberal outfits where you could subsidize anybody. I think I'm against that. If you want to do it in the Peace Corps, then that's your private thing. That's Kennedy."

LBJ preferred that Mayor Richard Daley run antipoverty programs in Chicago rather than the Urban League. "He's got heads of departments, and he's got experienced people at handling hundreds of millions of dollars." Though he envisioned his War on Poverty through the prism of the New Deal, LBJ ultimately permitted Moyers and Shriver to pursue their more unconventional and potentially disruptive initiative.

The antipoverty legislation that Shriver's group moved through Congress—the Economic Opportunity Act of 1964—ultimately contained six sections, or, in legislative parlance, "titles." The bill did in fact authorize the creation of the Job Corps, modeled in part after the New Deal–era Civilian Conservation Corps and NYA, with a mandate to relocate, socialize, and train tens of thousands of young men who were otherwise outside the labor force and lacking the basic skills to become gainfully employed. In addition, it established the Neighborhood Youth Corps, which would provide basic medical care, food security, and supplementary education to urban youth, and a work-study program for low-income undergraduates. The second, and by far the most controversial, section of the act authorized public and private organizations to operate government-funded community action programs. Critically, the bill required "maximum feasible participation" in such activities by local residents. The bill also authorized loans and grants to help impoverished farmers buy new tools and equipment—a provision that the Department of Agriculture strongly championed; provided funds for small-business loans and work-experience initiatives aimed at helping unemployed heads of households; and established Volunteers in Service to America (VISTA), a "domestic Peace Corps" that would deploy college graduates to help impoverished communities ameliorate their local conditions. In total, the measure devoted approximately $1 billion to LBJ's War on Poverty: $500 million in new funding, and $500 million that the administration redirected from existing programs. Most of its functions would be housed under the aegis of a new executive branch bureau—the Office of Economic Opportunity (OEO)—whose director, Sargent Shriver, would enjoy cabinet-level status.

In building the OEO's programs, Shriver was deprived of his most valuable asset: Adam Yarmolinsky. Southern congressmen who still fumed at his forced integration of military base towns now seized the opportunity to exact their price. Focusing on his alleged affiliation with a radical student group during his undergraduate days at Harvard, they insisted that Yarmolinsky was subversive—unfit to run the OEO (though, ironically, they voiced little objection to his return to the Pentagon). Shriver had only been able to secure passage of the Economic Opportunity Act by pledging that Yarmolinsky would play no forward role in the War on Poverty. It was an unfortunate development. Shriver excelled at vision and inspiration; Yarmolinsky, at organization. "Sarge's idea of administration is to give three guys the same assignment and see who finished first," an anonymous official told the syndicated columnists Rowland Evans and Robert Novak. Even as late as December, they reported, OEO officials routinely telephoned their former colleague at his Pentagon office, seeking direction and counsel.

From the start, the community action programs, which absorbed almost half of the OEO's budget for fiscal year 1965, proved a political lightning rod. Working within broad guidelines, organizations in and outside government—including public colleges, nonprofits, and municipal and county bodies—submitted grant proposals to deliver services as wide-ranging as health care, job training, child care, and housing assistance. To their credit, Shriver and his staff moved quickly to disperse money and initiate programming. "Sarge . . . and many others in the Congress were pressing the program people to get the money out and to go, go, go," recalled an OEO official. "It became obvious after a while that the only safety valve in the place was our office." By the end of the decade, over a thousand community action agencies participated in the initiative. Yet the safety valve was anything but tight. By early 1965, elected officials from across the country began complaining to Moyers,

Johnson, and Shriver that CAPs were bypassing their offices or, worse, organizing pickets, lawsuits, and political action *against* them. "Many mayors assert that the CAP is setting up a *competing political organization* in their own backyards," Charles Schultze confided to the president. (Indeed, in 1965 the U.S. Conference of Mayors pressed the administration to turn control of community action programs over to local political authorities.) He urged that *"we ought not to be in the business of organizing the poor politically."* Jim Rowe warned that local CAPs were "using public funds to *instruct* people how to protest." The implications of this dynamic were "obvious": the administration was providing antipoverty activists with funds to organize against the very same political machines that powered the Democratic Party at the state and local levels. Of course this approach was precisely how many of the OEO's framers understood the strategic value of community action. There could be no other purpose behind the grant to Syracuse University for a program that trained local poor people in the political organizing tactics of Saul Alinsky. In turn, they used their newly acquired skills to agitate for better sanitation services, rent subsidies, tenant rights, and parks and—in a move that raised the ire of the city's Republican mayor—to register voters. "We are experiencing a class struggle in the traditional Karl Marx style," the mayor complained, "and I do not like it."

When a CAP in Albuquerque organized pickets outside city hall, in demand of greater services for poor neighborhoods, Senator Clinton Anderson, a Democrat, called Shriver to complain. "The demonstration is being led by an ex-Peace Corps volunteer who's working in the Community Action Program now," he said with bewilderment. As Mankiewicz remembered the episode, it gave the senator cold comfort when Shriver replied, "Both of the agencies I'm running are successful. A guy who agitated the poor in Peru for two years took that training and used it and is now working for OEO to get the poor to demand that they be allowed to participate in city council meetings. That's what it's all about." Community programs in Newark, San Francisco, and other cities drew sharp scrutiny for their radicalism, financial irregularities, and palpable animosity toward established institutions, be they public or private. On the Lower East Side of Manhattan, Mobilization for Youth—one of the first products of the Ford Foundation's Gray Areas project—sued the New York Police Department and clamored for the establishment of a civilian review board. When a police shooting of a black teenager prompted riots in Harlem, conservative critics scored Mobilization for Youth as a radical and incendiary organization.

In Chicago, where the OEO insisted that the city government comply with the requirement that its program include "maximum feasible participation" on the part of local poor people, Mayor Richard Daley grew enraged. "What in the hell are you people doing?" he berated Moyers. "Does the President know he's putting M-O-N-E-Y in the hands of subversives? To poor people that aren't a part of the organization? Didn't the President know they'd take that money to bring him down?" Daley was an indispensable ally whose complaints resonated sharply within the West Wing, as was also the case with Sam Yorty and John Shelley, the Democratic mayors of Los Angeles and San Francisco, respectively. "Mayors all over the United States are being harassed by agitation prompted by Sargent Shriver's speeches urging those he calls 'poor' to insist upon control of local poverty programs," Yorty complained in mid-1965. Though in many instances the administration interceded on behalf of elected officials—including in Syracuse, where Shriver folded the controversial action program under an umbrella organization governed by municipal officials and old-line welfare agencies—there was no clear consensus about the definition of "maximum feasible participation" or even its very purpose. Hubert Humphrey, who often served as mediator with local officials after his election to the vice presidency in 1964, argued that the administration could ensure "maximum feasible participation" without antagonizing mayors. But many poor people who participated in community action initiatives explicitly set out to disrupt local politics.

In later years, Moynihan, who played a leading role in developing the War on Poverty as the Labor Department's representative to Shriver's interagency task force, would claim that "maximum feasible participation" was originally narrow in its intent—a safeguard to ensure that southern officials did not direct federal antipoverty funds toward segregated or all-white programs. Only later, when radicals inside the OEO leveraged the statutory language to enforce an adversarial agenda toward local institutions, did community action go off the rails. It was, Moynihan quipped, a singular case of "maximum feasible misunderstanding." Frederick Hayes, who served as assistant director of the agency's Community Action Program, agreed that the framers never intended to antagonize local governments and were surprised by the hostility that community action engendered. In most cities, "the program got off the ground smoothly and with enormous good results right away.... [I]t was only in Syracuse, New York, and Chicago and Mississippi and a few places like that where the cutting edge of the conflict was."

In its first year, community action programs accounted for roughly half of the OEO's authorized budget of $1 billion. Critics then and later would compare this total unfavorably with the New Deal, which authorized billions of dollars in jobs, housing, and relief programs. Yet despite Johnson's occasional inconsistency—"You tell Shriver no doles," he instructed Moyers, though on other occasions he envisioned the OEO as a latter-day National Youth Administration—the agency was never intended to furnish poor people with employment or income assistance. It all came back to the common understanding that if government managed economic growth and unlocked opportunity, poverty would recede. "I think it is a Liberal view, rather than a Conservative view, that there are too many Americans forced to live on our welfare rolls," Busby advised Johnson to say. The administration was addressing the roots, not just the symptoms, of poverty. "We have an obligation in our society... to support a principle of public policy which will permit every citizen not only to live at a certain minimum standard but to be able to live at a rising standard by his own effort and his own training and ability."

In cities as diverse as Oakland, Newark, New Haven, Durham, and Boston, a rising generation of elected officials cut their teeth as local program organizers. In 1977, a survey of black mayors, city council members, and state representatives found that 20 percent had been involved with community action programs in the prior decade, while many others worked or volunteered with a broader range of OEO initiatives. Some activists would complain that the "major beneficiaries of these programs have been non-poor persons who have been afforded the opportunity of executive, technical and professional positions in the program," a charge that Alinsky sounded when he denounced the "vast network of sergeants drawing general's pay." But such objections sidestepped one of the original intentions of community action: to empower individuals and communities to forge their own destiny. Ironically, though the Great Society did not create mass work programs for poor people, many of its major initiatives, including Medicare and Medicaid and aid to elementary and secondary education, required a larger federal and state workforce to administer. The resulting expansion of public-sector employment benefited a rising black professional class that now enjoyed protections against workforce discrimination. In the decades that followed Johnson's War on Poverty, government employment helped lift millions of African Americans—particularly teachers, social service workers, and nurses—into the middle class. In addition to serving poor clients, community action programs were both a fundamental training ground for black professionals and a powerful mechanism to grow black political power.

Almost as controversial as community action programs was the Job Corps, a program modeled after the New Deal's Civilian Conservation Corps and National Youth Administration, both of which provided temporary jobs to young men who repaired roads and national parks and provided labor to support land conservation and improvement. By 1967, its year of peak operation, the Job Corps employed forty-two thousand young people—mostly men—at a combination of rural work camps and urban skill centers, where enrollees learned basic carpentry, electrical wiring, welding, and other manual trades. The Office of Economic Opportunity blanketed poor neighborhoods with over 300,000 application cards and promotional pamphlets. From the start, the program's directors determined to accept "almost the toughest"—young men and women from blighted neighborhoods who lacked formal education or life and work skills. With the exception of recidivist criminals and applicants suffering serious mental or physical handicaps, the Job Corps drew its ranks from a group of Americans who otherwise seemed destined for prison or penury.

It was a noble endeavor, and for a small number of corpsmen like George Foreman, the future heavyweight boxing title holder, it was probably life changing. A native of Houston, where he grew up in slum conditions and, as a teenager, had already fallen into a pattern of petty crime, Foreman was, by his own later admission, destined to graduate to "robbing and armed robbing." But for the Job Corps, he "would eventually have moved to dope and . . . spent the rest of the days in prison." His journey from Texas to a job site in Oregon was eye-opening—"I had never been on an airplane," he remembered. "We didn't know airports existed." He had never owned a set of new clothes—non-hand-me-down—in his life, but at the program center administrators furnished him with black trousers and a blazer for formal occasions, work attire, and exercise clothing. "The Job Corps teachers . . . embraced me like I was a rich guy," he remembered. "They taught me how to read. They taught me how to build fences. They taught me how to construct a radio. I was so proud of that." Years later, Foreman still viewed the OEO director as a "celestial figure." When he visited their camps, "his hair tucked to the side of his head real neatly, and dressed very fancy," shaking the corpsmen's hands as though they were his own kin, this Kennedy family in-law became an "in-house hero to us. . . . All the boys felt that way about Sarge Shriver."

To many Americans, however, the Job Corps quickly assumed a different character. Lifting very poor young men—black and white, urban and rural, unskilled and uneducated, often from tumultuous home environments—from their neighborhoods and placing them in strange settings together was a risky undertaking, and it generated ample cause for concern. At Camp Kilmer in New Jersey, newspapers reported that corpsmen were habitually high on illegal narcotics and often stoned cars that drove past the work site. At Camp Atterbury in Indiana, several young men were arrested on sodomy charges. At a camp in western Kentucky, fighting broke out between black and white corpsmen. Neither was it apparent a year into the program's existence that the trainees left any better prepared to lead productive work lives than before they arrived. When a conservative senator scoffed that it would cost less to send a single corpsman to Harvard than to enroll him in the Job Corps for a year, Shriver quibbled with the math. In fact, he demonstrated, it cost the government just *two-thirds* the cost of a year at Harvard to train each corpsman. It was a well-intentioned rejoinder, but not one that was likely to quell the criticism.

Though community action would remain a lightning rod for criticism, perhaps the most enduringly popular of Johnson's Great Society programs, Head Start, began life as part of the CAP initiative. It also owed its conception, as was so often the case with programs emanating from the Office of Economic Opportunity, to a quick impulsive flash of Shriver's inspiration. Driving home to Timberlawn one evening in late 1964, Shriver pondered research that the Kennedy Foundation had funded into the use of early intervention to raise the IQs of children with intellectual disabilities. After consulting with Robert

Cooke, a physician at Johns Hopkins University who worked closely with the foundation, Shriver concluded that the same early exposure to education might prepare poor children to capture the advantages available to them as they progressed through school and entered the workforce. Many economically disadvantaged "kids arrive at the first grade beaten or at least handicapped before they start," he observed. "To use an analogy from sports, they stand 10, 20, and 30 feet back from the starting line; other people are way ahead of them. They don't get a fair, equal start with everyone else when they come to school at the age of six." By extending early childhood education to at-risk children, the government could level the playing field. It was a concept firmly rooted in opportunity theory and in the guiding principles that informed Great Society policy making. Over lunch at the Hay-Adams hotel, Shriver shared the idea with the widely syndicated columnist Joe Alsop, whom he considered "incorrigibly negativist" and therefore a likely skeptic. To his happy surprise, Alsop responded enthusiastically. "If Joe's not knocking the idea," thought Shriver, "it's not likely to be knocked."

Shriver hoped that if his office moved with haste, it could prepare and launch a summer pilot program in 1965 with 25,000 children. He instructed Dick Boone to begin planning. Twice each week in January and February, a dozen outside advisers and CAP staff members met to hammer out what would ultimately be designated the Cooke Report. Notably, very few members of the working committee were professional educators; most were medical professionals and psychologists. Their report suggested a comprehensive program of early childhood education, medical care, and nutritional services and—in keeping with the spirit of community action—heavy involvement from the parents of poor children. Jule Sugarman, one of Boone's deputies, recalled that the ad hoc committee far exceeded Shriver's original ambitions when it suggested that the OEO launch a sizable pilot program in the summer of 1965 across three hundred communities, reaching 100,000 youngsters. The proposal immediately excited both LBJ, who instructed Shriver to triple the size of the program, and Lady Bird, who lent the initiative a much-needed early endorsement when she hosted a tea at the White House to raise visibility and support. In attendance was a "large representation" of journalists, leading women in government and business, the wives of governors and big-city mayors, and prominent actors and entertainers. The result was an outpouring of interest from communities across the country. Instead of 100,000 children, the pilot program that summer ultimately served 560,000.

As with other OEO projects, Head Start posed enormous administrative challenges. Conceived in late winter, it would need to establish guidelines and curricula, process thousands of applications from local school districts and CAPs, hire thousands of staff members, and recruit half a million poor children in just a matter of months. Julius Richmond, a noted pediatrician and medical school professor, agreed to join the OEO as the first director of Head Start and quickly accepted Sugarman's suggestion that the program lean heavily on substitute teachers who were likely to claim college degrees and pedagogical training and who would be out of work during the summer and in need of a paycheck. The organizers further agreed that the program should focus on both four-year-olds and five-year-olds, because scarcely half of American children had access to public kindergarten. The OEO deployed 125 college volunteers to visit poor communities and enlist local service organizations, community action programs, school districts, and civic groups to sponsor and administer Head Start programs. A bipartisan group of congressional wives phone banked their districts "until they found somebody who was willing to talk about Head Start," Sugarman recalled. "Once they had that name then we'd send one or two of these young people off to sit down with them. They literally wrote the applications for most of these communities, and literally helped them to set up their centers even though they knew very little about it themselves." To train the summer staff and faculty members, the administration enlisted the participation of two hundred colleges and universities that sponsored six-day orientation programs for over forty-four thousand Head Start employees; to ensure the program's smooth operation and integrity, over two thousand health professionals, educators, and social workers formed an auxiliary "technical assistance corps" that fanned out across the country to help local organizations administer their programs effectively.

Despite the harried and ad hoc way in which it was conceived, Head Start proved immediately popular and became one of the untouchable legacies of LBJ's Great Society. Over thirty years later, the program served 900,000 poor children annually and in public opinion polls enjoyed the approval of over 90 percent of respondents. And of course, as early as 1969, there were critics who questioned the lasting value of early childhood education generally and

Head Start specifically. Some studies have concluded that whatever educational gains poor children made through the program quickly eroded by the time they reached grade school and middle school. Though other studies challenge this finding, in the decades after Head Start's launch, some consensus emerged that early intervention was not powerful enough in and of itself to reverse the combined challenges of single-parent households, persistent income and wealth inequality, neighborhood crime and deterioration, and failing public schools. Such criticisms implicitly call into question the underlying logic behind the War on Poverty—namely, that what was needed to break the cycle of poverty was opportunity, not cash transfers or income assistance.

But these criticisms miss the mark in a critical way. Head Start endeavored to close the gap in educational achievement, but that was just one of its mandates. The program also provided poor children with hot, nutritious meals each day, as well as medical and dental care (often for the first time in their lives). They learned and played in a stable and nurturing environment where their parents could act as full partners in their care and development. A government study found that among Head Start pupils in 1969, roughly one-third had not received their complete diphtheria, pertussis, and tetanus immunizations; nearly 40 percent had not been vaccinated against polio; and very few had received dental or eye exams. In Jacksonville, Florida, 52 percent of Head Start children were anemic; 31 percent suffered from hearing defects and 25 percent from eye problems. In South Carolina's Beaufort County, 90 percent of preschool-aged children had hookworm or roundworm. In Boston, 31 percent of eligible students endured major physical or psychological issues. More than just an early education program, Head Start provided its students services that materially narrowed the yawning wellness gap between poor and nonpoor youngsters. Although, as Daniel Patrick Moynihan later noted, Head Start proved so generally popular that most Americans never realized or soon forgot that it began life within the controversial Community Action Program, many of CAP's guiding principles were embedded in its playbook. Particularly in full-year Head Start programs, 90 percent of which were administered in the early years by local CAPs, parents and paraprofessionals from the community played an outsized role in staffing and maintaining local programs. Based on both firsthand knowledge and program data, Sugarman believed that "the non-professionals bring a different quality to the program than a program that's purely professionally run . . . it brings a dimension of sensitivity and concern that's better than you have in a purely professionally run program."

Julius Richmond would later recall one of his first encounters with Lyndon Johnson. In the spring of 1965, he accompanied Shriver to the White House for the announcement of the first round of Head Start grants. Entering the Oval Office, he shook the president's hand and instantly "did a double take" when LBJ pulled him close and confided, "You know, this whole thing is where I came in." Sensing Richmond's confusion, LBJ continued, "Well, you know, I'm a schoolteacher. I was teaching Mexican American children. This program is designed to do what we were trying to do way back then." Richmond observed that Johnson was "very intrigued and interested and very committed." Two years later, he had occasion to attend a White House screening of a documentary film, *Pancho*, about a Mexican American child who benefited from the Head Start program. During the screening, which the young boy's parents also attended, the president leaned over toward Richmond and "with tears in his eyes [said], 'This is all of what I used to see when I was teaching school down there in south Texas.'"

The brainchild of Sargent Shriver, it was up and running in a matter of months. It would later strike Richmond as remarkable that the administration never secured congressional approval to launch Head Start. It originated under the Community Action Program line in the OEO's budget and, as such, needed no such authorization and only later won permanent status from Congress. "I don't know of many other instances in the recent history of the United States . . . where anybody, anybody, anybody—I even include the president, almost—was ever able to start a program of national magnitude, involving, let's say, $70 million, without asking anybody for permission to do any of it."

CHAPTER 5

Frontlash

In July 1964, not even weeks after Johnson signed the Civil Rights Act into law, the venerated pollster Lou Harris described for readers of *Newsweek* an emerging and in many ways alarming development: in recent surveys of white ethnic voters in northern and midwestern cities, two-thirds of respondents feared "that most Negroes want to take jobs held by whites" and tended "to feel that the pace of civil rights is too fast"—that "Negroes are getting too 'uppity' for their own good." He warned that "the white backlash itself exists, lurking more or less menacingly in the background, but it is not yet a major force in the land." Harris did not coin the term "white backlash." That honor rested with the economist Eliot Janeway, who a year earlier forewarned that should automation and economic stagnation erode postwar gains in factory employment, white workers would perceive themselves in a zero-sum competition with African Americans and "lash back" in an ugly and potentially violent fashion. Though the concept—to say nothing of the phrase—was still unfamiliar to most casual students of current affairs, the savviest of politicians were already attuned to the shifting currents.

During a visit to East Asia several weeks earlier, Richard Nixon called on Henry Cabot Lodge, the U.S. ambassador to South Vietnam, who had been his running mate four years earlier. Nixon perceived a simmering discontent among "low income urban white groups" that stood to lose—or *thought* they stood to lose—in the wake of economic and social advancements by African Americans. Writing to his son, Lodge—a blue-blooded patrician who served in the U.S. Senate before losing his seat to John F. Kennedy over a decade earlier—reported that Nixon also "spoke of the practice known as 'bussing' whereby the white child is transported by bus from his suburban home into the slums to go to the slum school, and the Negro is transported by bus from his home in the slums to the school in the suburbs." In 1964, busing was still a new practice; it would not attract widespread adoption or scrutiny until later in the decade. But it testified to his limited political acumen that Lodge had not "read much about this in the papers."

Despite his recent string of victories—securing passage of the tax cuts, the Civil Rights Act, and the Economic Opportunity Act—Johnson was equally cognizant of the political headwinds he might face in the coming election. "If we aren't careful," he told George Reedy, "we're just gonna be presiding over a country that's so badly split-up that they'll vote for anybody that isn't us." The president had good cause to worry. As early as January, George Wallace, Alabama's arch-segregationist governor, began testing the waters for his own run for the Democratic nomination. In New England, skeptical audiences were startled to hear the southern populist speak in a calm and not altogether unconvincing tone about why "property rights are human rights, too." In California, he charmed local civic organizations and reveled in delivering sharp ripostes to liberal hecklers; in Berkeley, whose otherwise progressive voters had recently defeated an open housing referendum, he reminded the crowd that "they voted just like the people in Alabama." Though he attracted the scorn of Democratic officeholders during his swing through the Midwest's industrial belt—in Ohio, Senator Steve Young derided him as a buffoon; in Madison, Wisconsin, left-wing activists used Kool-Aid to engrave the frozen pond outside his guest quarters with the greeting "FUCK WALLACE"—local elected officials soon began to worry that the rabble-rouser might very well animate the fears and resentments of working-class, ethnic white voters.

They were right. After launching his campaign in Appleton, home to the late GOP senator Joseph McCarthy, Wallace canvassed the state's blue-collar wards with tireless discipline. In Milwaukee, over seven hundred working men and women packed the local American Serb Memorial Hall to hear Wallace confirm their suspicions that the civil rights bill then still pending in Congress would imperil their jobs, neighborhoods, and safety. "A vote for this little governor will let people in Washington know that we want them to leave our houses, schools, jobs, businesses, and farms alone," he roared to thunderous applause. The statute would "destroy the union seniority system and impose racial quotas." It would be "impossible for a home owner to sell his home to whomever he chooses." The crowd, which comprised mainly white residents of Serbian, Polish, Czechoslovakian, and Hungarian descent, had in recent years watched with guarded caution as the city's black neighborhood pushed up against their insular community of small, tidy bungalows, community schools, and ethnic churches. When a black civil rights protester garbed in a clerical collar taunted, "Get your dogs out!" the event's master of ceremonies, Bronko Gruber—a brawny military veteran and neighborhood bar owner—swept to his feet. "I'll tell you something about your dogs, Padre," he screamed. "I live on Walnut Street and three weeks ago tonight a friend of mine was assaulted by three of your countrymen, or whatever you want to call them. . . . They beat up old ladies eighty-three years old, rape our womenfolk. They mug people. They won't work. They are on relief. How long can we tolerate this? *Did I go to Guadalcanal to come back to something like this!?*"

Because initial polling had Wallace running at a negligible 5 percent, Johnson was rattled when Governor John Reynolds, his favorite-son proxy on the primary ballot, warned that Wallace might win as many as 175,000 votes, or over 15 percent of the projected turnout. Reynolds, whose successful advocacy of a state open housing law rendered him anathema in blue-collar neighborhoods, was inflating his real estimate to rally regular Democrats to action. Yet even his overestimation fell far short of the mark. On primary day, Wallace won 265,000 votes, or one-quarter of those cast. He prevailed in the governor's own district and took 30 percent of the vote in Milwaukee and 47 percent in the newly created Ninth Congressional District, which included some of the region's most prosperous suburbs. "We won without winning!" he boasted, a deed that he replicated weeks later in Indiana, where he took 30 percent, and again in Maryland, where 43 percent of the state's primary voters backed the outspoken segregationist. Disenchanted voters marched to the polls "with big grins on their faces," a newspaper editor observed. "I never saw anything like it." Senator Daniel Brewster, Johnson's proxy on the ballot in Maryland, fumed that Wallace's supporters had been hoodwinked by a "pack of mindless thugs," but there was little doubting that something was darkly amiss in the nation's heartland.

Wallace's speeches were laced with crude appeals to fear of crime ("If you are knocked in the head on a street in a city today," he warned, "the man who knocked you in the head is out of jail before you get to the hospital"), class resentment ("They're building a new bridge over the Potomac for all the white liberals fleeing to Virginia"), and race war ("Anyone here from Philadelphia?

You know, they can't even have night football games anymore because of the trouble between the races. And that's the city of brotherly love!").

If his rhetorical barrages were ugly and reckless, they were not random. Between 1910 and 1970, roughly 6.5 million African Americans left the South, swelling the population of northern, midwestern, and western cities. In that same space of time, the portion of black Americans living in the former Confederacy fell from 77 percent to less than 50 percent.

Though leaving Dixie presented them with comparatively greater freedom, including the unqualified right to vote, discriminatory employment practices limited black residents to some of the lowest-paying jobs and highest rates of unemployment. Racially restrictive housing laws—some enforced by a complex web of regulations handed down by federal mortgage agencies—consigned them to the worst, most cramped—yet paradoxically most overpriced—housing stock. And an absence of basic public services like reliable garbage removal, building inspection, and quality schools made them second-class citizens in most places where they lived.

Discrimination created a vicious cycle. Because African Americans faced rampant job discrimination, they tended to earn less cash income than their white neighbors and rely more heavily on welfare. Because discriminatory rental and mortgage practices sharply limited their residential options, black residents enjoyed little recourse when landlords in transitional neighborhoods consolidated and subdivided their properties, creating more cramped and run-down housing stock. As a result, many urban black neighborhoods came gradually to resemble wastelands—at least in the eyes of watchful, working-class white residents whose own tidy neighborhoods stood in proximity. Boarded-up, abandoned buildings seemed to dot every block, because landlords often found it more advantageous to pack more tenants in one property than to pay property taxes and maintenance on two. Such decay did, in fact, tend to attract a disproportionate share of drug dealers, vagrants, prostitutes, and vandals. In short, when residents of white ethnic enclaves in Gary, Indiana, or Milwaukee, Wisconsin, pointed to surrounding black neighborhoods with fear, they were reacting from genuine experience. In their assumption that ghetto residents *chose* to live in such degraded circumstances, they spoke from a position of willful ignorance—ignorance of the privilege they derived from the G.I. Bill's housing and educational opportunities, ignorance of their favored position in unionized industries, and ignorance of their superior access to public services. When they lashed out at white liberals, they had a point: no one was asking the residents of Georgetown or Chevy Chase to make personal sacrifices in the cause of civil rights. Even in the event that open housing laws prevailed, their neighborhoods were too expensive to attract large numbers of working-class black families. These contradictions would not be laid bare until later in the decade. But the early warning signs were already evident in the spring primary season. Wallace was a shrewd manipulator of public opinion and understood precisely how to broaden the appeal of his white supremacist agenda among urban and inner-ring suburban white voters outside the South.

LBJ's advisers were acutely aware of the challenge before them. Dan Rostenkowski, a Democratic congressman who represented heavily Polish American neighborhoods in Chicago, privately shared polling with Jack Valenti that suggested 78 percent of his constituents opposed the Civil Rights Act. "They are mostly Catholic," Valenti informed the president, "but in spite of the Church's emphatic stand on civil rights, they are very much opposed to the Negro advances. The Polish people are real estate conscious and worry about the value of their homes."

Richard Scammon, an influential political scientist whom JFK had installed as director of the census, warned Moyers that polling revealed a deep undercurrent of disaffection. "The American white majority's view of civil rights and race can only be labeled as confused, contradictory, and apprehensive." Most northern white respondents supported federal protection of civil rights activists, but they also believed that "mass Negro demonstrations are harmful." A commanding majority supported the Civil Rights Act, but "it is in such areas as street violence, the busing of school children, the right of a home owner not to sell to a Negro, the movement of Negro families 'onto this block,' and the movement of Negro workers 'into my job,' that the deep, gut-level apprehension bites into a super-structure of white tolerance and liberalism. While almost no whites would deny the Negro the right to vote, the majority would say: 'I'll be Goddamned if my kid has to ride a bus across this city to go to school in a Negro slum.'" Scammon found this sentiment increasingly evident among "lower middle class and working class families, many of them lifelong Democrats." By his assessment, the race issue could very well spell the difference between a blowout victory on par with Roosevelt's in 1936 or a narrow loss. "The vital importance of the race issue cannot be overestimated," he informed Moyers. Scammon observed that most Americans identified neither as liberals nor as conservatives but rather as "middle-of-the-roaders." Given his newfound zeal for civil rights and antipoverty measures, Johnson was almost assured solid liberal support. If he could fuse the vast middle of the spectrum to his left-wing base, he was assured to win. "[The] opportunities to identify the Administration with the viewpoints of moderation and of the middle-of-the-road seem obvious," he concluded.

Other presidential advisers agreed. In July, Horace Busby warned the president that "many in the Democratic Party apparatus have a naïve, immature, unreal view of what the Party is up against." Buzz worried that popular "euphoria" and "confidence" rested on the flawed assumption that since 1932 the Democratic Party had emerged as the presumptive "presidential party"; after all, it had won six of the last eight presidential elections, and it was easy to write off the Eisenhower interlude (1953–1961) as "an aberration, an interruption in an inexorable Democratic trend attributable solely to Eisenhower's unique 'war hero' appeal." These assumptions, Busby argued, did not hold up under an "unsentimental, hard-nose, reading of the political history." On the contrary, it was the Roosevelt era that was anomalous—the peculiar product of the Great Depression and World War II. In the sixteen presidential elections to date in the twentieth century, Republicans had racked up a cumulative plurality of 9.2 million votes, and not simply because of their predominant position in the first three decades of the century. Since 1948, their advantage in presidential elections amounted to an aggregate plurality of 13.9 million votes. While Busby conceded that Democrats did enjoy a massive advantage at the state and local levels, it was not lost on Johnson—or on any member of his team—that this point reflected artificial padding by southern Democrats, who since the late 1930s gradually came to hold little common ground with the rest of their party. Johnson had spent over twenty years in Congress carefully straddling the ever-widening chasm between the party's southern bloc, which was resistant to federal intervention in civil rights and the economy, and its northern and western blocs, which relied increasingly on the support of minority voters and organized labor. As a senator, Johnson had been more solicitous of the powerful southern committee chairmen who installed him as majority leader. As president, both hard electoral math and personal conviction required that he swing to the left.

Buzz believed that there was ample room to move leftward without losing broad support. He advised that Johnson abandon the interest group—or "bloc"—strategy that swept FDR into the White House in 1932 and that Harry Truman employed in his come-from-behind victory in 1948. Instead, Johnson should steer a clear course through the political center and "present himself not as a coalition leader of blocs but as a national interest leader." While John Kennedy had, on the surface, pursued a bloc strategy aimed at re-fusing Catholic voters (who had defected in sizable numbers to Ike) and southern Democrats (who had been wobbly in their party affinity since 1948), once he assumed the presidency, Busby argued, JFK moved away from Franklin Roosevelt's style, rhetoric, and electoral strategy and, "much to the surprise of some and the distress of others, attempt[ed] to broaden the Democratic Party's base of appeal." Johnson, he concluded, should do the same.

Heading into late summer, neither LBJ nor his aides harbored any illusions that the path to victory was clear. But the president held three trump cards:

Jack Valenti, a former Texas adman armed with a keen eye for packaging his candidate—and his candidate's opponent.

Bill Moyers, the bright-eyed preacher and Sunday school teacher who would prove an utterly ruthless and unforgiving campaign strategist.

And Barry Goldwater, the Republican nominee, who simply could not get out of his own way.

On July 13, 1964, the same day that Buzz penned his strategy memorandum to the president, moderate Republicans convened at San Francisco's Cow Palace determined to block the nomination of Senator Barry Goldwater of Arizona, the recognized leader of the GOP's archconservative wing, opponent of the Civil Rights Act, and hawkish supporter of military intervention against the Soviet bloc. "The hour is late," lamented the moderate New York governor, Nelson Rockefeller, "but if all leaders in the moderate mainstream of the Republican Party will unite upon a platform and upon Governor [William] Scranton"—an eleventh-hour entrant in the race—"the moderate cause can be won."

The hour was, in fact, too late. By virtue of early primary wins and a fortuitous meltdown on the part of Rockefeller, whose presidential bid fizzled out that spring over widespread disapproval of his divorce and remarriage, Goldwater had sewn up the nomination, but not before the convention broke into pandemonium. During a platform debate over immigration, a fistfight nearly ensued when a Goldwater supporter mocked Italian Americans, many of whom—including the moderate representative Silvio Conte of Massachusetts—took considerable umbrage at the insult. By a vote of 897 to 409, delegates flatly rejected a moderate amendment that would have strengthened the party's plank on civil rights, infuriating moderates from the Northeast whose states and districts included sizable black populations. Goldwater devotees grew increasingly vicious as the days wore on. It "wasn't just the galleries," recalled one moderate attendee. "It was the floor, it was the hall. The venom of the booing and the hatred in people's eyes was really quite stunning." A leader of the New York Young Republicans recalled the event as "horrible. I felt like I was in Nazi Germany." No less a party stalwart than former president Dwight Eisenhower called the gathering "unpardonable. . . . I was deeply ashamed."

What one historian later dubbed the "conservatives' Woodstock" reached its nadir not when Goldwater delivered his acceptance speech, in which he declared that "extremism in the defense of liberty is no vice," but when his delegates shouted down Rockefeller as he addressed the convention. "These extremists feed on fear, hate and terror," the New York governor intoned over the deafening jeers of the crowd. They offered "no program for America and the Republican Party . . . [they] operate from dark shadows of secrecy. It is essential that this convention repudiate here and now any doctrinaire, militant minority whether Communist, Ku Klux Klan or Birchers." In the wake of the convention, George Wallace formally dropped his own bid for the Democratic presidential nomination. "My mission has been accomplished," he explained.

Goldwater was a gift to Lyndon Johnson. A doctrinaire conservative and acknowledged leader of the Republican Party's right wing, he was a bundle of contradictions. Though he deplored government "handouts" and pined for a simpler day when "you either worked or you starved," Goldwater—the child of a wealthy department store owner—conveniently glossed over the strong links between his family's fortune and federal spending, which in his lifetime transformed Arizona from a desert backwater to a thriving Sunbelt powerhouse. I. F. Stone, the crusading left-wing journalist, would quip that Goldwater's base "likes to think of itself as rugged and frontier because [it is] Western and Southwestern. But the covered wagons in which it travels are Cadillacs and its wide open spaces have been air-conditioned." Bill Moyers aptly captured the conservative icon's charm when he told the president in confidence that "Goldwater has a basic appeal to people who want to return to America's 'Age of Innocence'—the days of county fairs, country bands, sawdust, candied apples, simple solutions to simple problems—days that never existed except in the minds of people who didn't live in them but wish they did."

Goldwater deplored the New Deal for its supposed creeping socialism, though he conveniently overlooked the $342 million in aid that Arizona collected from the federal government in those years—an era in which the state collected only $16 million in federal taxes. As a senator, he railed against the federal government but continued to champion federal spending on local infrastructure and water projects. Despite his personal fortune and his wife's considerable inheritance, he lived lavishly and beyond his means, even as he preached the politics of frugality and personal responsibility. Goldwater fashioned himself a conservative theorist, but even by his own admission he had been at best a middling student and exhibited very little intellectual curiosity. "There was nothing I did that made me a success," he acknowledged in a moment of candor. "You might say I was a success by being born into a successful family." His sister later observed, "I don't think he ever read a book growing up."

Covering Goldwater in the early primary state of New Hampshire, Teddy White observed that his "candor is the completely unrestrained candor of old men and little children." During his swing through the Granite State, the Arizona senator proposed authorizing NATO commanders to deploy atomic weapons. ("Let's lob one into the men's room of the Kremlin," he offered on another occasion.) He suggested that the Tennessee Valley Authority be privatized and Social Security transformed into a voluntary program. Goldwater discovered to his advisers' chagrin that statements he made earlier in his career now weighted down his candidacy—as when he dismissed the Eisenhower administration as a "dime-store New Deal" or offered that "this country would be better off if we could just saw off the Eastern Seaboard and let it float out to sea." Equally troubling, his movement earned the fervent support of far-right fringe groups like the John Birch Society. "We've got superpatriots running

through the woods like a collection of firebugs," groused one of his state organizers, "and I keep running after them, like Smokey Bear, putting out fires. We
just don't need any more enemies."

Goldwater defied tradition when he named William Miller—an obscure
congressman from upstate New York, armed with "a caustic tongue and a
dedication to conservatism"—as his running mate, rather than a more established officeholder at the state or federal level. Miller was little known (as a
popular ditty soon went, "Here's a riddle, it's a killer / Who the hell is William
Miller?"). To the few Washington insiders who actually *did* know him, he was
a cantankerous gadfly and prude who once took to the House floor to condemn the Kennedys for hosting a party at which guests danced the twist.
Goldwater enjoyed telling reporters that Miller "drives [Lyndon] Johnson
nuts." In truth, the incumbent scarcely knew who he was. The congressman
figured little in the fall campaign, appearing mostly at small venues in faraway
places, like Bangor, Maine. Based on intelligence from the field, Larry O'Brien
assured LBJ that he was a "complete zero."

His shortcomings notwithstanding, Goldwater aroused a growing portion
of the party's conservative base that rejected the politics of consensus and aspired to dismantle the New Deal. He channeled their fervent anticommunism
and resistance to the authority of the central state. Though personally opposed
to racial discrimination, Goldwater galvanized segregationists with his opposition to the Civil Rights Act and his rhetorical veneration of free enterprise
and association.

LBJ bore his opponent no personal ill will. The two men had enjoyed a
friendly rapport during their joint tenure in the Senate, though in a private
conversation with John Connally the president candidly sized up his opponent
as "just nutty as a fruitcake." In July, Buzz urged the president to assume the
high road—at least until after Labor Day—and scrupulously to avoid terms like
"whiffs of fascism" and "scent of Nazism," which could prove "explosive" and
turn the tide of public sympathy toward the Republican nominee. Goldwater's
extremism spoke for itself. By late September, however, Busby argued that
"the attack should be broadened on the extremes and factions. Republicans
should be told, in effect, that their party is being taken over not by Birchites
and Klansmen, but by the Reverend Billy Hargis"—an archconservative, segregationist preacher who pledged his support to Goldwater—"and all the other

Right Wing Kooks who can be fairly named. None of these things require your participation. You can remain above the battle. But these are real and valid issues." Instead, Bill Moyers and Jack Valenti would do it for him.

Johnson's staff ran the campaign out of the White House in an era with less stringent rules governing the separation between government resources and partisan activities. Teddy White later broke the president's organization into several categories. Team A comprised Moyers, Valenti, and Jenkins, the troika unquestionably in command of message, strategy, and execution. (White considered Busby and Goodwin worker bees, not leaders, of Team A.)

Team B included three well-regarded veterans of Democratic politics: Abe Fortas, Jim Rowe, and Clark Clifford.

Team C was "the Kennedy operational team"—namely, O'Brien and O'Donnell, who managed the campaign's state-by-state political operation and ground game.

Team D leaned on mid-level administration employees who, under Valenti's direction, drove the "Five O'Clock Club"—the first rapid-response operation in campaign history.

Finally, Team E—the Democratic National Committee and its operatives—contributed to the effort, though with less stature or consequence than in prior cycles.

Valenti and Moyers made the critical decision to retain Doyle Dane Bernbach (DDB), the upstart advertising agency that JFK had initially selected for his reelection effort. While larger shops on Madison Avenue debated the relative merits of David Ogilvy's method (research-driven, tasteful, possessing a "Big Idea," but not generally entertaining) and Rosser Reeves's (differentiation through a "unique selling proposition"), DDB threw out both playbooks and conveyed a smart, modern sensibility striking for its embrace of irony and sardonic wit. Its breakthrough campaign for the Volkswagen Beetle—"Think Small"—made it one of the country's most sought-after agencies. Though DDB had never worked on a political account, its principals understood better than rival agencies that the rules of communicating with voters—who were, after all, consumers—were changing. In the 1964 cycle, the major networks intended for the first time to sell advertising slots in the thirty-second and one-minute range *during* televised programs—a break with the standard five-minute or fifteen-minute follow-on spots. To capture and maintain viewer interest, they would need to appeal chiefly to emotion. "We're selling the President of the United States," a member of the account team offered.

The spots that DDB created under Moyers's and Valenti's supervision were like nothing the country had ever seen. In one, the camera lingered over a telephone with a flashing red light, conspicuously missing a rotary dial. "This particular phone only rings in a serious crisis," a narrator explained in a grave tone. "Leave it in the hands of a man who has proven himself responsible." Another depicted a young girl raptly engaged in an ice cream cone to a woman's troubling voice-over: "Know what people used to do? They used to explode bombs in the air. You know, children should have lots of vitamin A and calcium. But they shouldn't have strontium 90 or cesium 137." The narrator explained that reasonable leaders came together several years earlier to sign a test ban treaty, thus ridding the atmosphere of harmful nuclear radiant. "Now there's a man who wants to be President of the United States," she continued. "His name is Barry Goldwater. If he's elected, they might start testing all over again." From a distance, a Geiger counter clicked away with increased rapidity. In "Confessions of a Republican," an earnest, bespectacled young man—primly dressed and thoughtful in both voice and expression—offered that "I certainly don't feel guilty about being a Republican. I've always been a Republican. But when we come to Senator Goldwater, now it seems to me we're up against a very different kind of man." Midway through, he carefully pulled a packet from his suit pocket and lit a cigarette. Resting it between his right index and middle fingers, he continued, "I mean, when the head of the Ku Klux Klan with all those weird groups come out in favor of the candidate of my party, either they're not Republicans or I'm not."

On the evening of September 7, during NBC's *Monday Night at the Movies*, the campaign aired "Daisy Girl," a one-minute ad that featured a young girl picking petals off a flower while counting from one to ten. Midway through the spot, a man's voice supersedes the girl's with a countdown. The camera zoomed in on her eye, on which a giant, exploding mushroom cloud was reflected. "These are the stakes," LBJ's voice-over sounded. "To make a world in which all God's children can live, or go into the dark. We must either love each other or we must die." A narrator then warned, "Vote for President Johnson on

November 3. The stakes are too high for you to stay home." Minutes after the spot ran, the White House switchboard lit up with calls from across the country, complaining about the campaign's cheap appeal to fear and panic. "Holy shit!" the president screamed at Bill Moyers, whom he had summoned to the Oval Office. "What in the hell do you mean putting on that ad? I've been swamped with calls." Upon a moment's reflection, LBJ conceded with a laugh, "I guess it did what we goddamned set out to do, didn't it?" The spot aired only once, but the rival networks CBS and ABC reported widely on the controversy surrounding it. Days later, the chairman of the Republican National Committee lodged a formal complaint with the Federal Communications Commission, protesting that "this horror-type commercial implies that Senator Goldwater is a reckless man." Moyers was positively ecstatic when he telephoned Johnson to deliver the news. "That's exactly what we wanted to imply," he told the president. "*And we also hoped someone around Goldwater would say it, not us.*" Long after it aired, "Daisy Girl" would be remembered as one of the most vicious broadcast spots in American political history.

Much as Busby had suggested, the president's campaign would attempt to construct a vast, winning coalition spanning from center left to center right. The "soundest national approach," Dick Scammon advised Moyers, was "setting out that middle-of-the-road approach which seems to mark the views of three-quarters of our citizens. Firm support of a law-and-order, moderate program, guaranteeing citizen rights, and enforcing citizen duties. . . . Doubtless this policy should be accompanied by specific rejection of the views—and actions—of Klan hoodlums on the one side or liquor-looting hoodlums on the other." The president's campaign could thus argue that Goldwater and the Klan were tarred with the same brush, while avoiding the implication that LBJ drew support from "hoodlums" who had rioted that summer in Harlem.

Earlier in the year, the pollster Oliver Quayle coined a term to describe this strategy: "frontlash." Presidential advisers who had only recently braced themselves for a revolt by working-class white voters now perceived an opportunity to exploit the "much larger crack of moderate Republican 'frontlash' against Barry Goldwater," a reporter noted. By presenting themselves as the "party of stability and responsibility and calm judgment," they would make "it easier for moderate-minded Republicans to vote for President Johnson." Thinking principally of the immediate goal—racking up a commanding majority to satisfy

Johnson's desire to outperform even Franklin Roosevelt, who in 1936 captured 61 percent of the popular vote and 523 electoral votes, and building liberal majorities in Congress to enact more Great Society programs—"Team A" pursued their opponent without mercy. "We ought to treat Goldwater not as an equal, who has credentials to be president," Valenti urged. "We must depict Miller as some sort of April Fool's gag. . . . Practically all our answers ought to mantle in ridicule." (Indeed, Valenti reached out to Bob Hope's joke writers for material. The idea was to "whack [Goldwater] EVERY day with gags and humor that deny him any right to be called sane or stable.") That fall, DDB produced a darkly amusing spot that depicted a hand emerging from water and sawing off the Eastern Seaboard of the United States as the narrator reminded viewers that Goldwater had once advocated precisely this metaphorical outcome.

In a brutally direct memo to LBJ, Valenti contended that "[our] main strength lies not so much in the FOR Johnson but in the AGAINST Goldwater. . . . We must make him ridiculous and a little scary: trigger-happy, a bomb thrower, a radical . . . not the Nation's leader, will sell TVA, cancel Social Security, abolish the government, stir trouble in NATO, be the herald of WWIII." Moyers was in full agreement. The central message of the president's campaign was that Goldwater "*could* do these things—but only if we let him. Vote for President Johnson on November 3. The stakes are too high to stay home." The longer-term disadvantage of pursuing a "frontlash" strategy might not have been immediately apparent to the president's team. Writing that summer, the columnists Rowland Evans and Robert Novak observed that the White House was transforming the Democratic Party "into a non-ideological broad-based 'consensus' party cleansed of over-partisanship." The question was "whether these new Johnson voters, if even translated into a whopping majority in 1964, can be retained as Democrats in the future."

But Team A remained singularly focused. "We have a few more Goldwater ads," Moyers assured the president in the immediate wake of the "Daisy Girl" spot. It was a considerable understatement. They produced more spots than they could use. "Right now, the biggest asset we have is Goldwater's alleged instability in re atom and hydrogen bombs," Valenti offered. "We *must not* let this slip away."

Moyers and Valenti built an operation almost unprecedented in American presidential politics. The "Five O'Clock Club" deployed trackers to attend Goldwater's and Miller's public speeches and provided reporters with real-time retorts to the opposition's claims. They worked with friendly journalists to monitor Goldwater's off-the-record conversations with his press pool and put E. Howard Hunt, a CIA intelligence officer who would later gain notoriety for his role in the Watergate scandal, on the payroll to gather intelligence on the opposition. While presidential campaigns customarily relied on polling, Johnson's voracious hunger for data drove the White House to new extremes. In addition to conducting regular surveys of the two-candidate horse race, Moyers privately commissioned the Gallup organization to run "flash" polls that tested public reaction to specific speeches or messaging. Using dispersed call centers, Gallup could deliver results within twenty-four hours, at a cost of $4,000 per survey. This practice, which would later become standard, was wholly without precedent when Moyers first suggested it to the president.

In further pursuit of the "frontlash" strategy, Jim Rowe took leave of his law practice to organize seventy-two affinity groups, including the National Independent Committee for Johnson and Humphrey, an organization that drew together leading Republicans, including John Loeb, Sidney J. Weinberg of Goldman Sachs, Henry Ford II, Donald C. Cook of American Electric Power, two members of the staunchly Republican Cabot family of Massachusetts, and Bob Anderson, former Treasury secretary under Dwight Eisenhower, who chaired the organization. "Not since the 1920s," wrote the *Christian Science Monitor*, "has the businessman been so ardently wooed in a presidential election." The political humorist Art Buchwald noted that most of Rowe's committees—artists and authors, organized labor, women's groups, rural advocates—were fundamentally predictable. The only one that stood out, he wisecracked, was "Republicans for Goldwater."

Moyers was aware that "frontlash" was limited in its strategic value. If he did not take Goldwater seriously, he nevertheless cautioned the president not to ignore the GOP nominee's broader resonance with a large portion of the electorate. Moyers urged LBJ to make at least a symbolic gesture toward Americans who felt their country changing in ways that seemed menacing and unfriendly. He wanted to see Johnson "visit county fairs—be seen shaking hands—walking around among the people—talking to rural Americans." Wise counsel or not, Moyers could not—and LBJ would not—run such a campaign.

The issues confronting Americans were too grave, and the emerging divisions too wide, to escape.

Despite the early and trenchant success of the "frontlash" strategy, LBJ was not unassailable. His support for civil rights had opened an enormous chasm within the Democratic coalition.

On Friday, August 21, just days before the opening gavel of the Democratic National Convention, several busloads of black Mississippians arrived at the shabby, beaten-down Gem Motel, a mile from Convention Hall in Atlantic City. A reporter watching them assemble for a prayer session saw "a hymn-singing group of dedicated men and women, who feel as though they had temporarily escaped from a Mississippi prison and who think they may be jailed when they get back." They were sharecroppers, small-business owners, maids, and schoolteachers. Among them were a few whites, including the Reverend Ed King, the chaplain of Tougaloo College, a small black institution just north of Jackson. The Mississippians slept four to a room and dined frugally. They were "all dressed up in their Sunday-go-to-meeting best," recalled the veteran civil rights activist James Forman. They were representatives of the Mississippi Freedom Democratic Party (MFDP). On Saturday, they would appear before the convention's Credentials Committee and ask to be seated as the official Mississippi state delegation.

For more than three years, several civil rights groups, including the Student Nonviolent Coordinating Committee (SNCC), the National Association for the Advancement of Colored People, and the Congress of Racial Equality, had cooperated under the umbrella of the Council of Federated Organizations to run voter-registration drives in Mississippi. Even in the American South, where only 40 percent of eligible black citizens were registered to vote, the Magnolia State was exceptional. Of its several hundred thousand black voting-age residents, only 6.4 percent had managed to wade through the thicket of literacy and citizenship tests, poll taxes, and violence to register.

In 1963, the organizations switched tactics and coordinated the "Freedom Vote," an independent mock election intended to demonstrate that Mississippi's black citizens would vote if provided the opportunity. Some eighty thousand black citizens turned in mock ballots electing the state NAACP chief, Aaron Henry, governor and the Reverend Ed King lieutenant governor of Mississippi. The election was nonbinding, but it conveyed a powerful message: if given the opportunity, black Mississippians would readily exercise their constitutional right to the franchise.

Building on the success of the Freedom Vote, the organizers laid plans for two bold projects. First, they would bring a large contingent of white students to Mississippi in the summer of 1964 to register voters. Placing the sons and daughters of affluent middle-class whites from New York, Boston, and elsewhere in the line of fire would surely draw media attention to the violent injustice of Mississippi political culture, as well as provide sorely needed manpower. Second, they would sponsor another parallel election, this time to select delegates for the 1964 Democratic National Convention. To that end, the Council of Federated Organizations created the MFDP and invited every black and white citizen of voting age to participate in local, county, and statewide caucuses to choose delegates who would go to Atlantic City. They followed Mississippi election law to the letter, acting as though the MFDP were, in effect, the state Democratic Party. Because most black citizens were artificially disenfranchised, and because the MFDP opened its delegate caucuses to people of all races, the new organization would argue that it, not the regular state party, held rightful claim to Mississippi's slate of convention delegates.

The experiment in interracial cooperation drew enormous media attention. On Monday, June 22, just weeks into the project, Americans learned of the disappearance of three voter-registration workers—James Chaney, a twenty-one-year-old black native of Meridian; Michael Schwerner, a young, Jewish New Yorker; and Andrew Goodman, a summer volunteer from Queens College in New York City. Weeks later, after a massive and well-publicized manhunt, their bodies were found beneath an earthen dam.

By the opening gavel of the 1964 convention, it was clear that the MFDP enjoyed the strong support of liberal delegates. If the national convention agreed to seat the MFDP instead of the Mississippi regulars—and this was not entirely unimaginable after the chair of the delegation, Lieutenant Governor Paul Johnson, infuriated many northern Democrats by affirming that NAACP stood for "niggers, alligators, apes, coons and possums"—white southern state delegations might bolt the convention. To avert that possibility, Johnson dangled the vice presidency before the only Senate liberal with sufficient credibility to shut down the challenge: Hubert Humphrey. "I always had the feeling, and it was implicit," one of Humphrey's advisers later explained, "that if Humphrey messed this up, Johnson was not going to make him the running mate. It was a kind of test for him. If he couldn't do it, so much for Humphrey."

The MFDP's lawyer, Joe Rauh, was a veteran labor attorney and a close adviser to both Hubert Humphrey and Walter Reuther, the head of the United Auto Workers. Rauh had been a bitter enemy of Lyndon Johnson's throughout the 1950s but had recently closed ranks to help the White House secure passage of the Civil Rights Act. Now he found himself once again challenging Johnson on a matter of liberal conviction. His strategy was simple. He expected a majority of the convention's Credentials Committee to oppose seating the MFDP, but he needed only 10 percent of its members—eleven delegates—to force the drafting of a minority report, and then he needed just eight state delegations to request a formal convention-wide vote on the minority report. If he could carry the MFDP that far, he expected delegates outside the South would close ranks with the civil rights activists. To build momentum, he called a string of witnesses to testify before the Credentials Committee about the brutality of Jim Crow. Rita Schwerner, Michael Schwerner's young widow, spoke, as did Martin Luther King Jr., who told the committee that "if you value your party, if you value your nation, if you value the democratic process, then you must recognize the Freedom party delegation."

By far the most stirring testimony was that of Fannie Lou Hamer, a forty-six-year-old ex-sharecropper who was said to be SNCC's oldest but most dedicated field organizer. The youngest of twenty children, Hamer had spent all but two years of her life in Sunflower County, Mississippi, the home of the segregationist senator James Eastland. In 1962, when Hamer attempted to register to vote, the landowner she worked for had demanded that she withdraw her application. In a voice that was unschooled yet full of eloquent resilience, wearing new city clothes over her short, stout frame, and bearing an expression of both sadness and hope, Hamer told the Credentials Committee that "if the Freedom party is not seated now, I question America. Is this America, the land of the free and the home of the brave, where we have to sleep with our telephones off the hooks because our lives be threatened daily, because we want to live as decent human beings, in America?"

Watching the coverage from the Oval Office, Johnson realized the potential political danger of Hamer's testimony. He immediately called a press conference, diverting television coverage away from the credentials hearing. The networks were forced to change their live feeds, but the strategy backfired that evening when they rebroadcast her appearance before a prime-time audience. The next day newspapers ran photographs of Fannie Lou Hamer arm in arm with the family of Michael Schwerner in vigil on the Atlantic City Boardwalk.

Leaving nothing to chance, Johnson applied the full pressure of his office to whip liberal delegates into line. The president's campaign compelled the convention to accept a compromise stipulating that the MFDP would be accorded special guest status, along with two at-large, nonvoting delegates. The national party would also obligate subsequent national conventions to apply a strict nondiscrimination standard in accrediting delegate slates. Finally, the Mississippi regulars would have to pledge allegiance to the Democratic ticket before taking their seats at the convention. The MFDP refused the settlement. "We didn't come all this way for no two seats," Hamer told the packed MFDP caucus. So did the Mississippi regulars, who backtracked on their agreement and endorsed Barry Goldwater. LBJ—who ultimately rewarded Humphrey with the vice presidential nomination—was furious. He had sorely compromised his standing with the party's liberal flank and was now faced with the prospect of a mass revolt by southern delegates. "They're Democrats!" he said of the MFDP challengers in a private conversation with Carl Sanders, the moderate governor of Georgia. "These people went in and *begged* to go and participate in the convention. They've got half the population. They won't let them." The president had demanded that the convention ignore southern lawlessness—"You violated the '57 law, and you violated the '60 law, and you violated the '64 law, but we're going to seat you—every damn one of you"—and in return the regulars bolted.

Since May, Busby had beseeched LBJ to concentrate more effort on the South. He was particularly concerned that the White House had scheduled relatively few appearances by senior administration officials in the Old Confederacy and opted instead to concentrate efforts in the Northeast and the Midwest. A political realist, Johnson essentially resigned himself to losing at least some traditionally Democratic states in the South, as had Harry Truman in 1948 and Adlai Stevenson in 1952 and 1956. He had been willing to sacrifice the MFDP to avert a far-reaching crackup of the party, but he would not divert resources from his national "frontlash" strategy in the interest of courting hard-line segregationists who, in any event, would likely back Goldwater. But Busby was not alone in his reluctance to forfeit the South. Lady Bird Johnson insisted on conducting her own swing through Dixie. Over just four days, she traveled 1,628 miles by train and delivered forty-seven speeches from the back of her specially outfitted railcar. The reception was vitriolic. She was greeted by acid banners (BLACK BIRD GO HOME; JOHNSON IS A NIGGER-LOVER) and violent jeers. Resisting Busby's advice that she avoid controversial topics, she proudly proclaimed her support for the Civil Rights Act. In Columbia, South Carolina, she stared down an especially ugly mob. "This is a country of many viewpoints," she declared firmly in a southern drawl. "I respect your right to express your own. Now it is my turn to express mine. Thank you."

Over the years, LBJ had visited countless public and private indignities upon Lady Bird, but in their complicated relationship she was a trusted political adviser and close friend. He flew to New Orleans to join her final stop and dramatically walked half a mile to greet her train at the station. African American bystanders cheered wildly; white observers stood back several feet on the sidewalk, staring in silent loathing. Taking the stage at the Jung Hotel, Johnson launched into a passionate stem-winder in defense of the Great Society. "I want us to wipe poverty off the face of the South," he declared, "and off the conscience of the Nation. I want us to assure our young the best of education at every level, and the expectation of a good job in their home State when their schoolyears are through. I want us to assure our aged that when they need hospital care they will have it. I so much want us to maintain a prosperous, free enterprise economy, so your Governor can continue bringing in new plants and new payrolls and new jobs in the north and in the south of your State."

He then fixed his gaze on the crowd and addressed the one issue that he knew would cost him the state of Louisiana in November. "Whatever your views are," he said of the Civil Rights Act, "we have a Constitution and we have a Bill of Rights, and we have the law of the land, and two-thirds of the Democrats in the Senate voted for it and three-fourths of the Republicans. I signed it, and I am going to enforce it." What followed next left the crowd slack-jawed. Johnson told the apocryphal story of a visit that the late Sam Rayburn—his idol and mentor who had served for many years as House

Speaker—paid to a dying southern senator. Rayburn and the unnamed senator reflected on all that the Democratic Party had accomplished under Franklin Roosevelt—the schools and hospitals it had helped build, the relief jobs it offered to the unemployed, the electricity it delivered to rural farm families. "And [the senator] said, 'Sammy, I wish I felt a little better. . . . I would like to go back down there and make them one more Democratic speech. I just feel like I have one in me. The poor old State, they haven't heard a Democratic speech in 30 years. All they ever hear at election time is Nigger! Nigger! Nigger!'"

George Reedy, who had inherited Salinger's job as press secretary earlier in the spring, told Johnson that the speech left reporters "gasping." Jack Valenti, who was present, would describe the shocked reaction of the audience as "a physical thing—surprise, awe—ears heard what they plainly could not hear, a cataclysmic wave hit everyone there with stunning irreversible force." After a moment of dazed silence, African Americans in the crowd stood on their feet and—joined by many white bystanders—"rocked" the hall in "thunderous applause."

The newspapers promptly sanitized Johnson's language, but political professionals understood that he had invoked the crudest epithet in America's dark racial lexicon to implore a southern audience to resist the misdirection of Jim Crow demagoguery and rise above hate. The traveling press corps, previously lukewarm on LBJ, began evincing qualified "respect and admiration," his aides informed him. "The New Orleans (Negro, Negro, Negro) speech captured them," Busby gushed. "Thus overnight they are speaking of you—as once FDR—as 'the master,' 'the champ.'"

Though aimed at a southern audience, LBJ's speech in New Orleans represented a definitive embrace of frontlash and an acknowledgment that the solid South would inevitably fissure. Indeed, Goldwater ultimately carried Louisiana, as well as Georgia, Mississippi, Alabama, and South Carolina, which delivered forty-seven of his fifty-two electoral votes. Four years later, Wallace—running as a third-party candidate—would win the Goldwater states, while Richard Nixon would carry Florida, North Carolina, Virginia, Tennessee, Oklahoma, and Kentucky.

In stark contrast to Johnson, who gambled that he could win a changing map with an unorthodox racial calculus, Goldwater—who claimed to be personally opposed to segregation—played fast and loose with racial incitement.

The *New York Times* observed that as the fall campaign wore on, he "began to link directly his 'law and order' issue—in which he deplores crime and violence—with the civil rights movement, mentioning the two in juxtaposition." During a speech in Minneapolis, he "mentioned 'gang rape' and civil rights disturbances in the same paragraph." Speaking to campaign supporters in an all-white suburb of Philadelphia, he charged that "minority groups run this country" and "Americans are getting sick and tired of it." In southern states, his campaign aired a commercial that depicted a clean-cut, hardworking white youth losing his job to an "arrogant-looking Negro boy," as the president himself described the spot—courtesy of the Civil Rights Act.

Earlier in the year, the two candidates met in the White House, ostensibly to agree that neither side would stoke racial fears or resentments for advantage. Goldwater "came in, just wanted to tell me that he was a half-Jew, and that he didn't want to do anything to contribute to any riots or disorders or bring about any violence," Johnson told one of his cabinet members. "Because [of] his ancestry, he was aware of the problems that existed in that field, and he didn't want to say anything that would make them any worse." But Goldwater did not keep consistently to his pledge.

Most often, Goldwater's campaign exploited a wider constellation of grievances as proxy issues for race, as when it profited from a thirty-minute televised infomercial titled *Choice*, which juxtaposed imagery of women in topless bathing attire, striptease clubs, and pornographic literature with film footage of black urban rioters. Interspersed throughout scenes of lascivious pool parties, drug-addled youth, and dancing black children, a man veered wildly and at high speed in a Lincoln Continental, throwing beer cans out the driver-side window, willy-nilly, for added effect. The subtext was unmistakable: the same liberal forces that threatened to unravel the moral fabric of American society were driving racial minorities to lash out violently against public authority and private property. Or, for those who required direct narration: "Honest, hardworking America" was under assault. There were "two Americas, and you alone standing between them." The film was technically the work of Mothers for a Moral America, but just as Jim Rowe's seventy-two independent committees were not really independent, the GOP campaign played a hand in its production. Russell Watson, the communications director for Citizens for Goldwater, freely acknowledged that it would tap the "prejudice" of "people who were brought up in small towns and on the farms, especially in the Midwest."

If diverse issues like crime and morality were increasingly attractive proxies for racial appeals, Goldwater and Miller found an unexpected opening on October 13, when police sources in Washington, D.C., informed Republican campaign staff that Walter Jenkins had been detained earlier in the week on public indecency charges. After drinking several martinis at a party marking the opening of the new *Newsweek* building, the president's top aide had proceeded to the Washington YMCA, a notorious cruising locale for men seeking sexual liaisons with other men. There, he was arrested after an undercover police officer apprehended him in mid-act with an older man in a bathroom shower stall. Jenkins was booked, identified himself as a government "clerk," paid a $50 fine, and returned to the White House, where staff members thought nothing of his haggard appearance, because Jenkins often remained at his post until well after midnight. Goldwater's campaign sat on the information, unaware that the next morning several newspapers had also been tipped off and were seeking comment from Jenkins. In a panic, the chief of staff telephoned Abe Fortas, who found him "well off his rocker" and assumed that a combination of stress and fatigue had robbed him temporarily of his senses. Along with Clark Clifford, Fortas paid a series of urgent visits to the editors of the *Washington Star* and the *Washington Post*, both of whom agreed to hold the story out of consideration for Jenkins's family. The reprieve would prove temporary. That evening, the Republican National Committee issued a statement that accused the White House of "desperately trying to suppress a major news story affecting national security," and within half an hour UPI broke the news. It further materialized that Jenkins had been arrested several years earlier on similar charges. Under Fortas's direction, Jenkins committed himself for hospitalization and tendered his resignation. The White House put out a simple statement indicating that Moyers would assume his responsibilities, in effect elevating the young preacher to the untitled position of presidential chief of staff. In a striking conversation later that day, the First Lady firmly rejected her husband's instruction not to speak publicly on the matter and conveyed her intention to issue a "gesture of support to Walter." Hours later, her office released a statement. "My heart is aching for someone who has reached the end point of exhaustion in dedicated service to his country," she said, hewing closely to the official reasoning behind Jenkins's resignation.

For the most part, newspapers took a delicate approach to Jenkins's downfall, in no small part because he was a popular and sympathetic character to those on the inside. The columnist William White voiced mainstream consensus when he explained the episode as "a case of combat fatigue as surely as any man ever suffered it in battle." While Miller asked rhetorically "how a man of such convictions could be appointed to the highest councils of government," Goldwater did not wade into the Jenkins affair, preferring instead to speak more generally about Johnson's multiple conflicts of interest: his entanglement with Bobby Baker, the scandal-ridden former secretary of the Senate who had once been his protégé and trusted aide and now faced federal corruption charges; his accrual of massive wealth over years of Senate service; his relationship with several shady Texas businessmen. His followers eagerly drew the connection between perceived moral decay in society and corruption in the White House. Cries of "thief!" and "steal away!" rang out routinely when the candidate fulminated against LBJ's alleged venality. But the issue failed to gain GOP traction.

Lyndon Johnson ultimately won the fall election in a landslide, carrying forty-four states (and Washington, D.C.) with 61 percent of the popular vote. Larry O'Brien had predicted that many "Johnson Republicans" would "swing right back to the big R for the other state contests," but in fact the president's coattails were long: Democrats netted two Senate seats and thirty-seven House seats, delivering the largest majorities that the party had enjoyed since FDR's second term. O'Brien's prophecy would nevertheless prove correct in other ways. Shortly before Election Day, he told the president that few Johnson Republicans were "likely to become Democratic converts." The president's team won the election by convincing the country that Goldwater was "not a normal American politician," as Walter Lippmann observed, but rather a "grave threat to the internal peace of the nation." But it did not build a mandate for the Great Society. This was a strategic decision that would come back to haunt the architects of the Johnson landslide. Indeed, frontlash was a devil's bargain.

PART II

CHAPTER 6

A Frustrating Paradox

Joe Califano later recalled the whirlwind of events that swept him into Lyndon Johnson's close orbit. The Brooklyn-born son of an Italian American father and Irish American mother, Califano—young in appearance for his thirty-three years, with a full complement of dark, wavy hair, soft black eyes, and round face—was the product of Jesuit schools and Harvard Law School. Like so many of the nation's "best and brightest," in 1960 he caught the Kennedy fever fast and early and spent every spare hour knocking on doors in Manhattan, where he worked by day as an associate at the white-shoe firm of Dewey, Ballantine, Bushby, Palmer & Wood. Astonished to find that politics held his interest more than "splitting stocks" for clients, he gave up a hefty corporate paycheck and leveraged personal connections to secure a position at the Pentagon, where, as Eric Goldman would recall, "his sharp intelligence" and "ability to analyze a problem quickly and come up with clear alternative proposals" drew him to the attention of Secretary of Defense Robert McNamara, a number-crunching businessman with an abiding faith in process and empiricism. When Adam Yarmolinsky left his post as special assistant to the secretary, Califano took his place as well as his prized office, across the hall from McNamara's. One of his chief assignments was to act as the department's liaison to the White House.

In mid-1964, Bill Moyers made an abortive attempt to bring Califano into the White House. The defense secretary blocked the move. Still, it came as little surprise on July 8, 1965—not even six months into Johnson's new term as president—when Jack Valenti summoned him to the West Wing. In a brief meeting with Valenti and Moyers, Califano learned that he was to become a "general-utility infielder on the domestic scene," with a broad mandate to direct legislation and oversee the smooth enactment of LBJ's Great Society programs. Less than forty-eight hours later, he awoke at 3:00 on a Saturday morning for the short drive to Andrews Air Force Base, where he joined a small contingent that included Jack and Mary Margaret Valenti and Dick Goodwin for a flight aboard Air Force One, bound for the LBJ Ranch.

Still unaccustomed to the baroque rituals that governed life as a member of LBJ's White House staff, Califano changed on command into swim trunks and treaded water as the president, several inches taller and habitually wont to compel visitors into the deep end of the pool, where he could stand but they could not, jabbed him repeatedly with his index finger and spoke in an animated tone about the Senate's recent passage of his Medicare bill. Later that afternoon, still dressed in a damp suit and knit shirt, Califano rode shotgun as LBJ drove him at high speed around the sprawling ranch. From behind the wheel, the president was sipping Cutty Sark scotch and soda and would at irregular intervals stop the car, extend his left hand out the window, and rattle the paper cup, whereupon a Secret Service agent in the follow car would dash ahead and refresh Johnson's drink with ice and whiskey. There was a helicopter ride to the Haywood Ranch, a nearby property that the Johnsons also owned, lunch aboard a thirty-seven-foot yacht on Lake LBJ, and waterskiing (the president drove the motorboat, "faster and faster, zigging and zagging around the lake," as Califano held on for dear life. "He threw me only once"). Returning to dry land, the president beckoned his new aide into a small blue convertible—top down—and once again took the wheel. Moments later, as the vehicle began veering wildly toward the lake, LBJ cried, "The brakes don't work! The brakes don't work! We're going in! We're going under!" Califano braced for impact, only to find that the small blue convertible was an Amphicar: half car, half boat. "Did you see what Joe did?" the president bellowed in laughter to other guests. "He didn't give a damn about his President. He just wanted to save his own skin and get out of the car."

There was ample serious conversation that weekend about domestic policy—particularly, the imperative to fight a dual-front war at home (against poverty) and in Vietnam (against communism) without sacrificing one priority to the other. For Califano, the maiden voyage to the LBJ Ranch was in the main a lesson about the eccentric strains and stresses of his new life. As they walked from the lake into one of the nearby guest cottages, he later remembered, "the President stopped in a bright shaft of sunlight in the living room. He unbuckled his belt and twisted toward his right side as he lowered his pants and pushed down his undershorts, trying to look at his increasingly bare right buttock. 'Something hurts back there,' he said, now exploring the surface with his right hand. 'Is that a boil?'" Califano reluctantly glanced at the president's backside and confirmed that it was. The president nodded, made a mental note to contact the White House physician, and pulled his trousers up.

In winning his own term in office, Lyndon Johnson at last felt at liberty to fashion his presidency rather than complete Jack Kennedy's. He exercised this freedom in ways large and small, from reconstituting his staff to refurbishing his office. For all the glamour and sparkle that Americans had come to associate with Camelot—an image that often seemed at odds with the coarser, less polished air that the Johnsons, Texans born and bred, brought to the White House—the West Wing during JFK's tenure had been a shabby, dilapidated affair. Teddy White remembered the "business lobby" entrance as "a huge room, in the center of which is an enormous table of Philippine mahogany, normally festooned with coats, cameras and news gear in an untidy pile; on the walls, some of the uglier paintings of American art; about the sides, black easy chairs and oversized black sofas for lounging." The press room was small, dark, and cramped. In early 1965, under Lady Bird's direction, the Johnsons refurbished the West Wing. In consultation with Bill Walton, an abstract expressionist painter and art critic whom the Kennedys had appointed chairman of the U.S. Commission of Fine Arts, they enlarged the press room and redecorated the public hallways and entrances. "Newly lit and painted," White reported, "its ugly oil paintings replaced by fresh American art, the lobby has seen the removal of its old furnishings and their replacement by glittering green leather armchairs and sofas in the style called 'Dallas Modern.' It is a gayer, pleasanter place, but the atmosphere and gossip remain the same."

The "Fish Room"—later redubbed the Roosevelt Room during Richard Nixon's tenure—was "exceedingly drab and unattractive," Horace Busby remarked to Liz Carpenter. It was an "embarrassment as a waiting room for visitors coming to see the President." At Walton's suggestion, the staff remodeled the room with a bright, plush red carpet, fresh paintings, and walls lined with "items of historical interest, together with books and other materials giving it a semi-library tone and quality."

The Oval Office, too, underwent physical transformation. Gone was the bright red rug that Jackie Kennedy ordered installed during the trip to Texas—a surprise gift for her husband, who never lived to see or pace the length of it. In its place was a gray-green substitute, with the new seal of the United States—completed by two extra stars (for Hawaii and Alaska) surrounding the eagle—woven into its textured surface. The oatmeal curtains in red trim that Jackie had also selected remained in place, but the walls now featured a selection of American art from the Smithsonian, including a Gilbert Stuart portrait of George Washington above the fireplace, on whose mantel sat a vermeil tureen from the Margaret Biddle collection, flanked on each side by a pair of Chinese export vases—all of it carefully curated by Lady Bird and Bill Walton. LBJ's tall wooden rocking chair—not dissimilar to Kennedy's—faced the fire place. On side tables and bookshelves rested color photographs of his wife and daughters. There was a grandfather clock, with silenced chimes, to furnish the office with a constant metronome sound that Johnson found calming. And of course, a long console that housed three televisions—one for each network—and a news-wire ticker concealed within a custom wood credenza.

Of the many doors leading to and from the Oval Office, one led to an outer chamber where the president's secretaries kept watch, which in turn emptied into the ornate Cabinet Room. Another door on the west end of the Oval opened into a side study that the president used for reading or for hosting small conclaves with staff members and visitors. Outfitted with a couch and easy chair, each upholstered in a deep shade of green (LBJ's favorite), the room was lined with historic relics, including a framed letter penned by Sam Houston to Johnson's grandfather and autographed photographs of FDR, Harry Truman, and Dwight Eisenhower. That study, in turn, led to Kenneth O'Donnell's office—later bequeathed to Marvin Watson, a Texan who joined the administration in 1965—which opened next into Jack Valenti's lair, then to another room housing Valenti's small staff, then to a small office where Horace Busby set up shop, and finally to a spacious corner suite that housed Busby's team. Though each office had doors to its adjacent rooms, enabling LBJ to ramble from one to the other unencumbered, it also had a front entrance that spilled into a long, red-carpeted corridor running past the Fish Room and the West Lobby. On the other side of the wing were Moyers's palatial suite (since the early 1980s, the vice president's office), a small nook designated for the Secret

Service, and the press room. The indoor swimming pool, where Johnson so often held court in his natural element, occupied the runway from the West Wing to the mansion. In later years, the Nixon administration built a floor above it and converted it into a more modern briefing room for the press.

Walton transformed the once-featureless hallways into a veritable art gallery, with most of the pieces borrowed from the Smithsonian. The work ranged from Frederic Remington's depictions of cowboys and western landscapes and James McNeill Whistler's atmospheric paintings to a series of prints by Currier and Ives. For his own book-lined office, Buzz selected sixteen miniatures and silhouettes by early American artists. The walls in Valenti's office were framed by a series of paintings by the American artist Childe Hassam, whose work was deeply influenced by the European impressionists. Finally, there was Bill Moyers—first among equals since Walter Jenkins's departure, and the one aide, according to the *Washington Post*, who did not need to borrow his art. He brought his own, including a "dramatic" modern piece titled *Carnival* by the Mexican painter Alfredo Santos and a "striking canvas" that comprised "geometric designs in reds, orange and black"—the work of an unknown artist from an island off the coast of Panama. Behind his semicircular desk, three floor-to-ceiling windows offered a direct view of the Executive Mansion's front lawn.

"Intriguing designs and soft or brilliant colors of a new décor snap, crackle and pop in the renovated Presidential offices at the White House," a newspaper feature began. Presidential advisers, who "give more hours of their day to their country than to their own families, have brought a look of home-away-from-home to their workaday world."

Not long after LBJ's victory, Charles Roberts of *Newsweek* remarked that members of the White House press corps regarded LBJ as "a frustrating paradox—the most accessible and yet the most thin-skinned of Presidents. He encourages contacts with them, then reacts indignantly when their stories don't come out as pro-Johnson." Serving as a buffer between Johnson and the press was in most regards a losing proposition, but there were few people less suited to the role than George Reedy, a "friendly, pipe-smoking, contemplative man" who had been in the president's service for over a decade. Reedy was completing his third week of hospitalization for a weight-loss regimen in May 1964 when Walter Jenkins summoned him to the White House.

Upon arrival, he stumbled across Bill Moyers, who "made some inane remark like, 'Congratulations!'" (Reedy's enmity for Moyers was extreme and only grew with time.) Pierre Salinger had resigned as press secretary, and the role would now fall to Reedy, a former newspaperman who, in addition to his many other responsibilities as a member of Johnson's Senate and vice presidential staff, had been the principal liaison with the media. "I didn't know what he was congratulating me on," Reedy would recount, "but the tone of it sounded to me like I was being led to the Last Supper. And I remember my response was something equally inane like, 'If it weren't for the honor, I'd just as soon walk.'" He huddled with LBJ and Salinger in the small study adjacent to the Oval Office and reluctantly accepted the assignment. "I knew the President quite well. . . . And I had come to the conclusion many years previously that if he ever did become President, one of his greatest problems was going to be his handling of the press simply because he would want the press to do things that it would not do and could not do, and I didn't want to be the man caught in the middle on it." When Reedy entered the hospital, he weighed over 275 pounds. By the spring of 1965, he was down to approximately 200 pounds. Much of the weight loss owed to his weeks of hospitalization and a rigid, thousand-calorie-per-day diet to which he subsequently committed. But Roberts was certain that the "cruel and unusual punishment to which press secretaries are subjected" had a good deal to do with his reduced frame. ("Poor George," the president once told a group of reporters. "He can't drink and he can't eat. All he has in life is to take a beating twice a day from those White House correspondents.")

Roberts sized up Reedy as "more erudite" but "not so fast on his feet as either of his predecessors." Eisenhower's press secretary, Jim Hagerty, brought reporters to heel with his stern glower and habit of publicly discomfiting those who posed questions that the administration preferred not to answer. Salinger, by contrast, relied on demonstrations of wry wit and charm and turned daily press briefings into clever verbal jousts. Reedy took another tact altogether—periphrasis. "Your question is assuming some conclusions based upon some facts of which I am unaware," he might offer in response to a direct query, lit pipe in hand, a plume of smoke surrounding his jowly face. "As a casual

newspaper reader, I have some awareness of the stories to which you have al-
luded. As I can gather from these stories, I know of no particular occasion that
could be identified from them on which I was present. Consequently, I cannot
draw conclusions on a series of facts which are not known to me." If Reedy's
default style was ponderous and indirect, many newspapermen who covered
the administration blamed the president rather than his press secretary for
their information deficit. Johnson "tended to view reporters as so many enemies to be told as little and manipulated as much as possible," Eric Goldman
believed. "He kept a tight rein on what his Press Secretary could say." LBJ es-
chewed regular press conferences for hastily arranged briefings with select
newsmen or awkward, brisk strolls around the White House grounds, the journalists struggling to keep pace with the president's long stride even as they
scribbled notes.

Reedy would later characterize his relationship with LBJ as "stormy"
throughout his tenure as press secretary. The president ridiculed him for being
overly solicitous of reporters. "His attitude toward me was that I was being
grossly abused by the press," Reedy surmised. "I think he really meant it. And
I would try to explain to him that I had no problems at all that he wasn't creating for me, but that didn't help any." He considered his role partly as a liaison
between reporters and the White House. Reporters had a job to do, and the
administration could either help or—to its detriment—impede them. Ultimately, they would write stories, with or without the cooperation of the
president's staff. Reedy was capable at staying on message, delivering official
spin, or practicing bare-knuckle politics. As press secretary during the
campaign—there was no separate political press office—he regularly savaged
Barry Goldwater to brutal effect. When in the wake of the Harlem riots the
GOP nominee attempted to soften his image by meeting with LBJ to reach a
joint agreement not to stoke racial tensions, Reedy acidly offered that "as a
man who has asked for observance of the civil rights law and who has signed
the law and who is implementing the law, the President would not do anything
to incite or inflame tensions." Johnson, he continued, did not require a meeting to avoid provocation. Perhaps Goldwater did.

But the president faulted Reedy for what he perceived as abject servility to
the press corps. "He thought, and I was never able to disabuse him of this, that
my whole strategy was to make the press happy by seeing that their bags were

carried and that they had airplane space and adequate hotel space," Reedy concluded in retrospect. "He thought I was pampering the press. I wasn't. I was just trying to set up rational procedures so that the press could cover him." Indeed, reporters increasingly resented receiving the eleventh-hour notice of presidential travel—to the ranch, from the ranch, to random destinations—that they were required to cover. "The White House press corps wasted literally thousands of hours sitting on its baggage in Washington, Austin, Texas, and way stations waiting for the President to move," Charles Roberts mordantly observed. Reedy understood that reporters relished their access and dined out on tales of their frenetic lifestyles. He also appreciated that they were human beings who needed to manage their lives.

Even during the 1964 campaign, when Johnson earned an outsized share of positive coverage, there gradually emerged a trust deficit between reporters and the White House. It would later be termed the "credibility gap." As Goldman candidly acknowledged, the "press was growing increasingly suspicious of what was told them. Too often President Johnson was making statements that did not check out and denying rumors which turned out to be facts." Reporters did not generally hold Reedy accountable, though not for reasons that would have flattered the official White House secretary. Simply put, they believed that the "big, rumpled panda man" was the "last to know of White House developments." Though on the surface, the staff ran a tight operation— a reporter noted that a journalist making "an inquiry of Mr. Valenti or Mr. Moyers is much more likely to be referred back to the press secretary Mr. Reedy than he was in the old days of Pierre Salinger"—in truth, Goldman believed, "the LBJ White House was one vast sieve." Aides interacted regularly with reporters; on some occasions they kept Reedy informed, and on others they did not. It was of no help that Johnson would often encourage staff members to back channel information to journalists on his behalf, with an unspoken agreement to keep such interactions confidential. "George Reedy was a Press Secretary with a severely limited amount of information that was authoritative to announce," Goldman continued, "while other statements were constantly making their ways to the press." Sympathetic reporters agreed. "Mr. Johnson has given increased freedom to his staff except for George E. Reedy, his press secretary, whom he has not given the chance to do his job either freely or well," the New York Times reported in June 1965.

The deterioration in his relationship with LBJ pained Reedy. A stalwart veteran of the inner circle, he had been a loyal retainer in both the heady days when Johnson ruled the Senate with an iron fist and the gloomy years when the vice presidency stripped him of all power and prestige. Asked in later years whether Johnson kept him "adequately informed" during his tenure as press secretary, Reedy answered, "No . . . which I think was kind of unfortunate because I have been an extremely close adviser of his for many years on political problems and any other types of problems. And in a sense the mere fact that I was press secretary placed me in a category that in his mind took me outside his problems."

Reedy was also out of step with Moyers and Valenti, whom the president increasingly trusted to shape and guard his image, and even with Busby, who, he believed, shared their love of "gimmicks." Reedy advocated staging more televised presidential press conferences, a tactic that Salinger and JFK pioneered, initially to some criticism but ultimately to their advantage. He argued that such formal engagements, when offered at a regular cadence and with a minimum of ground rules in place, extended more control—not, as LBJ feared, less—over message. Such had been the case for John Kennedy, who at the urging of Pierre Salinger became the first president to stage regular briefings in front of television cameras. Many of JFK's other advisers opposed this approach at first, to say nothing of officials at the State Department and Department of Defense who feared that a spontaneous presidential remark might trigger a global crisis. But Salinger knew his boss to be a cool customer—witty, at ease with himself, and fully in command of policy. His clean disposal of Richard Nixon during their televised presidential debates in 1960—Salinger believed that Kennedy came across as a "mature, knowledgeable, attractive man," while Nixon looked the part of "an actor reading a toothpaste commercial"—established the importance of keeping JFK front and center. Unfortunately, Reedy had no such asset with which to work. LBJ as president was little better at his role than Nixon had been as a candidate.

Though Reedy believed that a head of state had a civic obligation to submit himself to public scrutiny by representatives of all of the national daily papers, wire services, and broadcast outlets on a regular basis, he was by no means in the thrall of journalists. He regarded press conferences as mostly stagecraft; "questions become highly rhetorical because they're intended to put the newspapermen on television more than they are to elicit information."

Valenti and Moyers advocated a different sensibility. Theirs was modish, where Reedy's was old-fashioned. In the same way that they embraced leading-edge methods in broadcast advertising to frame the stakes of the 1964 election, they encouraged the president to turn his press interactions into performance art that *he*, not the reporters, could control. One favored device was the wandering press conference. To Reedy's chagrin, the concept soon caught on, as did "haystack press conferences"—quite literally, availabilities staged beside a stack of hay at the LBJ Ranch—and "Saturday morning press conference, simply because when he'd wake up on Sunday morning he'd pick up the *New York Times* and the *Washington Post*, and there would be nothing in the papers except his press conference. This was an idea that came to him from Jack Valenti." Reedy believed that few Americans did more than gloss over the Sunday morning paper; they were too preoccupied with church, family leisure time, and children's sporting activities to deliberate over political affairs. He also fielded recurring complaints from editors and publishers about the logistical complications of amending their Sunday editions on short notice. "A press conference like that would cost the *New York Times* around $600,000," he fumed. "From a mechanical stand point, newspapers are really not geared to handle a large influx of unexpected news for the Sunday morning paper—about 85 percent of the Sunday paper is printed on Thursday."

Reedy was not above the occasional "gimmick." He once arranged a news conference on the South Lawn to which the children of the press corps were invited. After his question-and-answer session, Johnson jubilantly posed for photographs with the daughters and sons of his jousting partners. The reporters greatly appreciated the gesture. But he felt caught between a rock and a hard place. "Reedy rarely got a respite from the demands of his job," Roberts wrote. He was at the beck and call of the president (who insisted that he install a news ticker in his office bathroom, lest he skip a beat), on the one hand, and a press corps that grew increasingly skeptical of the administration's credibility, on the other.

In the immediate wake of his landslide victory against Barry Goldwater, Alan Otten of the *Wall Street Journal* reported that LBJ's relationship with the press had reached its nadir. "Mr. Johnson does not enjoy great personal affection or respect from many editors and Washington correspondents," the paper concluded. "Many resent his vanity, his corniness, the tendency of the

President and his aides to slant or even twist facts." During the fall campaign, most political reporters muted their dislike for LBJ out of genuine fear of a Goldwater victory. With that "threat now removed, it's likely that large parts of the press will now flip-flop and become highly critical of Mr. Johnson." In a portent of what was to come, Otten noted that, however unsuccessful Goldwater proved at the ballot box, he succeeded in sowing considerable doubt about LBJ's trustworthiness and personal credibility—doubt that would follow him throughout the duration of his presidency. Merriman Smith of UPI agreed, observing in mid-1965 that Johnson, who "enjoyed a longer political honeymoon than most chief executives, is now experiencing the slings and arrows of outrageous criticism that invariably go with high office." His quirky personality traits, which reporters initially regarded as the "colorful folkways" of a larger-than-life, southwestern politician, now seemed unbefitting the most powerful man in the country. Particularly loathsome to some members of the political press was Johnson's addiction to raw polling data, a tendency that, in the opinion of one reporter, made him seem like "a man goaded by an insatiable need for public acclaim." The charge was essentially fair—a fact that did not make Reedy's job easier.

Given the abundance of former newspaper reporters, editors, sometimes speechwriters, and image makers on the president's staff, there was no shortage of public relations counsel. Early in his White House tenure, Busby encouraged LBJ to exude a more "relaxed demeanor—and a willingness to smile at questions. Visible good humor is especially desirable in responding to the usual 'iffy' questions about politics." He also looked with disfavor upon Reedy's practice of providing friendly columnists with the first bite at newsworthy information. Such columnists, by definition, would inevitably place the information in a favorable light, while the "younger front page byline reporters resent favored status of such highly-paid columnists and tend to regard most of them as non-critical apologists." Instead, the White House should cultivate their favor by conducting more regular background briefings that provided the administration's "line" on breaking news. Such practice would inevitably reduce the press secretary's role in controlling the flow of information and empower the senior special assistants to speak more freely with the media.

A year later, Buzz—who, with Johnson's knowledge (and, quite possibly, encouragement), often circumvented Reedy to gauge the outlook and

disposition of the White House press corps—warned that "the newsmen, almost universally, feel these are 'worrisome times,' and offer as supporting evidence what they describe as the 'president's withdrawal.'" A combination of
"fewer public appearances, less visible ebullience [and] uncharacteristic 'subdued' appearances" left the journalists with a critical outlook on the president's
leadership.

Valenti believed that television offered the president an opportunity to circumvent the opinion makers and communicate directly with the American
people. He also understood that his principal was ill at ease with the medium.
"You know the old cliche, but it was true," he later acknowledged, "in a small
room with a hundred people or ten people Johnson was magnificent—the most
persuasive man I have ever met. But when he went before television, something happened. . . . He became kind of stiff and foreboding." He encouraged
LBJ to forgo his teleprompter and consulted several Hollywood producers to
solicit their advice about how best to add production value to the president's
broadcast appearances. The initiative went nowhere. Johnson also rejected an
offer by Fred Friendly, the president of CBS News, to produce a year-end television special for distribution on all three major networks, despite the assurances of one senior aide that Friendly was "the best in the business and has a
proper sense of respect for the Presidency."

Increasingly, the president came across in media reports as a slippery
character—his words calculated for maximum effect, his appearances overly
staged and intended to manipulate public opinion, his lofty speeches unconvincing. By early 1965, to repair his public image, Johnson would need to think
anew about his relationship with the Washington, D.C., press corps, and that
process, in turn, would necessitate a change in personnel.

Harry McPherson, who served alongside Reedy on LBJ's Senate staff and
later joined the White House as chief counsel to the president, sized up his
colleague as hopelessly out of step with the vigor and bold experimentation
that the Great Society hoped to project. "He was an old UPI fellow from Chicago," McPherson coldly explained. "He had a lot of liberalism in him, but
[not] of the radical kind. He was just not the guy to be the spokesman. For all
the complaints that people have made about Moyers, self-serving, serving
himself as against Johnson and all the rest of it, he was a far better proclaimer

of the Great Society message, far more in tune with that kind of politics than George would have been."

In July, the White House announced that Moyers would replace Reedy in the role of press secretary. The official explanation for the switch was that Reedy required surgery to correct his chronic hammertoe, a condition that often left him in debilitating pain and unable on some days to walk. That much was true. The outgoing press secretary would remain a special assistant to the president without portfolio. Within the corridors of power, it was widely assumed that Moyers had sidelined Reedy and added the press office to his already swelling portfolio of responsibilities. Reedy would inculpate his colleague for playing a perpetual game of "court politics." When later asked whether he thought the young theologian was "just specifically out for your job," Reedy replied without hesitation: "No, he was out to be [the] number one man, and succeeded."

Publicly, the White House maintained that Moyers had been reluctant to accept the job, a posture that Reedy and others dismissed as pure fiction. On his first day in the role, reported the *Los Angeles Times*, the "youthful" Moyers—just thirty-one years old and now entrusted with a broad mandate that included domestic policy, White House administration, and the press office—"showed his virtuosity by easily fielding questions and reeling off facts so fast that only shorthand reporters could follow him." At once earnest and urbane, he charmed a press corps that, in the main, felt warmly toward George Reedy but viewed Moyers as a more contemporary fit for the role.

Moyers was on the rise. Reedy was out (out of the press office, in any event). Califano was in. And so was Harry McPherson, a thirty-five-year-old attorney whom Bill Moyers lured from his post as assistant secretary of state for educational and cultural affairs. A "tall, handsome and personable" man, by Charles Roberts's description, McPherson was a native of Tyler—an East Texas town not far from Marshall, where Moyers grew up. Though the local economy relied principally on oil and livestock, Tyler hosted a vibrant junior college and the East Texas Symphony Orchestra. Harry, whose father worked in advertising and whose mother was an aspiring novelist, grew up in a home rich with culture and art. Unlike other LBJ protégés, he bypassed the University of Texas at Austin, training ground for generations of the state's business and political leaders, preferring instead to attend the University of the South at Sewanee, Tennessee, still celebrated as the center of the southern agrarian literary movement that had captured the national imagination briefly in the 1930s. McPherson aspired to become a poet. After completing his undergraduate degree in 1949, he relocated to New York and began a graduate program in literature at Columbia University. The Korean War changed his plans. Harry enlisted in the air force and served for three years as an intelligence officer in Wiesbaden, Germany, where he assessed Soviet troop deployments. Still intending to pursue a life of letters, he was stunned when, in 1953, Roy Cohn and G. David Schine—Senate staff members in the employ of Joseph McCarthy—visited his base while on a whirlwind inspection tour of American military installments in search of communists (or at least communist books in libraries maintained by the U.S. Information Agency). "Maybe my sense of history was bad," McPherson would later remark, "but McCarthy and his witch-hunting looked to me like a real threat to liberty. I saw us going into a sort of McCarthy Era, where everyone's rights would be in danger. I decided then that I wanted to be a lawyer."

After his discharge, Harry attended law school at the University of Texas, where he "graduated a quick-minded, agreeable young man with soft good looks, strong ties to the Episcopal Church, and a questing way of talking about 'social consciousness,'" Eric Goldman wrote. He authored two plays—*Ground Zero* and *Missing Person*, "staged in an Episcopal church and filled with social significance"—and had not entertained a career in politics. But when a relative on Johnson's Senate staff informed him that the Senate Democratic Policy Committee, the legislative arm of the leadership office, was in need of an assistant counsel, he jumped at the opportunity. Though a year earlier McPherson and his wife had fired off a hostile telegram to Johnson, sternly disapproving of his rhetorical support for the right-wing China Lobby, he had never met LBJ, who was then the Senate minority leader. Liberal in outlook, McPherson did not regard LBJ as a "bomb-throwing ally. But at the same time, there was a good deal of respect for him and considerable feeling that he might be an instrument of good, once you put that phrase in quotes. . . . And given Texas politics, he was certainly the most progressive senior public official on the scene." He would spend six years learning political craft from LBJ, first as assistant counsel and later as counsel to the Policy Committee. Early in the Kennedy administration, McPherson served a tour at the Pentagon as deputy undersecretary of defense, where he became one of McNamara's bright young men, and later at the Department of State. By virtue of his apprentice-ship at LBJ's side, by his early thirties he was world-wise, if not world-weary, well acquainted with and known by the nation's most senior lawmakers and administration officials and skilled at the craft of legislative draftsmanship and government and administration.

McPherson was in Japan on State Department business when a military aide phoned him at 5:30 a.m., Tokyo time, to inform him that John Kennedy had been assassinated. "You know, to wake up, to come out of a deep sleep in a part of the world with which you're very unfamiliar, where your bearings are quite foreign to you, and to hear that kind of hallucinatory statement, boggles the mind," he later remembered. Arriving in Washington on Saturday eve-ning, he caught a few hours of sleep and proceeded the next morning, as he did every Sunday, to attend services at St. Mark's Episcopal Church on Capi-tol Hill. Unbeknownst to him, the Johnsons chose to worship there as well that morning. Lady Bird was fond of both the minister and the congregation. "The place was swarming with Secret Service agents," McPherson remembered. "God, there must have been twenty in the church, and there were cops on the top of the Library of Congress Annex with rifles, and a massive crowd out-doors." After the service—the Reverend Bill Baxter "preached a hell of a ser-mon" titled, simply, "America"—the Johnsons surprised the congregants by joining them in the parish hall for coffee. "The Secret Service was going crazy," but LBJ and Lady Bird took strength from the moment, as did the churchgoers. "It was very comforting to him, quite obviously, to shake hands. Very plain people, old women and kids and everybody just going up and taking his hand. And a lot of people crying and holding his arm. It was immensely strengthening." After some time, the president and his onetime aide stole off to a quiet corner of the room and "stood toe to toe for a long time and we just talked very quietly about what he was doing." At LBJ's behest, McPherson walked him to his motorcade when, suddenly and without warning, a Secret Service agent brought a heel down on his foot and delivered a sharp elbow blow to his stomach, as two other agents hustled the president away. There would be no repeat of Dallas. As the president's entourage sped away, Harry returned to the vestry, where a fellow congregant informed him that Lee Harvey Oswald had been shot.

At the White House, McPherson owned a broad portfolio of responsibilities, though nominally he would serve as assistant counsel—and later as counsel—to the president. Though he had known LBJ for many years and owed his personal career advancement to the president, like many other young men who had been part of the New Frontier, even McPherson felt a melancholy sense of loss upon first entering the Oval Office as a staff member. "In 1965 one could still feel John Kennedy's presence in the White House," he later wrote. "I walked out of the mansion one cold, starry night, headed for my office in the West Wing, and imagined I saw that little figure standing in the Oval Office, his back to the window; but it was only an aide."

Rounding out the new senior staff were Marvin Watson and Douglass Cater, two individuals vastly different in background and temperament. A native of Montgomery, Cater was the son of an Alabama state legislator but early in life left the South behind, to attend first boarding school at Exeter and then college at Harvard, where he interrupted his undergraduate studies during World War II to serve as a Russian specialist with the Office of Strategic Services, the precursor to the postwar Central Intelligence Agency. After returning to Harvard, where he completed a graduate degree in public administration, Cater served as the Washington editor of the *Reporter*, a nationally influential magazine of news and opinion, and oversaw the outlet's searing coverage of Joseph McCarthy and full-throated advocacy of black civil rights. Time and again, he took leaves of absence from the magazine to author several books on national politics or to serve as a consultant to various government agencies, including a tour as special assistant to the secretary of the army. He was on sabbatical, serving as a visiting scholar at the Center for Advanced Studies at Wesleyan University in the spring of 1964, when Bill Moyers summoned him to the White House for a meeting. At the time, he was forty years old.

Cater had known LBJ for almost ten years, though by his own admission he was "never an intimate." He arrived at the White House expecting simply to lunch with Moyers but instead found himself paddling around in the pool with LBJ, Valenti, and Moyers—all in the buff—and discussing the president's declaration of a war on poverty. "It was exceedingly hot water," he told an interviewer some years later, "and it caused me almost to fall asleep at lunch because it was so soporific." He had little inkling that his visit was something approximating a job interview. Weeks later, he again flew to the capital at Moyers's request, where he was offered the post of special assistant to the president, with a vague and nondescript portfolio. At first, he concentrated on campaign work, drafting stump speeches and compiling an anthology of LBJ's most notable addresses for release in the fall. He soon emerged as the administration's point man on health and education, a mandate that would assume outsized importance after 1965 and that would also create repeated overlap with Califano's growing empire. He was a "tall man with a thatch of bushy hair and a slow Southern drawl," a newspaperman observed. "Cater puffs meditatively on a cigar, paces around his office or props his feet on his desk as he talks, occasionally twirling in his big swivel chair. He speaks with a good deal of reserve, evidently cherishing his status as one of the White House's backroom boys." Eric Goldman remembered him as equipped with "a well-stocked mind and readily adaptable to the main chance." Cater was "one of the few figures of the American intellectual or quasi-intellectual world who seemed ready to be a thoroughgoing LBJ man." (The warm sentiment was not mutual. In a private oral history conducted after Johnson left office, Cater identified the Princeton historian as one of the few "prima donnas" in an otherwise mainly harmonious staff.) Cater, McPherson, and Califano became LBJ's unofficial emissaries to the nation's universities and think tanks and populated the administration's task forces with some of the country's sharpest minds, exceeding the Kennedy White House by a mile in its engagement of public intellectuals.

Operating first out of a palatial suite in the Executive Office Building, and later from a basement office in the West Wing, Cater served as the chief liaison between the White House and the Department of Health, Education, and Welfare, the cabinet-level colossus responsible for implementing key Great Society programs. A southern liberal, Cater was genuinely committed to civil rights and used his administrative authority over federal education and health-care funds to effect a thoroughgoing desegregation of schools, hospitals, and universities. Both a scholar and a pragmatist, he believed—as did most historians and political scientists of his generation—that the lessons of the

Reconstruction era counseled both moral certitude and flexibility. "It was a failure of men and institutions" that led the U.S. government into constitutional crisis, he counseled the president. "Equally tragic, war freed the slave but failed to set conditions by which he could become a free man." In his dealings with local and state authorities, Cater wielded both carrot and stick with equal conviction.

Cater's function in the White House was important but also "contingent," McPherson noted. "You have the power to speak for the President so long as the President gives it to you, so long as your water is not cut off; and you speak as the President and you bring a Presidential perspective to bear on the problems of various departments." LBJ never did cut off Cater's water, and in his four and a half years on staff the onetime editor and professor would play a leading role in expanding the American welfare state.

At the time of his appointment to the White House staff in 1965, Marvin Watson was a forty-year-old steel company executive—"a dark, green-eyed, squarely built 180-pounder," as Charles Roberts remembered him. A conservative Texan, he had worked on LBJ's presidential campaign in 1960 and then stepped in four years later to run logistics at the 1964 convention. As Valenti increasingly assumed a larger portfolio of responsibilities, LBJ invited Watson to assume the role of appointments secretary, installing him in an office adjacent to his private study. "Marvin is a hard-nosed, hard-shell, nondrinking, no-nonsense Baptist," a Johnson aide said. "He's all business and he gets things done. He is not afraid to make decisions, where some people around here are afraid to go to the bathroom without asking the President." The only "frippery" that Watson indulged, said a fellow aide, was attire: "He was a natty dresser, given to hand-tailored seersucker suits, color-checked shirts, flashing gold cufflinks and a jewel-flecked triangular watch."

Two qualities set Watson apart: his politics, which were out of step with the liberal spirit that pervaded Johnson's White House, and his personality, at once gruff and provincial. "Watson is a conservative in every sense of the word," a friend observed, but as a reporter noted, "as the man whose office is closest to the President's, he has been required to speak for the most liberal pieces of the Great Society legislative program," an agenda that included the repeal of right-to-work provisions in the Taft-Hartley Act, which Watson supported, and the adoption of rent subsidies for the poor, which he opposed. As keeper of the gate, Watson brandished his power with far greater gusto and less discretion than Valenti, who attempted to preserve LBJ's access to a wide variety of ideas and voices. Busby, who had no great love for his new colleague, would later refer disdainfully to "the totalitarian days of Marvin Watson," when, as another insider noted, one could not so much as "buy a postal stamp without getting his O.K." Francis Keppel, the erudite former dean of Harvard's Graduate School of Education who served from 1962 to 1965 as the commissioner of education, held most of Johnson's staff in high regard, but not Watson. Cater, Califano, Moyers, O'Brien—"they were excellent. . . . It was just that 'glupp' [Watson] I didn't like."

McPherson described Watson as "a tremendously industrious person, totally loyal to the President, a literalist, who had to learn the hard way that the President doesn't always mean exactly what he says." That literalism—an inability to discern between what the president said and the outcome that he wanted—in addition to his "provincialism" caused Watson trouble in his early days at the White House. It was "not so much a Texas provincialism," McPherson qualified, "as a limitation in understanding of tides in American history." Tasked with reading the FBI files of prospective administration officials, Watson knew too little about the ways of Washington to regard J. Edgar Hoover and his organization with an appropriately skeptical eye. "The FBI reports are a disaster," McPherson categorically declared, and Watson read them as gospel. "We had some real battles over particular appointments."

Watson resented the influence that McPherson and Joseph Califano exerted on LBJ; he felt that "the President should not be going as swiftly and as vigorously toward the left as he was going." McPherson, in turn, sized up his fellow Texan as "conservative," though "by no means a Bircher or that sort"— someone who was "educable" and "liberalized his views about a lot of things" since joining LBJ's staff. "But essentially Marvin is an organization man," "a man of . . . tremendous personal loyalty." Valenti, who turned over the quotidian functions of his job to Watson but retained higher-level input into LBJ's schedule, argued that his colleague "was not abrasive. Marvin was tough. Marvin was able, competent." This assessment was kind. Though loyal to the president and hardworking in the extreme, Watson was generally unsympathetic to the Great Society and played little role in conceiving or executing its component parts. He was an enforcer of discipline in the West

Wing—important in his own right, but never particularly critical to domestic policy discussions.

Loyalty to LBJ did not ensure camaraderie or uniformity of thought. By 1965, according to Goldman, "Cater, Califano, Goodwin and McPherson moved principally in Moyers' orbit"—which was to say, on the outer left edges of the Great Society. "Valenti and Watson worked in uneasy relationship to each other, and both to Moyers. Busby and Reedy were off by themselves, sometimes functioning together, mostly singly." Factions and rivalries inevitably emerged, and while some were driven by ideology, others—particularly the toxic relationship between Reedy and Moyers—owed to the contest between so many aides over a finite amount of power. Such antipathies were inescapable, Valenti thought, "in a place where you're sitting amid power and the celebration of power.... You're going to have bruised egos, you're going to have a kind of Machiavellian jostling and crawling and pushing and vaulting.... Practically all of these fellows who work in the White House are men of some ego, and they are all looking for ways to enhance their own reputations as well as their power."

Califano, who promptly established himself as the administration's domestic policy czar, was particularly adept at the game. "Nothing in Joe Califano's original writ over here gave him the authority to do what he has subsequently come to do," McPherson noted with admiration. "He's an extremely capable and aggressive guy, who has taken the responsibility." When Daniel Patrick Moynihan once asked him how one obtains power in the White House, Califano replied nonchalantly, "You take it. There are vacuums everywhere, and if you do it, if you take it and seize it and run with it, it's yours, and you develop a certain right of adverse possession to responsibility."

Doug Cater found himself occasionally struggling to protect his remit. More interested in advancing policy than accruing power, he took the position that "as long as I was kept informed so that I wasn't ignorant of what was going on I was perfectly content to let" Califano and his staff members work on specific policy issues with HEW staff. "If I had been sensitive that any time anybody else spoke to HEW they were stepping in my territory, it could have caused a problem."

When Valenti surmised that every White House operated with an "inter-play of egos and clashings of ambitions, all sort of like satellites circling the sun," his reference point for the bright star at the center of the solar system was, of course, Lyndon Johnson, an enormously complicated individual whose re-lationship with his staff members was a study in contradiction. To serve LBJ as a special assistant to the president came with perks: a salary of $28,500 (equiv-alent in 2016 to over $215,000—far in excess of the top salaries that latter-day White House aides earned); chauffeured town cars to shuttle them to and from work or about town; frequent use of air force planes to traverse continents or simply hop to a nearby city for a brief meeting; and privileged status in elite social circles in Washington, D.C., and beyond. But, a newspaper informed readers, "he works you like a dog. He does not tolerate mistakes. He inspires fear and trepidation. He has a hair-trigger temper." Unlike Kennedy's staff, those in Johnson's employ were "treated like a member of the family, like a nephew, a niece or a brother. . . . [H]e is demanding, but that can bring out the best in a person." But along with the prestige of having a "PL" installed in one's home—the famous private line that only Moyers, Valenti, Busby, Watson, and McGeorge Bundy, the national security adviser, could boast—came the understanding that the president would use it at all hours. The human toll was considerable. Bill Moyers developed an ulcer from the stress, the president would inform visitors with satisfaction. Implicit in his pride was the under-standing that Moyers would work through the pain.

Johnson's dislike of staff structure and organization ("The President isn't a flow-chart man," explained one staff member. "We do what he tells us, never mind the rank and titles") was not dissimilar to the management style prac-ticed by his idol, Franklin Roosevelt. Like Valenti, Busby was a general utility player and became increasingly involved in foreign policy matters as 1965 gave way to 1966. McPherson was technically the top lawyer at the White House but also conferred with LBJ on Vietnam. The *Boston Globe* once proposed a movie script about the Johnson presidency in which Valenti played the part of the "image maker," Busby, the "licensed rhetorician in residence," and Moy-ers, the "auxiliary social conscience." In truth, each staff member was ex-pected to wear multiple hats.

Jim Rowe sized up Johnson as "an overpowering man," "a hard man to argue against, face to face." Without "really wanting to do it, he intimidated his staff a little too much, just with the force of his personality. When he wanted information, he was the best listener I've ever run into. . . . When he didn't want information . . . [if] I am trying to sell him something that does not interest him, I might as well be talking to a wall." Contrary to Johnson's famed vulgarity, Cater did not think that the president's "humor or his anecdotes were that much different in their crudeness from that of most men who are anecdotalists. He could tell a lusty story on occasion. He was not all that given to four-letter words. If a four-letter word fitted naturally into a story he would use it but he did not adorn them with four-letter words." Not everyone agreed. Once, when the White House received sustained, critical coverage from a female member of the press corps, LBJ informed Harry McPherson that "what that woman needs is you. Take her out. Give her a good dinner and a good fuck." According to Califano's memory of the incident, "McPherson sighed, shrugged, and continued with his conversation," but the president continued for weeks to hector him on the matter. Weeks later, Johnson told a group of senators acquainted with McPherson from his service on the Policy Committee staff that Harry was "a fine young man, but I'm a little concerned about his family. You know, Harry's been taking out this bitch reporter and screwing her, and I worry about his wife and children." Not dissimilarly, when James Gaither, a rising star on Califano's staff, informed the president that he was facing opposition on a particular matter from Edith Green, the formidable chairwoman of a key House subcommittee on education, LBJ instructed Califano to have him "take her out, give her a couple of Bloody Marys, and . . . spend the afternoon in bed with her and she'll support any Goddamn bill he wants. Now if he wants to help his president, that's what he should do instead of writing these whiney memos every night."

LBJ was testing his staff. As Cater noted, it was less Johnson's boorishness that placed him in a category of one (after all, John Kennedy, for all his polish, had treated women with nearly unparalleled disrespect) than his single-minded expectation that staff members submit fully in mind, body, and spirit to his indomitable will. He had no interests outside politics. He did not read books. He played no sport. What he did was work—eighteen hours each day, unceasingly—and he expected his aides to be as wholly consumed by the art of politics as was he. Charles Schultze, who succeeded Kermit Gordon as budget director, recalled that LBJ "relaxed in ways that would tire me." On the ranch, he drove his guests at frenetic speeds and talked politics. On the presidential yacht, the *Sequoia*, he cornered captive friends, staff members, and congressmen and talked politics. "It isn't that Johnson abuses people," a holdover from the Kennedy administration told Teddy White. "He simply dehydrates them." Much of the pressure was self-directed. An anonymous presidential assistant told the *New York Times* that "there is no real privacy in this job, and the demands are constant. All you have to do is go to dinner with the wrong person or have a drink with the wrong person or check the wrong box or write the wrong memo, and the president is in trouble. I could land him in boiling water 10 times a day."

By mid-1965, Washington columnists and opinion makers began to worry openly that Johnson might drive his closest aides to nervous breakdowns, much as they believed he had ruined Walter Jenkins. But for those closest to the president, it turned into their finest, most productive two years—a space of twenty-four months that left a lasting mark on American history and society.

CHAPTER 7

Completing the Fair Deal

S ince the 1930s, federal aid to primary and secondary education had been a foundational aspiration of American liberals. It was "shocking," Harry Truman told Congress in 1949, that "millions of our children are not receiving a good education. Millions of them are in overcrowded, obsolete buildings. We are short of teachers, because teachers' salaries are too low to attract new teachers, or to hold the ones we have." Truman requested direct federal appropriations to assist local schools in upgrading their facilities and paying their teachers and proposed that the various government agencies responsible for administering federal health, education, and welfare programs be accorded cabinet-level status. Congress did agree to consolidate existing agencies under the new cabinet-level Department of Health, Education, and Welfare in 1953, but in the absence of a more sweeping mandate the tiny and moribund Office of Education—which fell under HEW—remained a stodgy resting place for government bureaucrats with no appreciable connection to presidential power or authority. As had been the case for most of the nation's history, state and local governments bore the primary responsibility for funding and administering elementary and secondary schools, resulting in vast disparities between wealthy and poor districts, segregated and nonsegregated jurisdictions, and rural and urban areas. As the baby boom generation swelled America's schools, creating massive teacher and classroom shortages, efforts to pass a bill providing for federal aid to local education stalled repeatedly.

Some Republicans supported the idea, including the conservative senator Robert Taft and President Dwight Eisenhower. "We have helped the states build highways and local farm-to-market roads," the former general offered. "We have provided federal funds to help the states build hospitals and mental institutions." Why not classrooms? But most GOP leaders agreed with Barry Goldwater that "if the camel once gets his nose in the tent, his body will soon follow." The moment that local government became reliant on Washington, "supervision, and ultimately control of education," would fall into the hands of "federal authorities." The House minority leader, Gerald Ford, warned of "federalized schools, text books, and teachers, federalized libraries, laboratories, auditoriums, and theaters," while even Richard Nixon, a relative moderate, predicted in 1960 that when "the federal government gets the power to pay teachers, inevitably, in my opinion, it will acquire the power to set standards and to tell the teachers what to teach."

In addition to conservative opposition, efforts to secure federal funding for K-12 education met with the pointed resistance of Catholic political and religious leaders, who insisted that any aid bill include the vast network of diocesan and parish schools that the church had meticulously constructed and nurtured over the better part of a century. In the early postwar era, many white ethnic communities remained tightly bound and organized around a sweeping array of separate institutions—youth clubs, sports teams, fraternal organizations, newspapers—that all led back to the neighborhood church. Primary and secondary schools, which educated five million Catholic children each year, formed a mainstay of this religious network. Catholic Democrats were disinclined to support legislation that might create wider disparities in classroom funding and teacher salaries than already existed between parochial and public institutions. For their part, liberal Protestants steadfastly agreed with the National Council of Churches that it was neither "just" nor "lawful that public funds should be assigned to support the elementary or secondary schools of any church." The religious question constituted a major impediment to progress.

Finally, the issue of race proved a stumbling block for advocates of federal aid. Whenever the issue of aid to education came to the House floor, liberals of both parties routinely supported efforts by Adam Clayton Powell, a black clergyman and lawmaker from Harlem, to bar funds to school districts that were out of compliance with the Supreme Court's decision in *Brown v. Board of Education*. Without the amendment, liberals could not vote for the broader legislation; with it, southerners would not support it.

Liberals persisted in their argument that the country was in dire need of additional education funding. In any given year, American schoolchildren suffered a shortage of 304,000 classrooms. Many schools in poor areas lacked gymnasiums, lunchrooms, or libraries. To double up on space, administrators shifted fifth and sixth graders into middle schools and ran double-shift days. In Kentucky, over half of all pupils attended overcrowded classes—many with more than sixty children per room—and, according to the state superintendent of instruction, over 40 percent of facilities were "outmoded or unfit or should be abandoned." Unsurprisingly, student achievement reflected these broad disparities in resources and facilities. In 1960, the high school completion rate for young adults in the wealthiest five states and five poorest states in the country differed by twenty percentage points. For African Americans, who were substantially less likely than their white peers to finish secondary school, the disparity between residents of wealthy and poor states was 27 percent. It was precisely this fundamental opportunity deficit that enabled LBJ and his administration to slice through the Gordian knot that was federal education policy.

In the wake of his sweeping victory over Barry Goldwater, LBJ intended to use the Democratic Party's commanding majorities in Congress to break the dam that had for decades stalled the expansion of the welfare state. Resolving the impasse over education funding—a seemingly unending stalemate to which there was no obvious answer—took priority.

In December, LBJ, a consummate pragmatist who was more intent on reaching a deal than preserving a barrier between church and state, asked Doug Cater why the administration could not simply allocate funds to non-public schools in equal proportion to the percentage of children they educated. The idea was a nonstarter, his aide replied. Catholic schools had seen enrollment growth of 129 percent in the prior decade, resulting in pupil-teacher ratios that were far out of balance when compared with public institutions. Any aid package that subsidized this growth would draw liberal opposition. "Federal policy should be to improve the excellence of education for all children," Cater insisted. "But it should not encourage continued growth of the parochial school system at a faster rate than the public system." Yet behind closed doors, there appeared for the first time in many years to be room for compromise. Meeting with a dozen Catholic monsignors in December, administration officials learned that given the Supreme Court's increasingly liberal disposition, the church was not eager to force a judicial case that might definitively close the door on broad categorical aid to parochial schools. Legislation that went too far in funding religious schools would surely trigger such a legal test. The clerics assured Francis Keppel, the commissioner of education, that they would treat federal aid as supplemental rather than as an offset for their current education budgets. It finally appeared that a reasonable compromise might be in sight.

Meeting earlier that month with John Hay Whitney—newspaper publisher, diplomat, and scion of a wealthy Republican family (his grandfather had served as Abraham Lincoln's private secretary and, later, as secretary of state under William McKinley and Theodore Roosevelt)—the president explained that he was eager to reach an accommodation on the "church-state dispute," given the increasingly charged debate over school desegregation. In fact, enactment of the Civil Rights Act was a blessing as well as a curse to the cause of education reform. While it would soon enmesh thousands of school districts in contentious negotiations with the Department of Health, Education, and Welfare and in federal court cases, it removed a hot-button issue from debate. Liberals in Congress would no longer insist on the poison pill that was the Powell Amendment, because it was no longer necessary. The new civil rights law already stipulated that segregated institutions were ineligible for federal aid.

As late as 1962, William V. Shannon of the *New York Post* wrote that "religious and philosophical antagonisms engendered by school questions are so bitter that a solution through normal . . . methods is no longer possible." Now the door seemed to budge, if just a crack. Johnson's War on Poverty would provide the wedge to jar it wide open. On December 1, Keppel proposed shifting the formula from general aid to "categorical" aid. Rather than disburse funds to schools, the government could use the schools as pass-through agents for the disbursement of resources to economically disadvantaged children, whether they attended public, private, or parochial institutions. "The great majority of all school districts in the Nation would receive payments under the proposal," the commissioner advised, making the new formula politically difficult to resist. The idea was not new. Congressman John Dent, a Pennsylvania Democrat who helped steer the administration's antipoverty bill through the House in 1964, believed that the same allocation formula applied to community action programs might work for elementary and secondary education: the federal government could calculate the number of poor children in a particular area and disburse funds proportionally according to need. Senator Wayne Morse, a liberal Democrat from Oregon, had already suggested such an idea. In later years, Johnson's aides would disagree about the provenance of the formula. Wilbur Cohen, a veteran civil servant of the New Deal era who played a leading role in shepherding Johnson's education and health-care agenda through Congress, was certain that the proposal was his. Keppel recalled differently: "The NEA [National Education Association] thinks they thought it up, and the Catholics think they thought it up, and I think I thought it up. I don't know. It just got put together."

Regardless of who originated the idea, the president quickly approved it. For one, it was consistent with his long-standing core belief that education was a key to unlocking opportunity. It was both strategically and tactically convenient inasmuch as it aligned a perennial liberal aspiration—aid to primary and secondary education—with the guiding principles of the Great Society and circumvented the religious question by associating money with students rather than schools. In addition, the formula appealed to LBJ's pragmatism; the president understood that he would enjoy just one crack at the problem. Keppel and Cohen were waiting in the Fish Room in January 1965 when the president bounded in, "looking cheerful as he can be," the commissioner remembered. Johnson surveyed the room and abruptly turned the mood. "Look," he implored, "we've got to do this in a hurry. We've got in with this majority of sixteen million votes in the Congress. It doesn't make any difference what we do. We're going to lose them at a rate of about a million a month." Urging both men to expedite legislative action on education and health care, the president "turned around with that characteristic gesture," Keppel would recall, "and said, 'I want to see a whole bunch of coonskins on the wall!'"

In its final form, the Elementary and Secondary Education Act (ESEA) broke the long-standing impasse by providing compensatory education dollars to each state based on the number of children in households earning less than $2,000 annually. Title I provided aid to public schools to support supplemental programs that would benefit poor students (including those who attended private institutions). Title II funded textbooks and libraries in public and private schools alike. Title III underwrote supplemental programs in music, science, remedial skills, and physical education for poor children. Ultimately, less than

13 percent of funds supported private school students—enough to mollify the Roman Catholic Church, but wrapped in the War on Poverty in such a way as to make the scheme palatable to liberal Protestants. Critics would later dismiss the ESEA as a convoluted effort to fund education by making it an antipoverty program; the problem, they claimed, was that by traveling so circuitous a route to political compromise, the administration neither attacked poverty nor improved educational outcomes. In this assessment, alleviating poverty required lifting incomes through cash transfer programs, and improving education outcomes demanded a less targeted, more holistic approach to spending. Many low-performing students were not, in fact, poor, while in many districts local officials simply used Title I funds to offset or supplement regular budgetary expenses, thus obviating the intent of Congress to target programming to economically disadvantaged youth. Because the funding formula left states with broad discretion as to how and where they allocated funds, by 1977, according to one study, almost two-thirds of students benefiting from the program were not poor and over half were not low achievers.

The administration viewed matters differently. At the time, Keppel spoke for the president as well as for most administration officials when he argued that "income correlates highly with the number of years of schooling completed." He sincerely believed, as did most of the Great Society's architects, that additional funds "could interrupt the cycle of poverty where we have a fighting chance." Only in later years did policy makers focus on a multiplicity of cultural phenomena, including the disintegration of two-family households, and structural economic conditions—like stagflation and the decline of manufacturing and organized labor—that contributed in outsized proportions to poverty's growth and sustenance. At the time of the bill's passage, it was still an article of liberal faith that more education funding generated better educational outcomes and that better educational outcomes would lift children out of poverty. The very logic behind this thinking lay at the heart of opportunity theory.

Moreover, if liberals sincerely believed that broader access to education would help poor children break the cycle of poverty, they also believed that the federal government had an obligation to shoulder a portion of the nation's primary and secondary education burden. If tying aid to the number of poor children in a particular state or district was the mechanism by which to achieve this goal, then it was a method worth embracing. As one congressman later acknowledged, "In 1965, the issue was not good education policy versus bad. The question Congress had to settle in 1965 was whether there was ever going to be federal aid to the elementary and secondary schools of this nation. . . . The 1965 bill, in all candor, does not make much sense educationally, but it makes a hell of a lot of sense legally, politically, and constitutionally. This was a battle of principle, not substance, and that is the main reason I voted for it." In big cities especially, federal assistance proved critical, and officials could make the case that even offsets of ordinary course expenditures benefited poor children. As Benjamin Willis, the superintendent of schools in Chicago, explained to Congress, urban centers had in recent years attracted "large families from the rural South"—white and black alike—who "have little education and limited vocational skills." Their children "require specialized programs of education if they are to overcome the disadvantages imposed upon them by their limited background." More so than small towns and suburbs, "a large portion of the tax dollar in the great cities is required for non-school governmental services," including public transportation, police and sanitation, and public welfare. (Willis might have added that few conservatives raised concerns when the federal government funded a sprawling interstate highway system that primarily benefited suburbanites.) "Site and construction costs are considerably higher in the large cities than in smaller communities." Metropolises like Chicago could spend more on educating disadvantaged youth if they had more money—full stop.

Between 1958 and 1968, federal spending on primary and secondary education rose from $375 million to $4.2 billion, or from less than 3 percent to over 10 percent of total education funding. As Johnson predicted, once institutionalized, it would likely grow. By 1985, the federal government's share of all K–12 school spending rose to 16 percent; the percentage provided by state governments rose from 41 percent to 55 percent; and the portion shouldered by local governments fell from 51 percent to 31 percent. Because many local and state governments rely heavily on regressive property and sales taxes, in many cases these swings shifted some of the burden for funding schools from working-class and poor families to middle-class and wealthy income taxpayers. Furthermore, in the early 1970s Congress plugged some of the loopholes in the program by imposing "maintenance of effort" requirements on states and localities; to continue receiving ESEA funds, local and state governments must set their own education budgets at a high fraction of the prior year's appropriation, thus ensuring that federal dollars were truly supplementary. As the federal government gradually imposed additional regulations and restrictions governing the allocation of Title I money, state authorities centralized and professionalized their education departments and school systems to ensure ease of compliance and the continued flow of federal dollars. Partly as a result of this steady evolution, the number of independent school districts in the United States, which stood at 150,000 at the beginning of the twentieth century, fell to 15,000 by 1990.

At the bill signing in Johnson City, Texas, at the small one-room schoolhouse he had attended as a child, LBJ believed "deeply no law I have signed or will ever sign means more to the future of America."

"As a son of a tenant farmer," he told the nation, "I know that education is the only valid passport from poverty. As a former teacher—and, I hope, a future one—I have great expectations of what this law will mean for all of our young people." Much as conservatives once feared, and as liberals had long hoped, Washington, D.C., came to play a greatly expanded role in K-12 education. Even if federal education policy did not achieve the dramatic reduction in poverty that Great Society planners once prophesied, it did, as LBJ promised, "put into the hands of our youth more than 30 million new books, and into many of our schools their first libraries . . . reduce the terrible time lag in bringing new teaching techniques into the nation's classrooms [and] strengthen state and local agencies which bear the burden and the challenge of better education." ESEA contributed to a vast upgrade in facilities, teachers' salaries, library access, and supplementary programming for economically disadvantaged young people, and later for broader categories. By those measures, it achieved much of what its framers set out to do.

Charles Roberts, who covered the White House for *Newsweek* under both John Kennedy and Lyndon Johnson, observed that "where President Kennedy used to use his staff *against* the bureaucracy, President Johnson puts greater store in the wisdom and experience of his Cabinet officers and career government workers." Having risen politically during the New Deal era, when great power resided among hundreds of high-ranking departmental and agency leaders, LBJ understood the utility of governmental veterans who knew how to make programs work. Kennedy once told Roberts that "when things are noncontroversial, bureaucratically coordinated and all the rest, it may be that there is not much going on"; Johnson grasped the impossibility of the White House, with its relatively small staff, executing the Great Society's grandiose legislative agenda alone. This appreciation for agencies and bureaucrats knew some limits. LBJ expected the cabinet departments to do his bidding. Horace Busby, whose portfolio of responsibilities included serving as cabinet secretary (the White House official responsible for corralling members of the cabinet), earned plaudits for his success in giving the executive agencies a real seat at the table, as had not been the case in many years. "His choir-like directions of cabinet meetings," observed a reporter for the *New York Times*, "has turned them into precision affairs rather than rambling sessions."

In later years, Califano was the administration's undisputed orchestrator of domestic policy, but in 1965 and early 1966, when LBJ's prize initiatives—the education act and Medicare—were on the verge of launching, Doug Cater was (as Harry McPherson would recall) the "liaison man" with the Department of Health, Education, and Welfare, a sprawling and patchwork organization that comprised siloed fiefdoms—the Social Security Administration (SSA), the Office of Education, the Public Health Service—with little internal cohesion. In 1964, the office of the secretary of HEW totaled just sixteen professionals. Of the department's roughly eighty-three thousand employees, approximately seventy-one thousand were functionaries in the Public Health Service and Social Security Administration. HEW was effectively "a holding company for highly independent administrations and bureaus," a White House commission informed the president. "While its program burdens are enormous, the department is grossly understaffed at the top." A reporter who covered the department argued that it was "utterly ridiculous to be trying to run a $6 billion and $7 billion business with only a handful of people." Within HEW, no function was more inadequate to the task than the Office of Education, a small, hidebound outfit that was "not well equipped to administer effectively its many new responsibilities and that does not get strong support from the Secretary's office in solving its administrative problems," according to one observer. With roots in the late nineteenth century, the U.S. Office of Education employed a small army of professionals—most of them former public school teachers and principals—whose principal role was to compile data from state and local education officials and churn out arcane and generally uncontroversial studies about pedagogy. A government study found that its functionaries were "dedicated to servicing local, State and institutional policies rather than a national policy."

So irrelevant was the office that when John Kennedy learned from news reports that his first commissioner of education had quit his post, he replied with exasperation, "What's all this about this fellow resigning as Commissioner of Education, apparently by way of Capitol Hill? What's going on! I never heard of the fellow!" McGeorge Bundy, the president's national security adviser, replied coolly, "Mr. President, that's exactly the trouble. You never heard of the fellow!"

If Kennedy was indifferent to the workings of government bureaucracy, LBJ was not. With Califano's and Cater's support, Francis Keppel, who served as commissioner of education between 1962 and 1965, initiated a major overhaul of the office—"an old agency largely devoted to data-gathering and operating in deference to State and professional groups" that would now bear the operational burden of ESEA. Though some advocates called for the establishment of a cabinet-level Department of Education, the Johnson administration was already in the process of creating the Department of Housing and Urban Development and the Department of Transportation. There was no political will to create a third. Moreover, Keppel advised that if the White House elevated his office to cabinet level, conservatives would howl anew at the specter of federal control. In fact, he argued, there was so much convergence between the Great Society's education, health, and antipoverty programs that it made sense to house them under one umbrella department, albeit with a radically overhauled Office of Education. Over the course of several months, he smashed a number of bureaucratic idols and, in the process, alienated many people and organizations—especially state educational officials—who were invested in the status quo. "The anguish can only be imagined. The ensuing, if temporary, administrative chaos was shattering. For days and weeks, people could not find each other's offices—sometimes not even their own. Telephone extensions connected appropriate parties only by coincidence.... Those who could not live with the status loss resigned. And all of this came at a time of maximum work load."

Under Keppel and his successor, the Office of Education underwent sweeping personnel changes. It would take another decade and a half before Congress unraveled HEW and created a cabinet-level Department of Education, but in that time the Office of Education developed the operational know-how to oversee a growing budget, as successive Congresses grew the federal government's aid budget and established over a hundred new buckets of categorical assistance, including grants for migrant children, students for whom English was a second language, delinquent children, and children with physical and mental disabilities. As Cater and Keppel anticipated, the administrative burden associated with managing these programs—issuing annual guidelines for individual programs, monitoring eligibility and compliance, negotiating with states and school districts to ensure proper maintenance of effort, and, most notably, compelling schools to integrate their student and faculty bodies—would demand a more muscular and activist staff. In the first year after the enactment of the administration's education programs, the office's personnel grew by an astonishing 50 percent. LBJ's White House advisers were attentive to the art of governance and, in ways that were often invisible to the public at large, built capabilities that would ensure the lasting success of the administration's domestic policy achievements. In so doing, they also oversaw rapid growth in the federal bureaucracy that would later open them to sharp criticism.

As early as 1934, when Franklin Roosevelt's Committee on Economic Security first contemplated but ultimately rejected including health insurance in the original Social Security Act, liberals aspired to make access to affordable health care a fundamental right of citizenship. In the 1940s, Senator Robert Wagner and Congressmen John Dingell Sr. and Reid Murray introduced legislation that would have established a national program for hospital and medical insurance. It went nowhere, as was also the case with Harry Truman's efforts after 1949 to achieve the same result. At every turn, powerful opposition from the American Medical Association (AMA) and its Republican supporters in Congress stymied progressive efforts. The AMA alone showered $1.5 million on lobbyists and public relations professionals to defeat Truman's program—a staggering sum in its day. In 1952, when the GOP platform roundly denounced "federal compulsory health insurance, with its crushing cost, wasteful inefficiency, bureaucratic dead weight, and debased standards of medical care," Dwight Eisenhower—the very model of moderation—scored Democrats who would foist "socialized medicine" on an unsuspecting public. There was little room for bipartisan compromise.

It did not help the liberal argument that increasing numbers of working-class voters who might have been inclined to support national health care no longer needed it. After World War II, major employers began extending unprecedented benefits to workers—blue-collar and white-collar alike—including paid vacations, annual cost-of-living adjustments to wages, defined benefits pensions, and private health insurance. Liberal industrial unions endorsed this new model for labor-management relations. During the Great Depression, the United Auto Workers had staged dramatic sit-down strikes and demanded shop-floor democracy in the form of employee representation in management decisions. Now, reflecting the new reality of postwar prosperity, in 1950 the union signed a pathbreaking contract with General Motors—dubbed "the Treaty of Detroit"—which offered controls against strikes in return for generous employee benefits. "GM may have paid a billion for peace," wrote the sociologist Daniel Bell, then a columnist for *Fortune*, "but it got a bargain." What many liberals once assumed government would need to do for its working-class citizens, private industry now offered on a contingent basis. By 1960, 100 million Americans enjoyed access to private health plans.

While many Americans did not enjoy access to such perquisites—including most African Americans, Latinos, and women; most nonunionized workers; the unemployed; and children of uninsured adults—ardor cooled within organized labor on the subject of comprehensive health insurance. Instead, by the mid-1950s, Democrats turned their focus to a narrower subset of the population that, by definition, would not benefit from employer-based health programs: senior citizens, most of whom were no longer in the workforce. At a hearing in 1959, a retired blue-collar worker from Tampa told a Senate subcommittee that he and his wife got by on just $1,500 each year. "Well, we are old people and we don't require much," he offered. "But I want to ask you . . .

what do we do if . . . we need medical care . . . ? I will have to seek some charity institution and submit to the humiliation of what they call a necessity, and pronounce to the whole world that I am only a pauper, a beggar." A seventy-five-year-old woman from Boston shocked the panel with her tale of waiting "in line like a lot of cattle" at a charitable clinic, because she and her husband could not afford to spend $7 to visit a private doctor. "We pay $1.75 or $2 for a ticket to get in," she complained. "Then they write out a prescription. . . . $11 prescription. How in the world can I pay $11 for a prescription?" As a Senate aide to Lyndon Johnson, George Reedy had urged the majority leader to take up the cause of health care for the elderly. The "problem of aging amounts to a collective responsibility," he insisted. "America is no longer a nation of simple pioneer folk in which grandmother and grandfather can spend their declining years in a log cabin doing odd jobs and taking care of the grandchildren."

Legislation providing hospital insurance for the elderly first surfaced in 1951 and bore the common sobriquet Medicare as early as 1950. The bill that John Kennedy first proposed would have updated the 1935 Social Security Act by establishing a contributory hospital insurance program for every recipient of Old-Age, Survivors, and Disability Insurance—OASDI, or what is commonly known as Social Security. Workers would pay an additional payroll tax and enjoy the benefit upon retirement. Even this stripped-down proposal drew the angry opposition of the nation's physicians. The AMA spent $50 million—and hired seventy publicists and twenty-three full-time lobbyists—to kill the legislation. Every member of the organization—which is to say, most doctors in America—received a propaganda poster, SOCIALIZED MEDICINE AND YOU, intended for prominent display in their offices, as well as a supply of informational literature to place in the hands of patients. When the American Nurses Association broke with the physicians and endorsed the bill, individual members reported widespread, "rather unethical pressure" from their doctor-employers. The AMA's campaign worked. Though Kennedy tried to appeal to the country's generous spirit—"I can't imagine anything worse . . . to sap someone's self-reliance than to be sick, alone, broke," he declared—like the rest of his domestic agenda, his Medicare bill died prematurely in Congress.

Even in the aftermath of LBJ's landslide victory in 1964, when it became clear that the president would enjoy majorities sufficient to push Medicare through the House and the Senate, the AMA opted for vocal opposition rather than accept a seat at the drafting table. "We do not, by profession, compromise in matters of life and death," the organization's president announced. "Nor can we compromise with honor and duty." But the die was cast. Through labyrinthine negotiations between Wilbur Cohen and Wilbur Mills, the chairman of the House Ways and Means Committee, the final legislation combined three different concepts into one bill: Medicare Part A, which provided automatic hospital insurance for all recipients of OASDI. Under this section, seniors were entitled to ninety days of hospitalization per year, per illness, with a $40 deductible to cover the first sixty days and $10 per each subsequent day of inpatient care. The hospital insurance was financed by an increase in Social Security taxes. Medicare Part B, originally a Republican alternative to the Kennedy-Johnson plan, provided voluntary medical insurance to cover physician visits; for $3 each month, Americans over the age of sixty-five, whether eligible for OASDI or not, could buy coverage, which the government further subsidized. Finally, the bill established Medicaid insurance for indigent Americans of all ages, including dependent children; states would administer the program, with a sliding-scale match from Washington, D.C.

Officially called the Social Security Amendments of 1965, Medicare and Medicaid glided through Congress in early July. With the exception of southern holdouts, Democrats overwhelmingly supported the plan; Republicans in both the Senate and the House were more evenly divided. Johnson insisted on staging the formal bill signing at the Truman Presidential Library in Independence, Missouri, as a tribute to the aging former president but also to emphasize the continuity between the New Deal, the Fair Deal, and the Great Society. Several of LBJ's aides, including Busby, Cohen, and Cater, urged Johnson to relocate the ceremony to the White House or, as an alternative, to Hyde Park, given the upcoming thirtieth anniversary of Social Security. Truman's original bill had been a "close parallel to Great Britain's 'socialized medicine,'" Buzz observed. (Indeed, at the time, the AMA had deemed it a "monstrosity of Bolshevik bureaucracy.") After years of positioning Medicare as a moderate program well within the boundaries of existing political norms, the symbolism behind traveling to Independence would pose a "grotesque distortion with unhappy and impolitic overtones." Busby was particularly concerned that the AMA might shun both the ceremony and the program itself—a fear grounded in reality: the Ohio Medical Association, with a membership of ten thousand physicians, had already endorsed a Medicare boycott, as did most of the twenty-five thousand AMA members who had convened the prior month in New York for the association's annual conference. Moreover, Truman was renowned for his extreme candor. There was no telling what jabs he might throw at the medical profession in return for its years of stubborn opposition. Johnson insisted on his original plan. Neither was he particularly concerned about the possibility that the AMA would attempt to kill Medicare before its implementation.

"George, have you ever fed chickens?" the president asked George Meany, the president of the AFL-CIO who shared Cohen's concern about a physician boycott. "No," replied Meany. "Well, chickens are real dumb," LBJ explained. "They eat and eat and eat and never stop. Why they start shitting at the same time they're eating, and before you know it, they're knee-deep in their own shit. Well, the AMA's the same. They've been eating and eating nonstop and now they're knee-deep in their own shit and everybody knows it. They won't be able to stop anything." When the organization's leaders gathered at the White House on June 29—weeks before the signing ceremony—the president delivered the full "Johnson Treatment." He flattered his visitors, rained praise upon their chosen vocation and calling, and applauded their patriotism. Referencing the war in Vietnam, he asked whether the AMA would honor its civic duty by endorsing a voluntary initiative to send doctors for short tours of duty to help build the local medical infrastructure in South Vietnam. "Your country needs your help," he implored. "Your president needs your help." When the doctors signaled their agreement (for what else could they have done?), Johnson snapped for the press corps. A reporter led with the obvious question—would the AMA cooperate in the execution of Medicare?—and the president, as though on cue, feigned anger. "These men are going to get doctors to go to Vietnam where they might be killed," he lectured the newspapermen and broadcast outlets. "Medicare is the law of the land. Of course they'll support the law of the land."

Nothing like Medicare had ever been attempted in the United States: a new national health-care plan, financed by payroll taxes and voluntary contributions, offering roughly twenty million seniors automatic hospital coverage and an affordable, government-subsidized insurance program to cover doctors' visits. Not long after he signed Medicare into law in July 1965, LBJ cautioned John Gardner, who replaced Anthony Celebrezze as secretary of health, education, and welfare in August 1965, that the department's successful implementation of the program would be every bit as critical as the legislative achievement itself. "If you're wrong in your calculations," LBJ warned, "we're both going to look like the worst kind of damn fools."

The possibilities for failure were vast. In a day when "communications technology" meant printed mail and the rotary telephone, the new Medicare administration would have to find those seniors, tell them about the program, and get them to sign up. Some wondered whether the government could ever achieve its critical enrollment targets. Others, like the *New York Times* reporter Nona Brown, wondered if there would be "lines of old folks at hospital doors, with no rooms to put them in, too few doctors and nurses and technicians to care for them." It was by no means clear that doctors would participate, given the AMA's staunch opposition, and individual physicians were under no obligation to accept Medicare insurance—or that it would be possible to establish a working reimbursement system in so short a time. As Johnson later recalled, "There were predictions . . . that the system would collapse under its own weight." Yet after it launched, on July 1, 1966, no such calamity ensued. On the contrary, by the start date over nineteen million senior citizens had enrolled and immediately enjoyed the security of knowing that they would not go bankrupt by getting sick. Hospitals and doctors joined the Medicare network, and private and nonprofit insurance carriers stepped in to manage disbursements. In short, the system worked.

In constructing Medicare, the Johnson administration faced a number of daunting challenges. Though all Social Security recipients would be automatically enrolled in Medicare's hospital insurance program (Part A), roughly eight million seniors were not eligible for Social Security, either because their job sector was excluded or because they hadn't worked or accrued credits. These seniors needed to be located and registered. All seniors were also eligible to enroll voluntarily in the doctors' insurance program, Part B, which gave them access to routine medical care at a cost of $3 per month, but they, too, would have to be signed up one person at a time. Additionally, officials had to work with tens of thousands of scattered nursing homes, hospitals, and home health agencies to certify them and bring them into the system. Then there were the doctors—more than 200,000—who could elect to participate in Part B. They, too, needed to be briefed and enrolled.

In these days before mass electronic record keeping, it required vast human efforts to reach potential Medicare recipients. Under the leadership of HEW, multiple government agencies—including the Social Security Administration, Public Health Service, Internal Revenue Service, Civil Service Commission, General Services Administration, National Park Service, and Postal Service—dedicated tens of thousands of professional staff members to the challenge. The career officials who helped draft and implement the law brought decades of collective expertise to the task. They chose July 1, rather than January 1, to launch the program, because hospitals were often strained to capacity during the winter months, when senior citizens were likely to suffer from weather-related illness. The Postal Service hung billboards at each of its locations, announcing enrollment deadlines and processes. The Forest Service sent rangers into woods in search of remote, off-the-grid men and women who could not be reached by mail. The SSA sent over 19 million punch cards out to seniors and, at peak, processed 800,000 each week, routinely checking the responses against the Bureau of Data Processing and Accounts' magnetic tape records, so that eligible seniors who had not replied could be canvassed either in person or by mail.

Wilbur Cohen, whom LBJ elevated to the position of undersecretary of HEW, called it the most sweeping governmental maneuver since D-day. By July 1, 1966, between 90 percent and 95 percent of eligible individuals (nineteen million) were enrolled in both Part A *and* Part B. "I doubt if ever in history has there been such a comprehensive and successful program of communication with older people," crowed one official. At the same time, federal officials selected and prepared private insurance carriers to administer the new systems for hospital and doctor payments, consulting with groups as diverse as the American Nurses Association, the American Hospital Association, and Blue Cross organizations to help medical facilities meet the program's standards.

At first blush, the Johnson administration's success in launching Medicare in just eleven months—even as it took on the simultaneous task of desegregating health facilities throughout the South—seems to stand in sharp contrast to the trouble that successive administrations experienced in enacting various health-care reforms. But Johnson's White House worked from a position of comparative advantage.

For one, LBJ was able to rely heavily on state governments for cooperation. The White House asked governors—Democrats and Republicans, southern and northern alike—to designate state agencies to govern certification of insurance carriers in their jurisdictions. Even in the face of enforcement of Title VI of the Civil Rights Act, which many governors loathed, the states promptly stepped in to assume these administrative responsibilities. By contrast, half a century later, when Barack Obama implemented the Affordable Care Act (ACA), many Republican governors dug in their heels and flatly refused to implement it. Thirty-five states refused to establish health exchanges where, as the law intended, citizens could buy private health insurance plans and instead relied on Washington to operate exchanges for them; nineteen states also refused federal dollars to expand Medicaid coverage for poor residents, as the act also encouraged. Many governors refused to use state resources to enroll eligible citizens, and some even took the Obama administration to court. As divided as the country was during Johnson's term in office, this magnitude of political obduracy was largely unthinkable in the political culture of the day.

In the 1960s, there was also no ecosystem of business lobbies and conservative think tanks to engage in a guerrilla war against Medicare. Though the American Medical Association had long resisted the law, and while hospitals and individual physicians were under no obligation to participate in the program and see Medicare patients, most health-care providers largely acquiesced after its passage, joining with hospital organizations, insurance carriers, and religious and lay groups to help implement the program. Reflecting on the achievement many years after the fact—but well before enactment of the ACA—a Johnson administration official noted that "in Medicare we never had a class action suit in the first or second year. . . . There were no strong advocacy groups following our every move . . . and there was little litigation, except on the basis of individual claims, that went past the appeals process. By the time Medicare was implemented, major interest groups were involved—the AFL-CIO and senior citizens' organizations for example—but worked with us for change rather than filing suits." Obama's ACA met with organized resistance at every turn; by contrast, Medicare's early foe—the American Medical Association—soon accepted the program as established law and learned to live with it; indeed, many doctors soon discovered that it was a golden goose.

Finally, Medicare had a far narrower mandate than certain later initiatives. The program came under early and heavy criticism for its out-of-control costs, and indeed between 1966 and 1971 annual Medicare spending jumped from $3.5 billion to $7.9 billion, well in excess of what the Johnson administration initially projected. Detractors then and later would fault Medicare, with its fee-for-service model, for fueling runaway medical inflation across the board. Some of that criticism was fair, though hospital costs had already been sharply on the rise before Medicare, jumping 149 percent between 1950 and 1963, compared with a hike of just 27 percent in the consumer price index. In effect, medical inflation began outstripping general inflation well before Medicare. More fundamentally, Medicare was never intended to overhaul the health-care economy. The program used existing insurance carriers as administrative agents—that usually meant large, established companies that could demonstrate "unquestionable capability to administer effectively and efficiently . . . for a beneficiary group of significant size" and the ability to effect "prompt and proper payment under the concept of 'reasonable charges'"—and deliberately took a light hand in enforcing delivery and price controls. As an administration official later noted, Medicare "accepted the going system for the delivery of care and the program structure was modeled on previous private insurance arrangements. Reimbursement of institutions followed the principle of cost reimbursement that had been worked out with the American Hospital Association and the majority of Blue Cross plans. Physician reimbursement followed the direction of private commercial insurance, making payments based, by and large, on what physicians charged their other patients." The program was constructed solely to extend medical care to seniors, and because so many seniors availed themselves of its blanket coverage, costs soared. It simply "wasn't possible in 1965 to put cost controls in. It would never have passed Congress," Wilbur Cohen affirmed. "Even if we could have, no one knew how to do it in 1965." By contrast, Obama's ACA was designed to extend coverage *and* control costs and in this regard has a much more ambitious mission. In short, Americans expected more of the ACA—and in some case feared the ACA more—because the program was sold as a transformative measure.

In 1961, Ronald Reagan ominously warned that passage of Medicare would constitute "a short step to all the rest of socialism." In fact, LBJ relied on private insurance carriers, to the chagrin of liberals who might have preferred to bypass the entrenched medical establishment. The irony was not lost on the authors of a contemporary study who noted that "Medicare . . . began with an apparent paradox. Private enterprise had failed, markedly, to provide adequate health insurance for the elderly: hence the passage of Medicare. Yet private insurance was chosen to administer the new governmental system." Doctors, whose lobby had steadfastly resisted the program, learned to love it: their incomes rose approximately 11 percent each year over the first seven years of implementation. For most seniors, it soon became impossible to fathom a world without Medicare. As Johnson predicted, it became a third rail in American politics that only the most outspoken entitlement hawks dared attack. Its enduring success owed in no small measure to its smooth launch.

CHAPTER 8

Get 'Em! Get the Last Ones!

When Lyndon Johnson decreed in New Orleans that the Civil Rights Act of 1964 would be the guiding law of the land—"I signed it, and I am going to enforce it," he pledged in his most famous campaign speech—skeptics could be forgiven their incredulity. Throughout his tenure as Senate majority leader, LBJ earned a well-deserved reputation for prevarication and avoidance on the subject of civil rights. During his service in the House of Representatives, from 1937 to 1948, he voted reliably with the southern bloc against federal antilynching laws, equal employment measures, and the elimination of the poll tax. In the Senate, he devoted his maiden speech to a full-throated defense of the South's political traditions. In 1957, he maneuvered the first meaningful civil rights legislation through Congress in almost a century but only after he stripped it of its enforcement mechanisms. Though in his first months as president he lent considerable muscle to the fight for a new, more comprehensive civil rights law, by no means was it clear that he would compel compliance. Many liberals regarded him at best as a new convert to the cause and at worst as an opportunist who had no intention of enforcing its more controversial provisions. But Johnson proved good to his word, if not better, and his administration began with that most taboo of public spaces: schools.

It had been over ten years since Chief Justice Earl Warren—his eyes fixed downward on a prepared text, his full shock of white hair set sharply against the top of his long black judicial robes—stunned the world on May 17, 1954, when he announced in stark, unyielding terms that "in the field of public education, the doctrine of 'separate but equal' has no place." The ruling was stunning and led many observers to declare premature victory. The reaction to the Court's unanimous decision in the case of *Brown v. Board of Education*—arguably, the first major legal blow leveled against Jim Crow—elicited cries of anguish and outrage from the Deep South, shocked disbelief from the nation's most experienced political observers, and a surge of optimism from African American communities throughout the country. The *Chicago Defender*, a venerable black newspaper, optimistically predicted that *Brown* meant the "beginning of the end of the dual society in American life and the system . . . of segregation which supports it," while the author Ralph Ellison hoped that "another battle of the Civil War has been won. The rest is up to us and I'm very glad. . . . What a wonderful world of possibilities are unfolded for the children." "We assumed that *Brown* was self-executing," recalled Julius Chambers, then a teenager in North Carolina who would one day become director-counsel of the NAACP Legal Defense Fund, the organization that argued the case before the Supreme Court. "The law had been announced, and people would have to obey it. Wasn't that how things worked in America, even in white America?" he later reflected.

That was of course not how things worked. After the Court ruled in a subsequent decision in 1955 (dubbed *Brown II*) that local authorities should proceed with "all deliberate speed" in desegregating their facilities, most southern school districts evaded the letter and intent of the decree by using a variety of methods to avoid full compliance with the Court's decision, including "pupil placement" plans, which assigned students to schools by means of racially biased testing criteria, and open enrollment plans, which placed the onus on individual black students to apply for transfers into white schools. Lower federal courts gave the South wiggle room by distinguishing between desegregation, which mandated an end to formal rules separating white and black students, and integration, which involved the deliberate achievement of racial balance. In 1960, less than 1 percent of black students in the South attended majority-white schools; in 1964, still less than 5 percent. In Alabama, Mississippi, and Louisiana, less than 1 percent of all black children attended school with even one white student—a testament to the Deep South's dogged maintenance of dual education systems.

Southern resistance to integrated schools cannot be measured in numbers alone. It was a story that played out in hundreds of school districts among thousands of actors—many of them children—every day.

It was the story of Dorothy Counts, a fifteen-year-old who in 1957 enrolled as the first and only black student at Harding High School in Charlotte, North

Carolina—an ostensibly moderate, "New South" city with a thriving business community that endeavored to distinguish itself from retrograde "Deep South" hamlets in Alabama and Mississippi. Though municipal officials intended her enrollment to meet a token measure of compliance with *Brown* (she was one of just four black students assigned to all-white schools and the only black pupil at Harding), Counts met with a firewall of violent resistance. On her first day of class, white residents—many of them adults several multiples of her age—greeted her with jeers, shoves, and a barrage of sticks and small rocks. They spat on her and vomited ugly racial epithets. Dorothy stayed home from school for two days and then steeled herself for a return. Her classmates shoved and elbowed her in the halls, vandalized her locker, and pelted erasers at her head. The mob shattered a window in her father's car as he attempted to drive her home. The Counts family had had enough. They moved north to Philadelphia, where she attended a nonsegregated high school.

It was also the story of Ruby Bridges, who in 1960 became the first black student to attend William Frantz Elementary School in New Orleans, after the federal district judge J. Skelly Wright, a native Louisianan, ordered the city to comply with *Brown*. Dressed immaculately in a starched white blouse, dark skirt, and polished Mary Janes, Ruby—a six-year-old girl in pigtails—walked quietly and with cool resolution as four U.S. marshals escorted her through an angry mob of 150 white protesters, most of them housewives, who pelted her with rotten eggs and vegetables and chanted the vicious doggerel "Two, four, six, eight. We don't want to integrate. Eight, six, four, two. We don't want a chiggeroo." One of the federal lawmen who protected her that day remarked that "she showed a lot of courage. She never cried. She didn't whimper. She just marched along like a little soldier, and we're all very very proud of her." White parents withdrew their children from the school and placed them in "private" academies supported by public funds. Throughout the fall, Ruby maintained her public composure, but she was rattled when one of the white women who heckled her each morning outside the school door threatened to poison her food. At the end of the semester, her teachers found Ruby's locker crammed with uneaten sandwiches that her mother had prepared for her lunch.

Shortly after John Kennedy's assassination, Burke Marshall, the head of the Justice Department's Civil Rights Division, observed that the South's decade-long campaign of "massive resistance" to the Supreme Court was "testing . . . the durability of the federal structure." State and local governments patently refused to desegregate their school systems, requiring the Justice Department to file individual suits that wound their way slowly through the federal court system. "It is as if no taxpayer sent in a return until he personally was sued by the Federal government," Marshall lamented. "The crisis is more deplorable, of course, because it is not private persons . . . who are failing to comply with laws, but the states themselves." It was precisely this moral and legal crisis that LBJ was determined to surmount.

Lyndon Johnson had an "abnormal, superstitious respect for education," George Reedy confided to an interviewer. He also believed with every fiber of his being that access to education should be color-blind. At age twenty-one, he taught elementary school in Cotulla, a small town on the South Texas plains, where all of his students were Mexican Americans. He was appalled by their dire poverty. Most of his students went hungry in the afternoons because their parents lacked the wherewithal to pack them off for the day with lunches. Over the single academic year he spent as a teacher, he championed his students, pushing them to learn and dream big. "Those little brown bodies had so little and needed so much," he painfully recalled. "I could never forget seeing the disappointment in their eyes and seeing the quizzical expression on their faces—all the time they seemed to be asking me, 'Why don't people like me? Why do they hate me because I am brown?'" As president, he now wielded power to right a wrong that had haunted him for decades, and he would make good use of it.

Title VI of the 1964 Civil Rights Act empowered the executive branch to cut off school funding for districts that still practiced de jure segregation. The 1965 Elementary and Secondary Education Act, which increased federal funding for public schools from just $2.7 billion in 1964 to $14.7 billion in 1971, rendered that enforcement authority more important. Federal funding now amounted to upwards of 30 percent of some southern districts' prospective budgets. If local officials insisted on maintaining dual school systems, not only might they face Justice Department suits and, potentially, court orders; the administration could also summarily withhold a large portion of their eligible federal education funding.

In theory, Title VI relieved the courts of the responsibility for enforcement. As one administration official observed, it offered a "golden opportunity for taking the intolerable pressure of the school cases off the federal judges by introducing a powerful new force for school integration." In reality, the aggressive means by which the Johnson administration administered Title VI spurred federal judges to involve themselves more, not less, in local school desegregation battles. Wielding two sticks—Title VI enforcement, which enabled the administration to cut off federal funds, and Justice Department lawsuits, which could result in judicial orders that federal law enforcement authorities would be compelled to enforce—the administration quickly showed its determination to bring the era of "all deliberate speed" to a close.

The Office of Education began driving southern districts to comply with Title VI even before the president signed ESEA into law and in many cases—such as Georgia, where Governor Carl Sanders, a relative moderate, sharply rejected the administration's scrutiny of districts that he deemed desegregated—bumped up against local resistance. Not just Douglass Cater and Joe Califano, but even Vice President Hubert Humphrey, who for a time acted as the administration's senior policy coordinator on civil rights, carefully oversaw negotiations between HEW and the Justice Department, on the one hand, and southern governors, on the other. Despite complaints by southern governors and members of Congress, Johnson gave his aides free rein in demanding that thousands of school districts submit clear desegregation plans to the commissioner of education, who alone would certify their compliance with the law. No White House had ever involved its staff in so granular, expansive, and consistent a review of civil rights compliance.

Within two weeks of ESEA's enactment on April 11, Doug Cater informed Johnson that HEW and the Department of Justice had decided to issue firm guidelines to districts that maintained dual school systems—which was to say, most localities in the former Confederate states, as well as many towns in the border states. "The problem was simply this," Cater informed LBJ. "Approximately 500 districts have submitted plans, most of them considered by the Commissioner of Education to be unacceptable. . . . It would be impossible to negotiate with each administration on an ad hoc basis. In fact, there has been evidence in negotiations attempted thus far that many districts are holding back on making commitments until they determine whether the Office of Education means business." The administration's parameters applied to all school districts that were not under court desegregation orders (such judicial decrees superseded HEW's authority) and required that they integrate at least four grades by the start of the 1965–1966 school year and all grades by the fall of 1967. Districts were permitted to use two mechanisms: geographic rezoning or "freedom-of-choice plans" that permitted parents to select the school they preferred for their children. Cater acknowledged that civil rights activists would look with disfavor upon the allowance of choice plans, which resembled the very mechanisms that white officials had used for over a decade to circumvent *Brown*. But the guidelines emphasized that "performance not paperwork is the ultimate measure of a plan's adequacy." Cater regarded the means by which districts desegregated as less important than the end. If the administration enforced its own requirements, choice plans could in fact operate as a powerful desegregation tool.

Much of the onus fell on Francis Keppel, who served by his own admission as the administration's "chief SOB with the Southerners." With only five months until the start of the new school year, his office was responsible for coaxing, cajoling, and haggling with over 5,000 individual districts throughout the South. "I had a whole crew of fellows trying to talk these Southern school districts into changing," he remembered. "They'd put up a plan—we wouldn't like it, and we'd [send] it back. I used to have to go over with Joe Califano about every three days, just as if you were reporting on your hunting trip, saying, 'We've now got 3,200 of them,' and, 'We've now got 3,800 of them.' We finally got down to a hundred of them or something." During his regular meetings at the White House—sometimes held in the Fish Room, sometimes in Califano's basement-level office suite—the president would routinely "wander in and out saying, 'Get 'em! Get 'em! Get the last ones!' We were going absolutely nuts. But it was a kind of political game. He wanted them all in the bag, you know, by September."

Meeting with Attorney General Nicholas Katzenbach, White House counsel Lee White, and Keppel, Califano emphasized that LBJ was "anxious to put all the states in such condition under Title VI that he will not have to withhold federal funds from a single county." The president's objective was to desegregate schools, not punish local communities. Indeed, he intended ESEA funds to help lift underprivileged communities in the South and elsewhere out of the cycle of poverty. He wanted "to make sure that we are doing everything possible so that he does not have to withhold funds from a single school district." To aid in the process, the Office of Education organized seminars for local education officials to help them design plans that would pass muster with the administration's guidelines. The program cost $7 million over the course of several months—"money well spent," White observed. Keppel would later claim that he "never had any doubts" about Johnson's sincerity on the question of school desegregation. "I don't know his life well," he allowed, "but certainly by the time I was connected with it, every time that we came up with a rational procedure to get on with it, we were supported. I never sensed any hesitation when the thing got near the president." Despite the steep price that he paid in lost political capital, Johnson was "no-nonsense" on the question of Title VI.

Many newspaper editorialists, local business leaders, and public education professionals in the South greeted the administration's school desegregation drive with "resignation," as the *Atlanta Constitution* characterized the response of its own state's education officials. In Alabama, the superintendent of education convened a meeting with most of the state's 117 district officials and instructed them to file desegregation plans with HEW and the Department of Justice. In Mississippi, Governor Paul Johnson affirmed that "obedience to our laws is not optional"—a stark concession by a fiery defender of Jim Crow whose home state reveled in its long tradition of flouting federal laws and the constitutional rights of its citizens, both black and white. In Virginia, elected officials were "taken aback" by the specter of "mixed schools," but the state did not contemplate shuttering its public school system, as it had done in the immediate aftermath of the *Brown* decision as a means to resist integrated classrooms. The *Birmingham News* roundly deplored the administration's guidelines but cautioned readers that "distasteful as these requirements still are to a majority of whites in Alabama, to react to them in anything but the utmost realism would be a tragic disservice to the State and its children." There were, as always, holdouts. Senator Strom Thurmond of South Carolina, an unreconstructed segregationist who formally switched parties in 1964, wired the secretary of health, education, and welfare to express "shock" at the administration's determination to "force integration" of classrooms. But some local school officials quietly communicated their appreciation to Keppel, Cater, and Califano for devising parameters that provided clarity around how to develop plans that were in compliance with HEW's expectations.

Despite the absence of widespread "massive resistance" (the organized efforts to stop integration in the years immediately following the *Brown* decision), administration officials soon discerned two clear impediments to school
desegregation. First, as Cater predicted might be the case, two-thirds of school
districts *not* under court order adopted freedom-of-choice plans as their primary mode of compliance with HEW guidelines; the onus fell almost entirely
on black families to overcome white hostility and bureaucratic roadblocks at
the local level. Second, officials in many towns and cities *preferred* being
placed under court order. As an assistant secretary of HEW observed, it was
"politically more comfortable" for a mayor or school board chair to be compelled to undertake certain actions than to comply—or seem to comply—
voluntarily. It was easier to blame unelected federal judges for school integration
than to enter into a phased desegregation agreement with the Office of
Education. Moreover, "HEW regulations governing the voluntary plans or
compliance agreements demand complete desegregation of the entire system," observed the *Shreveport Journal*, "including students, faculty, lunch
workers, bus drivers, and administrators, whereas the court ordered plans can
be more or less negotiated with the judge."

By early 1966, the loudest critics of the administration's school desegregation efforts were not southerners—though proficient race baiters like George
Wallace made a show of barring Alabama's school districts from filing plans
with HEW—but liberal northerners who voiced dismay with the slow pace of
progress. The White House "was not stringent enough" in demanding real
change, Congressman William Fitts Ryan of New York complained. A writer
for the liberal outlet the *Nation* fumed that "the Guidelines were, in short, a
farce: a blank map to nowhere." In early 1966, the leadership of eight State
Councils on Human Relations—interracial civil rights organizations throughout the South—urged Keppel to consider that "'the free choice plan' can only
serve to prolong the segregated school system, not to end it." As progressive
southerners, the council directors maintained from personal experience that
"every 'fearsome' change in the course of progress at which [local administra-
tors] threw up their hands in horror proved a timid lion when addressed affir-
matively. Most experiences to date unmistakably point to this fact: headaches
are fewer and not so long if system desegregation is planned and implemented
at the same time." The message to LBJ's staff was clear: move more quickly.

Roughly around the same time, representatives of the Student Nonviolent Coordinating Committee, now a more radical organization than in its earlier incarnation, admonished John Gardner: "We think time is running out. Negroes in increasingly large numbers are losing faith in the ability and will of the Federal Government. . . . Hope has turned to despair, trust has turned into suspicion, and understanding has turned into bitterness."

In early 1966, with White House involvement, HEW prepared revised guidelines for the following school year. "While freedom of choice plans will be accepted again this year," the department informed Cater, "districts electing this type of plan will have to demonstrate that their school systems will not be substantially segregated again next fall." For the first time, HEW identified "the percentage of Negro children in the district who will be attending desegregated schools" as a legitimate benchmark in determining whether local officials had satisfied their obligations under Title VI. The administration would require districts that did not meet these targets to extend their "freedom of choice" enrollment periods, provide extended police protection to black families who sought to enroll their children in predominantly white schools, cooperate more closely with parents and civic groups, or—in the most recalcitrant of cases—end choice plans altogether and adopt more aggressive measures. This policy broke new ground. Before 1966, officials at the White House, the Department of Justice, and HEW insisted that their sole aim was to dismantle the South's dual education system. Ending compulsory, state-enforced segregation—not replacing it with state-mandated integration—was their guiding principle. But the failure of choice plans to bend the South's inelastic race line compelled a reconsideration of this policy. Too few black students had been enrolled in majority-white schools. Drawing on multiple decisions that federal district and appellate court judges had issued in the preceding months, the general counsel of the OEO concluded that the courts "recognized that the discriminatory effects of almost a century of compulsory segregation and the many years of involuntary servitude that preceded that" demanded more than just the formal removal of barriers. The same legal logic that underscored the *Brown* decision—that the very act of segregation injured the personalities of black children and deprived them of their due process rights as citizens—now demanded that the government require schools to integrate their student bodies and to demonstrate their compliance with this more stringent standard through hard numbers and percentages. "The fact that schools remain identifiable as intended for Negro[s]" because of the racial makeup of their staff and student bodies would now be held as proof of non-compliance with Title VI and would render such schools ineligible for federal education funds and subject to lawsuits. Schools where black children made up 8 to 9 percent of the student body in 1965 and 1966 would be encouraged, if not required, to double that ratio the following year; those with student bodies that comprised only 4 or 5 percent minority children would be asked to triple their share. HEW and its Office of Education drove the process; Cater and Califano played a supportive role.

Predictably, many white southerners complained that HEW was essentially compelling local authorities to produce "racial balance" in public schools. Phil Landrum, the powerful Georgia congressman who had sponsored LBJ's Economic Opportunity Act in the House of Representatives, found "nothing in Title VI of the Act and nothing in the legislative history of the Act requiring such drastic and precipitous new regulations"; indeed, he strained to point out, the legislation stipulated that "desegregation shall not mean the assignment of students to public schools in order to overcome racial imbalance." The administration not only placed the burden of proof on individual districts. It also insisted that staff and faculty ratios—not just student ratios—were a fair measure of a district's good-faith effort to comply with the law. The superintendent of schools in North Carolina maintained that Title VI "speaks in terms of *exclusion*. The guidelines seem to adopt a posture of *forced inclusion*," and he challenged the government's authority to mandate that "race, color or national origin may not be a factor in the hiring or assignment to schools of teachers or other professional staff." Despite the widespread resistance of southern districts to the integration of teachers and paraprofessionals, in its revised guidelines HEW also set hard targets for the integration of school staff members and threatened to cut off funds and file federal lawsuits against those districts that failed to comply.

When southern members of Congress protested that the administration was imposing quotas and compulsory integration, LBJ strained credibility by responding personally that the "guidelines are not designed to compel desegregation beyond that inherent in a fairly working free choice plan. . . . The percentages to which you take exception are designed simply as an administrative guide to assist the Department in reviewing over 2,000 separate school districts." This claim was technically true but fundamentally disingenuous. Local jurisdictions that failed to meet HEW's "guides" and goals—both for student and for staff placement—could be denied federal education funds, a result that very few districts were willing to risk. By mid-1966, Lyndon Johnson no longer even feigned solicitousness toward southern segregationists, even those like Richard Russell, his friend and Senate mentor, whom he reminded, "You have advocated acceptance of the law and urged people to adjust themselves to it." Later that summer, Cater informed the president that the Office of Education planned to cut off fifty districts in Alabama, Georgia, Mississippi, and Louisiana, with more likely to follow. "It will be impossible to avoid political controversy on this, particularly during the election season," he explained. "The best policy . . . is for HEW to proceed with no evasion of responsibilities, but with every attempt to be conciliatory rather than belligerent." Johnson made no effort to stop the department.

Much in the same way that HEW and the White House looked to appellate court decisions to justify their imposition of hard targets, judges—beginning in 1965, with the Fifth Circuit's decision in *Singleton v. Jackson Municipal Separate School District*—invoked HEW's new administrative rulings as legal grounds to issue more proscriptive rulings. Writing for the appellate panel, Judge John Minor Wisdom—one of four members of the Fifth Circuit who would earn the enmity of their fellow southerners for aggressively enforcing civil rights laws in the 1960s and 1970s—"attach[ed] great weight to the standards established by the Office of Education. The judiciary has of course functions and duties distinct from that of the executive, but in carrying out a national policy we have the same objective. There should be a close correlation . . . between the judiciary's standards in enforcing the national policy requiring desegregation of public schools and the executive department's standards in administering this policy. Absent legal questions, the United States Office of Education is better qualified than the courts and is the more appropriate federal body to weigh administrative difficulties inherent in school desegregation plans." In effect, the Johnson administration's embrace of integration targets provided federal judges with the justification they required to issue similarly proscriptive rulings.

The combination of administrative and judicial firepower worked.

Between 1965 and 1968, the number of black students in the South who attended majority-white schools rose from roughly 2.3 percent to almost 23.4 percent. That ratio would continue to climb over the following two decades until it peaked at 43.5 percent in 1988. More arresting still, between 1968 and 1980 the portion of southern black children attending deeply segregated schools—schools where they made up over 90 percent of the student population—fell from 77.5 percent to 26.5 percent. In those same years, the portion of white southern students attending deeply segregated public schools dropped from 68.8 percent to 26 percent.

Southern compliance testified to the success of LBJ's carrot-and-stick method. But many southern school districts attempted to comply minimally with HEW's requirements or played sleight-of-hand games—for instance, clustering black students in the same classrooms—that invited closer scrutiny. That scrutiny became more standard in 1967 when the Fifth Circuit, whose jurisdiction then extended to the Deep South states of Texas, Louisiana, Mississippi, Florida, Alabama, and Georgia, ruled in *United States v. Jefferson County Board of Education* that freedom-of-choice and pupil placement plans were invalid and that districts had an "affirmative duty" to achieve racial balance in their schools. In 1968, the U.S. Supreme Court went a step further, ruling in *Green v. County School Board of New Kent County, Virginia* that jurisdictions with dual school systems "must be required to convert promptly to a system without a 'white' school and a 'Negro' school, but just schools." In effect, the Court signaled that the time for "all deliberate speed" had unquestionably ended.

It was one matter to integrate southern schools, where local officials had for the better part of a century flagrantly maintained racially segregated and unequal systems. It was another matter to monitor districts outside the Deep South, where segregation appeared more coincidental in nature. As Califano, Cater, and HEW devised new guidelines for the 1966–1967 school year, the state of affairs in northern and western states influenced the Johnson administration's thinking about race and education nationwide. Writing to Cater, Peter Libassi, a special assistant to HEW's secretary, John Gardner, affirmed that there was in fact widespread segregation in non-southern schools, though most of the segregation in these states appeared to be the result of de facto residential segregation rather than the willful maintenance of dual systems.

Libassi acknowledged that the department knew less about the situation outside the South. "While we are investigating complaints of discrimination against Northern and Western schools," he explained, "we simply have not had enough experience in these areas to issue guidelines of general applicability."

There were hard limits to LBJ's tolerance for action outside the South. In the summer of 1965, a coalition of civil rights organizations filed a complaint with HEW that charged the city of Chicago with maintaining separate school systems for black and white pupils. The accusation was both compelling and a harbinger of the deep complications that liberal Democrats would confront when the black freedom movement set its sights on northern cities, where a powerful complex of discriminatory banking, residential, and employment practices concealed itself behind the curtain of de facto segregation. In Chicago, many blue-collar unions aggressively locked African Americans out of well-paying building trades and industrial jobs—jobs that directly and indirectly relied on the public sector's spending power and recognition of collective bargaining rights. African Americans were also consigned to the worst, most cramped, and most overpriced housing stock—not because black residents chose to live in all-black neighborhoods, but because no landlord in a white ethnic neighborhood would rent to them, and banks would not issue mortgages in integrated neighborhoods, per the federal government's long-standing custom of redlining such census tracks as undesirable. As in thousands of cities and towns throughout the North and the Midwest, de facto segregation was a direct by-product of state-sanctioned and state-sponsored housing and employment discrimination.

If Chicago's de facto segregation was in reality no accident or expression of natural preference, city officials nevertheless went the extra mile to maintain dual schools for black and white children. Under the leadership of Superintendent Benjamin Willis, a close ally of Mayor Richard Daley's, hundreds of classrooms in white neighborhood schools lay vacant, while schools in black neighborhoods were dangerously over capacity, aging, and decrepit. In cases where overcrowding stretched even the moral limits of the city's white leaders, school authorities furnished schools with mobile trailers—which civil rights activists dubbed "Willis Wagons"—rather than reassign black students to all-white classrooms. Though the Board of Education did not sanction a "junior high" tier between elementary and high school, when student populations at black primary schools swelled, authorities created "upper grade centers"—a blunt conceit that effectively manufactured ad hoc junior high schools to avoid busing black children to white neighborhoods. When authorities did authorize new construction (between 1951 and 1962, the city built two hundred schools), they concentrated efforts in primarily black or white neighborhoods in a manner that perpetuated the city's dual system. Black schools often lacked gymnasiums, had inferior library facilities, and employed a higher ratio of non-certified teachers. Few offered honors or advanced placement courses in English, chemistry, algebra, biology, physics, or American history. Vocational schools, which the city operated in coordination with trade unions and which functioned as a pipeline to well-paying trade occupations, were almost all lily-white. At the start of the 1964–1965 school year, over four-fifths of Chicago's elementary schools and almost three-quarters of its high schools were either "absolutely segregated" or "segregated"—meaning over 90 percent of their student populations comprised one race. More arresting still, 90 percent of the city's black children and teenagers attended such institutions.

Local civil rights officials, who operated under the auspices of the Coordinating Council of Community Organizations, encouraged the White House to view Chicago's willful maintenance of a dual school system, and its misappropriation of Title I funds, as a threat to the Johnson administration's broader educational agenda. "The Elementary and Secondary Education Act is a program too crucial to national survival to be weakened through disbursement of its funds in a manner contrary to the requirement of the Act," they implored Cater, "and for educational programs which are inadequate to achieve its goals."

In the early fall of 1965, Keppel's office instructed Willis to respond to allegations that he had earmarked Chicago's Title I funds for white children who were not poor. His team afforded Chicago officials no more leeway than they extended to southern officials. For every school in the city, the Johnson administration demanded student enrollment figures by race; average class sizes, daily attendance, and student-teacher ratios; open or over capacity; information on available courses and curricula; an accurate count of classrooms, gymnasiums, libraries, and lounges; dropout statistics; and faculty backgrounds. When the superintendent gave him the cold shoulder, Keppel informed Willis on

September 30 that his office would defer the delivery of federal funds—$32 million in total—pending a resolution of the complaint. He struck the same collaborative, encouraging tone that HEW assumed with southern governors and school districts—Keppel informed the Illinois state superintendent of schools that he would send teams to Springfield and Chicago to help local officials meet federal guidelines—and forewarned Doug Cater of his action. The next day, Cater informed the president that he might receive blowback over HEW's action in Chicago. An initial investigation found that "a couple of vocational schools might be in violation," but Keppel "believed the whole matter can be worked out swiftly."

Keppel was acutely aware, as he told an interviewer several years after the fact, that "northern school districts were practicing discrimination by subvisible means. . . . [I]t's a national problem, but it's a lot harder to catch the boys up north, because down south they said, 'Sure, we've got black schools and white schools. What are you fellows talking about? We treat them all equally.'" The challenge in the North was "not only more subtle" but "much more of a public policy problem to handle—much more!" Two days after Cater informed him of the Chicago affair, LBJ flew to Manhattan, where he was scheduled to sign a sweeping immigration reform law. Daley was in town and secured a private audience with the president, during which he unleashed his rage at Keppel and other bureaucrats in HEW. LBJ promptly instructed Wilbur Cohen to travel to Chicago posthaste and "fix the problem." The assistant secretary complied, squeezing a few minor concessions from Daley's office but effectively walking back the administration's position. In early 1966, Johnson appointed Keppel to the post of assistant secretary of HEW and tapped Harold Howe, a career educator, to replace him as education commissioner. On paper, it was a promotion; in reality, Keppel would later observe, "I was fired. . . . I was the chief SOB with the Southerners. And then you get to be a chief SOB with the Northern Democrats in one city! Come on—you're useless! Get out!"

Howe would take a more diplomatic tact with Daley, but by December 1966, just months into his tenure, his office informed the mayor and his superintendent that the city's schools were out of compliance and at risk of losing their funds. For Johnson, as for any Democratic president, Richard Daley represented a unique case. Joseph Califano instructed Howe to work directly with the mayor; HEW should not publicize its findings, he ordered, but should make strong recommendations to the Board of Education (ending apprentice-ship programs with unions until black students were admitted in proportionate numbers; engaging pupil placement specialists to reduce segregation in neighborhood schools) that would bring them back into compliance with Title VI. By then, white voters in Chicago—as in many northern cities—were in full backlash mode against the Johnson administration and liberal judges who appeared to threaten the integrity of their neighborhoods and local institutions. That trend would eventually speed the dissolution of LBJ's sweeping 1964 electoral mandate and pave the way for conservatives to chip away at the Democratic coalition of black and white working-class voters—a coalition dating back to Franklin Roosevelt's tenure.

David Seeley, the official responsible for civil rights compliance within the Office of Education, would later deny that "the reversal of the withholding action" in Chicago was as much "an example of unwarranted political interference by Mayor Daley" as "an example of the danger of taking strong governmental action in a politically sensitive area like civil rights." It was unclear to administration officials in 1965 that the law empowered them to withhold funds where it was not manifestly evident that the state or city maintained dual school systems. "As head of the Office of Education civil rights enforcement program during this period," he maintained, "I can attest to many situations in which President Johnson was under considerably stronger and more persistent political pressures to undercut our enforcement efforts and in which he displayed admirable backbone in resisting them."

Schools might have been the most controversial, but they were not the only institutions that the Johnson administration desegregated during the Great Society's general rollout. In March 1966—less than four months before Medicare was due to launch—the Public Health Service, a division of HEW, sent a questionnaire to over ten thousand participating hospitals, nursing homes, and qualified health-care facilities, inquiring whether they were in compliance with the new civil rights law. Traditionally, many hospitals and doctors' offices across the South either pointedly refused to care for black patients or consigned them to segregated and often inferior wings within the same building. In many cases, they even designated separate emergency rooms and nurseries for each race. Just as Title VI of the Civil Rights Act made federal education funds unavailable to segregated schools, it required that health providers participating in Medicare integrate their facilities and file the very same 441-B forms certifying compliance that schools submitted to become eligible for compensatory education dollars. In effect, even as it set about constructing the single largest health program in the nation's history, the Johnson administration also faced the challenge of integrating hospitals and nursing homes throughout one-third of the nation. This task was not merely an administrative nuisance: it was a threat to the entire system. Southern health-care providers could very well have opted out of the new program, effectively killing Medicare in one-third of the states.

HEW dispatched more than a thousand inspectors to visit hospitals directly and ensure they were complying with Title VI. Close to seven thousand facilities swiftly acquiesced; another fifty-five hundred fell into line after inspection. Unsurprisingly, most of the noncompliant facilities were in four Deep South states: Mississippi, Louisiana, Alabama, and South Carolina. As with schools, HEW kept Califano and Cater informed of the most granular details on a weekly and sometimes daily basis. Having learned the hard way a year earlier that it was essential to issue clear and concise guidelines, the department produced a fifteen-minute film in coordination with the American Hospital Association that outlined the metrics that institutions were required to meet and enlisted charitable organizations like the National Social Welfare Assembly to encourage obedience to the law among grassroots members and activists.

The guidelines were sweeping. All people were to be admitted for inpatient and outpatient services without regard to color, race, or national origin. Where there was a "significant variation between the racial composition of patients and the population served," the hospital had an affirmative obligation to justify that variance to federal officials. Each facility's "rooms, wards, floors, sections, and buildings" must be integrated; officials were not to ask patients whether they wished to share quarters with someone of a particular race. "Employees, medical staff and volunteers of the hospital are to be assigned to patient service" on a color-blind basis. Training programs were to be fully integrated. The guidelines required that hospital employees apply "courtesy titles" like "Dr.," "Mrs.," and "Mr." without regard to race and that formerly segregated institutions conduct proactive outreach to nonwhite physicians, nurses, and civil rights organizations—and take out advertisements in local media outlets—announcing the change in policy. The Johnson administration was not merely forcing hospitals to extend access to black citizens. It was enforcing a mandatory shift in how medical professionals treated African Americans as patients, colleagues, and human beings and placing new quantitative and qualitative obligations on local institutions.

In the same way that the Office of Education enjoyed discretion over the disbursement of ESEA funds, the Public Health Service—under the direction of Surgeon General William Stewart—was responsible for certifying hospitals compliant with Title VI. In a hopeful dispatch to hospital administrators just prior to Medicare's rollout, the surgeon general affirmed that the "transition has not been as difficult as some feared. To the contrary, it has contributed to better patient care and in addition has proven to be both administratively and economically advantageous." But the administration would remain vigilant. "Your participation in the Hospital Insurance for the Aged program," Stewart warned, "even if you are otherwise certified as eligible," was wholly dependent on compliance with Title VI. The administration dispatched Stewart to negotiate personally with municipal and hospital officials in a number of cities, including Memphis, New Orleans, and Shreveport, hosted twenty state hospital associations for an instructional conference in Washington, D.C., and conscripted major employers and labor unions to exert economic and peer pressure on recalcitrant institutions.

In May 1966, HEW's secretary, John Gardner, informed the president that roughly 15 percent of all hospital beds in the nation were still in nonconforming institutions and that most nonconforming institutions were heavily concentrated in several Deep South states. On the eve of the program's launch in July, only 34 percent of hospital beds in Mississippi were in compliance with Title VI. There were holdouts—even at the end of LBJ's term as president in 1968, an official at HEW conceded that a "handful of hospitals, largely in the Delta area of Mississippi and Alabama," remained out of step with the law (and therefore ineligible to accept Medicare dollars). But for the most part, the administration's commitment to enforcing the civil rights law, and its willingness to withhold federal dollars from hospitals that could scarcely afford to lose them, compelled sweeping changes. Arthur Hess, a career administrator at

HEW, recalled a memorable visit to a southern hospital. When he and other federal officials informed hospital officials that their facility was still noncompliant, and that it would not be permitted to participate in Medicare, administrators and board members began "ranting and raving" in a noisy display of resistance. Yet as Hess and his colleagues left the meeting, one board member quietly sidled up to them and said, "Keep the heat on." Local hospital boards needed to use federal compulsion to cover themselves with their own elected officials and community members. In effect, the Johnson administration was engaged in an elaborate pantomime. The pressure worked. By the end of the decade, the number of black and Latino hospital patients grew by 30 percent, while the portion of hospitals that employed minority doctors or dentists rose by 61 percent.

Unlike hospitals, nursing homes would not be eligible to participate in Medicare until January 1, 1967, but the administration began its education and enforcement activities the summer before. Of fifteen thousand extended-care facilities in the United States, HEW estimated that only six thousand would elect to participate in Medicare and only three thousand would earn certification. Nevertheless, it was imperative that the department issue firm guidance across the board. Unlike hospitals, whose patient populations were by definition transitory, nursing homes were residential in character and would prove a more bitter battleground, north and south. Furthermore, Peter Libassi, the general counsel of HEW, informed Cater and Califano that while "most of the hospital discrimination was in the South, discrimination in [nursing homes] is more widespread. Many institutions in the North have been admitting patients of only one race until this time." Just as the Office of Education had carried its Title VI compliance efforts into Chicago and other northern cities, HEW applied the law with equal force and consistency both above and below the Mason-Dixon Line. Libassi was confident that the rollout would progress smoothly, as indeed it did the following year. The department had increased its dedicated compliance staff and had "learned a great deal during these last five months and expect to put our experience to good work."

Wilbur Cohen scarcely exaggerated the point when he observed that on "the day before Medicare went into effect, in every hospital in the South, over every drinking fountain, over every bathroom, over every cafeteria, there were signs reading 'White' and 'Colored' for separate but presumably equal facilities. On the day that Medicare went into effect in the South, all those signs and separate facilities began to come down." In reality, most hospitals removed those signs two years earlier, after passage of the Civil Rights Act. But the scale of change was breathtaking. No president before or after LBJ attempted to introduce a major, new government entitlement while at the same time using that very benefit to break down long-established patterns of de facto and de jure discrimination. On the contrary, while a handful of New Deal initiatives either expressly or incidentally undermined Jim Crow, for the most part Franklin Roosevelt—Johnson's hero—struck a devil's bargain that left many African Americans outside his administration's protective embrace. The context in which LBJ operated was starkly different, but a lesser president might have temporized in the interest of ensuring an orderly rollout of Medicare and ESEA. Johnson knowingly assumed great risk.

Weeks before Medicare's launch, a correspondent warned the president that southern hospitals were just as much hot spots as schools. The administration was demanding an overnight end to practices that had been in place for as long as most people could remember. "And they won't [comply] Lyndon. You know that. Do you want to be responsible for closing St. Francis Hospital in Biloxi, Mississippi? That's what will happen if you put this thing into effect. . . . Doctors won't treat the coloreds, and the nurses won't treat them."

"It was a great gamble," remembered Harry McPherson. "Whatever he decided, thousands of people, either the elderly or the blacks, might have been deprived of hospitalization." Johnson wagered a big bet—and he won.

CHAPTER 9

The Fabulous Eighty-Ninth

Two weeks after LBJ outlined his vision of the Great Society in 1964, Dick Goodwin and Bill Moyers traveled on presidential instructions to Cambridge, Massachusetts, where they met with thirty professors from the Boston area. Over a long lunch at the home of John Kenneth Galbraith, the young White House aides solicited the formal participation of America's public intellectuals in task forces that would help design the themes and substance of Johnson's domestic agenda. The outcome of the meeting was fourteen committees that met and corresponded over the coming months to propose policy and legislation concerning transportation, natural resources, urban life, the environment, agriculture, civil rights, health and welfare, and infrastructure. Though John Kennedy enjoyed a reputation as the thinking man's liberal, it was LBJ—not his predecessor—who fully leveraged the talent and imagination of the country's academics. The original task forces that Goodwin and Moyers assembled included top administrative and faculty talent from the University of California, the Carnegie Corporation, the Brookings Institution, Harvard, MIT, and Princeton. Unlike ceremonial committees before and after, the LBJ task forces exerted tangible influence on policy making. Their members interacted freely with designated White House liaisons—including Cater (transportation), Lee White (natural resources, civil rights), Goodwin (education, natural beauty, metropolitan and urban problems), and Heller (intergovernmental fiscal cooperation)—and the output of their labors enjoyed wide circulation and consideration within the West Wing.

Shortly after the election, on November 10, Moyers, Goodwin, Cater, and Myer Feldman, a holdover from Kennedy's staff, reviewed the task force reports and flagged the most promising and feasible of proposals for the president's consideration. "If we had adopted all of their ideas," an aide observed, "we would have had to come up with a budget of [tens of millions of dollars]." Moyers and his colleagues presented an abridged twelve-hundred-page version of the task force recommendations to Johnson at the LBJ Ranch over the Thanksgiving and Christmas holidays. Some of the ideas rehashed legislation that JFK had already submitted to Congress—Medicare, aid to education, immigration reform—but that had languished in committee. Others were entirely new, including enhancements to public culture and pathbreaking environmental initiatives, preschool initiatives, work-study programs, library services, instruction in the arts and sciences, federal aid to college and graduate students, preservation of scenic areas adjacent to federal highways, formalized revenue-sharing arrangements with states, health care for poor children, and a broader safety net for workers who were not covered by Social Security.

Though Johnson did not pursue all of his task forces' recommendations, in launching his ambitious domestic policy agenda in 1965, he enjoyed wide majorities in Congress and, equally important, a liberal resurgence within the House and Senate Democratic caucuses. Though in his years as majority leader LBJ aligned himself more firmly with southern conservatives and frequently thwarted measures important to civil rights groups and organized labor, he now relied on the left wing of his party to shepherd the Great Society through Congress. It took very little time before liberals asserted themselves. On the opening day of what Johnson later dubbed the "Fabulous Eighty-ninth" Congress, House Democrats stripped Mississippi's John Bell Williams and South Carolina's Albert Watson of their seniority in response to their endorsement of Barry Goldwater the year before. It was the first such disciplinary action against a sitting congressman since 1911 and effectively deprived the apostate members of their committee assignments and perquisites. The caucus also took aim at Rules Committee chairman Howard Smith when it voted to reinstate the "twenty-one day rule," a measure that allowed any committee chairman whose bill had been mired in the powerful Rules Committee for more than three weeks to bring the legislation directly to the floor. Though it is unclear whether the caucus passed the measure at the president's behest, two days after the election LBJ had instructed Bill Moyers to raise the issue with congressional leaders. In the Senate, reformers faced steeper challenges in weakening the filibuster, but by sheer numbers alone the combination of liberal Democrats and moderate Republicans provided a powerful check against the southern caucus. Thus did the Johnson administration begin its full term in a position of strength that earlier presidents would have envied.

These advantages notwithstanding, LBJ's White House left nothing to chance. In pursuit of his legislative agenda, Johnson benefited from a well-oiled legislative liaison office that Larry O'Brien had first assembled under Kennedy but that enjoyed little success until Johnson inherited the presidency. In the weeks immediately following JFK's election in 1960, O'Brien consulted a wide swath of White House veterans from earlier Democratic administrations, including FDR's former administrative aide, Jim Rowe, and Clark Clifford, David Bell, and Charles Murphy, all of whom had served in senior roles on Harry Truman's staff. O'Brien soon discovered that "there had been no formalization" of the legislative liaison role "at any time. It was just sort of seat-of-the-pants. The President might make a call or send somebody to see someone. But it wasn't organized." The first presidential aide officially tasked with congressional relations had been Bryce Harlow, who performed the function for Eisenhower and generously offered O'Brien counsel on how to organize his office. On the afternoon of Kennedy's inauguration, amid a bitter-cold snap of winter weather, the seasoned Boston political organizer walked over to the White House. "I'd never been in the building, even as a tourist," he would recall. "So we walked in, with the staff, and looked around the two floors. I don't think I even knew the basement was there. And I found this corner office on the second floor, and I noted that there was space for two secretaries and a conference room, and about three offices. So I planted myself in the center office and my staff on each end. And that's how the office was established."

Under O'Brien's leadership, the office of legislative liaison pulled all the available levers of presidential influence and persuasion. During his first year in office, JFK held thirty-two private "leadership breakfasts" with the top brass in each house of Congress, ninety group meetings with various senators and congressmen, and dozens of "coffee hours" attended by five hundred legislators—"the entire Congress," O'Brien remembered, "at one time or another." There were bill signings. Personal letters from the president to each member on his or her birthday. When members of Congress were out of range for important votes, the White House sent military planes to transport them back to Washington, D.C. O'Brien also made good use of the *Sequoia*, the official presidential yacht, which set sail on the Potomac several times each week. "We'd have a buffet dinner and maybe an accordion player, at times, or a sing-along. We would leave the dock at 6:00 p.m., return at 9:00. And that became the greatest tool available to us, and I utilized it to the fullest. It became a great bore to be on that Sequoia for my wife for three hours, sometimes two and three times a week," he later recounted with a laugh.

Yet no charm offensive proved sufficient to break the deadlock. Conservative Republicans and southern Democrats enjoyed sufficient numbers to bottleneck the legislative process throughout Kennedy's presidency, and JFK, despite having served for six years in the House and eight years in the Senate, had never enjoyed "the kind of seniority in either the House or Senate, obviously, to be a prime mover," O'Brien observed. "He was very much junior to all his former colleagues, and how do you utilize him?" His clout was limited, in part because he was naturally cooler and more aloof. "Jack Kennedy would not force the issue with a group of senators or congressmen." Recognizing Kennedy's more passive approach, O'Brien was deliberately measured in his use of the president's influence, taking care never to put JFK in a position of asking for a vote that he could not secure. "I would be very, very careful to make it only when I had determined we'd exhausted every possibility and there was one last opportunity and that was the President."

O'Brien learned early in his tenure as Lyndon Johnson's congressional liaison that the new president operated in a starkly different fashion. Once, when the administration lost a close vote in the House during a late-night session that wound into the early hours of the morning, O'Brien stopped at a twenty-four-hour cafeteria for breakfast and waited until an appropriate hour—6:30 a.m.—to phone the president. "Why didn't you call me?" LBJ demanded. "When you're up there bleeding, I want to bleed with you. We have to share these things." "I never got over that," O'Brien recalled.

Though Johnson continued to speak constantly with his former congressional colleagues, he took care to consult O'Brien before directly involving himself in legislative lobbying. But he was an aggressive advocate who "would devote an inordinate amount of time to the sales pitch, and he would put it on a truly personal basis: 'I'm pleading with you. You've got to help me. You can't walk away from this. Come on, you've just—' And that would get to the arm around the shoulder, the close proximity and the pitch that could be lengthy at times. A member would be pretty exhausted. And that was basically the difference in style." On a typical evening, the president and his legislative liaison sat inches apart, knee to knee, in the small study adjacent to the Oval Office, and dialed almost two dozen members of the House to resolve a fine point around the Washington, D.C., appropriations bill. "I couldn't stop him," O'Brien told an interviewer years later. "He proceeded to pick up the phone and gave the White House telephone operator the names of the twenty-two and chased them all over town. I don't recall he had caught all twenty-two by the time I went home, but he stayed with it."

These were the high-water days of the Great Society, before the Vietnam War began to eat away at the government's resources and undermine the public's faith in the unbounded capacity of their government to solve large, vexing problems like poverty and disease. Years later, O'Brien still displayed with pride a framed collection of some sixty bill-signing pens spanning his service in both the Kennedy and the Johnson White Houses. The vast majority dated to the "Fabulous Eighty-ninth."

The "Fabulous Eighty-ninth" began its work against a dramatic backdrop. By early 1965, Martin Luther King Jr. had already determined to stage his next campaign in Selma—the seat of Dallas County, Alabama, where black residents made up over half the population but only about 2 percent of registered voters. King's strategy was at once simple and complicated. Since Congress passed the Civil Rights Act six month earlier, the movement had renewed its focus on voting rights—a giant piece of the civil rights puzzle that still required legislative remedy. From a numbers perspective, the decision made sense. As King explained to readers of the *New York Times*, "Selma has succeeded in limiting Negro registration to the snail's pace of about 145 persons a year. At this rate, it would take 103 years to register the 15,000 eligible Negro voters of Dallas County."

Most liberals understood that securing access to the ballot box necessarily constituted an important part of the Great Society. In a phone conversation with King on January 15, LBJ named voting rights as a centerpiece of the civil rights agenda but signaled his intent to wait until Congress passed his health-care and education packages before introducing legislation. He was confident in his strategy and counseled King to galvanize support by "find[ing] the worst condition that you run into in Alabama, Mississippi, or Louisiana, or South Carolina.... And if you just take that one illustration and get it on radio and get it on television and get it in the pulpits, get it in the meetings, get it every place you can . . . then that will help us on what we're going to shove through in the end." Unbeknownst to LBJ, King had already found his "one illustration": Selma, Alabama.

King's own notes explained his thinking: (1) "nonviolent demonstrators go into the streets to exercise their constitutional rights"; (2) "racists resist by unleashing violence against them"; (3) "Americans of conscience in the name of decency demand federal intervention and legislation"; (4) "the Administration, under mass pressure, initiates measures of immediate intervention and remedial legislation." Selma was a hornet's nest of racial violence. The Student Nonviolent Coordinating Committee had been active there since 1962, but now King's Southern Christian Leadership Conference planned to join the fray and "dramatize the situation to arouse the federal government by marching by the thousands to the places of registration."

True to form, local authorities under Dallas County's sheriff, Jim Clark, took the bait. They clapped over two thousand activists in jail in the first weeks of the campaign and rained unspeakable violence on peaceful protesters. On February 18, state troopers beat and shot Jimmie Lee Jackson, a twenty-six-year-old voting rights demonstrator. When Jackson died eight days later of his wounds, movement leaders conceived a fifty-mile march from Albany to Montgomery, where they would voice their grievances on the steps of the state capitol. The campaign's climactic moment occurred on Bloody Sunday—March 7, 1965—when state and county law enforcement officers savagely attacked roughly five hundred peaceful marchers as they attempted to cross the Edmund Pettus Bridge.

In 1965, news footage still needed to be flown to New York for national broadcast. That evening, ABC won the race. The brutality was stomach turning. Mounted policemen employed tear gas, electric prods, horse whips, and batons wrapped in barbed wire. They pursued marchers who were running desperately in retreat. When the network broke into its regularly scheduled program—the television premiere of *Judgment at Nuremberg*—millions of viewers were confronted with gut-wrenching scenes that jarred the nation's conscience. Two more marches ensued: one, led by King, in which protesters proceeded to the bridge, knelt, prayed, and turned back; and another, which culminated in a historic trek to Montgomery.

Bloody Sunday dealt a profound shock to the American conscience. House Speaker John McCormack denounced the police brutality as a "disgraceful exercise of arbitrary power." A Michigan congressman called it "a savage action, storm trooper style, under direction of a reckless demagogue." Behind the scenes, the administration was engaged in tense negotiations with Everett Dirksen, the Senate Republican leader whose support had been critical in securing passage of the Civil Rights Act and who controlled a sufficient bloc of moderate votes to ensure passage of a voting rights bill.

Days after the massacre at the Edmund Pettus Bridge, the two sides reached an agreement: the proposed bill would create automatic triggers that suspended discriminatory practices like literacy tests in states where a given portion of eligible voters did not participate in federal elections. It empowered federal examiners to monitor polling stations and in certain cases replace county registrars, stipulated that poll taxes were unconstitutional, required states that qualified for the trigger to preclear any changes to their voting process with the Department of Justice, and established criminal penalties for officials who interfered with citizens' right to vote.

Inside the White House, aides urged Johnson to use the presidential pulpit in support of the measure. "The public knows you are for the enforcement of civil rights," Harry McPherson told LBJ. "The Deep South knows it; that is why it went for Goldwater." The American public felt the "deepest sense of outrage" and "want you to express your own, present sense of outrage," he urged. Even Abe Fortas, a "reasonable man" not usually given to displays of emotion, wanted to impose martial law on Alabama. The moment demanded executive action. It took little convincing. Dick Goodwin later recalled that "America didn't like what it saw. And neither did Lyndon Johnson, who witnessed not a revelation (he had grown up in the South), but an affront to the sensibilities and moral justice of the country he now led."

Johnson addressed a rare joint session of Congress on March 15 and called for the passage of voting rights legislation. After a long build in which he situated the black freedom struggle in the historical arc of democratic struggle dating back to the American Revolution, he proclaimed, "This time, on this issue, there must be no delay, no hesitation and no compromise with our purpose.... There is no moral issue. It is wrong—deadly wrong—to deny any of your fellow Americans the right to vote in this country. There is no issue of States rights or national rights. There is only the struggle for human rights." Speaking in a slow, steady Texas drawl to a near-silent chamber, the president told Congress, "Their cause must be our cause, too. Because it is not just Negroes, but really it is all of us who must overcome the crippling legacy of bigotry and injustice. And we shall overcome."

Goodwin, who drafted the speech, later wrote that there "was an instant of silence, the gradually apprehended realization that the president had proclaimed, adopted as his own rallying cry, the anthem of black protest, the hymn of a hundred embattled black marchers." He observed tears streaming down the Senate majority leader Mike Mansfield's face and Emanuel Celler, the seventy-six-year-old chairman of the House Judiciary Committee and a stalwart supporter of equal rights, "cheering as wildly as a schoolboy at his first football game." With bipartisan support, but again in the face of southern opposition, Congress swiftly passed the Voting Rights Act, and Johnson signed it into law on August 6.

As with its strict enforcement of the Civil Rights Act, the administration signaled its unwavering intent to force compliance with the new voting rights law. Not an hour after the bill-signing ceremony, LBJ instructed Joe Califano to ensure that the attorney general "immediately mounted an all-fronts attack on poll taxes and litcracy tests." Four days later—the ink barely dry—federal examiners descended on twelve counties in Alabama, Louisiana, Mississippi, and Georgia. By the following January, they added over ninety thousand voters to the rolls in those jurisdictions alone. Violence and intimidation persisted, but for the most part southern authorities acquiesced in the face of strong executive enforcement.

Alongside the Civil Rights Act, the Voting Rights Act of 1965 reordered daily life in the eleven former states of the Confederacy, as well as border states like Kansas, Maryland, Missouri, Oklahoma, and Delaware. As late as 1965, only 6.7 percent of African Americans in Mississippi and 19 percent in Alabama had surmounted the complex of legal and extralegal measures in place to prevent them from exercising the franchise. But southern resistance crumbled in the wake of congressional action. By 1970, roughly two-thirds of African Americans in these Deep South states were registered to vote, and most were able to exercise this right without interference. White southerners now had to grapple with the long-term prospect of black representation at all levels of government and with the more immediate reality of political power sharing. Edgar Mouton, a state legislator from Louisiana, marveled that he had "never shook hands with a black person before I ran for office . . . the first time I shook hands it was a traumatic thing." The Voting Rights Act did not just redistribute power; it compelled white southerners to rethink their relationship with their black neighbors.

If the administration's aggressive enforcement of civil rights moved the country toward a new pluralism, it also took other steps that would fundamentally change the meaning of what it meant to be an American. In October 1965, Lyndon Johnson signed into law the Immigration and Nationality Act, a measure that opened the floodgates to new immigrants—the vast majority of them from Latin America, Africa, and Asia. At the time, non-Hispanic white citizens constituted over 85 percent of the American population. Fifty years later, that portion was just 62 percent and falling. Alongside civil rights enforcement, immigration reform was the realization of a decades-long liberal aspiration and fundamentally changed not only the demography of the United States but the very meaning of American citizenship. Before the Great Society, the concept of full citizenship was deeply bound up with race. After 1965, that would no longer be the case.

Between 1820 and 1924, roughly thirty-seven million European immigrants came to the United States. Proportionally, this migration was unprecedented (the population of the United States in 1850 was just twenty-three million). Northern Europeans—Irish and Germans, especially—predominated in the first wave, between 1820 and 1880. The second great wave, between 1880 and 1924, drew newcomers from southern and eastern Europe, including large numbers of Italians, Greeks, Slavs, Poles, and Jews from the Russian Empire. Smaller numbers of immigrants also came from China, Japan, and other Asian countries. By the early twentieth century, immigrants and the children of immigrants constituted upwards of 75 percent of the population in major cities like New York, Chicago, Boston, Cleveland, and Detroit.

Since 1790, when Congress passed the nation's first immigration act, prevailing law had restricted naturalized citizenship to "free white persons." What constituted a white person was by no means clear. While in later years it seemed intuitive to classify German, Irish, or Italian Americans as white, in the mid-nineteenth century many native-born Protestants regarded newcomers as unwhite and therefore unfit for citizenship. In establishment outlets like *Harper's Magazine*, editorialists lampooned Irish immigrants as drunken, lazy, and idle, while cartoonists portrayed them as possessing apelike, subhuman physical attributes.

With "whiteness" such a crucial attribute, many immigrants—including Irish Catholics in large, northeastern cities—worked aggressively to draw a sharp distinction between themselves and free African Americans. Black-face minstrelsy, a popular form of entertainment among new immigrants, enabled racially suspect Europeans to establish that they were, in fact, white (after all, only a white person needed to "black up" to play the part of an African American) and to project onto African Americans the same vicious stereotypes that nativists ascribed to Catholic newcomers.

By the late nineteenth century, America's new cultural and civic diversity—a result of immigration from southern Europe, eastern Europe, and Asia and the emancipation of black slaves—gradually resulted in a popular classification of humans along hierarchal lines. In 1911, a government commission impaneled to investigate the potential effects of mass immigration broke the population into "45 races or peoples among immigrants coming to the United States, and of these 36 are indigenous to Europe." Bohemians, the report determined, were "the most advanced of all" Slavic racial groups. "The ancient Greeks were preeminent in philosophy and science, a position not generally accredited to the modern Greeks as a race . . . they compare with the Hebrew race as the best traders of the Orient." Further, "the Gypsy resents the restraint of higher social organization . . . to him laws and statutes are persecutions to be evaded." The southern Italian was "an individualist having little adaptability to highly organized society." Whereas German and Irish newcomers seemed distinctly unfit for citizenship in the mid-nineteenth century, scientific racial analysis now considered them a higher category of white than southern and eastern European newcomers, most of whom were Catholic or Jewish.

The era's nativism rested on a bedrock of labor competition, religious intolerance, and fear of anarchism and communism. But scientific racism supplied its intellectual justification. "The welfare of the United States demands that the door should be closed to immigrants for a time," a leading congressman declared at the time. "We are being made a dumping ground for the human wreckage of [World War I]." Immigrants from southern Europe and Asia suffered "inborn socially inadequate qualities," a prominent scientist offered. They were responsible for a hike in urban crime, social disorder, and neighborhood decay. Such ideas formed the foundation of the Immigration Act of 1924, which limited the annual number of immigrants from any given country to just 2 percent of the total number of people born in that country and residing in the United States in 1890. By using 1890 as a benchmark, the law favored older immigrant groups from northern and central Europe. For Jews, Italians, Greeks, Slavs, Poles, Croatians, and Russians, the door effectively swung shut. (For the Chinese, that door had been closed since 1882, when Congress passed the Chinese Exclusion Act.)

The year 1924 was the high-water mark for scientific racism, which became increasingly unpopular in Depression-era America. The Columbia University anthropologist Franz Boas and his protégées Margaret Mead and Ruth Benedict were among the first to blast away at the edifice of "race," proving in a series of devastating monographs and articles that human behavior and intelligence were products of environment, not blood, and that no "pure" races could even be said to exist. This shift in thinking also emerged as a response to the excesses of Nazi Germany. Although many Americans in the 1920s regarded eugenics and other forms of racial engineering as good science and solid public policy, revelations of Germany's euthanasia program targeting mentally and physically handicapped children inspired a scientific repudiation of eugenics in the United States. More generally, Nazi race policy and anti-Semitism delegitimized racialist thinking in nearly all of its popular incarnations, influencing works like Ashley Montagu's *Man's Most Dangerous Myth: The Fallacy of Race*, a celebrated volume that argued race was a scientifically "artificial" and "meaningless" invention. In 1938, the American Psychological Association and the American Anthropological Association broke new ground in formally repudiating scientific racism. Other academic organizations followed, and ever since biologists, chemists, and geneticists have steadfastly maintained that race is, at best, a social phenomenon; at worst, a lie. Certainly, few scholars of any repute continue to believe that race is determinative of behavior, intellectual endowment, and physical capacity.

Even as scientific racism came under cultural and academic assault, the 1924 law restricting immigration remained on the books. Ironically, it might have aided the mainstreaming of ethnic Americans by cutting off the supply of newcomers who spoke in foreign tongues, wore strange clothing, and listened to unfamiliar music. The new faces of ethnic America were the children of immigrants who grew up speaking accentless English, became fanatical baseball fans, and wore American garbs. That generation's contribution during World War II drove a final nail in the coffin of scientific racism.

In the postwar years, northern liberals clamored for both civil rights *and* immigration reform. As Jim Crow came under increased fire, it became possible to attack the national origins standard (the very backbone of the 1924 law) for what it was: in the words of the Democratic Party platform in 1960, "a policy of deliberate discrimination" that "contradicts the founding principles of this nation." The same coalition of churches, liberal organizations, and labor and industry groups that championed the Civil Rights Act of 1964 also backed immigration reform.

In the wake of the Republican Goldwater's defeat, Democrats seized the opportunity to pass the Immigration and Nationality Act, landmark legislation that did not take effect until June 1968—the waning days of LBJ's presidency—but that fundamentally transformed the country in ways that even the president might not have anticipated. The new law favored newcomers with specialized skills and education or existing family relationships with American citizens or residents and substituted the national origins standard with annual hemispheric limits: 170,000 immigrants from the Eastern Hemisphere, 120,000 from the Western Hemisphere—a breakdown that reflected lingering bias toward Europe. (That provision was later eliminated and replaced with a simple, annual cap of 290,000 immigrants.) Critically, the bill exempted from these caps all immigrants with immediate family members in the United States.

In signing the law, Johnson affirmed that the national origins standard violated "the basic principle of American democracy—the principle that values and rewards each man on the basis of his merit as a man." While the bill's champions, including LBJ and New York's congressman Emanuel Celler, were committed to ethnic and racial pluralism, they anticipated that most of its beneficiaries would hail from Europe. Celler assured his colleagues that as a matter of pure numbers "the effect of the bill on our population would be insignificant," while Edward Kennedy, JFK's youngest brother and the initiative's chief whip in the Senate, maintained that the "ethnic mix of this country will not be upset," because the legislation would "not inundate America with immigrants from any one country or area, or the most overpopulated and economically deprived nations of Africa and Asia." The *Wall Street Journal* agreed, arguing that the family unification provision "insured that the new immigration pattern would not stray radically from the old one."

The story played itself out differently, and in ways that neither Kennedy nor Celler, Lyndon Johnson nor the *Wall Street Journal*, anticipated. As Europe's economy finally emerged from the ashes of World War II, fewer residents of Ireland, Italy, or Germany moved to the United States, while those residing in the Soviet bloc found it all but impossible to try. But tens of thousands of educated professionals—lawyers, doctors, engineers, scientists—from Asia and Central America did avail themselves of new opportunities in the United States and established roots in the United States legally. So did tens of thousands of refugees from Cuba, Vietnam, and other repressive regimes. By 1972, the Association of American Medical Colleges found that 46 percent of all licensed physicians were foreign-born, with large numbers emigrating from India, the Philippines, Korea, Iran, Thailand, Pakistan, and China. Because the law exempted many categories of family members from the hemispheric caps, these new citizens were soon able to bring their relatives to join them. Many more immigrants than expected thus came to the United States, and those who did so created a much more diverse population. In the first decade of the bill's enactment, an average of 100,000 legal immigrants *above* the cap relocated annually to the United States; by 1980, the annual number soared to 730,000. Fifty years after the bill's passage, foreign-born immigrants made up roughly 13 percent of the total population, approaching the all-time high of 14.7 percent in 1910. Another 20 percent were born in the United States but had at least one foreign-born parent, bringing the proportion of first- and second-generation Americans to near-historic heights. Unlike earlier waves, 90 percent of new Americans after 1965 hailed from outside Europe—from countries like Mexico, Brazil, the Philippines, Korea, Cuba, Taiwan, India, and the Dominican Republic. As a consequence, demographers projected that by 2050 non-Hispanic white Americans would constitute less than half of the U.S. population.

The bill itself did not take effect until shortly before Johnson left office. It was the rare example of Great Society legislation whose long-term consequences neither the president nor his White House staff was able to presage. Yet alongside the administration's vigorous enforcement of civil rights laws, immigration reform catalyzed a new electoral alignment—which some political scientists have dubbed the "Great Society coalition"—that comprised African Americans, Latinos, and well-educated white voters (many of whom unknowingly benefited from the legacy of Johnson's higher education policies). This coalition, though not ascendant for at least a quarter century after LBJ left office, would in later years prove a powerful counterweight to the forces of white backlash. On October 3, 1965, the day that LBJ signed the immigration act into law, those days lay far in the distance. The politics of white retrenchment, however, were just around the corner.

The magnitude of Johnson's legislative and administrative accomplishment in 1965 and 1966 was astonishing by earlier and later comparisons. In addition to civil rights and voting rights, immigration reform, the education act, Medicare, and Medicaid, LBJ's White House, with the full support of an overwhelmingly Democratic Congress, unleashed a tidal wave of liberal reform. Some of these measures exerted a lasting and positive influence on American life. Others would prove noble but failed experiments.

When he launched the Great Society at the University of Michigan, Johnson emphasized the imperative of ameliorating conditions in America's cities. At his urging, in 1965 Congress created a new cabinet agency, the Department of Housing and Urban Development (HUD), and assigned it a broad mandate to oversee not only federal housing initiatives but the delivery of better social services, infrastructure assistance—including mundane but critical areas like water and sewage systems—and slum rehabilitation. To lead the new department, Johnson appointed Robert Weaver, the administrator of the Housing and Home Finance Agency and now the nation's first black cabinet member. A year later, after considerable pressure from the White House, Congress authorized the Model Cities program, originally intended to target aid to six demonstration cities—Washington, Detroit, Chicago, Philadelphia, Houston, and Los Angeles—where HUD would work in close coordination with municipal, civic, and religious leaders to overhaul schools, hospitals and health centers, transportation services, and low-income and middle-class housing. The program would bring to bear "all of the techniques and talents within our society on the crisis of the American city."

In the end analysis, politics proved the undoing of its mission. Members of Congress did not permit the administration to discover what a handful of demonstration cities could accomplish with a sizable, narrowly targeted infusion of cash and strong benchmarks and oversight from Washington. Instead, explained the *New York Times* several years later, "every legislator had to have a slice of the pork. The few cities became 75, then 150. Eventually the money was shoveled around only a half-inch deep anywhere. The program was destined to fail." Despite the failure of the Model Cities program, the Johnson administration gave American urban dwellers a seat at the cabinet table and ensured that their interests would at last receive the same consideration that rural Americans had long enjoyed through the Department of Agriculture and the Department of the Interior.

The Johnson administration's education initiatives extended far beyond aid to primary and secondary schools. The graduate of a public university, LBJ believed passionately in the cause of higher education and, like many liberal Democrats of his age, had long pressed for stronger federal assistance to college students. In the early 1960s, institutions were under mounting strain to accommodate the rising generation of baby boomers who flooded American campuses. At half of the country's four-year colleges and over 80 percent of junior colleges, libraries fell short of minimal standards. Moreover, few poor children were able to afford tuition and fees, resulting in a notable disparity between the portion of middle-class (78 percent) and working-class (33 percent) high school graduates who attended college. Over one-fifth of students who began postsecondary studies had to drop out for want of financial wherewithal. For many black families, whose median income was little more than half that of white families, postsecondary education was essentially out of reach. Average tuition, room, and board at a four-year public university ate up

14.5 percent of a typical white family's income but 26.3 percent of income for a typical black family. The corresponding figures for private four-year institutions were even more staggering: 30.4 percent and 55.1 percent, respectively.

With faith that access to a quality education would help poor people achieve their share of American prosperity, the Johnson White House secured passage in 1965 of the Higher Education Act (HEA). The legislation appropriated funds to support library expansion at private and public universities and established work study, grant programs, and reduced-interest loans to make tuition and fees affordable for poor and working-class students.

In real (inflation-adjusted) dollars, the federal government's annual spending on postsecondary student expenses increased by over 10,000 percent between 1963 and 2010. When Johnson signed the Higher Education Act into law, he intended its benefits to flow primarily to poor people. "The important role of the federal government is somehow to do something for the people who are down and out," he affirmed, "and that's where its major energy in education ought to go." Despite this original intent, as tuition and fees at both public and private institutions began to climb sharply in the 1980s, successive Congresses and administrations gradually expanded eligibility to include more middle-income students. Upon signing a reauthorization of HEA in 1992, President George H. W. Bush proudly asserted that it "gives a hand up to lower income students who need help the most. But it also reaches out into the middle-income families, the ones who skipped a vacation and drove the old clunker so that their kids could go to college." Through various, subtle means— including the exemption of home equity in calculating a family's eligibility for assistance and the gradual shift from grants (which made up roughly half of all student aid in 1965 but today account for less than 30 percent) to loans—the law gradually morphed into a middle-class subsidy that also happened to help those poor families able to capture its benefits.

Despite this departure from the bill's founding principles, Johnson left a vital legacy. Today, federal grants account for 10 percent of the total operating budget of all four-year institutions, while subsidized loans underwrite a substantial portion of the tuition and fees that universities and colleges collect. Just as critics identified Medicare as a driver of medical inflation, skeptics of federal education policy cited federal grants and loans—particularly those that flowed to middle-income students—as a primary culprit in the skyrocketing cost of college. Yet as higher education emerged as an entry key to employment in the modern information economy, the role of federal support in broadening access—particularly to groups traditionally locked out—was undeniable.

One indisputable triumph for the Great Society was its lasting contribution to providing food security to the most vulnerable Americans. When a team of researchers surveyed hunger in poor communities in the early 1960s, they found "children whose nutritional and medical conditions we can only describe as shocking—even to a group of physicians whose work involves daily confrontation with disease and suffering. In child after child we saw: evidence of vitamin and mineral deficiencies . . . in boys and girls in every county we visited, obvious evidence of severe malnutrition, with injury to body's tissues—its muscles, bones and skin as well as an associated psychological state of fatigue, listlessness, and exhaustion. . . . We saw homes with children who are lucky to eat one meal a day . . . who don't get to drink milk, don't get to eat fruit, green vegetables, or meat."

During World War II, roughly half of all counties in the United States participated in a federally subsidized food stamp program that enabled poor people to purchase discounted coupons that could be redeemed for food. The program ended in 1943. Under John Kennedy, the government reinstituted it as a pilot initiative in just eight regions of the country. The 1964 Food Stamp Act took what had been a limited test program and created a new entitlement. Under its provisions, poor families were eligible to purchase cut-price food stamps. The requirement that recipients pay for the coupons was consistent with LBJ's mandate that there be "no doles" in his War on Poverty, but more fundamentally it represented the administration's belief that the poor required qualitative assistance to realize their fair portion of the nation's abundance, not cash transfers. Yet when Congress eliminated the purchase requirement, the food stamp program—whose rolls grew from roughly 500,000 recipients in 1965 to roughly 13 million in 1974—evolved into both a nutritional assistance program and a hidden form of income support. Because food stamps qualify in budgetary terms as a "near-cash" benefit—meaning, they are not technically income—the federal government does not include their value when measuring poverty. Using the alternative Supplemental Poverty Measure (SPM), which counts the value of such benefits as part of household income, census figures in 2010 revealed that food stamps cut the child poverty rate by 3 percentage points. The program also accomplished much of its original mandate to help alleviate hunger and nutritional deficiency among poor people. Though some families may use food stamps—later renamed SNAP (Supplemental Nutrition Assistance Program)—to defray grocery purchases they would otherwise have made, studies establish that the program afforded poor people and particularly poor children greater access to nutritious food.

At Johnson's urging, Congress also passed the 1966 Child Nutrition Act, which substantially expanded a preexisting, subsidized school lunch program for poor children and established a pilot breakfast program. Both initiatives experienced steady growth under successive Democratic and Republican initiatives: between 1970 and 2010, the number of disadvantaged youth benefiting from free or subsidized breakfasts grew from 450,000 to 11.7 million, while those receiving free or reduced-price lunches grew from 22 million to 32 million.

Aside from the very real contribution that school meals play in providing food security for poor children, census data report that they account for a 1 point decrease in child poverty rates when accounting for the cash value of the benefit. In absolute numbers, food stamps and school meals together reduce the total number of children living in poverty today by approximately 15 percent.

In his signature address at the University of Michigan, LBJ had declared that the Great Society was "a place where the city of man serves not only the needs of the body and the demands of commerce but the desire for beauty and the hunger for community." It was a "place where men are more concerned with the quality of their goals than the quantity of their goods." Such sweeping rhetorical flourishes reflected the imprimatur of New Frontiersmen like Dick Goodwin and Bill Moyers on the Great Society's agenda. (They also drove Horace Busby and George Reedy to distraction.) Fighting poverty and completing the nation's frayed and patchwork safety net were legacy items from the New Deal and Fair Deal years; expanding the liberal agenda to include environmental, consumer, and workforce protections reflected the concerns of younger LBJ aides who presaged the "New Politics" movement of the 1970s. Over the course of his presidency, Johnson signed roughly three hundred such measures into law. The Water Quality Act of 1965 established standards for interstate lakes and rivers and held states accountable for enforcement. The Clean Water Restoration Act appropriated over $3.5 billion to remediate lakes and rivers and created regulations to stem the flow of sewage and industrial waste. The Air Quality Act of 1967 established some of the first emissions standards for automobiles and industrial plants. A highway beautification bill—an initiative that Lady Bird tirelessly championed, the passage of which became "a matter of personal honor" for the president—limited the placement of billboards along federal highways. Such measures—pioneering in their time—were fundamental building blocks on which the modern environmental movement later established a more stringent regulatory apparatus to safeguard America's water, air, and land. "No longer is peripheral action—the 'saving' of a forest, a park, and a refuge for wildlife—isolated from the mainstream," declared Secretary of the Interior Stewart Udall, who served under both Kennedy and Johnson. "The total environment is now the concern, and the new conservation makes man, himself, its subject. The quality of life is now the perspective and repose of the new conservation."

The Great Society was also on the vanguard of consumer protection and health and safety reform, emerging concerns among liberal interest groups. At the administration's urging, in 1966 Congress passed the Fair Packaging and Labeling Act, which required manufacturers of consumer goods to label the "net contents, identity of commodity, and name and place of the product's manufacturer, packer, or distributor." The law also empowered the Federal Trade Commission and the Food and Drug Administration to impose additional rules governing the disclosure of ingredients, package size, and pricing.

With the support of overwhelmingly Democratic majorities in the House and the Senate, LBJ secured passage of two new federal agencies—the National Endowment for the Humanities and the National Endowment for the Arts—with a mandate and budget to promote American cultural achievement. He also signed into law the Public Broadcasting Act of 1967, which established the Corporation for Public Broadcasting, an agency with dedicated federal funding that helped local public television and radio stations create and broadcast quality programming. The broadcasting act spurred the creation of both the Public Broadcasting Service (PBS) and National Public Radio, which launched in 1970. In his memoirs, Johnson was critical of PBS. "Considering that the thrust of the Great Society in general was toward the poor and minorities," he concluded, "it is worth saying that the emphasis in public broadcasting turned out to be toward an elite audience." He was correct inasmuch as local stations devoted a large portion of airtime in the system's early years to costume dramas and television plays produced by the BBC. But Johnson, who died in January 1973, did not enjoy the opportunity to witness the lasting influence of PBS on quality children's programming.

In 1968, Joan Ganz Cooney, a New York–based public television producer who had won an Emmy for her documentary on the achievements of the Head Start program, founded the Children's Television Workshop (CTW). Convinced that television had an important role to play in preparing low-income children for school, Cooney received backing from the Carnegie Foundation to plan an educational show targeted to children between the ages of three and five. The concept was generally uncontroversial, but its approach was highly unorthodox. "If we accept the premise that commercials are effective teachers," Cooney wrote in her Carnegie report, "it is important to be aware of their characteristics, the most obvious being frequent repetition, clever visual presentation, brevity and clarity." In the course of a two-hour time slot, television viewers—young and old alike—were exposed to as many as fifty thirty-second advertisements. Rather than fight this tendency, the fledgling production shop would build advertising techniques into its premier effort, *Sesame Street*. Each hour-long episode featured upwards of twenty-five short, educational segments "sponsored" by letters and numbers ("Today's show was brought to you by the letter J and the number 7"). *Sesame Street* broke new ground in its use of an inner-city street set and knowingly spoofed the bland daytime game shows and soap operas that children invariably took in over the course of their preschool years; it had its own white-toothed game-show host, a Muppet named Guy Smiley, and a man-on-the-scene reporter named Kermit the Frog. Occupying the 9:00 a.m. time slot, when 20 percent of children aged three to five were already seated in front of the television, *Sesame Street* drew almost half of the nation's preschool population within a year of its debut. The generation of children raised in the 1970s was the first to learn its numbers and letters—and some of its values—from public television.

Not everyone shared the enthusiasm of so many young viewers. In Mississippi, public television stations initially refused to air the show because it featured a racially integrated cast, while in England, BBC's children's programming director declined to run *Sesame Street* because he was "worried by the program's authoritarian aims. Right answers are demanded and praised." Some education experts also argued that *Sesame Street* socialized kids to learn by rote memorization rather than creative thinking and deduction. CTW remained defiant in the face of these criticisms, insisting, as did one producer, that "we've proved [that] kids will watch quality shows and will choose them over sleazy competition." By numbers and brand recognition alone, they were right.

In every sense, CTW and *Sesame Street* were children of the Great Society.

Despite the sheer breadth of his achievement, Johnson sustained mounting criticism from liberal intellectuals and journalists, particularly those who identified most closely with the New Frontier and viewed Robert Kennedy as the true heir of his brother's legacy. Many of these critics had never accepted LBJ as one of their own and could not intellectually reconcile his emergence as a liberal icon. Speaking before the annual conference of Americans for Democratic Action (ADA) in April 1965, *after* LBJ's historic address on voting rights and with ESEA and Medicare gliding their way through the legislative process, Arthur Schlesinger baldly claimed that the Great Society had been Dick Goodwin's doing—not just the phrase, but the very concept. LBJ's brain trust— Valenti, Busby, and Reedy—had resisted it with unbending will, believing that its "dreamy vague proposals would be interpreted as a hangover from the Soviet Union's series of unsuccessful five-year plans." It was only by virtue of Goodwin's intellectual probity and towering influence that the forces of goodness had scored "a clear victory of the liberal cause of American politics over the messianic conservative complex of the President's Texas mafia." Earlier that year, Schlesinger privately recorded his opinion that LBJ was "living intellectually off the Kennedy program." Anything worthwhile emanating from the Johnson White House had been the handiwork of "the Kennedy people."

Johnson was acutely aware of this perception and increasingly wary of

Kennedy loyalists who sought to diminish his standing. When the historian William Leuchtenburg visited the White House to interview LBJ at the conclusion of the first session of the Eighty-ninth Congress in late 1965, he found the president—whom he had never met—irritable and on edge. "Mr. President, this has been a remarkable Congress. It is even arguable whether this isn't the most significant Congress ever," he began by way of opening. "No, it isn't," LBJ snapped. "It's not arguable. You can perform a great service if you say that never before have the three independent branches been so productive. Never has the American system worked so effectively in producing quality legislation—and at a time when our system is under attack all over the world." Johnson was wound up "like an old Victrola" and let go a two-hour volley of grievances against the Kennedys, "ADA liberals" generally—Arthur Schlesinger specifically—and the press. It was a remarkable display of annoyance and resentment.

At the time of the interview, Lyndon Johnson stood at the height of his power and accomplishment. Arthur Schlesinger might not admit to the world what he acknowledged in his diary: LBJ was likely destined to greatness. But in ways that were not then apparent, Johnson and his inner circle had already committed themselves to decisions that would nearly prove the undoing of the Great Society.

PART III

CHAPTER 10

Guns and Butter

I don't want to be known as a war president," Lyndon Johnson insisted in the summer of 1965. Franklin Roosevelt would forever be remembered for leading the nation to victory in Europe and the Pacific, but Johnson vividly recalled how the exigencies of mobilization and combat had forced FDR to transform himself from "Dr. New Deal" to "Dr. Win the War," effectively drawing to a close a decade of liberal domestic reform and forestalling the completion of the nation's safety net. It was the story of every Democratic president in the twentieth century, from Woodrow Wilson, who largely sidelined progressive economic and social reform after America entered the European conflict, to Harry Truman, who became bogged down in Korea and ultimately spent down his political capital to raise armies and manage a wartime economy rather than pursue his Fair Deal programs. Foreign adventures had also consumed the Kennedy administration, much to the detriment of the Democratic Party's domestic policy agenda. Johnson was acutely aware of this cumulative history and remained determined not to fall into the same trap. Yet in the early months of his full term, he made fateful decisions that proved his political undoing.

Before the early 1950s, few Americans had heard of Vietnam, a onetime French protectorate in Southeast Asia that fell under Japanese control during World War II and emerged after the war as one of many nations eager to shake off the yoke of European colonialism and achieve political independence. A nationalist guerrilla army, the Vietminh—led by a longtime communist insurgent, Ho Chi Minh—engaged in a ten-year struggle with the French, who fought to reimpose control on their former province. It was around this time that the U.S. government took an interest in Vietnam. Prevailing foreign policy wisdom held that if one country were to fall to the communist bloc, a "domino effect" would soon topple nearby democratic or colonial governments, thus emboldening communist China and depriving Americans and their allies of access to raw materials, markets, naval bases, and strategic positions throughout Asia. The Eisenhower administration watched with concern—but did not intervene—when the Vietminh defeated the American-backed French army at Dien Bien Phu. In subsequent peace talks held in Geneva, Switzerland, the United States stepped in as the lead Western power seeking to check the influence of Ho's nationalist movement. By agreement, the country would be temporarily split in two at the seventeenth parallel, with reunification and free elections to follow two years later.

The United States subsequently installed a new leader in South Vietnam—Ngo Dinh Diem, a Catholic civil servant from the old French regime—and attempted to prop up his government with military and financial aid. With American consent, Diem canceled the scheduled elections in 1956. In the coming years, he would prove an expensive and troublesome client of the United States. Corrupt and inept, his government alienated large numbers of Vietnamese peasants and soon fell into open, armed conflict with southern remnants of the Vietminh, now rebranded the National Liberation Front (NLF), or Vietcong (VC). Courtesy of Ho's government in Hanoi, the NLF enjoyed a steady supply of materials that flowed down the "Ho Chi Minh Trail," a winding network of footpaths and tunnels that extended over six hundred miles through Laos and Cambodia.

Frustration with Diem's government led JFK to sanction a military overthrow in 1963; in the American-backed coup, just weeks before Kennedy's assassination, Diem and his brother were killed and a new military junta installed. The United States had already committed billions of dollars in assistance to the Saigon government and had over fifteen thousand military advisers in place. Such was the state of American involvement when Johnson became president.

At three critical junctures, LBJ and his foreign policy advisers led the country further down a path to war: in August 1964, when, in response to a suspected North Vietnamese attack on an American gunboat in the Gulf of Tonkin, Congress authorized the administration to use "all necessary measures to repel any armed attack against the armed forces of the United States and to prevent further aggression"; in February 1965, when American forces began a massive bombing campaign against North Vietnamese and NLF targets—later dubbed "Operation Rolling Thunder"; and in July 1965, when Johnson committed combat troops to root out the NLF and prop up the weak and disreputable government in Saigon. Until late 1967, LBJ's advisers were near unanimous in their conviction that South Vietnam must not fall. "If I don't go in now and they show later that I should have," LBJ lamented, "they'll push ... Vietnam up my ass every time." Even later, when some of his national security advisers arrived at the conclusion that the war could not be won, Johnson remained adamant that the political costs of capitulation were too heavy to bear. A communist victory "would shatter my Presidency, kill my administration, and damage our democracy. I knew that Harry Truman and Dean Acheson had lost their effectiveness the day that the Communists took over in China."

The administration's lone dissenter of consequence was George Ball, the undersecretary of state, whose work as a director of the Strategic Bombing Survey in 1945 led him to believe that the United States would gain little advantage through the indiscriminate bombing of a preindustrial country (North Vietnam) with precious few vital targets. Ball also questioned America's ability to win a ground war against well-stocked guerrilla fighters. History would later prove him right, though at the time his was a lone voice. By the end of 1965, over 150,000 servicemen were stationed in Vietnam; by 1968, over 500,000.

In World War II, the average American combat soldier was twenty-six years old. In Vietnam, he was nineteen. From the very start, his exposure to war was surreal. Rather than send servicemen by military transport, the government contracted with commercial airlines to shuttle fresh troops to Southeast Asia. The sleek civilian jets were "all painted in their designer colors, puce and canary yellow," remembered one veteran. "There were stewardesses on the plane, air conditioning. You would think we were going to Phoenix or something." Another serviceman remembered that "you could cut the fear on that plane with a knife. You could smell it. The guy sitting next to me was married. I'm sure he was worried sick about his family back home. The stewardess came by and gave us sandwiches ... and he started crying. He couldn't eat his sandwich. He just sat there and cried."

For grunts on the front line, Vietnam was a grim battleground. Over 60 percent of the country's topography consisted of densely vegetated highlands where Vietcong guerrillas successfully camouflaged themselves among the million or so Vietnamese citizens who dwelled in sparsely settled hamlets. Most American combat troops spent their days "humping" the hills and mountains amid scorching heat and humidity and carrying out "search and destroy missions," the aim of which was to kill as many NLF fighters as possible. Unlike past wars, in which the objective was to capture and hold territory, Vietnam required combat units to rack up a body count. Contending with the thick heat and heavy rain, working on little sleep but an excess of stress, suffering hundreds of paper-thin cuts from the elephant grass, which sometimes climbed ten feet tall, and enduring painful blisters, swelling, and skin decay on their feet, servicemen had to make life-and-death decisions in the blink of an eye about which Vietnamese to regard as noncombatants and which to regard as VC. Because the enemy made a practice of hiding among civilians and brutally coercing noncombatants into providing them aid and cover, many American combat units stopped differentiating altogether. According to the rules of engagement, in so-called free-fire zones they were permitted to shoot anyone or anything without compunction. "When I got to Nam," explained one veteran, "it was like black had turned into white because I was totally unprepared. . . . You're so scared, that you'll shoot at anything."

"I went to Vietnam a basic naïve young man of eighteen," remembered a combat paratrooper who served with the 173rd Airborne Division in 1969. "Before I reached my nineteenth birthday, I was an animal." Like many grunts, under the strain of combat he descended into wanton, criminal violence. He cut off the ears and fingers of VC dead and wore them on a string around his neck. He shot civilians, whose deaths only drove up his unit's body count. He participated in the gang rape and murder of a young, pregnant Vietnamese woman. "After a while, it really bothered me," the soldier told a reporter. "I started saying to myself, What would I do if someone would do something like this to my child? To my mother. . . . I was in charge of a group of animals, and I had to be the biggest animal there. I allowed things to happen. I had learned not to care. And I didn't care."

The most famous example of American war crimes in Vietnam involved Lieutenant William L. Calley, the commander of Charlie Company's first platoon—a unit attached to Task Force Barker of the American Division's Eleventh Infantry Brigade. In March 1968, Calley received orders from his direct superior to clear out the small hamlet of My Lai 4. Though most of the villagers at My Lai were women, children, and elderly men, and though an official inquiry later found that Charlie Company did not draw enemy fire from the town, Calley's troops unleashed an orgy of violence and destruction, rounding up and summarily gunning down anywhere between 350 and 500 innocent civilians. The murder victims included scores of young children. Military officials concealed the details of the slaughter until late 1969, when the independent journalist Seymour Hersh broke the story. In March 1971, Calley was convicted of twenty-two counts of murder and sentenced to life in prison. Richard Nixon promptly commuted the sentence to five years of house arrest, of which Calley served only three.

Philip Caputo, who later earned acclaim for his war memoirs, wrote that "out there, lacking restraints, sanctioned to kill, confronted by a hostile country and a relentless enemy, we sank into a brutish state." The mother of Private Paul Meadlo, a participant in the My Lai massacre, spoke for many parents when she mourned, "I gave them a good boy, and they made him a murderer."

For those working-class teenagers who served in the war, what might have been the best years of their lives became a nightmare that many later found impossible to shake. Leroy Quintana, who served in the 101st Airborne Division, remembered facing a long line of armed Vietcong soldiers. "I was shivering in the mud," he said, "and this is how bad it was: I wanted my mom. . . . When it's really, really down, everything becomes primal." Michael Herr, a reporter for *Esquire* who chronicled the lives of ordinary servicemen in Southeast Asia, once observed that "it was never easy to guess the ages of the Marines at Khe Sanh since nothing like youth ever lasted in their faces for very long."

Enduring the stress, alienation, and depression of combat service was sometimes as difficult as dodging enemy bullets. Grunts lived for those rare "bennies" like a letter from home, a C ration of canned fruit, a hot shower at the rear, or ice cream. They also turned to drugs, especially in the latter years of the ground war. Southeast Asia was fertile ground for narcotics cultivation, and Vietnamese marijuana had THC levels between five times and twenty times that of American grass. Suppliers regularly emptied out cartons of tobacco cigarettes and filled them with potent, homegrown marijuana. By 1969, roughly 60 percent of all combat troops were smoking marijuana on a regular basis. In the 1970s, heroin also became widely available. Unlike the expensive, diluted product sold on American streets, heroin in Vietnam was 95 percent pure, and it was cheap. Small vials that sold for $200 in the United States cost only $2 in Vietnam. By 1971, roughly 10 percent of combat troops were heroin addicts, while another 20 percent were recreational users.

Any administration would have been hard-pressed to manage the political fallout of a morally controversial war that claimed the deaths of over thirty thousand servicemen between 1965 and 1968 alone and whose horrors were nightly on display in every American living room, courtesy of extensive television news coverage. But Johnson and his aides ensnared themselves in a trap of their own making. Initially certain that the conflict could be won in six months—and loath to rally popular support for a war that might deflect attention, will, and resources from its cherished domestic agenda—the administration downplayed Vietnam at every critical juncture. Initially, neither LBJ nor any senior cabinet member or White House aide announced or acknowledged that the president had committed ground forces to Southeast Asia. When reporters observed marine landings at Danang and Phu Bai and a buildup of soldiers and airmen elsewhere in South Vietnam, the administration dissembled, insisting that the mission had not changed. "American troops have been sent [to] South Vietnam recently with the mission of protecting key installations there," the State Department answered casually. Only in June 1965 did the department's spokesperson acknowledge that the government had committed to lend "combat support to Vietnamese forces," though, when asked when the president had granted that authorization, he answered, "I couldn't be specific but it is something that has developed over the past several weeks." The inevitable swell of coverage obligated George Reedy, who was then still the White House press secretary, to issue a clarifying statement. Yet Reedy backtracked, insisting that there had been "no change in the mission of the United States combat units in Vietnam in recent days or weeks. . . . The primary mission of these troops is to secure and safeguard important military installations." Offhandedly, Reedy acknowledged that General William Westmoreland, the American commander on the ground, enjoyed the authority to "employ these troops in support of Vietnamese forces faced with aggressive attack . . . when in his judgment, the general military situation urgently requires it." His non-denial denial was so fundamentally dishonest that even Westmoreland later judged it "a masterpiece of obliquity."

The response to the administration's dissimulation was swift and

overwhelmingly negative. But the White House soon compounded its problems. If Johnson would not acknowledge that he had committed the nation to
war, he certainly could not disclose its cost. In 1965, LBJ buried Vietnam
expenditures—which totaled roughly $5 billion—in the Pentagon budget. It
would shock members of Congress when, six months later, in the middle of the
fiscal year, the administration was forced to request a sizable supplementary
appropriations package to cover the swiftly mounting costs of the war. By December 1965, when Murrey Marder of the *Washington Post* first introduced
the term, the idea of the "credibility gap" had become a fixture of opposition to
the administration. It was a pattern that continued through Johnson's presidency. "The old C&O canal which runs north from Georgetown is bounded
by the Cumberland Gap at one end and the Credibility Gap at the other," one
satirist noted. By 1967, even as LBJ continued to downplay the budgetary implications of Vietnam, war costs approached $26.5 billion for the budget cycle
that began in July. Public polling revealed that a majority of the population
regarded LBJ as a "conner." "The President," McPherson lamented, "is simply
not believed."

As antiwar sentiment took root on college campuses and in communities
across the country, and as the press grew ever more skeptical of Johnson's
tangled approach to the truth, the burden of dissemblance fell squarely on the
shoulders of Bill Moyers, who served as White House press secretary from
mid-1965 through January 1967. The clean-cut preacher proved supremely
capable of playing hardball. When CBS News aired a televised report that
showed American servicemen cold-bloodedly torching the village of Cam
Ne—the troops used Zippo lighters to burn civilians out of their small, bamboo
huts, ostensibly to root out NLF fighters—the White House press operation
swung into full tilt. Moyers summoned Frank Stanton, the president of CBS
News, to the Oval Office, where, as journalist Morley Safer later wrote, "Johnson threatened that, unless CBS got rid of me and 'cleaned up its act,' the
White House would 'go public' with information about Safer's 'Communist
ties.'" Moyers would later deny the details of the meeting, though at the time
he privately assured the president that he would explore "steps we can take to
improve coverage of the Vietnam War." He warned that "we will never eliminate altogether the irresponsible and prejudiced coverage of men like Peter
Arnett and Morris [*sic*] Safer, men who are not American and who do not have

the basic American interest at heart." (Safer was Canadian-born; Arnett, from New Zealand.)

By late 1966, some members of the press spoke openly of the "Moyers Gap"—that yawning aperture between truth and dissemblance, particularly on the administration's Vietnam policy. Others inside the White House quietly agreed. "The credibility gap was purely a Moyers invention because he'd answer too damned many questions," Jake Jacobsen, an LBJ intimate from Texas who joined the senior staff in 1966, believed. "He wouldn't ever say, 'I don't know.' He just had to have an answer for everything, and that creates a credibility gap. Whether it was the President's answer or his, you never did know that." As the administration continued to obscure the mounting human and financial costs of the war, Moyers found himself in an impossible bind—particularly as he grew uncomfortable with the administration's policy in Vietnam. He became "less and less successful as Presidential Press Secretary," Harry McPherson observed, in no small part because he engaged in frequent "background" discussions in which he attempted to represent the president as fundamentally conflicted about the war. The result was confusion among the press corps: Should reporters believe what the president said, what Moyers said publicly, or what Moyers said privately? Or none of the above?

As the press grew more sharply critical of his Vietnam policy, LBJ became more distrustful of Moyers—his onetime favorite, who now seemed to garner better coverage than the president—and of his media-friendly aides. He ordered McPherson to file weekly reports with Moyers, detailing every conversation he had with members of the press, and for a time prohibited him altogether from speaking with reporters. When the *New York Times Magazine* assigned a profile of Califano, Johnson forbade his domestic policy chief to cooperate. "You just tell these reporters you're not in the interview business," he snapped. "Then you don't have to worry about getting misquoted." The policy likely cut against Johnson's best interests. As more reporters were apt to doubt that Moyers was furnishing them with a complete view of the truth, their inability to speak with top aides like Califano and McPherson, who refused to return their calls, created an atmosphere of diminishing trust.

So wary was the president of high-level leaks that in late 1965 he ordered Marvin Watson to keep a log of all inbound calls to senior White House aides—a highly inadvisable scheme that Watson, true to fashion, launched with gusto. It took little time before reporters understood that the switchboard logs were intended to surveil their contact with administration officials. When members of the press corps challenged Moyers on this "gum-shoe tactic," the press secretary deflected, rejecting the charge as a "very clever, but inaccurate and unwarranted description." But Moyers evidently thought the operation foolish. The following January, he quietly shut it down. Watson, he explained with thinly camouflaged contempt, had "finished whatever he wanted to study and they're not doing it anymore."

The more the credibility gap widened, the more mistrustful LBJ grew. When in 1967 the *New York Times* ran an inside story about the administration's education task force, the president called Doug Cater on the carpet and berated him for rank disloyalty. Infuriated, Cater sleuthed around the West Wing to determine who had leaked the report.

"I did," Califano told him with bemusement.

"Well, I'll never tell him," Cater assured his colleague.

"*He* told me to put it out!"

The president had in fact forgotten his instruction to Califano that the commission's report be made public.

Charles Schultze would later observe that when he replaced Kermit Gordon as budget director in June 1965, "it was still the general economic opinion, not really having any appreciation of what the expenditure requirements on Vietnam were going to be," that the economy would continue to hum along with steady growth and low inflation. Even that fall, Secretary of Defense Robert McNamara had assured Americans that it was a "myth that education, or welfare, or health or other civilian needs have to be cut back to meet our defense requirements. This is a rich and powerful country, and we can do whatever needs to be done to educate our people and fight poverty and at the same time we can spend what needs to be spent to assure an adequate national defense." The intellectual foundation of the Great Society assumed that if the president's economists pulled the right levers, they could manufacture uninterrupted growth and full employment at low inflation. Later events would call this wisdom into question, but when McNamara informed the president in December that he would need to request an $11 billion supplemental appropriation for the *current* fiscal year—almost double the amount that Congress had originally appropriated—his aides worried for the first time that the economy might quickly become overheated, leading to runaway inflation. Worse still, the war would require an even greater commitment of resources for the 1967 fiscal year, which would begin on July 1, 1966. Reluctant to acknowledge how swiftly the conflict had escalated, Johnson downplayed McNamara's forecast and requested $10.3 billion; by the end of the fiscal year, in June 1967, the total climbed to roughly $20 billion.

A former economics professor who had served in the 1950s as a staff member at the Council of Economic Advisers and, later, as assistant budget director under both Kennedy and Johnson, Schultze had very little direct exposure to the president before Gordon recommended him as his successor. As he strode into the Oval Office to accept the position, he assumed that he would spend "half an hour, an hour," with Johnson. The role of budget director would place him at the nexus of domestic and foreign policy, at just the moment when the economic assumptions undergirding the Great Society threatened to come loose. LBJ merely grunted and said, "How are you? Will you take the job?" When Schultze indicated that he would be honored to serve, Johnson replied curtly, "Good. Glad to have you. Next appointment."

In the coming two years, Schultze bore the thankless task of paying for both steadily rising costs associated with the war in Vietnam and a growing roster of Great Society programs, all while trying to keep inflation in check. "A lot of this was not only additional troops, but the fact that aircraft attrition was a little bit higher, and that was something you'd make a new estimate maybe every month on," Schultze explained. "Ammunition consumption was a little higher. It was a gradual revision of this production schedule, of that production schedule, a few more troops here, a few more troops there." Having worked as a staff economist at the Office of Price Stabilization during the Korean War, he understood that military conflicts were inevitably difficult to forecast with accuracy or precision. The Truman and Eisenhower administrations had submitted cumulative requests for $45 billion in supplemental appropriations above and beyond what Congress authorized for Korea. In the end analysis, Vietnam ultimately came in closer to budget than either Korea or World War II. "The real problem here," Schultze argued, "was, for all sorts of reasons, an unwillingness to admit publicly the war was going to cost a lot more." LBJ feared that if he admitted the full scope of engagement—or if he embraced the advice of both Schultze and Gardner Ackley, the chairman of the CEA, that the administration raise personal and corporate income taxes to prevent the economy from overheating—he would box himself into a corner with Congress. "Because obviously the whole game of the Republicans, naturally, would have been, 'Why the devil should we give you these extra taxes when you won't tell us how much more the war is going to cost?'"

Asking for the tax increase necessarily exposed the administration to Republican demands that Johnson trim domestic spending—something that he was singularly opposed to doing. "He had no stomach for it," Lady Bird later said of her husband's outlook on Vietnam. "It wasn't the war he wanted. The one he wanted was on poverty and ignorance and disease and that was worth putting your life into."

Unable—or unwilling—to ask Congress for a tax increase, Johnson worked every other lever available to him. Not until January 1967 did LBJ ask for a tax surcharge, and not until mid-1968 did Congress approve one. In the meantime, the White House relied on a hopeless jawbone strategy. "Johnson pushed me constantly to move on some price or another," Califano wrote, "as he read reports from the Council of Economic Advisers, or noticed some increase on the AP or UPI wires. Shoe prices went up, so LBJ slapped export controls on hides to increase the supply of leather. Reports that color television sets would sell at high prices came across the wire. Johnson told me to ask RCA's David Sarnoff to hold them down. Domestic lamb prices rose. LBJ directed McNamara to buy cheaper lamb from New Zealand for the troops in Vietnam." The president ordered the government to cease new furniture purchases in order to reduce aggregate demand for (and thus the price of) lumber. He instructed Califano and the CEA to "move on household appliances, paper cartons, newsprint, men's underwear, women's hosiery, glass containers, cellulose, chlorine, air conditioners, and caustic soda, which is used to make soap and paper." When the price of eggs began to climb, he encouraged government officials to voice concerns about the health effects of high cholesterol.

LBJ also vigorously jawboned labor and business into holding down prices and wages. He personally intervened in negotiations between the United Steelworkers of America and the major steel companies in late 1965. The union demanded a 5 percent wage hike; the operators warned that such a contract would necessitate price increases above the administration's 3.2 percent guidelines. "No price increase," the president ordered Califano, gesturing with his right hand (thumb and forefinger held in a tight circle). "None. Zero." Convinced that his labor secretary, William Wirtz, was too closely in sympathy with the USWA, he enlisted the UN ambassador, Arthur Goldberg, a former labor secretary, and Clark Clifford, who served as counsel to Republic Steel, to hammer out a settlement. When the president announced an agreement on September 3, Walter Heller, the former chairman of the CEA and architect of both the Kennedy-Johnson tax cuts and the War on Poverty, congratulated him on a "masterful" resolution of the "steel crisis. . . . You struck a key blow for continued cost-price stability and the country's economic health." Heller's laudatory note was premature. Increasingly, the administration found that no amount of jawboning could restrain the inflationary effects of mounting budget deficits—the direct impact of a war whose costs continued to climb unabated. Arthur Okun, who became chairman of the Council of Economic Advisers toward the end of LBJ's presidency, later acknowledged that "within the administration, there were no illusions: it was clearly recognized that the public budget and not private action was the engine of inflation." Yet when New York's mayor, John Lindsay, agreed to a new contract with city transit workers that provided a 6.3 percent wage hike, the president censured such an "irresponsible action" that would "only bring on an inflation that would damage us all." When in 1966 steel manufacturers walked away from their prior year's pledge and raised prices, Ackley decried their disregard for the "public interest." Later that year, the major airlines agreed to a 4.9 percent wage increase in contract negotiations with the International Association of Machinists and Aerospace Workers (IAM) union, effectively smashing "all existing wage and price guidelines now in existence," the IAM's president acknowledged. Even the president admitted to his cabinet that he had "no power to tell either party what they had to take. . . . This is a complicated and difficult problem."

Throughout 1966 and 1967, the administration plied this "nickel-and-dime" strategy, in Schultze's words, to slow federal spending by delaying preauthorized initiatives. "You would make them wait a month between getting a new contract, or you would tell them to go slow on putting the power house in. But technically it is just difficult." Try as they might, White House officials could not tell local officials who had already issued bonds, cleared land, and completed site remediation for the construction of a new federally subsidized hospital that they would have to wait another year to break ground. The politics associated with such decisions were impossible.

It did not help matters that liberal congressmen continued to authorize spending on Great Society programs at levels far in excess of what the administration requested or approved. The administration had raised "great expectations," a Democratic congressman admonished John Gardner. Liberal Democrats expected the president to make good. Hugh Carey, a Democrat from New York, lamented that Congress was being "forced to make a choice here between books and bullets." After all, polling suggested that while wide support still existed for the war effort in Vietnam, fully 72 percent of Americans opposed cuts to domestic programs as a trade-off for increased military appropriations. In pledging that America could do it all—have guns and butter, fight poverty and communism, ensure sustained economic growth with low inflation—the president had promised more than he could deliver. James Scheuer, a congressman from New York, attributed liberal frustration to the administration's "own eloquence and your own creativity in whetting our appetites."

In mid-1966, Califano and Cater were able to delay for one year a scheduled increase in the formula that determined eligibility for ESEA Title I funds, from a family poverty floor of $2,000 to $3,000. But Congress added new buckets of categorical aid for handicapped children and children in foster homes and thereby blew through the administration's budget authorization figure by $1.7 billion—or 39 percent of the original request. Such actions confirmed Johnson's long-standing conviction that once implemented, government programs were difficult to extinguish. He was certainly disinclined to veto the reauthorizations of his signature programs. But as prices and wages began to climb, the White House found itself in the unusual position of urging restraint—in part because of the need to keep inflation in check, in part out of the recognition that it would require the buildup of bureaucratic muscle memory to administer programs already on the books.

In a sharp memorandum to Califano in December 1965, Schultze urged against a flurry of *"new legislative proposals. . . .* Adequate funding will be a very difficult problem *even if there are no new programs. . . .* In the present budget situation I see very little hope of *significant* expenditure building up on *existing* Great Society programs. . . . As I see it, the situation will get *worse instead of better* unless we decide to *digest what we already have on our plate* before reaching for more." When Schultze warned that "raising hopes and crushing them because of budgetary limitations is worse than leaving the public in the dark about the new programs," McPherson wondered if the administration should preemptively broadcast that it was "not closing the door on the Great Society; we are just muting our welcome to it because of Viet Nam. These programs—Medicare, education, area development, are after all going into effect, and we could gain some mileage from identifying ourselves with them more meaningfully. Also, it would take the edge off the limited program we will offer this year." They were stuck in a corner, unable to square with the public but under pressure from powerful liberals like Andy Biemiller, a former congressman and now the top lobbyist for the AFL-CIO, who delivered a hard warning from the federation's boss, George Meany: "The Great Society programs must not be gutted because of the war in Vietnam." In a flash of anger, Johnson snapped at his domestic policy chief. "[We're] getting the hell beaten out of us" on Capitol Hill, he barked. It was Califano's responsibility to keep spending in check. When Califano replied that he would confer with Larry O'Brien, the president erupted in rage: "I'm talking to you. You do it. You've got to mount this Congress like you mount a woman."

Despite these entreaties, the unemployment rate dipped from a high of 5.7 percent when LBJ took office to 3.5 percent in mid-1968—well below the full employment threshold. Inflation, which hovered around 1 percent throughout most of JFK's term in office, cracked 5 percent as Johnson left the White House in 1969—nowhere near the heights of the "Great Inflation" of the 1970s, but still striking in the context of recent memory. Califano and others worried that the administration's obfuscation of the hard and soft costs of the war—most notably, LBJ's refusal to request a tax increase—"was taking a toll on his credibility. Many economists were beginning to wonder whether he was serious about reining in inflation. . . . Rising war costs and funds for Great Society programs were stretching the outer limits of the President's ability to manipulate the federal budget."

By the end of 1967, many stalwart defenders of the Great Society grew despondent over the administration's tightfisted approach to budgeting. In

December, after the Budget Bureau took "some real whacks" at the HEW budget, Secretary John Gardner—a respected education specialist under whose leadership the department had breathed administrative life into some of Johnson's most cherished programs—flew to the LBJ Ranch to plead for a restoration of funds. Huddled with LBJ in the First Family's living room, Gardner seemed a man in "turmoil," in Douglass Cater's recollection. The secretary was "always a little bit reserved around the President. He's a quiet kind of man, and they never had an easy conversational relationship." The meeting unfolded poorly. As he escorted them to their plane for the flight back to Washington, the president threw his arm around Gardner's shoulder and, with apparent sincerity, assured him that the days of austerity would soon come to an end. "Don't worry, John. We're going to end this war and then you'll have all the money you want for education, and health, and everything else." Cater and Gardner said very little on the journey home, but it was clear that the secretary "had lost faith that Johnson could stay on top of the situation." Within three months, he resigned his post. LBJ nominated Wilbur Cohen to replace him.

Sargent Shriver, too, requested a larger appropriation for the Office of Economic Opportunity. As early as December 1965, when Schultze first began to impose restraint on domestic spending, Moyers wired Johnson that the OEO director was "tired and disheartened," convinced that he was on the president's "—— list." "I again tried to disabuse him of this," Moyers continued, "and told him not to let your firmness on budget be taken for personal ill will. If this were [the] case every official in Washington at this time of the year would think that he is on that —— list." Two years later, Congress took a 14 percent bite out of Shriver's proposed budget for the coming fiscal year; after meeting with Schultze, the OEO director determined that he would likely need to "take a rather sizeable (15-20%) cut in ongoing local programs" in order to maintain initiatives already live in the field. Doing so would carry political consequences, he warned Johnson. However controversial some community action programs were, mayors generally supported the bulk of his office's initiatives and wanted "more jobs programs," "more day care programs," "more help for the aged," and "more Follow-Through with Head Start children." On a visit to the LBJ Ranch, Shriver implored the president to consider committing between $6 billion and $8 billion annually to the War on

Poverty. Still a true believer, he remained firm in the conviction that the administration's programs were "reaching something like a third or a quarter" of poor people. "Look, Mr. President," he began, "that is what is needed financially to eliminate poverty in our country. With this amount of money, I think we really hold out the hope of eliminating poverty over a ten-year period." Johnson was dumbstruck. "Sarge," he replied incredulously, "we can't go from a program of one billion or one billion and a half to six billion." One of the director's aides would later affirm that Shriver honestly "believed that this nation was wealthy enough to wage both a War on Poverty—on a much bigger scale than the war we were waging on poverty in terms of dollars and cents—and also the war in Vietnam [with] the amount of resources it was taking at that period of time." Johnson disagreed. Like Gardner, Shriver stepped down in March 1968.

Reporters who had grown skeptical of the administration's honesty also began to note the war's deadening effect on the Great Society. A well-placed journalist frankly advised McPherson that "a lot of the Congressional dissatisfaction with the Administration stemmed from the fact that domestic programs were being under-financed as a result of the Vietnam War" and believed that the White House could make few further strides in civil rights "so long as money is being drained off at such a rate for the war." Even as popular backlash against the Great Society gathered in 1966, influential columnists remained firm in their support for the opportunity theory that underlay much of Johnson's domestic agenda. That year, Joseph Alsop privately urged a "colossal" commitment of resources aimed at providing residents of urban ghettos with better jobs and housing and a "massive school building program, intensive recruitment of teachers, high pay, better school books." Many members of the fourth estate worried that Vietnam—the financial scope of which the administration continued to obscure—would limit the president's course of action. White House aides assured friendly journalists that "there was no reason to believe that Congress would take Vietnam expenditures and put them into social programs" if the United States were summarily to pull out of Southeast Asia. But the argument fell on deaf ears.

The White House understood that the war had also undercut the administration's standing with some of its most natural allies in and out of government. Even before he joined the White House staff in mid-1965, Califano—who was then still Robert McNamara's chief aide at the Pentagon—warned Horace Busby that many of his peers in the other cabinet agencies "move in liberal circles" and were "not supporting the President's position in Vietnam." Months later, when Califano, McPherson, and Cater visited college campuses to enlist prominent academics in a new round of domestic policy task forces, they met with stony resistance. "So long as the President persists in these policies," wrote a prominent historian, "there is no hope at all for expanding the Great Society. So count me out." Another scholar lamented that "the war has contributed to a profound alienation from this Administration of intellectuals and social scientists whose efforts would be essential to the domestic revolution required." Though he was "very enthusiastic" about the Great Society, the poet Robert Lowell publicly embarrassed the administration when he rejected an invitation to attend the White House Festival of the Arts. "How nice it is to have a man who gives what liberals have asked for for generations," the *New Republic* derisively observed of such displays, "plus the fun of kicking him around too."

McPherson privately fumed at those "neurotic and demagogic 'intellectuals' whose stock in trade is opposition to the Establishment," but he considered theirs a minority opinion. In addition to its partnership with leading academics in the formation of domestic policy, the Johnson White House was quietly establishing itself as the greatest patron of the arts and sciences in modern American history. The administration was spearheading the establishment of the John F. Kennedy Center for the Performing Arts and the Hirshhorn Museum and Sculpture Garden; it was vastly expanding the scope of the Smithsonian Institution and funneling money into space exploration, medical research, and the humanities. McPherson was optimistic that "a beautiful and creative Washington will benefit generations born long after the Viet Nam conflict is stilled." But in the short run, he vastly underestimated the potential for Vietnam to isolate the LBJ White House from the very artists, intellectuals, and scientists it had worked so assiduously to benefit.

Economics made Lyndon Johnson's presidency and now threatened to kill it. "Stable, rapid, noncyclical, noninflationary growth" was the "underpinning of the Great Society," James Tobin, a consultant to the CEA, later argued. Arthur Okun added that as "long as the economy was growing rapidly and making progress, [Johnson] really did see an opportunity for shifting things to the public sector, for shifting the distribution of public services toward the disadvantaged without having anybody feel it very much because it would be sharing the gains rather than asking for belt-tightening." Between 1962 and 1972, the proportional cost of social welfare programs rose from roughly 25 percent to 41 percent of the federal budget and in the same time more than doubled as a portion of GDP, from 4.3 percent to 8.8 percent. But the very same faith in the limitless potential of a "robust noninflationary economy"—as Califano later termed it—led LBJ and his advisers to assume they could also fight a war in Vietnam without anybody feeling it. Liberals in the Kennedy administration had openly spurned Dwight Eisenhower's New Look policy, which assumed that American resources were finite and that the country would have to pick and choose its ground battles carefully. The same logic carried over into the Johnson White House. "Let no one doubt for a moment that we have the resources and we have the will to follow this course as long as it may take," LBJ insisted. When the days of noninflationary growth came to an end, the administration could no longer promise guns and butter. It had to choose.

From the earliest days of their acquaintance, Lyndon Johnson reviled Robert Kennedy, who was then a lowly Senate staff aide, as a "snot-nosed little son-of-a-bitch." Ever eager to diminish others to aggrandize himself, he would greet Bobby in the hallways as "sonny boy." It is difficult to pinpoint the moment when the two men developed their all-consuming hatred for each other. It might have been in late 1959, when Jack dispatched his brother to the LBJ Ranch in Texas to determine whether Johnson intended to run for the Democratic presidential nomination the following year. In a deliberate attempt to humiliate JFK's younger brother, Johnson took him deer hunting and purposely handed him a high-caliber rifle with an especially powerful recoil. It knocked Kennedy to the ground. "Son," Johnson said, "you've got to learn to handle a gun like a man."

It might also have been several months later, when LBJ's campaign spread (factually correct) rumors that Jack Kennedy was concealing a serious illness and reminded liberal delegates to the Democratic National Convention that the candidate's father, Joseph P. Kennedy, had opposed Franklin Roosevelt's war preparedness policies in the late 1930s. "Lyndon Johnson has compared my father to the Nazis, and John Connally . . . lied in saying my brother is dying" of Addison's disease, Bobby complained to one of Johnson's close aides. "You Johnson people are running a stinking damned campaign, and you're gonna get yours when the time comes."

After JFK secured the nomination, he offered Johnson the vice presidential slot. Johnson accepted it, and then Bobby—apparently on his own authority, or because of a miscommunication with his brother—attempted to rescind it. The story leaked widely and caused Johnson considerable embarrassment, for which he never forgave RFK.

As vice president, Johnson stoically and without public complaint weathered almost three years of endless humiliation at the hand of Bobby Kennedy. Though JFK insisted that his staff members accord LBJ all of the consideration and courtesy due to the vice president, Bobby and his loyalists were uniformly dismissive and impolite. They frequently disregarded instructions that LBJ be included in key policy and security conclaves. At cabinet and interagency meetings, Bobby took every opportunity to single out the vice president for a public scolding. Lyndon and Lady Bird Johnson were rarely granted invitations to parties at Hickory Hill, Bobby's estate in Northern Virginia and the unofficial social capital of the New Frontier. On those few occasions when they were included, Ethel Kennedy seated them at the "losers' table." Hugh Sidey, a leading journalist, recalled their treatment at Hickory Hill as "just awful . . . inexcusable, really." At one party, staff aides presented Bobby with a cloth effigy of Johnson, with pins sticking out of it. The story inevitably got back to LBJ. On another occasion, Johnson attended a small gathering of Kennedy staff members and appointees. When he attempted to exchange greetings with Ron Linton, a senior Pentagon official, and John Reilly, the president's nominee to chair the Federal Trade Commission, the two men continued in private conversation as though LBJ were invisible. Observing that Johnson had retreated in search of someone who might deign to speak with him, Linton thought better of their brush-off. "John," he told Reilly, "I think we just insulted the vice president of the United States."

"Fuck 'im," Reilly replied loudly.

Johnson stopped dead in his tracks and turned for a moment toward the men, wearing an icy, defiant scowl. He said nothing and walked away. (Just weeks after the encounter, Lyndon Johnson would take the oath of office at Love Field.)

Dick Goodwin later observed that "Bobby symbolized everything Johnson hated. He became *the* symbol of all the things Johnson wasn't . . . with these characteristics of wealth and power and ease and Eastern elegance; with Johnson always looking at himself as the guy they thought was illiterate, rude, crude. They laughed at him behind his back. I think he felt all of that." Johnson miserably accepted that such disgrace would be his lot in life for eight years—unless the Kennedys dumped him from the ticket in 1964, a fear that haunted him nightly. It was an open secret that Bobby coveted the 1968 nomination for himself. He was, according to all the newsmagazines, the "No. 2" man in Washington. "When this fellow looks at me," said the *actual* No. 2 man, "he looks at me like he's going to look a hole right through me, like I'm a spy or something."

In a particular moment of weakness, the vice president cornered Bobby inside the White House residence and pleaded, "I don't understand you, Bobby. Your father likes me. Your brother likes me. But *you don't like me*. Now, why? Why don't you like me?" According to a bystander, RFK "agreed to the accuracy of all this." It was the ultimate twist of the knife.

When, on November 22, 1963, fate reversed their fortunes, Johnson tried at first and of necessity to be gracious to the man who was now *his* attorney general. He had to serve out John Kennedy's remaining thirteen months in office before he could lay claim to his own mandate. But the relationship, already bad, grew poisonous from the first instance. Bobby deeply resented that LBJ insisted on flying back from Dallas on Air Force One, rather than on the vice presidential plane, and he believed—though he was not entirely correct—that LBJ had treated Jackie Kennedy shabbily that day. While LBJ consciously avoided the Oval Office until after President Kennedy had been buried, on the morning of November 23 he instructed JFK's secretary to clear out her office so that his secretaries could move in, a callous gesture that inevitably traveled back to Bobby. That afternoon, RFK observed his brother's iconic rocking chair stacked upside down in the corridor. Unaware that it had been removed *before* the assassination so that a new carpet could be installed in the Oval, he assumed incorrectly that Johnson had already begun installing his furniture and belongings. For the next several weeks, he would show up late to cabinet meetings and openly brood or stare with open aggression at the sight of the new president sitting in his brother's seat. "Our President was a gentleman and a human being," Bobby told an interviewer in confidence. "This man is not. . . . He's mean, bitter, vicious—an animal in many ways."

Despite his hatred for Johnson, Bobby was eager to reclaim the Kennedy family's power base and made overtures for the vice presidential spot in 1964. When LBJ turned him down, Bobby resigned his post and ran for the Senate in New York. It proved a tougher race than everyone expected. In the closing days, RFK had to swallow his pride and ask the president—who was then riding high and on his way to a landslide victory against Barry Goldwater—to campaign with him in the Empire State. The photographs show a very glum Senate candidate hating every minute of their joint appearance. Yet in 1965, even at the height of his power, LBJ feared that his onetime tormentor would swerve to the left and challenge him for the presidency in 1968. Goodwin thought that the president was "always afraid of Bobby. It was more than hatred. It was fear."

Johnson's concern was not entirely misplaced. Very late to the twin causes of civil rights and the War on Poverty, RFK—who earned a reputation as a relatively conservative anticommunist during his formative years as a Senate aide in the 1950s—now reinvented himself as a liberal. "What does [Johnson] know about people who've got no jobs, or are undereducated?" he asked Dick Goodwin in a remarkable display of cognitive dissonance. "He's got no feeling for people who are hungry. It's up to us." In the wake of his brother's death, and as a freshman senator from New York—a state whose impoverished urban ghettos and rural hamlets stood in stark contrast to prosperous neighborhoods in Manhattan, Westchester, and the suburbs of Long Island—RFK developed genuine concern for the plight of poor people and minorities. But it stung Johnson loyalists when Kennedy denounced Johnson's urban policies. "It's too little, it's nothing," RFK barked at senior administration officials during an intimate dinner party. "We have to do twenty times as much." In early 1967, Bobby and two other members of the Senate Subcommittee on Employment, Manpower, and Poverty embarked on a widely publicized fact-finding trip to study food insecurity. Though Johnson had vastly expanded food support programs for poor children and families, the press lavished attention on Bobby's pained expression as he shook hands with starving farmers and city dwellers.

The empathy was real. As Marian Wright, founder of the Children's Defense Fund, later observed, he "did things that I wouldn't do. He went into the dirtiest, filthiest, poorest black homes . . . and he would sit with a baby who had open sores . . . I wouldn't do that! I didn't do that!" Johnson, who had become almost "paranoiac" about the prospect that Bobby might challenge him from the left, dug his heels in and resisted Kennedy's call for an expansion of the administration's food stamp program. Liberals scorned the president for placing politics above policy—"Why would he respond so coldly when he knows thousands of desperate people are depending on him for relief?" the *Nation* asked rhetorically. "Because, simply, he is incapable of rising above personal politics. Look at the subcommittee that made the request: one man he hates (Robert F. Kennedy); one man he thoroughly dislikes (Edward M. Kennedy)." Bobby, the editors asserted, "could put aside personal politics for mercy's sake. . . . President Johnson could not."

It was not just intense abhorrence or fear of Bobby Kennedy that drove Lyndon Johnson. On the contrary, as Califano explained in a private memorandum, the secretary of agriculture—whose department administered food stamps—did "not want to upset the entire program by either giving food to these negroes in the delta or by lowering the amount of money they have to pay for food stamps until he has the food stamp program through Congress." Typical of senators and congressmen, Kennedy rattled his saber without acknowledging or understanding that the administration faced numerous obstacles in securing funding reauthorization from Congress. A near-cash benefit, food stamps upended traditional patterns of social and economic deference, particularly in the South, and thus engendered opposition from conservative Democrats and Republicans. Equally important, the mounting costs of war—costs that Johnson labored assiduously to hide or obscure—created an imperative to hold the line on domestic spending. The trade-off between Vietnam and the Great Society was one of his own making, but he was not incorrect to hold Bobby Kennedy partially responsible for his bind.

From 1965 through the end of 1967, Bobby—like many of his Democratic congressional colleagues—attempted to find middle ground on Vietnam. He opposed outright withdrawal, because such "a course would involve a repudiation of commitments undertaken and confirmed by three administrations." Neither did he advocate an intensification of America's war effort. "Let us not deceive ourselves: this would be a deep and terrible decision," he warned. Egged on by his young staff members, who were stridently opposed to the war and vehemently hostile to Johnson, Bobby supported a temporary halt in bombing ("If we regard bombing as the answer in Vietnam, we are headed straight for disaster," he argued on the Senate floor) and advocated the inclusion of the NLF in negotiations—a position that was sharply at odds with the administration's position. Permitting the NLF to participate in peace talks "*may* mean a compromise government." Newspapers pounced on this line. "Viet Coalition Rule, Including Vietcong Urged by Kennedy," the *New York Times* announced. "Ho Chi Kennedy," the *Chicago Tribune* offered less charitably. Speaking for the White House, Hubert Humphrey decried Kennedy's idea as a "dose of arsenic" that would destroy the democratic aspirations of the South Vietnamese people.

Of LBJ's aides, Bill Moyers enjoyed the closest relationship with the Kennedys, and by 1966 his seeming dual loyalty was fast becoming a liability. In the wake of Bobby's call to include the NLF in peace talks and potentially in a coalition government, Moyers strained to close the gap between LBJ and RFK. He telephoned Bobby to assure him (without basis) that the president would ultimately come around to his position and urged the senator to dial back his support for including the NLF in a coalition government—a request with which Kennedy attempted to comply in a series of incoherent follow-up interviews and statements. At the same time, Moyers confided to Johnson that "Kennedy has managed to create the image of division among us, thus escaping the necessity of clarifying his own positions." To journalists, he offered a tangled assurance that "if Senator Kennedy did not propose a coalition government with Communist participation before elections are held, there is no disagreement." Moyers was playing a dangerous game, attempting at his own peril to serve two masters at once. It did not escape notice. The *Washington Star* spoke for a skeptical press corps when it observed that the "Kennedy-Moyers pact did not appear to rest on entirely solid ground." In fact, Kennedy's position was tortured. Though in favor of a bombing halt and more favorably inclined to negotiate with the NLF, Bobby was no less willing to lose Vietnam than the president. When college students taunted him with hand-drawn signs that read, KENNEDY: HAWK, DOVE, OR CHICKEN, they mordantly called out his vulnerability. His opposition was rooted more in style (and antagonism to

Johnson) than in substance. This point was cold comfort to the president. From his perch in the Senate, Bobby could swerve to LBJ's left without the burden of offering a substitute plan that would de-escalate the war and free up funding for an expansion of Great Society programs.

It did not escape LBJ that his press secretary and untitled chief of staff enjoyed a direct line to Bobby and used it liberally. "God . . . he was on the phone every day with Moyers!" marveled Joe Dolan, one of Kennedy's top aides. "That's the trouble with all you fellows!" the president once snapped at his press secretary. "You're in bed with the Kennedys!" Keeping a watchful eye from Bobby's Senate office, Dolan was every bit as suspicious of the relationship as the president. He wondered how Moyers could possibly "serve two masters" and would later rue that it was not "a proud moment in Robert Kennedy's life. . . . How does he defend talking to the president's press secretary when he's supposed to be at war with the president?" It was especially unhelpful when the *New York Times* cheerfully observed "interesting parallels between Moyers and Robert Kennedy (the two are, in fact, friendly despite the disaffection between Kennedy and Johnson)."

On occasion, the president also suspected Harry McPherson of conflicted loyalty. A veteran of his Senate leadership staff, McPherson had begun political life as a Johnson acolyte but glided with ease into the New Frontier, which he served as deputy undersecretary of the army and assistant secretary of state. Sensing early that LBJ looked with disfavor upon his cordial relationship with the Kennedys, he chose an opposite course from Moyers. Rather than try to bridge the personal and political gap between Bobby and the president, he urged Johnson essentially to ignore RFK. He argued that Bobby was an intellectual lightweight and liberal poseur who tacked to the left "to put himself into a position of leadership among liberal Senators, newspapermen, foundation executives, and the like. Most of these people mistrusted him in the past, believing him (rightly) to be a man of narrow sensibilities and totalitarian instincts." But liberal intellectuals were warming to Bobby and probably would continue to do so, for "as we know the intellectuals are as easy a lay as can be found," McPherson argued. "The Kennedys are handsome and dashing, they support many good causes. And to some people their rudeness and ruthlessness is exciting. . . . There is an air of tragic loss about them now." He suggested that there was little use in testing the loyalty of former Kennedy officials who

now served in Johnson's administration, men like McNamara and Katzenbach. "The test of our people should be whether they are smart, imaginative
and working to carry out your policies," he continued. "You have the office, the
policies, the personal magnetism, the power to lead and inspire, and above all
the power to put good ideas into effect. An obsession with Bobby and of the
relationship of your best people to him may, I believe, distort policy and offend
the very men you need to attract."

McPherson's advice went unheeded. Throughout 1966 and 1967, the two
antagonists alternated between cautious efforts to keep their feud at a low
simmer—Johnson was fearful of pushing Bobby into a direct confrontation
that might result in a primary challenge in 1968; RFK was wary of appearing
too calculating or disloyal to the Democratic Party—and angry flare-ups that
made for splashy headlines. Privately, the president's obsession with Kennedy
only intensified. Matters came to a boil in 1967 when William Manchester, a
reporter and book editor, published his long-awaited account of JFK's assassination. In writing *The Death of a President*, Manchester had exchanged access to Jackie Kennedy for broad editorial rights over his final work. Months
before the book's serial debut in *Look* magazine, Kennedy aides sounded an
alarm. The draft portrayed Lyndon Johnson in a dramatically poor light, so
much so that family loyalists feared it would boomerang on Bobby and jeopar-
dize a future presidential bid. An odd sideshow ensued, whereby Jackie sued
Manchester in an ill-fated attempt to forestall publication. The author ultimately agreed to modest revisions, but the final work proved no less incendiary.
Particularly cruel were chapters that portrayed Johnson and his entourage as
boorish interlopers on the flight back from Dallas and in the days leading up to
Jack Kennedy's funeral. Seething with rage, LBJ set his staff about the task of
identifying all of the book's factual errors. But he maintained public silence,
preferring to advance his position through targeted, unattributed leaks. "The
President, his family and his associates are indignant about this [portrayal],"
reported *U.S. News*, "feeling that he has no recourse, no proper forum, no
legitimate way to clear the air and set the record straight in connection with
derogatory reports that have gained wide credence." To Moyers, Johnson confided, "I don't want to debate with them. I don't think the president of this
country, at this time, ought to. It's just unthinkable that my whole morning
would not be spent on Vietnam or anything else but be spent on this kinda

stuff." But this declaration was probably intended for wider dissemination. The president had earlier informed Abe Fortas that he was now convinced that whatever he told Moyers "becomes known to Schlesinger immediately," and then to William Manchester, and then to liberal columnists and other "agents of the people who want to destroy me." Johnson was paranoid, but he was not wrong.

Weeks later, during an official visit to Paris, Bobby accepted an invitation to meet with Étienne Manac'h, a minor official in the French Foreign Office. Accompanied by John Gunther Dean, a State Department official who translated in real time, RFK seemed perplexed as Manac'h relayed word from a source in the North Vietnamese government that were the United States to halt its bombing campaign, Hanoi *might* agree to peace talks. Bobby thought little of the conversation, which he had trouble following despite simultaneous translation. When he arrived back in the United States, he was stunned to learn that word of the discussion had leaked to *Newsweek* and the *New York Times*. While Kennedy was not at fault—*Newsweek* had learned of the meeting from a low-level State Department official who was in possession of a routine cable that Dean had transmitted—the president and his secretary of state, Dean Rusk, were incensed. As a matter of course, the administration received such "feelers" on a monthly basis. Most were either baseless—the handiwork of amateur legates "eight months pregnant with peace," as Rusk fumed—or designed to embarrass the government. Rusk's staff nevertheless pursued each inbound proffer with care. Now Bobby had—seemingly for political glory and gain—presumed to engage in slapdash diplomacy in a stunning violation of the separation of powers. The resulting "diplomatic hubbub," the *New York Times* observed, "added another strain to the already taut political relations between President Johnson and Mr. Kennedy." The *Times* further informed readers that a subsequent Oval Office meeting between LBJ and RFK "was reported by White House aides to have been serious, even-tempered and constructive, if not precisely fraternal. But it was acknowledged that it had not served to narrow the breach between the two leading figures in the Democratic party."

This last point was an understatement. Bobby had haughtily insisted that the leak came from "your State Department," to which the president exploded, "It's not *my* State Department, goddamnit. It's *your State Department*. . . . I'll destroy you and every one of your dove friends. You'll be dead politically in six months." When Bobby urged Johnson to halt the bombings during Tet, the Vietnamese New Year celebration, LBJ accused his antagonist of providing the impression that the American government was buckling and thereby encouraging Hanoi and its NLF allies to continue inflicting harm on U.S. servicemen. "Look, I don't have to take this from you," Bobby retorted. The meeting ended with a tense agreement that Kennedy would deny ever having received a backdoor overture from the North Vietnamese. "We never receive any peace feelers at all," Johnson barked. "Isn't that right?" Stranded in a corner by his own action, RFK sullenly walked into the West Lobby and assured awaiting reporters that the news stories had been exaggerated.

The country remained doggedly supportive of the mission despite over thirty thousand casualties—including those dead, wounded, or missing in action. Only 31 percent of respondents to a Gallup poll believed that it had been a "mistake" to commit ground troops, and not until the end of the summer of 1968 did a majority of respondents come to view the ground war as a blunder. It was little wonder that pollsters dubbed 1967 "the year of the hawk," with one-quarter of Americans even registering support for a nuclear attack on North Vietnam to speed the end of the conflict. But the war was already limiting the administration's range of action domestically, even as other forces combined to challenge the continued expansion of the Great Society.

CHAPTER 11

Backlash

On the evening of August 11, 1965—just five days after Lyndon Johnson signed the Voting Rights Act into law—a white California highway patrolman cruising the South Los Angeles neighborhood of Watts pulled over two brothers, both African Americans, under suspicion of drunk driving. An altercation ensued when several bystanders rushed to the men's assistance. More white police officers arrived. When one of the uniformed lawmen struck a black woman to the ground and kicked her in the stomach, the neighborhood erupted in rage. The riot proper began the next evening as black city residents shattered white-owned shopwindows, burned cars and buildings, looted, and engaged in urban warfare with heavily armed state and local police officers. Though comparably less disadvantaged than other big-city ghettos, Watts—its neat, tree-lined streets and tidy bungalow houses notwithstanding—bore many of the same scars: residential segregation that created population density four times the city average, employment discrimination that left deep pockets of economic privation, persistent law enforcement brutality that fostered a culture of animosity and distrust between the police and the citizenry, and a growing sense that America's prosperity and promise had bypassed the city's black residents. Jarring footage shot from helicopters showed blocks of burning buildings and giant smoke plumes, a bitter repudiation of the racial harmony that LBJ heralded in his many speeches favoring civil rights.

Watching the news from his ranch, LBJ was uncharacteristically paralyzed by the violence. He authorized Moyers to inform the press that he found the riots "tragic and shocking" but for two days refused to accept calls from his domestic policy chief, Joe Califano. As the president blocked out reality by strolling around his property and entertaining guests, Califano fielded a frantic plea from California's lieutenant governor, Glenn Anderson, standing in for Governor Pat Brown, who remained abroad on an extended European holiday. After consulting with Katzenbach and McNamara, both of whom were vacationing on Martha's Vineyard, Califano took the unusual step of authorizing the army to supply the California National Guard with food, trucks, tear gas, and ammunition. It required almost fourteen thousand guardsmen to end the riot, which resulted in thirty-four deaths, a thousand injuries, four thousand arrests, and $35 million in property damage (equivalent to over $250 million in 2016 dollars). Valenti was immediately alarmed when he learned of Califano's approval of federal military assistance.

"I had more authority to deal with civil disturbances when I was in the Pentagon," Califano protested.

"The stakes were lower there," replied Valenti. "Here, when you act, you're acting for the President."

When LBJ finally returned Califano's many telephone calls, he sounded "more sorrowful than angry. . . . He feared that the riots would make it more difficult to pass Great Society legislation and threaten the gains we'd already made." He instructed Califano to set Dick Goodwin about the task of writing a brief presidential statement. When, thirty minutes later, he called to inquire about the draft, Califano "told him the Coast Guard was searching for Goodwin, who was also sailing in the waters off Martha's Vineyard. 'We ought to blow up that Goddamned island,' Johnson said."

If smaller disturbances in Harlem and Philadelphia had been the warning shot, Watts let loose the volley. The following year, 1966, witnessed thirty-eight urban riots, including deadly disturbances in Chicago, Cleveland, and San Francisco. In 1967, violence broke out in dozens of cities, most notably in Newark and Detroit, where police officers unleashed a fury of extralegal violence against innocent black bystanders, while rioters themselves looted and burned thousands of buildings. By the summer's end, entire city blocks lay smoldering in ruins. Jerome Cavanagh, the mayor of Detroit, surveyed what was left of his city and saw only "Berlin in 1945."

The ghetto conditions that turned cities into tinderboxes were not accidental creations. They were the result of a toxic combination of decades of public-sector and private-sector discrimination that created dangerously impoverished, dense, and segregated urban neighborhoods. Though the U.S. Supreme Court declared restrictive housing covenants to be nonbinding in 1948, resistance at the grassroots level among homeowners and property agents effectively restricted African Americans to a handful of neighborhoods in most cities and barred them from all but the worst rental properties. Federal mortgage policies made matters worse. Beginning in the 1930s, most mortgages were underwritten by the Federal Housing Administration (FHA), a government agency that insured banks against losses from homeowners who defaulted on their loans. The FHA insured these mortgages in return for securing the banks' pledge to provide home loans at low interest rates and to spread interest payments over the term of the mortgage, to require only a small down payment for the purchase of a home, and, finally, to allow homeowners at least fifteen and as many as thirty years to pay back their loans. At minimal expense to the federal government and with only the pledge of default insurance, the FHA freed up unprecedented levels of capital and helped create a postwar social order in which 60 percent of American families owned and accumulated wealth in their own homes. In deciding whether or not to insure mortgages, the FHA rated every census tract in the country. Assuming that houses lost value in neighborhoods that were racially mixed or primarily populated by African Americans and Latinos, the FHA assigned such areas lower scores or "redlined" them altogether, refusing to insure mortgages in these neighborhoods or insuring them on unfavorable terms. This meant that most black Americans could not secure mortgages, because their mere presence in a neighborhood would choke off affordable credit.

The FHA could claim that it was simply following the logic of the free market. When African Americans moved into a neighborhood, white homeowners tended to flee en masse, thus glutting the local real estate market and collectively driving down the prices of their homes. In this sense, it was grassroots white racism, not government policy, that was to blame. But this logic was circular. White homeowners understood on some level that when black families moved into their neighborhoods, home prices dropped. Prices dropped in part because the FHA stopped insuring mortgages for prospective buyers in these newly heterogeneous neighborhoods, thus making loans more expensive and driving down the amount of money that buyers could reasonably offer. It was a vicious cycle, and one that kept the majority of black Americans trapped in a rapidly depleting and deteriorating universe of old housing stock, in majority-minority neighborhoods. These inner-city neighborhoods became dangerously overcrowded and received inadequate public services like sanitation and road repair. In a perverse twist, black residents had little recourse but to rent cramped, subdivided apartments in buildings whose white landlords often neglected repairs and upkeep, but the physical decay of their homes fed white Americans' suspicions that black residents *chose* to live in squalor. "I would just like to say that when these houses were built they did not come furnished with roaches," the Democratic congressman Wayne Hays of Ohio—normally a reliable administration supporter—said of the black ghetto neighborhoods of Cleveland. "What are we to do now? Go out and clean houses for these people?"

It was not just a matter of housing. Discrimination by employers and nepotism within trade unions had long excluded black workers from well-paying, blue-collar industries that gave rise to the postwar middle class. As George Meany, the president of the AFL-CIO, crassly admitted, "When I was a plumber, it never [occurred] to me to have niggers in the union!" Even in liberal bastions like New York City, African Americans in the postwar period constituted less than 5 percent of all dockworkers, skilled machinists, electricians, or unionized carpenters. The black unemployment rate was double that of the city's unemployment rate. And New York was better than most places. In Chicago, 17 percent of black adults were unemployed. In Cleveland, 20 percent. In Detroit, 39 percent.

The stark poverty and inequality that marred ghetto neighborhoods stood in sharp contrast to America's self-image as a prosperous society and influenced the way in which violence unfolded and was reported. Sociologists soon drew distinctions between the "commodity riots" of the mid-1960s and the "community riots" that preceded them. Unlike earlier racial disturbances, which saw white residents and law enforcement officers target African Americans (and African Americans attempt to defend themselves, in turn), commodity riots saw black urbanites destroy and plunder white-owned institutions in their own communities. To the average white television viewer, this inner-directed arson seemed self-defeating at best and dangerously criminal at worst. Members of the National Advisory Commission on Civil Disorders—also known as the Kerner Commission, after its chairman, Illinois's governor, Otto Kerner—later concluded that many black Americans, no less than their white neighbors, had internalized ubiquitous imagery linking the culture of postwar prosperity to citizenship. What they could not own, they were determined to loot or destroy in protest. As one young looter told the commission, "They tell us about pie in the sky but that pie in the sky is too damn high." In the aftermath of the Newark riots of 1967, the black arts poet Amiri Baraka told a state investigative commission that the "poorest black man in Newark, in America, knows how white people live. We have television sets; we see movies. We see the fantasy and the reality of white America every day."

Though liberals, including Lyndon Johnson, were sympathetic to the structural causes behind urban riots, many middle-class and working-class white voters reacted with fear and anger. They saw minority neighborhoods swelling to accommodate four million African Americans who made the great postwar migration from the Deep South to the urban North and Midwest, and as those neighborhoods pushed up against their own, they focused on the symptoms rather than the causes of urban blight. "The neighborhood was totally destroyed as soon as the blacks moved in," a typical white resident of a transitional Brooklyn neighborhood observed several years later. "Buildings started burning down, and we had more crime. My sister and two of my little cousins went trick or treating one night, and about six or seven niggers ripped them off. . . . I'm not saying it's all blacks. It's just that people have blacks living right next to them, and sure, they're nice people. In my old neighborhood we used to have blacks who were nice people and we were friends and everything." A homeowner explained that "it's the minority's right to move where they want. I wouldn't mind if a colored family moved next door if they were upstanding and fine like me. Educated and intelligent blacks, why not? They are people. Color shouldn't have any place there. But I don't want trash who will frighten me. My problem is walking in the streets and seeing people who I don't know whether they are going to bother me. There is no reason to walk in fear."

Many white Americans wore blinders when they commingled concerns about integration with fear of crime. But lawlessness was a real and growing problem. Between 1960 and 1970, the national crime rate increased by 176 percent, a trend that continued unabated into the 1970s. Whereas the annual murder rate held steady throughout the 1940s and 1950s, between 1963 and 1975 it nearly doubled. The decade also saw a pronounced increase in narcotics distribution and use. These trends were well in evidence by the time of the Watts riot. Ordinary people could feel them, if they could not yet quantify them, and it became all too easy to attribute them to the growth of black urban ghettos.

Even as crime rates and drug use were soaring, the judiciary was becoming ever more solicitous of the rights of the accused. In the 1960s the U.S. Supreme Court ruled that defendants must be informed of their constitutional rights upon arrest and could not stand trial without counsel. Other rulings made it more difficult for police officers to conduct searches and seizures without proper warrants. In some cases, the courts went so far as to assume control of entire state penal systems, many of which held prisoners in dangerous, inhumane conditions. However constitutionally sound these decisions might have been, they sat poorly with many Middle Americans who saw the courts as weighing in on the side of criminals rather than on that of law-abiding taxpayers. Further contributing to popular frustration, many legal authorities in the late 1960s embraced the work of liberal criminologists and sociologists who claimed that America suffered a "crisis of over-criminalization." Many judges meted out softer sentences, while some states began liberalizing their juvenile justice systems to mainstream thousands of young offenders.

Also vexing to growing numbers of white middle-class and working-class voters was the explosion of America's welfare burden, particularly the sharp rise in the number of people benefiting from Aid to Families with Dependent Children (AFDC). Part of the Social Security Act of 1935, the program originally intended to provide support to single mothers whose husbands had died of work-related injuries or unforeseen health problems. But by 1957 roughly 57 percent of recipients were divorced or abandoned mothers and their children. Between 1960 and 1968, the AFDC rolls almost doubled from 3.1 million recipients to 6.1 million. Roughly 46 percent of these recipients were black Americans. This upsurge in welfare caseloads owed partly to a steady rise in divorce and out-of-wedlock births, but it was also the result of a deliberate initiative on the part of the National Welfare Rights Organization (NWRO)—a group with 100,000 members—to encourage eligible adults, most of them single mothers, to enroll in the program and demand their full benefits. Some NWRO activists genuinely intended to overburden the system; they wanted it to collapse under its own weight in the somewhat naive hope that a more comprehensive system of income support might emerge in its place. But the organization's clients were legally entitled to collect benefits, and increasingly they did. A legacy program from the New Deal era, AFDC hardly afforded recipients extravagant support; average monthly assistance in 1960 was just $108, leaving welfare beneficiaries well below the official poverty level. But as the cost to taxpayers increased—from $3.8 billion in 1960 to $9.8 billion in 1968—so did the antipathy of many white voters who bundled welfare, crime, and civil unrest together in a nebulous but powerful rejection of liberal social and economic policies.

As the public increasingly came to associate the Johnson administration with its signature commitment to civil rights, many voters found it difficult to decouple the Great Society from the struggle for black equality. Programs that aided poor people seemed specially manufactured to transfer hard-earned tax dollars from thrifty white workers to shiftless welfare recipients in the black ghetto. It mattered little that most welfare recipients were white or that the primary drivers of black poverty were employment and housing discrimination. Perception became the new reality in politics. Many white northerners who supported civil rights when that commitment was confined to the desegregation of schools, public accommodations, and voting booths in the South instantly revolted against the Great Society when that struggle came to *their* schools, workplaces, and neighborhoods. The backlash that LBJ's team had feared in 1964 finally seemed primed to materialize, and in 1966 it crystallized around the issue of open housing.

The idea for an open housing bill had been in the works for over a year. "We've got to end this Goddamn discrimination against Negroes," the president barked at Joe Califano as the two men took a late afternoon swim at the LBJ Ranch during the summer of 1965. LBJ, who was tall enough to stand in the deep end, jabbed repeatedly at the shoulders of his young aide, who was paddling furiously in an effort to stay afloat. "Until people whether they're purple, brown, black, yellow, red, green, or whatever live together, they'll never know they have the same hopes for their children, the same fears, troubles, woes, ambitions. I want a bill that makes it possible for anybody to buy a house anywhere they can afford to. Now, can you do that? Can you do all these things?" Califano replied that he could. The legislation was ready by the time Johnson delivered his State of the Union address in January 1966, when he asked Congress to pass his new bill. Known eventually as the Civil Rights Act of 1966, the proposed measure was for the most part uncontroversial: it included certain items left uncovered by the 1964 civil rights bill, including a ban on racial discrimination in jury selection, and strengthened preexisting measures by granting the Department of Justice broader authority to bring desegregation lawsuits—steps that most moderates could support. But Title IV, an "open housing" provision that barred racial discrimination in the sale and rental of housing, proved explosive.

It drew the immediately opposition of Republican legislators, including Senate minority leader Everett Dirksen and House minority leader Gerald Ford, local community groups, and the real estate lobby. Throughout the spring and summer, congressmen received constituent mail by the bagful, demanding in livid terms the rejection of the open housing provision.

"As a citizen and a taxpayer I was very upset to hear about 'Title IV' of the so-called civil rights Bill S. 3296," a resident of Illinois wrote to Senator Paul Douglas, a liberal who was running for a fourth term that year. "This is not Civil Rights. This takes away a person's rights. We too are people and need someone to protect us."

Another voter complained that his family "designed and built our own home and I would hate to think of being forced to sell my lovely home to anyone just because they had the money."

"Do you or any of your friends live next door to a negro—why should we have them pushed down our throats?" another angry constituent demanded.

Douglas's home state was ground zero of the open housing battle that summer, as Martin Luther King Jr. led protests throughout the "bungalow belt" in Chicago's working-class white neighborhoods and the nearby blue-collar suburb of Cicero. Polish, Italian, and Irish residents who had once been staunch Democratic voters now erupted in fury against peaceful black marchers. They pelted protesters with rocks, beat them with clubs and fists, and, in unknowing emulation of urban rioters whom they decried, set the occasional object on fire. Cries of "White Power! White Power!" rang out in an angry rebuke of the "black power" mantra that many young, radical civil rights activists had adopted a year earlier. "Polish Power!" "Burn them like Jews!" "We want Martin Luther Coon!" "Roses are red, violets are black, King would look good with a knife in his back." King, who had moved his family into a rancid apartment in Chicago's black ghetto to signal his commitment to northern civil rights activism, was aghast at the ugly reception accorded his peaceful marchers. "I think the people of Mississippi ought to come to Chicago to learn how to hate," he mournfully remarked.

Weeks before the start of the fall campaign, an Illinois resident and "staunch Democrat" informed Douglas that he could not "help but whole-heartedly agree with Barry Goldwater.... I feel Mr. Johnson is much respon-sible for the present riot by his constant encouragement for the Negro to take any measure to assert himself and DEMAND his rights—Rights, and respect are earned!" The situation in Illinois was not an aberration. Back in Washing-ton, Harry McPherson sat down for an off-the-record conversation with Bob Novak, one of the country's leading political columnists. "We mostly talked about civil rights," he reported to Moyers. "He is convinced that the white backlash is growing as a response to the riots and the fair housing legislation. I acknowledged that there was a lot of this but I thought it coexisted in people's minds with a sense that there was a real emergency that could only be solved by helping the Negro become a part of our society. He said that this might be so, but negative reactions were spreading to the white middle-class from the white lower-class and this presented the gravest danger to progress the civil rights movement has yet faced." White House officials who had been so pleas-antly surprised at the relative ease with which southern states accepted the desegregation of hospitals and movie theaters did not anticipate how inviolate many white ethnic residents of northern cities and suburbs regarded their neighborhood boundaries. Weeks later, a correspondent for *Time* told McPherson that the "backlash" issue had overtaken Vietnam as the top con-sideration for white voters in Indiana and Ohio. Their warnings would soon prove prescient.

By early fall, conservatives in both parties perceived an opening and grasped it. George Smathers, a Democratic senator from Florida and LBJ confidant, openly asked why "when a colored boy rapes a white girl, he gets off easier." Congressman William Colmer, a Democrat from Mississippi, la-mented that the "Social Security widow in my district" would now be forced to rent a room to a black man. Gerald Ford more subtly insisted that "respect for law and order is basic to the achievement of common goals within our na-tion" and blamed Title VI for sowing the seeds of rebellion. "Since its incep-tion," he declared, "it has created confusion and bitterness. It has divided the country and fostered discord and animosity when calmness and a unified

approach to civil rights problems are desperately needed." In an editorial for
U.S. News & World Report that August, the former vice president Richard
Nixon taught his fellow Republicans how to fuse anxieties over housing, urban
riots, crime, and civil disorder with more nuance but no less precision. "Who
is responsible for the breakdown of law and order in this country?" he asked
rhetorically. He laid the blame squarely with well-meaning but sorely mis-
guided "public officials, educators, clergymen, and civil rights leaders" who
had incited African Americans with inflated expectations and expansive rights
consciousness. Quoting his political opponents wildly out of context, he
pointed to Vice President Hubert Humphrey, who claimed he could "lead a
mighty good revolt," the "junior senator from New York" (Robert Kennedy),
who argued that "there is no point in telling Negroes to obey the law," and "the
professor"—a catchall for the academic elites who populated LBJ's domestic
policy task forces—who, in raising a cry against "de facto segregation," unknowingly gave young people license to riot and revolt. Perhaps to the professor "it may be crystal clear where civil disobedience may begin and where it
must end. But the boundaries have become fluid to his students."

Practiced as he was at the art of rhetorical provocation, Nixon did not
choose the metaphor of professor and student without meticulous calculation.
It was a symbol bound to resonate with millions of men and women who instinctively knew the protests overwhelming America's college and university
campuses had something to do with their broader tangle of concerns, even if
they could not say precisely why or how.

Back in September 1964, roughly a thousand students who had participated
in Freedom Summer in Mississippi returned to colleges and universities
throughout the country. They were battle tested and with eyes wide open, and
they formed the spark that set off waves of campus demonstrations that began
at the University of California at Berkeley, where police attempted to block
civil rights activists from canvassing on campus.

One such Freedom Summer veteran was Mario Savio, the unofficial
leader of the Berkeley Free Speech Movement, who told his fellow collegians,
"Last summer I went to Mississippi to join the struggle there for civil rights.
This fall I am engaged in another phase of the same struggle, this time in

Berkeley. In Mississippi an autocratic and powerful minority rules, through organized violence, to suppress the vast majority. In California, the privileged minority manipulates the university bureaucracy to suppress the students' political expression." Savio encouraged his peers to perceive a real parallel between political repression in the South—the familiar images of police dogs, water hoses, and tobacco-chewing sheriffs—and the university administration's restrictive policies governing political advocacy on campus grounds. More viscerally, he tapped into an undercurrent of resentment about the everyday realities of student life.

Fueled by a massive influx of federal research dollars, universities in the 1960s grew to unprecedented size: Prior to World War II, no American higher education institution had a student population over fifteen thousand, but by 1970 more than fifty campuses were that large. Undergraduates at these schools were increasingly likely to take mass courses in which the professor was a distant pinpoint in the well of a lecture hall and a graduate teaching assistant, scarcely older than they, provided their only human interaction with an instructor. Young people raised in nurturing middle-class homes were now assigned IBM punch cards. "They always seem to be wanting to make me into a number," complained one undergraduate. "I won't let them. I have a name and am important enough to be known by it. . . . I'll join any movement that comes along to help me."

Further contributing to student resentment was the thick web of *in loco parentis* rules that regarded college administrators as proxy mothers and fathers. At the University of Illinois, undergraduates faced a weeknight curfew of 10:30 p.m. and a weekend curfew of 1:00 a.m. At the University of Massachusetts, women who broke curfew by five minutes lost privileges for the ensuing Friday night; ten minutes cost them Saturday night; fifteen minutes bought them a hearing before the women's judiciary committee. At Barnard College, a man could visit a woman's dorm room at set hours, but three of the couple's four legs had to be touching the ground at all times. Earlier generations of college students accommodated themselves to in loco parentis rules, which had governed college campuses in one way or another since the inception of modern American higher education in the late nineteenth century, but not the baby boomers. Having been raised according to the child-centered, "progressive" model preferred by middle-class parents and suburban schools in the early postwar era, many college students came to regard in loco parentis as a special form of oppression. The black freedom struggle and the Vietnam War gave them a way to understand this feeling of oppression. "If there is any one reason for increased student protest," recalled a journalist at the University of Utah, "it would probably be the civil rights movement. The movement... convinced many of them that nonviolent demonstrations could be an effective device on the campus. It also served to make them more sensitive of their own civil rights." "The American university campus has become a ghetto," claimed an activist at the University of Florida. "Like all ghettos, it has its managers (the administrators), its Uncle Toms (the intimidated, status-berserk faculty), its raw natural resources processed for outside exploitation and consumption (the students)."

At Berkeley, as on other campuses, the initial spark was administrative overreach: students were barred from exercising their right to canvass on university property (in the case of Berkeley, authorities prohibited political advocacy at the heavily trafficked intersection of Bancroft Way and Telegraph Avenue). Student activists understandably chafed at the suggestion that they leave their First Amendment rights at the college gates. They also perceived parallels between their personal and political marginalization and that of oppressed minorities at home and abroad.

Many if not most protesters were deeply sincere in their beliefs. But they also situated their own experiences within a broader spectrum of political repression and fought both for civil rights *and* for an end to in loco parentis, for draft resistance *and* for free speech on campus, against the Vietnam War *and* against the culture of benign neglect to which faculty and administrators subjected them. When they complained, as did one activist, that "Michigan State is the Mississippi of American universities," they risked incurring the perfectly valid charge that they were a favored cohort appropriating the legitimate struggle of less privileged people. They also invited unfavorable comparisons to less privileged people in their own backyards.

Twenty-seven million young men came of draft age between 1964 and 1973—the peak years of American military engagement in Southeast Asia. Of that total, 2.5 million men served in the Vietnam War. Roughly 25 percent of all enlisted men who served in Vietnam were from poor families, 55 percent from working-class families, and 20 percent from the ranks of the middle class.

In an era when half of all Americans claimed at least some postsecondary education, only 20 percent of Vietnam War servicemen had been to college, while a staggering 19 percent had not completed twelfth grade. "When I was in high school, I knew I wasn't going to college," remembered a typical recruit. "It was really out of the question. Even graduating from high school was a big thing in my family."

Among enlisted men who fought in Vietnam, roughly one-third were drafted, one-third joined entirely out of choice, and one-third were "draft-motivated" enlistees who expected to be swept up by the Selective Service and volunteered in hopes of choosing the branch and location of their service. Many recruits who joined of their own volition had few other options. Unemployment rates for young men hovered around 12.5 percent in the late 1960s (over double that figure for young black men), and even in places where unemployment was low, companies were reluctant to hire and train young working-class men, for fear they would soon be drafted. "You try to get a job," explained one such unemployed man, "and the first thing they ask you is if you fulfilled your military service."

By contrast, middle-class boomers enjoyed a host of options in avoiding the draft. The government extended deferments to students enrolled in college or graduate school, but only to those who were full-time students. "I was in school," recalled one working-class man. "But I was only carrying a course load of nine credits. You had to have 12 or 15 back then [to earn a deferment]. But I was working two jobs and didn't have time for another three credits." The Selective Service snatched him up.

Potential conscripts could also avoid the draft if they furnished military authorities with proof of psychiatric or medical ineligibility, but as a general rule few working-class families enjoyed regular access to private physicians who could furnish or fabricate evidence of long-term treatment for a qualifying disability. "Most poor and working-class kids who had physical problems had to rely on army doctors to pronounce them unfit for military service," explained a Detroit-based attorney who offered free draft counseling to local men. "Yes, there were doctors there, but their goal was to process as many people as possible. Day in and day out, people who had legitimate ailments under the written regulations put forth by the Selective Service System were approved for military service." Even something so simple as orthodontic braces were grounds for ineligibility, but few working-class men could afford to pay $2,000 for elective dental work.

Because of the built-in bias in the draft system, Vietnam split Americans by class and geography. Three affluent towns in Massachusetts—Milton, Lexington, and Wellesley—lost 11 young men in the war out of a total population of roughly 100,000. Nearby Dorchester, a working-class enclave with a comparable population, saw 42 of its sons die in Southeast Asia. A study conducted in Illinois found that young men from working-class neighborhoods were four times as likely to be killed in the war as men from middle-class neighborhoods, while in New York, *Newsday* studied the backgrounds of four hundred Long Island men who died in Vietnam and concluded that they "were overwhelmingly white, working-class men. Their parents were typically blue collar or clerical workers, mailmen, factory workers, building tradesmen, and so on." Where a man lived, who his parents were, and how he grew up mattered enormously. It was a reality that concerned some of Johnson's aides, including Harry McPherson, who early on proposed a compulsory national service system that would require all men of fighting age to enlist in either the military, the Peace Corps, VISTA, or the Job Corps. The idea went nowhere. Not until Richard Nixon ended the deferment system in 1971 would it become more difficult for privileged families to opt their sons out of the war, but within a year Nixon had pulled out all but twenty-four thousand men, rendering the issue almost moot.

Counterintuitively, public polls data consistently revealed very little daylight between working-class and middle-class voters on the issue of Vietnam. Bob Novak confided to Harry McPherson that "most people in the middle, classifiable neither as doves or hawks, are in despair over a solution." Yet even as opposition to the war increased, the parents of soldiers, marines, and airmen found it difficult to identify with, much less embrace, middle-class college protesters. "Here were these kids," a working-class father would later say, "rich kids who could go to college, who didn't have to fight, they are telling you your son died in vain. It makes you feel your whole life is shit, just nothing." A firefighter whose son died in the war told an interviewer, "I'm bitter. You bet your goddamn dollar I'm bitter. It's people like us who give up our sons for the country. . . . The college types, the professors, they go to Washington and tell the government what to do. . . . But their sons don't end up in the swamps over there. No sir. They're deferred, because they're in school. . . . Ralph had no choice. He didn't want to die. He wanted to live. They just took him—to 'defend democracy,' that's what they kept on saying. Hell, I wonder." Ralph's mother confessed that "my husband and I can't help but thinking that our son gave his life for nothing." Yet they despised the "peace crowd. . . . I told [my husband] I thought they wanted the war to end, so no more Ralphs will die, but he says no, they never stop and think about Ralph and his kind of people, and I'm inclined to agree. . . . I'm against this war, too—the way a mother is, whose sons are in the army, who has lost a son fighting it. The world hears those demonstrators making their noise. The world doesn't hear me, and it doesn't hear a single person I know."

These divisions were only beginning to emerge in 1966, but some politicians on the right already understood how to exploit them. Chief among them was Ronald Reagan.

When Reagan first signaled his intention to run for California's governorship in 1966, most political observers regarded his candidacy with mild bemusement. Though a drab, even gruff character, the Democratic incumbent, Pat Brown, was a liberal giant. He originally defeated California's powerful U.S. senator, William Knowland, in a hotly contested gubernatorial election in 1958 and four years later trounced the former vice president Richard Nixon, who bitterly told the press, "You won't have Nixon to kick around anymore, because, gentlemen, this is my last press conference." (It was a bizarre and ungracious performance. In its aftermath, ABC television aired a special segment titled "The Political Obituary of Richard M. Nixon." "Barring a miracle," *Time* magazine announced, "Richard Nixon can never hope to be elected to any political office again.") During his eight years in office, Brown stewarded the construction of a thousand miles of state highways, massive irrigation projects that watered the Southern California desert, funding for new hospitals and clinics, a school building initiative to accommodate millions of baby-boomer children who would come of age in the following decade, and an unparalleled higher education construction program that created one of the world's most formidable public university systems, whose campuses offered the children of California's growing middle class a top-flight college education, tuition-free. Ronald Reagan, a former actor whose glory days were already well behind him, claimed no experience in public office and was a political carbon copy of Barry Goldwater, the conservative ideologue whom LBJ humiliated just two years before. When asked what kind of chief executive he would be, Reagan flashed his winning grin and replied, "I don't know, I've never played a governor before." He was easy to dismiss, as when the political satirist Tom Lehrer recorded a song about George Murphy, the song-and-dance man whom Californians sent to the U.S. Senate in 1964. "Hollywood's often tried to mix / Show business with politics," Lehrer crooned, "From Helen Gahagan / To *Ronald Reagan?*"

Yet Reagan had been an avid student of politics since his tenure as president of the Screen Actors Guild in the late 1940s, when he walked in lockstep with other AFL and CIO officials in championing Harry Truman's Fair Deal. In 1948, he played a leading role in labor's drive to secure a victory for Truman in California and supported Hubert Humphrey in his successful bid for a seat in the U.S. Senate. In 1950, Reagan even backed Helen Gahagan Douglas, the left-wing actress turned congresswoman with whom he would later be lumped together in Lehrer's song, in her bitter, unsuccessful Senate campaign against Richard Nixon.

If Reagan had always been politically engaged, his ideology evolved over the following decade. He clashed with communist union infiltrators in the 1940s and 1950s and when his movie career fell into a steep decline—later Reagan features include such unmemorable flicks as *Law and Order* and *Castle Queen of Montana*—eagerly accepted an invitation to host General Electric's television hour. GE was then on the vanguard of the incipient conservative revival. It indoctrinated employees with company book clubs (the reading list invariably featured watered-down works by conservative economists and theorists) and cemented its public standing with its popular Sunday night television show. In need of the money, Reagan was happy to play the part, which came with a whopping salary of $125,000 per year, later raised to $150,000. The former trade union president became a company spokesman.

Part of his job was to tour GE plants and deliver political speeches to the employee base. He was a popular draw and used his celebrity to excite opposition to John Kennedy's proposed Medicare bill. "If you and I don't do this," he implored his audience, "then you and I may well spend our sunset years telling our children's children what it was once like in America when men were free."

("How much are they paying you for this shit?" asked one liberal skeptic during a routine plant visit.) Toward the latter part of his GE contract, Reagan returned to the presidency of SAG and proved a tough negotiator with the studios, even as he warned GE workers about the perils of their own union and perfected the contours of what later became known simply as "the Speech." Designed originally for internal GE audiences, Reagan retooled the presentation in 1964 to raise money for Barry Goldwater. "The Speech" signaled his full conversion from New Deal partisan to New Right crusader. Two years earlier, he switched his party registration, but it hardly mattered. He had not supported a Democratic presidential candidate since 1948.

Though Reagan's gubernatorial candidacy seemed improbable at first blush, political observers understood the high stakes involved. "California is the most populous state in the Union," remarked the conservative *San Diego Union*, "and a Republican victory in November would most certainly signal the beginning of the end of the political extravagances of the Great Society." Johnson was eager to forestall that possibility. "We've just got to go after him," he privately confided to Brown. "And . . . put him right where he belongs: with Goldwater around his neck."

"I spent all day Sunday reviewing Mr. Reagan's record," the governor assured LBJ. "And this fellow is part of the kook crowd in the United States. He's to the right of Goldwater!"

"No question about that," Johnson agreed. "He's got a better television personality and he's more effective. But he's more dangerous."

As was often the case, Johnson proved an apt political seer. On the hustings, Reagan took care to distance himself from the same extremists whom Barry Goldwater had, to devastating consequences, refused to renounce. When Brown's campaign issued attack literature tying the candidate to the John Birch Society, Reagan just shrugged. "If anyone chooses to vote for me, they are buying my views. I am not buying theirs," he insisted. He avoided Goldwater's angry dogmatism and reassured moderate residents when he acknowledged that "as the state grows, we must have growth in government services." He did not propose to shut down entire agencies, only that "there should be some proportionality." He assured voters that he "never advocated selling the Post Office or abolishing Social Security. Nor do I believe in some conspiracy theory that all who favored increased government planning and control are engaged in a devious plot." When he decried the state of affairs in Watts—still a raw memory among Californians just one year after the riots—he allowed that "ninety-nine percent of the people there are fine, responsible citizens and had no part in the trouble. We're talking about a one percent minority." With deft preparation—his staff typed out hundreds of index cards with issue-specific one-liners and ripostes, each of which the candidate committed to memory with his actor's discipline—Reagan sidestepped every land mine that Goldwater had tripped. "I disagree with almost everything he says," groused one of Brown's aides. "But dammit, I can't help but feel that he is basically a nice guy."

Nice guy or not, Reagan proved adroit at channeling backlash against seemingly unrelated conditions that troubled many white Americans. He blamed the riots in Watts on the "philosophy that in any situation the public should turn to government for the answer." He decried the "small minority of beatniks, radicals, and filthy-speech advocates" who "brought shame" to the University of California at Berkeley, one of the flagships of the state's higher education system—a system that should have been a crowning proof point for Pat Brown but that Reagan forced him to wear like an albatross around his neck. His audiences listened with rapt attention as he described an antiwar program at Berkeley, where two movie screens pictured "the nude torsos of men and women . . . from time to time, in suggestive positions and movements. . . . Three rock bands played simultaneously. . . . The smell of marijuana was thick through the hall. There were signs that some of those present had taken dope. . . . There were intimations of other happenings which cannot be mentioned." For millions of white middle-class and working-class voters who regarded campus unrest with disgust and disbelief—after all, had any generation of Americans ever known such privilege as the UC students who attended some of the finest colleges in the land, free of cost?—Reagan offered an identifiable cause (liberalism) and cure. "I'd like to harness their youthful energy with a strap," he said of juvenile delinquents. It was a line bound to draw approving nods from the crowd.

On no issue did Reagan hit home harder than on open housing. In 1963, at Brown's urging, the legislature passed a state law barring racial, ethnic, and religious discrimination in housing sales and rentals. Brown called it "one of the great victories of my career [and] the beginning of our struggle to attack the problem of the ghettos." The following year, even as Johnson carried California with 59 percent of the vote to Goldwater's 41 percent, voters passed Proposition 14, a provision that voided the open housing law. (In subsequent years, both the California Supreme Court and the U.S. Supreme Court would rule the proposition unconstitutional.) It was a canary in a coal mine, and running for reelection in 1966, Brown now had to answer for Lyndon Johnson's proposed *federal* open housing law—a law that would reimpose the same restrictions that Californians had recently rejected by a lopsided margin. "I have never believed that majority rule has the right to impose on an individual as to what he does with his property," Reagan argued. "This has nothing to do with discrimination. It has to do with our freedom, our basic freedom." It was a theme that he hammered with relentless consistency and to great effect, deploying phrases like "basic freedom" and "basic individual rights" with almost mechanic precision.

On September 14, less than eight weeks before the election, Senate liberals in Washington, D.C., failed to achieve cloture on a southern filibuster of the president's federal open housing legislation—a bill that he had already stripped down by exempting 60 percent of the country's housing units. It was the first major Great Society initiative to die in Congress. The defeat only strengthened Reagan's hand in California.

Pat Brown did little to help himself—he ran a hapless campaign—but in the end it probably mattered little. Reagan trounced the once-popular incumbent, winning 58 percent of the vote to Brown's 42 percent. Nationally, in the midterm races, Democrats lost forty-seven seats in the U.S. House and three in the Senate—including Paul Douglas, whom Illinois voters punished for his support for open housing—and saw reactionary candidates win several key gubernatorial elections. Some observers understood backlash as primarily a function of growing racial animosity on the part of working-class white voters. In a Gallup poll, 52 percent of white respondents agreed that LBJ was moving too fast on civil rights; only 10 percent thought he was not moving fast enough. These results represented a sharp erosion in support for the black freedom movement since 1962. "Go . . . into any home, any bar, any barber shop and you will find people are not talking about Vietnam or rising prices or prosperity," a Chicago congressman observed on the eve of the election. "They are talking about Martin Luther King and how they are moving in on us and what's going to happen to our neighborhoods." Reagan understood how to channel racial animosity into anger with Lyndon Johnson. "Now the wraps are off the Great Society," he remarked in the wake of his victory, decrying the "welfare state" and "unprecedented federalization of American life." Voters who had tolerated an expanded role for the federal government could be converted to opposition if they perceived the government as a threat to the privileges they enjoyed as homeowners and working-class or middle-class workers.

Working-class and middle-class white voters were not the only constituency that began to sour on the Great Society. By 1966, a small but influential group of public intellectuals had begun to question the efficacy of government programs designed to remedy social and economic problems like poverty. Though some of these critics made a swift and unambiguous migration to the conservative camp—Norman Podhoretz, the editor of *Commentary*, figured prominently in this group—others insisted that they remained committed liberals or, as the sociologist Daniel Bell wryly labeled himself, "skeptical Whig[s]." Eventually, the term "neoconservative" took root. Alongside onetime anticommunist liberals like James Q. Wilson, Nathan Glazer, Seymour Martin Lipset, and Irving Kristol, prominent essayists and social scientists openly challenged many of the tenets of Great Society liberalism, though in the pages of *Commentary* and the *Public Interest*—a journal devoted to public scholarship—they disagreed among themselves as much as they jousted with conventional liberal Democrats. Among this group, none was more influential or connected to the wiring of official Washington than Daniel Patrick Moynihan, an early participant in the Johnson administration's interagency poverty task force and assistant secretary of labor from 1963 to 1965.

A tall and voluble Irish Catholic who had affected an aristocratic accent ever since his postgraduate studies in England (and who later earned a Ph.D. in international relations to match the patrician drawl), Moynihan enjoyed a close friendship with Harry McPherson but was otherwise a second-tier member of both the New Frontier and the Great Society crowds. The Department of Labor was comparatively small, and his role—as assistant secretary for policy, planning, and research—was toothless: he was the in-house intellectual, given free rein to write reports and issue memorandums. Unlike most early architects of the Johnson administration's antipoverty agenda, Moynihan was skeptical of opportunity theory and believed that what poor people needed was not compensatory programs like education and job training but actual jobs. "The only way out of poverty for a man is employment," he urged. By 1965, his focus turned to the one group of Americans who had fallen most precipitously out of the labor market: black men, whose rate of unemployment was more than twice that of white men. In a series of sharp memorandums, he urged corrective measures to boost workforce participation, including the institution of twice-daily mail delivery (the U.S. Postal Service traditionally employed many black mailmen) and a loosening of military tests that excluded a disproportionate number of black men from the armed services. "The single most important and dramatic instance of the exclusion of Negro Americans from employment opportunities is that of the Armed Forces," he told McPherson. "Above all things the down-and-out Negro boy needs to be inducted into the male American society."

Moynihan was sharply critical of Aid to Families with Dependent Children, a program that grew at a rapid clip during the 1960s through no effort of Lyndon Johnson (indeed, the president kept wary watch as the rolls expanded). He believed that the program created a powerful disincentive to marriage by restricting eligibility to single-parent households—almost always headed by women. It "rotted the poor," he claimed. Rather than "pension the Negroes off," he urged a dramatic volte-face in the administration's poverty agenda. "Nothing would be more terrible, if it should come to pass. We have created an entire subculture of dependency, alienation, and despair. We have already done as much to whole sections of Appalachia, as I understand it, and also to the Indian reservations. It is in truth the way that we cope with this kind of problem. As against giving the men proper jobs and a respectable place in their community and family."

In 1965, Moynihan set about the task of writing a report on the relationship between family structure and unemployment in poor black communities. He read widely, beginning with the renowned black historian W. E. B. DuBois, who six decades earlier observed many of the same trends—high rates of joblessness, single-parent households, absentee fathers—and E. Franklin Frazier, one of the nation's leading sociologists (and arguably the most prominent

African American in his field), both of whom attributed the dissolution of black families to the social and psychological trauma of slavery. He also consulted the work of Horace Cayton, St. Clair Drake, and Allison Davis, black scholars who wrote about the traumatic aftershocks of urbanization on formerly rural African Americans. Like DuBois before him, Frazier devoted particular focus to charting rates of "illegitimacy" in poor black communities.

Of equal inspiration were two celebrated studies—*Slavery*, by the white historian Stanley Elkins, and *Dark Ghetto*, by Kenneth Clark, a black psychologist who first achieved public acclaim when the Supreme Court cited his earlier work to buttress its decision in the case of *Brown v. Board of Education*. Elkins drew heavily on studies by the child psychiatrist Bruno Bettelheim, who had argued that Nazi concentration camps deeply scarred their prisoners emotionally, reducing them to a docile, childlike state. Relying on plantation records kept by white slaveholders and oral histories of ex-slaves that the Works Progress Administration conducted in the 1930s, Elkins arrived at similar conclusions about the lasting effects of slavery on black Americans. Though he broke with a historiographical legacy of apologia and portrayed American chattel slavery as singularly brutal, he also concluded that this very inhumanity infantilized its subjects and destroyed the psyche of black American men. In a similar vein, Clark concluded that slavery had so degraded black men as to establish a "Negro Matriarchy," further perpetuated by the "continued post-slavery relegation of the Negro male to menial and subservient status." These scars carried over into the urban North, where black migrants crowded into the "dark ghetto"—an "institutionalized pathology; it is chronic, self-perpetuating pathology."

An engaging synthesizer but not an original scholar, Moynihan wove these themes into a powerful but inevitably controversial and flawed report. He argued that the "fundamental problem" in poor black communities was "that of family structure. . . . A middle-class group has managed to save itself, but for vast numbers of the unskilled, poorly educated city working class the fabric of conventional social relationships has all but disintegrated." Slavery and Jim Crow had destroyed black families—in particular, centuries of discrimination had broken the psyche of black men—and created a self-perpetuating cycle of joblessness, broken homes, and poverty. A close read of the report leaves no doubt that Moynihan strongly advocated a massive federal program to ensure that black Americans realized "equal results," not just equal rights. He intended to bolster not a conservative argument against intervention but rather a liberal argument for income maintenance and jobs programs. But in focusing so intently on black family structure and borrowing liberally from works of psychology, sociology, and psychohistory, he furnished conservative intellectuals with an arsenal of powerful rhetoric that they would later use to argue against the efficacy of antipoverty programs. The report's most provocative and memorable line identified a "tangle of pathology" that rendered working-class black communities damaged and in need of intervention. At the "center of the tangle of pathology," he wrote, "is the weakness of the family structure. Once or twice removed, it will be found to be the principal source of most of the aberrant, inadequate, or anti-social behavior that did not establish, but now serves to perpetuate the cycle of poverty and deprivation."

Harry McPherson, who remained Moynihan's closest ally inside the West Wing, later observed that as the administration shifted its focus from securing equality of opportunity to equality of outcome, it waded into murkier waters. Most northern white voters could agree that segregated buses and Jim Crow voting laws were morally reprehensible. They recoiled in collective horror at images of white policemen brutally assaulting peaceful protesters. But when it came to housing segregation, ghetto violence, and economic inequality, there were no apparent "villains—at least none that strangers could identify—in the broken homes of the Northern cities where men 'chose' to be unemployed, women chose welfare, and young people chose heroin."

Inside the White House, Moynihan's report circulated quietly for several weeks. It is unclear whether LBJ ever read it; his aides would later claim he did not. But it made an impression on the staff, who recognized both its powerful argument and its explosive potential. In May 1965, Moynihan was summoned to the West Wing, where he collaborated with Goodwin on the president's forthcoming commencement speech at Howard University. The speech was in large part a condensed and sanitized version of Moynihan's larger effort. Johnson acknowledged the centuries of systemic violence and discrimination against black men—the "long years of degradation and discrimination, which have attacked his dignity and assaulted his ability to produce for his family." He rehearsed the familiar themes of broken families, single-parent homes, and communities in disarray. But in his call to action, LBJ—reciting lines that

Goodwin and Moynihan penned for him—went further than the report in providing prescriptive guidance. He declared that "freedom is not enough. You do not wipe away the scars of centuries by saying: Now you are free to go where you want, and do as you desire, and choose the leaders you please. You do not take a person who, for years, has been hobbled by chains and liberate him, bring him up to the starting line of a race and then say, 'you are free to compete with all the others,' and still justly believe that you have been completely fair." The president announced that he would soon convene a conference of "scholars, and experts, and outstanding Negro leaders—men of both races—and officials of Government at every level," to propose a bold course of action that would remedy centuries of debilitating oppression. Titled "To Fulfill These Rights," the speech heralded a new phase in the Johnson administration's War on Poverty and drive toward black equality.

In the meantime, aides grappled with how to handle the report, a potentially incendiary document whose author, Moynihan, left the administration that summer to run for city council president in New York City. LBJ's aides intended to head off controversy by instructing the Government Printing Office to release the document under plain cover and make it available for purchase at forty-five cents per copy. If it were issued as just another document, perhaps it would not draw unusual attention. But in August, someone—perhaps Moynihan, perhaps another official—leaked the report to *Newsweek* and set off a firestorm of controversy. The magazine ran its review beside a photograph of children throwing glass bottles in an urban neighborhood, with a subtitle that read "A time bomb ticks in the ghetto." The report "has set off a quiet revolution in the basic White House approach to the continuing dilemma of race," claimed the author, who lent special focus to "the splintering Negro family," "the rising rate of non-white illegitimacy," the "runaway curve in child welfare cases," and the "disintegration of Negro families," which "may have fallen into a self-sustaining vicious cycle."

By the end of the month, Robert Novak and Rowland Evans dubbed it the "Moynihan Report"; most of official Washington was already familiar with its general contours. So were civil rights leaders and black intellectuals, many of whom took great umbrage at its thesis and immediately returned fire. The NAACP's official organ, the *Crisis*, announced "The New Genteel Racism." James Farmer, the leader of the Congress of Racial Equality, denounced

Moynihan for providing a "massive academic cop-out for the white conscience." It was, by his estimation, "the most serious threat to the ultimate freedom of American Negroes to appear in print in recent memory." Moynihan's implicit argument was that "Negroes in the nation will never secure a substantial measure of freedom until we learn to behave ourselves and stop buying Cadillacs instead of bread." Kenneth Clark, who originated the term "tangle of pathology," was one of a few prominent black scholars to defend Moynihan. "It's kind of a wolf's pack operating in a very undignified way," he complained. "If Pat is a racist, I am." But the stigma followed Moynihan for the better part of the decade, even as he took up a prestigious post at Harvard University. Though his report was meant to sound a clarion call for a family income floor—a measure far more radical and redistributionist than any contemplated by the Great Society—many liberals regarded him as a turncoat who furnished conservatives with a powerful rhetorical argument against antipoverty and civil rights initiatives. The "middle-class sense of fairness," McPherson observed, was "willing to free the Negro from certain obvious and obnoxious restrictions. Once that was done, the American idea was that every man was on his own. No one was supposed to get special treatment. The Irish hadn't; the Italians hadn't; the Jews hadn't. What made the Negro special?" Such was the argument that pervaded working-class neighborhoods in the Chicago bungalow neighborhoods and in prosperous Orange County, California, where voters in 1966 sharply rebuked Pat Brown. However unwittingly, Moynihan furnished opponents of the Great Society with an intellectually respectable means to sanitize backlash politics and make it seem both credible and reputable.

Despite its incendiary quality, the Moynihan Report reflected growing skepticism within the administration that qualitative measures could eradicate poverty. That fall, Sargent Shriver told the president that to "end poverty in the United States, as we know it today, within a generation," the administration ought to adopt a "negative income tax." Rather than pay taxes to the government, poor people would receive money back. Layering a minimum income support on top of existing antipoverty programs would cost at least $7.5 billion in incremental spending. It was a political nonstarter, though one of the internal proponents of this strategy nonsensically argued that "one of the attractive features of the Negative Income Tax is that it would automatically go away as the [poverty] problem is solved." Policy makers would revisit this concept sporadically, but only in the 1970s would a critical bloc of Democrats—and some Republicans—consider it seriously.

Moynihan's report was not the only challenge to the intellectual foundation of the Great Society. In 1966, a team of researchers led by James Coleman, a respected sociologist based at the University of Chicago, released a report titled *Equality of Educational Opportunity*. Commissioned by HEW, the "Coleman Report" studied a broad sample of 655,000 students and concluded that "school factors" were less instrumental in determining individual performance than "family background and socioeconomic factors." Coleman's team concluded that "the sources of inequality of educational opportunity appear to be first in the home itself and the cultural influences immediately surrounding the home; then they lie in the schools' ineffectiveness to free achievement from the impact of the home, and in the schools' homogeneity which perpetuated the social influences of the home and its environments." Conservatives pointed to the Coleman Report as proof positive that schools could not remedy more trenchant cultural pathologies that grew out of poverty and broken homes; thus, no amount of government largesse would make a difference. In the coming years, other studies would challenge or reaffirm Coleman's findings: the White Task Force on Early Childhood Development (1966-1967) found that early intervention of the Head Start variety was in fact instrumental in improving student outcomes and urged that more funding be directed to primary and secondary schools. By contrast, a government study issued in 1967, *Racial Isolation in the Public Schools*, found that deep patterns of residential segregation had isolated a critical number of black students; implicitly, the report argued that integration, not resources, would close the gap between black and white student performance. On some level, Title I of the education act, which allocated funds to school districts on the basis of how many poor students they served, had always operated as a mechanism by which to surpass the church-and-state dilemma that had long stymied federal aid to primary and secondary schools. But LBJ and his advisers genuinely believed that education was a key that poor people could use to unlock the door to opportunity. Alongside Moynihan's analysis, these reports supplied ammunition to congressional Republicans who in 1967 proposed bundling a substantial portion of categorical aid into block grants that the federal government would then return to states, much to the advantage of wealthier districts and the detriment of poor ones. As it had on prior occasions, the Johnson administration called on labor, religious, and civil rights groups to lobby on behalf of its legislative program. Congress reauthorized ESEA with its original formula intact, but not without protracted debate over amendments—ultimately unsuccessful—that would have prohibited the use of funds for busing and would have sharply restricted the ability of the Office of Education to withhold funds from districts that did not meet its Title VI enforcement guidelines.

In mid-1966, local Democratic leaders raised a hue and cry when the Child Development Group of Mississippi (CDGM), an all-black community action program that administered most of the state's Head Start programs, requested an appropriation of $41 million for fiscal year 1967—a large multiple of its current-year funding. Staffed in large part by veterans of the Mississippi Freedom Democratic Party who in their off time continued to take an active hand in voter registration and political organization, the CDGM raised the ire of the U.S. senator John Stennis, who denounced its leaders as "extremists." It did not help matters that an OEO audit found that the program could not account for thousands of dollars of questionable expenses, employed no white teachers or paraprofessionals, and had "been increasingly oriented toward the economic needs of adults rather than the education and development needs of children." Under fire from liberals, Shriver defended the OEO's decision to defund the program. "We see every reason in morality and public policy to encourage racially integrated groups in Mississippi," he insisted. "We intend to encourage such groups in Head Start and other programs." When the OEO announced Head Start funding for a new, interracial CAP whose leadership included Aaron Henry and Hodding Carter III, a liberal white newspaper editor, activists denounced the administration for impeding "the prospect of a self-emancipated Negro community." Shriver was deeply embittered by the criticism. "I'd never really seen him as moved and angry," Jule Sugarman remarked. "It was a terrible reflection on his personal integrity." Years later, Shriver spoke to the pain of being caught in the cross fire between black community organizers who in many respects embodied the expectations of community action—they were, after all, building indigenous organizations to lift their own communities out of poverty and dependency—and politicians who demanded moderation and accountability. "I was trying to defend CDGM," he insisted. "But those people were so zealous, so religiously dedicated to what they were doing—and not without good cause—on behalf of the black people in Mississippi, that that was all they could see. My critics thought I was not sufficiently interested in blacks, or in CDGM. They thought I did not understand the situation, or that I was gutless and couldn't take the political pressure."

Ultimately, Shriver hammered out a difficult compromise that divided jurisdiction over Mississippi's Head Start program between several organizations, including CDGM, which agreed to adopt stricter accountability standards and appoint several white people to its board. The agreement represented a victory for the state's poor children but exhausted the director's capital among increasingly skeptical members of Congress. The controversy was only one of many local firestorms over community action. In dozens of cities around the country, elected officials—many of them Democrats—complained loudly that community activists were using federal dollars to organize voters against the local machines.

Few people at the time knew that Shriver was fighting a multifront war. With the war in Vietnam commanding additional attention and resources, the administration approved a 1967 budget for the OEO that came in at just one-third of Shriver's original request and one-tenth of what experts believed was necessary to fund its initiatives at full capacity. In the same way that the president grew ever more wary of Robert Kennedy, he came to question Shriver's loyalty—a cruel irony, given Bobby's visceral disregard for his brother-in-law. There was also continued blowback from northern mayors who resented the autonomy and occasional hostility of federally funded community action programs. In Newark, Mayor Hugh Addonizio, a Democrat who had been elected with support from the city's black and Italian communities, complained loudly that the Newark Community Union Project was attempting to topple his government by organizing rent strikes and political protests demanding better public services and better oversight of the police. The same pattern was on exhibit in San Francisco, where the Democratic mayor, John Shelley, did battle with Citizens United Against Poverty.

At the LBJ Ranch on December 19, Califano delivered Shriver's handwritten resignation to the president. The director believed that it was in

Johnson's interest "and OEO's [to have] a new face and a new image." He had "exhausted his bargaining power in the Congress. I am out of IOUs up there." And "having been in this job for three years, I believe it is time for a change. There are certain jobs in which your capital is eroded faster than in others; this is one of them."

Alarmed by the damage that Shriver's departure would inflict on the administration's antipoverty program, Hubert Humphrey persuaded the president to reject his resignation. For the time, Shriver would remain at his post, with the promise that more funding would ensue as the military effort in Vietnam achieved steadier ground. That promise would prove ever more elusive as Americans flipped their calendars to 1967.

CHAPTER 12

You Aren't a Man in Your Own Right

Working in any White House is an exhausting and all-consuming endeavor. Most senior staff members reach a burnout point. This was
certainly the case in LBJ's administration. Even before the midterm elections
that weakened the liberal majority in Congress, the president's original slate of
White House aides began showing signs of enervation. Their lives, explained
the *New York Times*, had grown "extremely demanding. The hours are long
and the vacations are infrequent. The 12-hour day, the six-day week, with half
a day at the desk on Sunday, is routine. There does not seem to be much evidence that this pace by itself exhausts the special assistant. But many of them
do develop feelings of guilt because they feel they are neglecting their families." The grueling demands of the job wore heavily on all staff members, but
none more than Jack Valenti, whose ragbag of responsibilities—though lacking
cohesion—required that he shadow the president at all times and on all days.
He was, according to the veteran political reporter Tom Wicker, the "most
enigmatic and the most omnipresent of the Johnson men," the aide who saw
"Mr. Johnson first in the morning and last at night, and nobody in Washington
underestimates that privilege.... He can be seen passing notes to the President
at a news conference or alighting at his side from a helicopter." LBJ, who by
habit tested the limits of his aides' forbearance and devotion, once described
him as "more important than a valet and less important than an ambassador,"
with "some of the functions of each—and many in between."

Like Moyers and Busby, by 1966 Valenti increasingly found himself attending long foreign policy meetings—particularly on the sinking quagmire
that was Vietnam. The pace, as well as the burden of responsibility, was bound
to take a toll on his sunny disposition and eventually did. "You didn't take work
home," he remembered, "because I would usually arrive around 7:30 in the
morning...and would leave the White House anywhere from ten to midnight

or one. . . . You went home to sleep and then you were up the next day. . . . The hours were very long and very strenuous." With time, Valenti—who bore "the most stereotyped image of [LBJ's] staff members," one newspaperman wrote— came to resent his popular caricature as an intellectual lightweight and consummate bagman. "Every time I see a story about myself I'm described as a fast-talking Houston ad man who wears metallic suits," he grumbled in a moment of rare candor and pique with the press. "Goodwin isn't the only guy around here who has ever read a book."

His want of a defined portfolio also began to grate on Valenti. Moyers initially owned development of the Great Society agenda and later served concurrently as press secretary—a role that Valenti had once coveted for himself—and de facto chief of staff. Joe Califano hastily built a small empire headquartered in the basement of the West Wing, where he ran herd over domestic policy, overlapping at times with Doug Cater, who enjoyed sweeping influence over education and health initiatives. Horace Busby had a wide-ranging mandate that included his well-defined role as cabinet secretary. McGeorge Bundy was the staff man chiefly responsible for foreign affairs.

Which left Valenti a critical player without a real job. An accidental presidential adviser with no prior experience in government, he proved a quick study in the ways of Washington and a skilled practitioner in the art of administration. Inside the White House and in the corridors of the Capitol, few insiders doubted his value. But he remained the butt of jokes from critical reporters—he was the "valet," the gofer, the presidential sidekick. "When the crunches came from time to time with the press and inside the government," he later observed, "I did not have allies, because I was alone."

In June 1965—still in the heady days following Johnson's victory over Goldwater—Valenti had broken with habit and agreed to address the American Advertising Federation. He flew to Boston, delivered his speech, and returned to Washington, thinking little of the occasion. Upon his arrival at the White House, George Reedy, then in his final days as press secretary, phoned him and angrily asked, "What the hell did you say in that Boston speech?" It was then, Valenti would recall, that "the mortars began to land, and it was guerilla warfare in the West Wing." In the closing lines of his talk, Valenti told his audience that he slept "each night a little better, a little more confidently because Lyndon Johnson is my President." The reaction from newspapermen, editorialists, and capital cognoscenti was scathing. They lambasted Valenti as a simpleton and sycophant who lacked independence of thought or action. The speech inspired Herblock's depiction of the White House as a plantation, where the master (LBJ) whipped his slaves (staff) into submission. "Happy days on the old plantation," the caption read. "A sensitive man . . . a warm-hearted man . . . I sleep each night a little better, a little more confidently because Lyndon Johnson is my President." Outwardly, Valenti took the ribbing in good stride. Privately, he fumed in full knowledge that when Ted Sorensen compared his boss, John Kennedy—then still very much alive—to Saint Francis, the intelligentsia smiled and nodded with approval.

Though LBJ supported his aide through what UPI's Merriman Smith dubbed the "love-that-boss speech" incident—the president's "attitude, as described by one staff member, was essentially, 'Poor Jack'"—it contributed to Valenti's growing weariness. Early in 1966, Lew Wasserman, the president of the Music Corporation of America, and Edwin Weisl, a prominent attorney who had been close to Johnson since his days in the Senate, offered Valenti the presidency of the Motion Picture Association of America (MPAA), the powerful trade organization that represented Hollywood's movie studios both in the United States and abroad. The post was prestigious and lucrative; his starting annual compensation would be $175,000, a princely sum for the time and a large multiple of his government salary. In April, Jack and Mary Margaret joined the president and the First Lady in the private quarters for dinner. Valenti made his case for leaving the White House: he owed it to his young family to secure their financial future and to spend more time at home. At his personal insistence, the MPAA had agreed to a clause in his contract that allowed him to take leave whenever the president requested his assistance or time. Johnson graciously wished his aide well. "You have served your country with devotion and distinction," he wrote later that month, "and you can always be as proud, or prouder of that, as you are of your fifty-one missions. You served me, though—and I thank you, and love you, and am very proud of you."

True to their agreement, within months of leaving the West Wing, Valenti—in Rome for a meeting with Italian government officials—received an urgent telegram summoning him to Manila, where the president requested his participation in a diplomatic conference. Valenti packed a bag and caught a military flight to the Philippines.

Valenti's departure followed closely on the heels of the overlapping resignations of Dick Goodwin and Horace Busby. Goodwin's allegiance to LBJ had always been contingent. He was a New Frontiersman and Kennedy partisan above all, and it was less surprising that he parted ways with the president than that he waited so long to do so. Nevertheless, LBJ was deeply embittered by his departure and assumed that his aide intended to rejoin the Kennedy camp. When Moyers beseeched LBJ to bring Goodwin back on a onetime assignment to help draft the 1966 State of the Union address, Johnson begrudgingly consented to the request but patently refused to meet with his speechwriter. He ultimately left most of Goodwin's prose on the cutting room floor. The result—the first major speech of his presidency in almost two years that did not bear Dick Goodwin's imprimatur—was an uninspiring and prosaic work. It met with widespread diffidence.

Busby's exit prompted greater speculation. Though his position had not weakened, particularly as he took a more direct hand in foreign policy deliberations, he chafed under Moyers's growing power and influence and—as had been the case over his long association with Johnson—found it difficult to subordinate his personality to LBJ's overpowering ego. Eric Goldman observed that Busby "admired Lyndon Johnson in much the same way that George Reedy did, but unlike the unflappable Reedy, he found it impossible to take the lashings for any length of time." The president, in turn, was fond of Busby but "could make a remark like 'Buzz is a very sound, very solid, able, good boy.' The very sound and solid and able—and very adult and complex—Horace Busby would hear about the remark and flare." Eager to return to the business of making money, and ideologically out of step with Moyers and Califano, he took leave. As had always been the case, he would be back.

Though lacking a formal title or role, from early in Johnson's tenure in the White House Abe Fortas emerged as "probably the single greatest influence on the President," according to Arthur Goldberg, the former labor secretary whom JFK had appointed to the Supreme Court in 1962. Fortas edited major presidential addresses and provided counsel on the formation of Great Society legislation. As the administration increasingly found itself mired in Vietnam, he began attending meetings in the Situation Room. He enjoyed unfettered access to Johnson and, along with Clark Clifford and Jim Rowe, constituted the core of the president's kitchen cabinet.

Fortas was a complicated and contradictory figure. Clifford later described him as "a deep-seated dyed-in-the-wool one-hundred percent liberal. . . . He was a true-blood Roosevelt liberal." Trained in the tradition of legal realism at Yale, he believed that laws were living constructs whose evolution should be informed by science, sociology, and economics. He embraced an active federal state in the 1930s and advocated broadly for the rights of individuals and minorities, including Clarence Gideon's right to counsel (a right that technically appeared nowhere in the Constitution). He encouraged the president and his aides to move aggressively on civil rights and believed, as he once expressed in his draft of a presidential speech, that a civilized country should "provide our people with the facilities needed for their health, for the education of our children, for welfare, for the development of our national resources."

But Johnson's aides often questioned Fortas's political judgment. A brilliant but consummate lawyer, he often gave Johnson sound legal advice that clashed with good politics. "It seems to me I'm on opposite sides almost every time when we get down to some purely political decision that the President has to make," McPherson offered. "But on the great issues Abe Fortas is really just tremendous."

Though a committed liberal, Fortas also developed a second, quite different reputation as an unscrupulous fixer and corporate lawyer with a rapacious appetite for the good life. When Walter Jenkins was arrested at the YMCA, the president turned to Fortas and Clifford to try to squash the story, as well as the charges. Fortas was deeply entangled in the Bobby Baker affair (he served as Baker's counsel but resigned after LBJ became president) and crossed multiple ethical lines to help the president obtrude with inquiries into the Johnson family's wealth and finances. Fortas resisted a cabinet post because he was loath to abandon his practice during peak earning years; his wife, Carolyn Agger—a high-powered tax attorney in her own right—was immovably opposed to the idea for precisely the same reason.

In late 1965, LBJ finally persuaded Fortas to accept an appointment as associate justice of the Supreme Court, where he filled the so-called Jewish seat previously held in reverse succession by Goldberg, Felix Frankfurter, and Benjamin Cardozo. (To make room for his friend, he persuaded Goldberg to resign from the bench and accept an appointment as ambassador to the United Nations. An opponent of the war in Vietnam, Goldberg believed he might be able to influence the administration's policy in Southeast Asia.) When she learned of her husband's appointment, Carolyn Agger was furious with the president, who she believed, correctly, had strong-armed her husband onto the bench. The couple had recently purchased a rambling home in Georgetown, where they planned extensive refurbishments, including the installation of an inground pool. When friends suggested that they earned so much money— and paid such a large portion of it to the government—that Abe's cut in income would have little net effect on their lifestyle, Carolyn replied that "two big gross incomes equal two big net incomes." (Shortly after the appointment, Joe Califano paid a visit to the nominee. As he stepped into the handsome entry-way, Fortas pointed to a hole in the foyer ceiling. "That, my friend, was to have been our central air conditioning," he said with a smile. "Now we won't be able to afford it." It was, by Califano's recollection, "the first of several complaints I heard Fortas make about the income that he would forfeit from his private law practice.")

Monetary concerns aside, Agger believed that her husband would do better to wait until Earl Warren retired so that he could ascend directly to the chief justiceship. "You don't treat friends that way," she snapped at LBJ when he telephoned her law office to extend a conciliatory gesture. She then proceeded to hang up on him. In confidence, Fortas told one of his law partners that he had "never heard anybody talk to the President like Carol did."

As an associate justice, Fortas contributed to building on the Warren Court's formidable legacy of liberal jurisprudence, including rulings on civil rights, privacy rights, and the rights of the accused that infuriated conservatives of both parties who were already unnerved by LBJ's expansion of the federal welfare state and desegregation of southern schools, hospitals, and places of public accommodation.

Even as he sat on the Court, Fortas remained an informal presidential adviser, and like most of the staff he was unconcerned by the seeming impropriety of the executive branch and the judicial branch colluding on matters of policy and politics. In an earlier era, Felix Frankfurter remained an informal counselor to FDR, even after joining the Court. "The President has got too much respect for the independence of the Court for that and wouldn't want to embarrass Abe," McPherson added. "But he has asked him an awful lot of things, which probably have gone on occasion too far."

If the impropriety of a justice serving as an informal presidential adviser was not so clear in 1968 as it would be in later years, the continued intensity of their relationship was extraordinary even by contemporary standards. LBJ ordered a direct White House line installed in Fortas's home and office, enabling the president to reach him at all times of the day. Between November 23, 1963, and early July 1968, when the president nominated him as chief justice, Fortas met with LBJ at least 145 times in person and spoke with him on countless occasions by phone. As associate justice, Fortas violated a bright red line when he knowingly shared important information with the president concerning Court deliberations and weighed in on matters of policy and constitutional law. In one case, he advised the administration on a matter involving the Interstate Commerce Commission's approval of a railroad merger and then participated in a Court case on the very same matter.

When Congress sent a stringent anticrime bill to the president in November 1966, LBJ sought Fortas's counsel. While the FBI director, J. Edgar Hoover, and Nicholas Katzenbach, the former attorney general now serving as undersecretary of state, advised the president to sign the measure, Fortas agreed with the White House staff, which was almost unanimous in its support of a veto. The justice believed that several provisions, including an antipornography title and extended authority to interrogate witnesses and suspects prior to an arraignment, were patently unconstitutional. He allowed that a section providing for mandatory sentences would likely survive judicial scrutiny, even if it was ill-advised. As was usually the case, the president heeded Fortas's advice. The associate justice and Califano drafted the veto message, which LBJ issued verbatim.

Harry McPherson would later recall a moment late in the evening on July 24, 1967, when rioters in Detroit had exhausted the capabilities of Michigan's state police and National Guard. He entered the Oval Office, only to find Abe Fortas polishing a draft of the president's televised address to the nation, in which Johnson would announce the deployment of military personnel to restore order in Motor City. McPherson disagreed with the tenor of the draft, which he believed gave excess weight to framing the legal justification for sending troops at the expense of discussing the social and economic roots of urban riots. But he did not press the point. "I was intimidated by the stature and the brains and the judgment and the reputation and my own relationship with Justice Fortas," he explained. "I was very much the junior man and although I would have argued with the President alone about it, I didn't argue with Justice Fortas." Fortas, a sitting associate justice, helped the president of the United States frame his justification for a decision that could well have faced legal scrutiny in the federal courts. The episode foreshadowed a larger conflict of interest that would later haunt both men.

"We on the White House staff ought not to be public figures," Bill Moyers told a reporter in April 1966. "It is not in our interest to have what we do publicized. . . . You aren't a man in your own right when you are working for a President. To be most effective you need to have an umbilical cord character, nature, and personality." Moyers was by this time seemingly unable to follow his own sound advice. Over the course of many days, he sat for interviews with the *New York Times*, which published a lengthy and glowing profile of the thirty-one-year-old wunderkind adviser. "I am *not* the president's 'Good Angel,'" Moyers averred. "I am *not* the president's conscience, as some people have written. To say that implies that he does not have motives and instincts and values with which I can identify. It was the President who taught me that power must have a purpose." It was not an interview likely to endear Moyers to the small, growing—but, for the time, silent—group of administration officials who cast a wary eye on the preacher-politician. Behind his back, they dismissed him as a modern-day "Elmer Gantry" and derided his combination of staged authenticity and "stiletto tactics." "Whatever he does," one critic sneered, "he does with every assurance that he is carrying out the will of John the Baptist."

George Reedy, whom Moyers replaced as press secretary, believed that LBJ had "a rather unfortunate predilection to flattery, which accounted to a tremendous extent for the Bill Moyers syndrome. And also I think that he's a little bit over-awed by self-confident people." Even Moyers's allies, including Harry McPherson, acknowledged that several of Moyers's staff assistants were more loyal to the Kennedys than to the president in whose White House they served. "They made it appear that all that was good, all that happened, that

Bill was a good angel; that Lyndon Johnson was really a kind of an evil old man, who was inclined always to do the wrong thing."

When Moyers told reporters that he had "developed a relationship with Lyndon Johnson that it takes a man a long time to carve out; I can't forfeit that," and that he could "interpret what I knew to be the 'Complete Johnson' to the bureaucracy. I was certain I knew what the president wanted"—or when the *New York Times* likened him to "Sherman Adams, Harry Hopkins, Colonel House and other well-remembered presidential advisors of the past"—it rankled those of his colleagues who envied that rapport and harbored suspicions about his motive and character. "He's an individual, not a team player," an anonymous colleague told the press. "He's out for himself." Jake Jacobsen later confided to an interviewer that "Moyers was always undercutting somebody. Or he'd call you in on his own and say, 'Now, Jake, so-and-so is just fixing to write a mean article about you, and I stopped him from doing it.' Well, about half the time that wasn't true at all." With bemused wonder, he remembered that "Moyers treated me about as bad as a man could be treated. Every time he'd get a chance to take a swipe at me he would. I don't know why. I had no animosity toward Bill."

LBJ appeared to tolerate his aide's public persona as the good angel on his shoulder, though another aide remarked anonymously that the president hardly required such prodding on domestic issues: "He's way out in front of the country there." He might also have forgiven the presumptuousness in Moyers's remark "I work for him despite his faults, and he lets me work for him despite my deficiencies." But as Johnson's relationship with the press frayed, a rift gradually emerged between the president and his young aide. He was the "ideal press secretary," the *New York Times* reported. "The press has been good to Moyers, and Moyers has been good to the press." He was "informed, concise, quotable," "unexcelled in the art of the leak and in the trial balloon, and in coaxing columnists, charming publishers and converting skeptical reporters." LBJ valued this aptitude when it operated in his favor, but not when his press secretary began to enjoy better coverage than the president. "There was much talk of a 'credibility gap' during his tenure," the *Times* continued, "but reporters tended to blame Johnson, not Moyers, for alleged inconsistencies on Vietnam policy."

By no means did every member of the press corps let Moyers off the hook.

He was a "slick operator, but he isn't particularly trustworthy," one anonymous correspondent offered on background. "A very smart guy, a master at the snow job," another journalist added. When the *Austin American-Statesman* surveyed reporters on the presidential beat, it found support for this assessment, though they also conceded that he was "by far the best man for his exacting job. If they think he sometimes falls short of telling the truth, the whole truth, and nothing but the truth—an allegation he denies—they also think that no one else could come close to explaining the President." Yet Moyers had also grown "more irritable lately." In his early days on the job, he seemed to enjoy the easy repartee and good-natured jousting, but in his reflexive instinct to return every volley, he gradually exposed himself to critics who thought he "would sometimes be better advised to simply say 'no comment' to some questions than to give partial answers that may lead reporters astray," as the *New York Times* observed. It was in some respects an impossible position. When Moyers heeded such advice and pulled back, "saying less in public briefings," others censured him for secrecy. By the middle of 1966, it dawned on him that the role might be his undoing.

When newspapermen caught him planting questions among reporters favorable to LBJ before regularly scheduled press conferences, Moyers reacted with pique, asserting that these events should serve the "convenience of the President, not the convenience of the press." It was Johnson's prerogative to use press availabilities to convey information that he wished to convey to the public, and like his predecessors under earlier administrations Moyers felt no compunction about pointing friendly journalists in the right direction. As a pack, the press corps "tends to write its opinions of a matter, and then to seek out facts for it." Too often, coverage of the administration demonstrated "very poor judgment" and was "very poorly informed." Clearly feeling the sting of criticism that he was a chief culprit behind the credibility gap, he argued that the president was better served when he spoke "directly to the people through radio and television, than if the people have to decide upon what some other human being—a subject to all the frailties of human nature—interprets as his intentions or his policy."

In mid-1966, Moyers attempted to transition out of his role as press secretary. Foreign policy—particularly the war in Vietnam—consumed ever more of his time and interest. After McGeorge Bundy resigned his post as national security adviser in February, reports surfaced that with one eye on that job Moyers was actively recruiting his own replacement as press secretary. Though in April LBJ appointed Walt Rostow, a Kennedy holdover, to replace Bundy, press reports explained that the new aide would share Bundy's responsibilities with Valenti and Moyers and that Moyers would be chiefly responsible for the Vietnam portfolio. The reshuffle was maddening for those unaccustomed to Johnson's White House, where, as one columnist explained, "titles mean nothing... and salaries among the half dozen highest ranking or so are at the same level and there are no clearly defined duties." But to those who could read the tea leaves, Moyers and Valenti were clearly ascendant in the field of foreign policy. With clear ambition to shift into Bundy's seat, that spring Moyers hired Robert Fleming, the former head of ABC's bureau in Washington, D.C. He would begin as deputy press secretary and then assume full responsibility for the role. Unfortunately for the president—and for Bill Moyers—the transition was a flop. Fleming proved ill-suited to the position, his "flippant and often uncooperative style" an irritant to the press corps, which was already predisposed to question the official White House line. More difficult still, Johnson never took to Fleming and froze him out—a fate akin to professional death for a press secretary. By September, an unhappy Moyers was back at his perch in the press room.

Public speculation about Moyers's potential career path—perhaps national security adviser, perhaps ambassador to Vietnam—only served to poison further his relationship with Johnson. By Jack Valenti's recollection, Moyers campaigned too assiduously for promotion. When Valenti proposed his name as a replacement for Bundy, the president, "a little vexed" at the suggestion, replied tartly that Moyers did not "have the experience and the background for the job."

That autumn, it became conventional wisdom in Washington that Moyers was the administration's chief dove and had for some time urged the president to seek a peaceful way out of Southeast Asia. This narrative vastly overstated Moyers's independence from the administration's foreign policy consensus. At a dinner party toward the end of Johnson's presidency, Jack Valenti and his wife shared a table with Arthur Schlesinger, who grumbled that "LBJ had not listened to the war advice of Bill Moyers when he was a presidential aide." "But, Arthur," Valenti protested, "Bill held no such view, at least not before midyear 1966. He was as much in favor of massive intervention as the President. If he wasn't, he never let anyone know his true feelings. The president made it clear to me many times that with the exception of [Undersecretary of State] George Ball, no higher official in the government was opposed to our position and that includes *every* White House aide."

By late 1966, those nearest the president knew that he had tired of reading that Moyers was his "intelligent social conscience." He came to suspect that Moyers was the source of multiple leaks emanating from the West Wing, and indeed, as Harry McPherson would attest, "Bill had adopted a method of operation that included an awful lot of backgrounding on what the President was really doing, and most of it was intended to push the President—to show the President as a liberal and a bit to push the President as well." By George Reedy's estimation—and, increasingly, LBJ's—Moyers was interested less in pushing Johnson to the left than in convincing reporters of his own ideological independence from the president.

Moyers was "fairly near a snapping point," McPherson recalled. In late September, his older brother committed suicide at age thirty-nine, leaving Bill both deeply anguished and with an added financial burden to provide for his sister-in-law and her children. His own marriage was purportedly under strain, the natural result of punishing hours and unrelenting responsibilities. His "once-close personal relationship with Lyndon Johnson was crumbling," said another colleague. "His ambition," Jake Jacobsen believed, "just about ran him into the ground." Early in 1967, Moyers announced his decision to leave the White House for New York, where he would succeed the legendary Harry Guggenheim as publisher of *Newsday*, then still a nationally influential newspaper. The break with Johnson was bitter. "I don't think the President cried very many tears when Bill left," an aide recalled. The day after he departed the White House, Moyers accepted Bobby Kennedy's invitation to lunch at Sans Souci, a restaurant popular with the capital's power crowd. As they broke bread, a news photographer quickly snapped a picture of the two men.

Moyers remained ambivalent. In the coming months, even as he settled into his new life in New York, he sent feelers—first, to determine whether the president might appoint him to run the Peace Corps. When, "after a while that got to be not enough . . . he wanted to become Under Secretary of State very badly." The UN ambassador, Arthur Goldberg, and Secretary of Defense Robert McNamara were supportive of his aspiration and urged LBJ to bring Moyers back to Washington. But the president proved unbending.

When Moyers conveyed his torment over his break with Johnson, Abe Fortas advised that "it is always a mistake to think in terms of resuming a relationship, or any part of it, which has been characterized by such intimacy or interdependence." It was wise counsel. LBJ and Moyers would never repair the breach.

Even before Moyers's departure, it became increasingly clear that Joe Califano had emerged as the White House official chiefly responsible for managing, expanding, and—as Johnson's slip on power grew more pronounced—preserving the Great Society. He was a skilled political operator. He also showed little compunction about "inhaling other secretaries and staff people," according to Jacobsen, who privately regarded him as "an empire builder" and "would not trust him around the corner"—"nobody liked Califano," he claimed in a moment of candor—but conceded that he was "bright as hell" and "a fine assistant to the President." By 1967, he had assembled a crack staff that included James Gaither, a former law clerk to Chief Justice Earl Warren, who served as the principal liaison with the White House task forces; Fred Bohen, a young assistant dean at Princeton University's Woodrow Wilson School; and Matthew Nimetz, who graduated first in his class at Harvard Law School before clerking for Justice John Marshall Harlan II. Their average age was thirty-two, and by one colleague's estimation they "quite possibly topped anything the White House had ever seen. Writers, composers, lawyers, economists, dreamers, slaves—each of them was a little of all."

Despite his age, and that of his core staff, Califano brought managerial expertise that proved essential to the Great Society's ambitious expansion of the federal state. When he came to the West Wing, Califano carried over the Planning, Programming, and Budgeting System (PPBS) that Robert McNamara had initiated at the Pentagon, to great public acclaim. Before its adoption, different defense agencies with overlapping mandates jockeyed each year over funding for pet projects. It was an inefficient and costly way of budgeting. Originally the brainchild of researchers at the Rand Corporation, PPBS leveraged advanced quantitative modeling and economic analysis to establish long-range program goals and multiyear budget models. The system was meant to smooth out interagency rivalries, eliminate duplicative initiatives, and create spending and operational efficiencies. It was a "rational concept," McPherson believed, "but difficult to practice." It required skillful negotiations with members of Congress who viewed spending and procurement decisions as inherently political. Califano's management discipline proved critical as the administration shifted from imagining new initiatives to securing a durable future for them. Some of the Great Society's signature components required multiyear congressional reauthorizations and appropriations. Califano's insistence on more rigorous budgeting processes armed the administration with powerful tools in its successful effort to preserve and extend the life of these programs through the following decade.

By 1967, Califano's talents were in high demand. Faced with the need to placate liberals who demanded a steady expansion of existing Great Society programs and conservative Democrats and Republicans who in the aftermath of the off-year elections enjoyed renewed influence—particularly in the House—the administration had to show dexterity at the negotiating table. That year, Califano and Cater hammered out a compromise set of amendments to the Social Security Act that raised the payroll tax (much to the chagrin of liberals, who viewed this measure as a means to obscure and offset the war's drain on the regular budget) to fund a 13 percent increase in retirement benefits. This measure helped lift many elderly Americans above the poverty line. The amendments also loosened Medicare's reimbursement process—a boon to doctors, who could now submit "reasonable" charges for such procedures as X-rays and radiology directly to the government. But the White House had to swallow caps on Medicaid, an opening salvo in a decades-long effort by conservatives to constrain the program's growth, as well as new work training requirements for recipients of AFDC. The administration was even less successful that year in persuading Congress to approve a modest appropriation of $40 million to help cities pay for rodent control. "The knowledge that many children in the world's most affluent nation are attacked, maimed, and even killed by rats should fill every American with shame," the president told House and Senate members. The initiative quickly foundered as Newark erupted in flames. Conservatives seized upon the riots as confirmation that black ghetto residents were lawless and beyond redemption. "Let's buy a lot of cats and turn them lose," a southern Democrat cackled from the House floor. "Civil rats!" another member catcalled from the rear of the chamber. Martha Griffiths, a liberal congresswoman from Michigan, was appalled by her colleagues' insensitivity. "If you're going to spend seventy-nine billion dollars to kill off a few Vietcong," she intoned, "I'd spend forty million dollars to kill off the most devastating enemy that man has ever had." Her plea fell on deaf ears; the House rejected LBJ's proposal by a wide majority.

Fred Panzer, a staff assistant responsible broadly for research and analysis, likened the Republican Party's new approach to domestic policy to "the great Detroit-style wars of the late 50s when tailfins and chromium were the automakers' weapons of choice. To match all the new features of the LBJ-product—Medicare, war on poverty, model cities, federal aid to education, air and water pollution control, and extensive government reorganization—the GOP has unveiled its new 1967 'Kandy-Kolored, Tangerine-Flake, Streamline' model. What they have done is to bolt a flashy 'leopard' body onto their basic 'elephant' chasis [sic]. They are market-testing names for it right now." In place of ESEA, they offered block grants to states, with minimal federal oversight—a "handy gimmick" that Panzer rated "unsafe for school children." To supplant the War on Poverty, the GOP proposed a hollow "dismantling device" that they called the "Opportunity Crusade." Rather than public housing vouchers, the "Gerry[sic] Ford 'home ownership' clutch," which would effectively act as a subsidy for middle-class families and do little for impoverished urban residents. The administration successfully protected its programs from the newly resurgent congressional coalition of conservative Republicans and southern Democrats, but preservation gradually replaced innovation as a staff priority.

Despite increasingly trenchant backlash, Califano left a considerable mark in his tenure as domestic policy chief. At LBJ's urging, he played a driving role in creating a new cabinet agency, the Department of Transportation, that would streamline the efforts of over thirty disparate agencies and bureaus then dedicated to coordinating federal transportation policy. The president demanded a holistic approach that would improve the country's transportation infrastructure "radically, looking not only to the next year, but to 1980, the year 2000 and beyond." He aspired not just to restructure the existing collage of fiefdoms but to "invigorate" and "modernize" an ailing grid of roads, waterways, railroads, and airports that were built to support a smaller, more dispersed nation. Though Americans spent $120 billion in aggregate on transportation—accounting for one-sixth of economic output—Johnson maintained that the country's system of "aging and often obsolete plant and equipment" and infra-structure built to support a bygone agrarian economy would hobble future eco-nomic growth. A dedicated cabinet agency could act "as a full partner with private enterprise in meeting America's urgent need for mobility."

The negotiations, which stretched over the better part of 1966, proved thorny. The Treasury Department jealously held to its stewardship of the Coast Guard. ("[W]hat is it?" the president ribbed Secretary of the Treasury Henry Fowler. "Do you have a boat, a yacht, a plane you want to keep? Is it the Coast Guard mess you want to keep? Do you like to wear a Coast Guard uni-form?") Management and labor representatives from the waning maritime industry—with support from the AFL-CIO—looked with disfavor on consoli-dation, fearing it might cost them their public subsidies. John McClellan, the powerful senator from Arkansas whose committee claimed jurisdiction over the enabling legislation, demanded that the administration alter its criteria for approving waterway projects. In short, multiple constituencies threatened to scuttle the project over parochial concerns. When Califano caved on several of McClellan's key demands, LBJ rose from his chair and fixed his intense stare on the young aide. "Open your fly," he instructed. Califano laughed obligingly, "knowing he wasn't serious but surprised nonetheless."

"Unzip your fly," the president repeated, "because there's nothing there. John McClellan just cut it off with a razor so sharp you didn't even notice it."

The president proceeded to reach the errant senator by telephone. "John," he began, "I'm calling about Joe Califano. You cut his pecker off and put it in your desk drawer. Now I'm sending him back up there to get it from you. I can't agree to anything like that. You've got to realize that the transportation system of the country needs something besides more highways in Arkansas."

The legislation, which Johnson signed in October 1966, was a singular accomplishment, as was the Traffic Safety Act, which Congress sent to LBJ's desk several weeks earlier. It provided grants to states to improve road design and safety, required automobile manufacturers to enhance safety perfor-mance, and established a national research and test center for highway safety. Califano, who was instrumental in securing passage of both measures, would play an equally critical role in overseeing the creation of the Department of Transportation and the growth of its mandate and resources.

· · · · ·

If Califano played the driving role in expanding and securing the administration's Great Society initiatives in 1966 and 1967, his closest collaborator was Harry McPherson. Ostensibly the president's chief counsel—a role in which he served as legislative and administrative draftsman and primary liaison to the Department of Justice—he gradually assumed an enhanced portfolio that included mediating labor and industry disputes and, alongside Califano, coordinating rapid response during the perennial outburst of urban riots during the "long hot summers" between 1965 and 1968. In what became a painfully familiar routine, the White House would dispatch Deputy Secretary of Defense Cyrus Vance or Deputy Attorney General Warren Christopher to coordinate with local elected officials and to serve as the administration's on-site liaison to National Guard units called up to quell the disturbance. During the first wave of uprisings, the administration found itself at a disadvantage. For several years, the Department of Justice had "operated a very extensive network throughout the South," McPherson explained. When violence erupted in a southern city like Selma or Meridian, it had informants on the ground—a "lawyer or a judge or an elected official" who would "call from that part of the country and say there is going to be trouble tonight, and there is going to be physical violence." But that was in the South. No such web of local contacts and informants existed in the North, where most urban riots occurred. Determined to build better relationships and understanding, in late 1967 and early 1968 McPherson traveled with White House colleagues on a fact-finding tour of ghetto neighborhoods in New York, Chicago, Cleveland, and Baltimore, among other cities. He acknowledged that it was a "desultory way of getting information about the black poor to the President": "We knew we could not learn much about [the communities] in the course of a long weekend. What we hoped to gain was a sense of how the people who lived there felt about their future: specifically, whether they thought conditions might be improved through peaceful processes or only through violence; or that nothing would help." Still expecting that Johnson would serve a second full term and that the war would come to an end in the foreseeable future, the White House staff continued to look for ways to quell urban unrest.

Goodwin left the White House in late 1965; Valenti, Busby, and Moyers, in 1966. All four aides had played a leading role in helping the president articulate his vision. In their absence, McPherson gradually assumed unacknowledged status as Johnson's chief speechwriter, in addition to his role as chief counsel. "My job was to make staying with it in Vietnam, and in the ghettos, sound compelling and necessary," he remembered—objectives that were increasingly difficult to meet as LBJ entered the last year of his term.

After leaving the White House, Moyers privately credited McPherson with keeping a "steady hand on an erratic wheel"—a role, he claimed, that "has never been fully explained or understood. Perhaps it never will be except to a few of us." In acknowledgment of his own reputation for political cunning, he suggested that had McPherson "only been a former preacher and a few years younger, with a calculating penchant for intrigue, you might have gained the notoriety which your personal talents deserve, but then you would not have been Harry McPherson and you would not have lasted as long or been as effective as you have." George Christian, who succeeded Moyers as press secretary, would later agree with this confidential assessment. McPherson was less interested in power than in "peace of mind. He dodged the power struggles as best he could and concentrated on influencing the President with the written word; his hand was in virtually every Presidential utterance on major policy." He also succeeded, where no others did, in "living a private life of his own." McPherson "occasionally left home with his family without telling the White House switchboard where he was going. More importantly, he was the only one who got away with it."

LBJ once told McPherson that it did not "matter what kind of a majority you come in with. You've got just about a year when they treat you right, and before they start worrying about themselves. The third year, you lose votes; if this war goes on, I'll lose a lot of 'em. A lot of our people don't belong here, they're in Republican seats, and the Republicans will get them back. The fourth year's all politics. You can't put anything through when half the Congress is thinking how to beat you. So you've got one year. That's why I tried. Well, we gave it a hell of a lick, didn't we?" Johnson had knowingly spent down his political capital on civil rights and the Vietnam War. He exited 1967 in full knowledge that his reelection was far from inevitable. For his aides, this uncertainty lent added urgency to their efforts to build a secure future for the president's Great Society legacy.

CHAPTER 13

The Thirty-first of March

By the close of 1967, over 500,000 American troops were bogged down in Southeast Asia. More than 15,000 had been killed in action. Within twelve months, the casualty count would almost double. The war was "all people talked about at cocktail parties or across the back fence," recalled Senator George McGovern of South Dakota. "It was the transcendent issue in American politics. If you lived in Washington, it was the only issue." As Lyndon Johnson's approval rating plummeted from 61 percent in early 1966 to 38 percent in October 1967, the former vice president Richard Nixon, now earning a lucrative salary as managing partner of a prestigious New York law firm, slowly rebuilt his political base. The consummate campaigner, Nixon had traveled the country on behalf of Barry Goldwater in 1964, delivering over 150 speeches in thirty-six states and accumulating goodwill among grassroots conservatives who resented the refusal of moderate and liberal Republicans to work for the party's right-wing nominee. In 1966, Nixon accelerated his political activities, headlining dozens of fund-raisers for congressional candidates and delivering over 600 speeches in forty states. When the party netted 540 state legislative seats, 47 House seats, and 3 Senate seats that year, Nixon—whose political operation already employed full-time advance men and speechwriters—emerged as a leading contender for the presidential nomination in 1968. He was conservative enough to please many Goldwater supporters but moderate enough to calm the nerves of centrist Republicans. Rumors of his political demise, it turned out, had been greatly exaggerated.

Dick Scammon, the former census director whose survey work informed Moyers's and Valenti's messaging strategy four years earlier, conceded the likelihood of Nixon's nomination but considered him "a born loser." The race would likely be very close—Republican candidates had won two of the past four presidential elections and racked up a cumulative advantage of roughly

100,000 votes out of roughly 262 million cast. In effect, the LBJ landslide in 1964 had been an outlier event. The default setting in American politics was near deadlock. But by no stretch of the imagination was the race unwinnable. The key to besting Nixon (or Ronald Reagan or Nelson Rockefeller) was to focus intently on the middle-American voter. "He is un-young. He is un-black. He is un-poor," Scammon said. As Doug Cater explained to the president, "This suggests that campaign strategy should be carefully aimed at the white, middle-aged, middle-class voters—'the people,' in Scammon's phrase, 'who bowl regularly.'" Pointing to recent backlash votes against open housing in California and a police review board in otherwise liberal New York City in 1966, Scammon advised a centrist approach to the two topics that would almost certainly dominate the coming election: Vietnam and urban riots. To win, the president would have to steer a middle course on the war and "couple any 'help the ghetto' programs with a campaign to 'get tough with rioters.'" In effect, Scammon discovered America's "Silent Majority" two years before Nixon coined the very term. But as an incumbent president weighted down by war, riots, campus unrest, and an inflationary economy, Johnson was not well positioned to appeal to the sensibilities of that broad center of the national electorate.

A consummate political animal, Johnson proved unusually slow to focus on his reelection effort, his days increasingly given to urgent meetings with his national security advisers. In late 1967, his aides implored him to act. "I believe we are going to have a real battle for survival next year," cautioned James Roche, a political scientist who joined the White House staff the year before. Robert Kennedy was still an untested and undeclared candidate for the Democratic nomination, but Roche believed that any attempt to challenge an incumbent president for the party's nomination would inevitably result in a Republican general election victory. Above all, he implored, it was time to "break the administration out of the 'siege' mentality which is a form of defeatism.... The 1968 campaign is going to be a real slug-fest and your supporters should get in training." In November, Johnson begrudgingly convened a group of trusted hands—Marvin Watson, who would run the campaign's operations; Larry O'Brien, who would direct its political shop from his new perch as postmaster general; Jim Rowe, the mastermind of Harry Truman's improbable victory some two decades earlier; and other members of the senior staff—to assemble the shell of an organization. But the president himself cast only one eye on politics as he searched despairingly for a way out of the Vietnam quagmire.

LBJ's advisers firmly believed that the standard political playbook would prove unequal to the new dynamic—a dynamic that Larry O'Brien confidentially laid out for the political reporter Teddy White as the year wound to a close. "New forces were changing the country," White recalled. "The middle class now included all of the working class, too—why, Walter Reuther now had strikes without pickets, no passion. Workingmen used Labor Day to clean out the basement or fix up the playroom, and the traditional political kick-off of a Democratic campaign before the auto workers in Detroit on Labor Day meant nothing; last time the unions couldn't even fill up Cobo Hall." Even if Scammon's centrist messaging was correct, the president's team would need to develop an entirely fresh approach to engaging newly affluent working-class and middle-class families who had turned against the Great Society's civil rights agenda and who were deeply divided over the Vietnam War. More perplexing to O'Brien were twelve million first-time voters—young men and women in their early twenties—who would be eligible to participate in the election. "These were the uncommitted children of the middle class, seeking new causes," White related. "You had to go out after them and bring them in. Yet even O'Brien's perceptive analysis was oriented only to the clash with the Republicans in the November elections . . . it was unthinkable that a sitting President of the United States could be un-horsed within his own Party either by primaries, conventions or riot in the streets."

The one person of consequence who first perceived an opportunity to "un-horse" the sitting president was Allard K. Lowenstein, a thirty-eight-year-old veteran organizer and Yale-educated attorney who had spent the better part of fifteen years moving from one university teaching or administrative post to another, all the while insinuating himself in various civil rights and antiwar campaigns. Teddy White sized him up as a "permeant youth leader. Wiry yet frail, balding early, his eyes compelling behind their black horn-rimmed eyeglasses, a non-smoker and non-drinker, Lowenstein was a one-man excitement wherever he moved." Throughout the late summer and fall, Lowenstein traveled the country, coalescing antiwar party activists and students at the local level into a loose coalition that would seek to deny Johnson renomination the following year. "I said we'll build the base first, [then] the candidate will come along," he explained. Building the base was easier than expected. Recruiting a credible challenger proved more daunting. He approached first Robert Kennedy, who took the meeting out of courtesy to his young staff members, then George McGovern, then the retired lieutenant general James Gavin, a liberal who had served briefly as ambassador to France and who now argued that America was squandering resources in Vietnam that could be put to better use in the urban ghetto. All three men turned him down. Finally, Lowenstein approached Eugene McCarthy, the senior senator from Minnesota. It took several conversations, but when McCarthy asked, "How do you think we'd do in a Wisconsin primary?" Lowenstein knew he had found his candidate. "I was ecstatic," he said. "It was like music, like an organ welling up in my ears."

When McCarthy formally announced his candidacy, most observers believed that he was on a suicide mission. There was good reason why he was Lowenstein's last call. A devout Catholic and former college instructor, though he had won election five times to the House and twice to the Senate, he was a cold, aloof character. A loner who seldom partook of the capital's lively social scene, he often holed himself up in his Senate office, reading poetry, appearing on the floor only to cast a vote before returning to the solitary confines of his hideaway, which he preferred to the glad-handing ways of the Democratic cloakroom. Notwithstanding the normal challenges of unseating an incumbent president, McCarthy was a lazy and diffident candidate. He refused to appear before the multitude of state organizing conferences that were desperate to meet their newly anointed standard-bearer and kept Lowenstein and his staff at arm's length. Disengaged from campaign strategy and unfamiliar with many of the staff members and local activists whom Lowenstein recruited for the effort, he had to be cajoled into canvassing on his own behalf. During his fifteen-day campaign swing through New Hampshire, he routinely skipped scheduled events, refused to make obligatory early-morning appearances at factory gates ("I'm not really a morning person," he explained), and delivered dry, pretentiously cerebral speeches that tended to anesthetize, rather than galvanize, his audiences. When Johnny Carson, the host of NBC's popular *Tonight Show*, asked what sort of president he would be, McCarthy replied, "I think I would be adequate." Polling initially had him below 10 percent, and even his staff members found his lackluster performance uninspiring. Many of them would have much preferred to work for Bobby Kennedy. But Kennedy was not running.

On January 30, 1968, the political winds shifted. Some sixty-seven thousand Vietcong troops launched a massive invasion of South Vietnamese cities on the eve of the Tet New Year's celebration. Known thereafter as the Tet Offensive, the military campaign lasted several months and ultimately cost the Vietcong enormous troop losses, but it fundamentally shook the confidence of many Americans who had believed the administration's assurances that the United States was turning the corner in Southeast Asia and that the enemy's resources were nearly spent. For weeks on end, television viewers absorbed the shock of evening news reports that portrayed the enemy as well stocked, resilient, and nowhere near surrender. Support for the war plummeted sharply. A Gallup poll showed that the portion of Americans describing themselves as "hawks" dropped from 60 percent to 41 percent, while the portion of those calling themselves "doves" rose from 24 percent to 42 percent. Antiwar activists who had long represented minority opinion now saw an opportunity to build a broad-based coalition in opposition to the war. Suddenly the unthinkable seemed possible.

If McCarthy was disengaged—on one occasion, inquiring newsmen in search of the candidate, who had failed to appear at his own event, found him dining alone in a hotel restaurant with the poet Robert Lowell—his young staff and volunteers were anything but. From their headquarters at the Sheraton-Wayfarer hotel in Manchester, Dick Goodwin—a fervent critic of the war who was now determined to force his ex-boss into retirement—assumed day-to-day control over the ragtag, amateur operation. Suddenly there were professional and disciplined radio and television spots saturating New Hampshire's airwaves and a massive field operation well suited to New Hampshire's peculiar brand of retail politics. Students from Harvard, Yale, Amherst, Smith, Mount Holyoke, and other New England colleges flooded the state—by some estimates, three thousand strong. "They came with sleeping bags and ski boots," White wrote, "like a Boy Scout camp-out, bringing with them the youthful talent for improvised organization. . . . Bearded students had sacrificed their beards so as not to alarm the citizens on their rounds; blue jeans and sweatshirts were also proscribed. . . . All were as neat, tidy and wholesome as their parents had ever hoped they would be." Sympathetic locals housed them in spare bedrooms, in church and synagogue basements, and on living room floors. "What is happening is that violet-eyed damsels from Smith are pinning McCarthy buttons on tattooed mill-workers," observed the veteran political journalist Mary McGrory, "and Ph.D.s from Cornell, shaven and shorn for world peace, are deferentially bowing to middle-aged Manchester housewives and importuning them to consider a change in Commander-in-Chief." On-site to cover the primary, White found that "Hampshiremen and their wives loved it." "These college kids are fabulous," the chairman of the Nashua Democratic City Committee crowed. "There are so many people who have kids of their own of the same age, and they can't talk to their own kids, it's another generation. These kids knock at the door, and come in politely, and actually want to talk to grown-ups, and people are delighted."

On March 12, McCarthy scored a stunning near upset in the New Hampshire primary, winning 42 percent of the vote to Lyndon Johnson's 49 percent. The candidate was, as always, confident but wryly diffident. "I think I can get the nomination," he told reporters. "I'm ahead now. We'll be able to finance our Wisconsin campaign after what happened here yesterday, we'll be able to pay our hotel bills."

While McCarthy's team picked up stakes and headed for Wisconsin, Robert Kennedy remained racked by uncertainty. Since December, his inner circle had hotly debated the merits of challenging LBJ. His young aides Adam Walinsky and Peter Edelman strongly favored entering the race. Kenneth O'Donnell believed that Bobby would likely lose but argued that some things were worth losing for. Others were less certain. Edward Kennedy and Ted Sorensen feared that Bobby would accomplish little other than to divide the liberal camp in two and tarnish his own reputation as an antiwar leader. Larry O'Brien—still a member of Johnson's cabinet and deeply involved in the president's reelection campaign—kept a respectful distance from the deliberations. Outside RFK's inner circles, signals were equally mixed. From California, Jesse Unruh, the powerful speaker of the state assembly, urged Bobby to enter the fray. In Chicago, Mayor Richard Daley—who opposed the war and had warned Johnson that it would prove the undoing of the Great Society—signaled an unwillingness to break with the president. In late January, even in the wake of the Tet Offensive, Bobby maintained his public insistence that he would not be a candidate.

And then came the New Hampshire primary. That evening, Kennedy telephoned McCarthy's headquarters to congratulate his colleague on a stunning upset. Goodwin, who answered the call, was elated by the returns but delivered an uncomfortable ultimatum: The hour had come to make a definitive decision. Bobby must enter the race or endorse McCarthy. Four days later, Kennedy announced his candidacy from the same Senate Caucus Room where JFK launched his own campaign in 1960. "We woke up after the New Hampshire primary, like it was Christmas day," said a young McCarthy volunteer. "And when we went down to the tree, we found Bobby Kennedy had stolen our Christmas presents." Though Goodwin immediately quit the campaign and joined Bobby's team, most McCarthy staff members and foot soldiers were appalled by what they perceived as RFK's ruthless and self-serving ambition. Over the next eight weeks, the two antiwar senators would hurl more fire at each other than at the president whom they had both grown to loathe and mistrust.

Six days after the New Hampshire primary, Harry McPherson outlined his understanding of the race in a lengthy memorandum to the president. Of the six likely candidates for president—Democrats Johnson, McCarthy, and Kennedy; Republicans Rockefeller and Nixon; and independent George Wallace—LBJ carried the most political baggage. The 1968 cycle would culminate in a change election, he argued, and as "the incumbent president you are (to some degree, at least) the natural defender of the status quo. You represent things as they are—the course we are following, the policies and programs we have chosen. Therefore, you are the most conservative of the six—the man who is not calling for change, but resisting it. This is a tough position today." Consider, he said, the others: Wallace, the candidate of rage and backlash (McPherson dismissed his base of support as "unreachable by us"); Nixon, a "modified version of the Wallace change"; Rockefeller, the "Republican Kennedy"; McCarthy, the only proponent of an "all-out dove policy"; and Kennedy, who would pledge to "bridge the gap" between hawk and dove, black and white, business and labor, and who—as his brother had done to Nixon and

Eisenhower eight years earlier—would position himself as the candidate of "vitality" against Johnson, the very image of "staleness and weariness." He urged the president to break out of the pack by announcing a sharp change in tactics in Vietnam—with more focus on holding key cities and less emphasis on racking up body count—as the first step in a wider de-escalation. "It seems to me that we are not going to win a military victory, in the ordinary meaning of that term." He further counseled an emergency summit of fifty big-city mayors to identify a wide range of measures to reduce tension within minority communities and to restore law and order. "You should try to be neither the toughest police chief in the country, nor sympathetic with rioters because of the conditions they live in." In a nod to the depressing reality of recent years, McPherson assumed that there would be riots that summer and that these riots would assume political importance in the lead-up to the fall campaign. The president, he believed, should keep rhetoric to a minimum but demonstrate strong leadership by committing troops to restore order at the earliest instance of violence. Finally, he advocated a heavy travel schedule. Johnson could not run an Oval Office or front-porch race. He would inevitably have to "risk a lot of heckling and picketing. Otherwise the contrast with McCarthy, Kennedy, Rockefeller and Nixon will be obvious and damaging—they can speak to the American people, you cannot." LBJ should arrange rallies and speeches in cities like Philadelphia, Charlotte, New Orleans, Albuquerque, Denver, Memphis, Rochester, St. Louis—anywhere there was not a "large activist campus or peace movement in town"—and "create the impression that you can go anywhere."

The president's other aides and advisers were equally restive. Jim Rowe warned that the president must take "dramatic and exciting" action immediately. The "dove" position had gained irreversible traction in recent weeks, and if Johnson did not transform himself from the "Win the War" candidate to the "Peace with Honor" candidate, he might lose the upcoming Wisconsin primary. The committee had canvassed 400 party officials nationwide, of whom 399 had committed to the president's campaign. But a popular rejection at the polls would cause many of those leaders to reconsider their course.

Several weeks earlier, Clark Clifford replaced Robert McNamara as defense secretary. Increasingly despondent and certain that the war had been a tragic mistake, McNamara had left office an emotional wreck. His successor, a hardened veteran of Washington politics who had consistently supported LBJ's war policy in his capacity as a private adviser, spent his first days at the Pentagon taking stock of the situation. He quickly determined that what the generals were requesting to "win" the war—an additional 206,000 combat troops and an additional $12 billion in budget (above and beyond the existing appropriation)—was politically untenable. The South Vietnamese government had proven itself unwilling to pull its weight. Regional allies in Asia were reluctant to enter the fight. McNamara had arrived at the right conclusion: the time had come to de-escalate. Johnson's circle of security advisers and "wise men"— Omar Bradley, Walt Rostow, Dean Rusk, George Ball, Arthur Dean, McGeorge Bundy—all agreed. The only holdouts in the group were Abe Fortas and Maxwell Taylor, the former chairman of the Joint Chiefs of Staff. The president assigned McPherson the task of preparing a dramatic, televised address in which he would announce a sharp curtailment of bombings and an offer to cease the bombings altogether and return to the peace table with North Vietnam. For one of the few times in his presidency, LBJ would also speak in complete candor to the American people about the financial costs of the war and the resultant need to pass a temporary tax surcharge and reduce nonmilitary expenditures in the coming year.

On Saturday, March 30, the president phoned Horace Busby to inform him of the pending announcement, which he planned to make during a televised speech the next evening. "I was jubilant," Busby remembered. "Such a startling reversal of American policy must mean that Hanoi had already sent assurances that the proposal would be accepted."

"No," the president replied, "we have heard nothing from Hanoi, not a whisper, not a wink. . . . It's only a roll of the dice. I'm shoving all my stack on this one." Johnson asked his former aide to review McPherson's draft. "I am going to send a driver out to your house for Sunday night," he explained. "It'll take him at least an hour to get there. While he's on his way, I wish you would sit down and write out for me what you and I were talking about in January. Have the driver bring it back in here to me. I want to look it over, and I may consider using it."

Busby remembered very well what he had discussed with the president in January.

Johnson understood what Harry McPherson did not: he could not engage in a hard-fought campaign to retain the White House while also attempting to negotiate peace in Vietnam. He certainly could not travel from city to city, where he would meet with enraged protesters, and govern a country that was on the cusp of yet another long, hot summer marred by urban violence. When Busby arrived at the White House on Sunday—a secretary had called him shortly after midnight with instructions to arrive early that morning—he found Johnson drained and weary but still undecided as to whether he would use the new, concluding paragraph. "The biggest reason to do it is just one thing," he murmured. "I want out of this cage."

LBJ had already telephoned Hubert Humphrey with news of his potential withdrawal from the race. The vice president doubted that he could take the nomination away from Bobby; this factor, too, weighed on Johnson's mind. Without an office, Busby camped out in the Treaty Room, where he polished his proposed conclusion. Gradually, the president informed other staff members of what he was considering. "Are you for it?" Busby asked Marie Fehmer, one of Johnson's senior secretaries. "I am not," she replied "firmly and coolly." Marvin Watson, too, was "visibly unhappy." Early that evening, as Buzz sat outside Johnson's bedroom door, Watson approached with a glower and opened the door to the inner sanctum. "I see you have had a very good day," he barked. "I knew what this meant," recalled Busby. "Marvin Watson would express himself clearly and unmistakably, but also with faultless propriety. . . . Since morning, I had had more than my share of time alone with the president; Marvin Watson deserved time alone now. I made no move to follow."

At 9:00 p.m., the president began his televised address. Forty minutes later, as he concluded, Lyndon Johnson announced that he would not seek or accept his party's nomination for another term as president.

Throughout the spring, as Nixon solidified his delegate count and plotted a general election strategy, Kennedy and McCarthy battled it out in several hotly contested primaries. It would prove to be one of the bloodiest seasons in American political history. In early April, an assassin gunned down Martin Luther King Jr. in Memphis, where the civil rights leader had joined striking sanitation workers. His death sparked another wave of urban unrest, including riots in Washington, D.C., that were visible from the White House. Two months later, Bobby Kennedy was assassinated in the kitchen of the Ambassador Hotel in Los Angeles, just moments after declaring victory in California's hard-fought primary. "The world has never been more disorderly within memory of living man," the journalist Walter Lippmann wrote that year.

By August, when the Democratic National Convention opened in Chicago, well over two-thirds of primary voters had supported either McCarthy or Kennedy, candidates who called for a negotiated settlement of the war in Southeast Asia. By contrast, only 2.2 percent of voters had supported Hubert Humphrey, Johnson's heir apparent, who reluctantly echoed the administration line on Vietnam and who had not competed in a single primary. Others had cast their votes for favorite-son candidates who could be expected to support the incumbent president or his chosen successor.

If the will of the voters determined the outcome, the Democrats would have nominated an antiwar liberal. But in 1968 only fifteen states chose their delegates by primary. Almost three-fifths of convention delegates were selected by county committeemen, state party apparatchiks, and elected officials. As early as June 2, even before Kennedy's assassination, the vice president's advisers had sewn up enough delegates to secure the nomination. Humphrey did not need grassroots support to win; he only needed the party bosses.

Given the sharp divisions within the party—hawks versus doves, young against old, blue-collar versus white-collar, McCarthy supporters against Kennedy supporters, McCarthy *and* Kennedy supporters against Humphrey's machine—it was almost inevitable that the Democrats would fight and fracture, as indeed they did. Amid reports that various groups planned to disrupt the convention's proceedings, Richard J. Daley, the legendary Chicago mayor and party fixer, mobilized twelve thousand city policemen, five thousand National Guardsmen, and six thousand federal troops to stand watch over the city. Ironically, Daley had gradually evolved from hawk to qualified dove. He no longer felt the war could be won, and he feared that the war might hurt down-ballot Democratic candidates in the fall election. But he was a party man through and through, and he would not brook disruption or dissent—not in his city and not on his watch.

It was true that several organized groups intended to demonstrate in Chicago. Under the direction of Abbie Hoffman and Jerry Rubin, the "Yippies," a motley band of agitators who combined New Left politics with street-theater tactics, had all sorts of wonders planned for the benefit of Humphrey's supporters. Among their designs: having one thousand nudists stage a float-in in Lake Michigan, enlisting 230 "hyper-potent" men to seduce the wives and daughters of prominent delegates, injecting LSD into Chicago's water supply, and sending hundreds of activists into the streets to throw handfuls of rice at passersby. Slightly less menacing—but only just—were members of the National Mobilization Committee to End the War (the MOBE), who had orchestrated the highly successful 1967 spring demonstration that drew hundreds of thousands of antiwar protesters into the streets nationwide. Finally, there were Gene McCarthy's supporters, who were deeply embittered that the party was about to crown a man who had not competed in a single presidential primary.

The convention descended into chaos. Inside the hall, city policemen treated pro-McCarthy delegates brutally, refusing entrance to Lowenstein, who was not only a delegate from New York but also a Democratic nominee for Congress that fall, and roughing up Alex Rosenberg, a delegate who headed New York City's most important Democratic reform club. "I wasn't sentenced and sent here!" Rosenberg screamed as the police dragged him away. "I was elected!" When the CBS reporter Mike Wallace tried to cover the mayhem, a policeman punched him in the face.

The convention turned positively rancorous when Lyndon Johnson's representatives managed to scuttle a compromise plank on Vietnam. As the *New York Times* noted, LBJ had "left Vice President Humphrey more tightly bound than ever to Administration policy and gave the doves the rallying cry that the Vietnam plank in the Democratic platform was directed by the White House." And rally they did. Upon hearing of the adoption of a hard-line plank on Vietnam, several thousand MOBE protesters, Yippies, and McCarthy supporters began marching toward the convention hall, only to be violently blocked by Chicago police.

As Daley's police force brutally attacked the young protesters, inside the liberal senator Abraham Ribicoff of Connecticut took to the podium to denounce the "Gestapo tactics on the streets of Chicago." Television viewers who had already been mesmerized by live feeds of the riot engulfing the city's streets were then treated to an unusually vivid spectacle as Mayor Daley, seething with rage, pointed his right index finger in Ribicoff's direction and bellowed out a string of inaudible expletives. Seasoned lip-readers had little trouble discerning his words: "Fuck you. You Jew son of a bitch!"

"How hard it is to accept the truth," Ribicoff taunted in reply. "How hard it is."

At the end of the week, Hubert Humphrey collected his prize. He would be the Democratic nominee in the November election. But he trailed Richard Nixon by twelve points in the polls, and his party lay in shambles.

At the White House, Johnson and his advisers quickly learned what life was like in a lame-duck administration. In June, some three months after LBJ shook the political establishment with his retirement announcement, Chief Justice Earl Warren—fearing that Richard Nixon, a fellow Californian whom he had long despised, might win the White House—conveyed to the president his decision to step down from the bench. "Johnson saw the Court as a means of perpetuating his social reform, particularly racial justice," explained Joe Califano. "He also wanted the Court to uphold the compromise he had reached with Catholics on funds for parochial schools, as well as his consumer, health, and environmental legislation." The president expected that all of these issues would "play out in the courts long after he left the White House, and he intended to win them as well after he had gone."

The plan called for elevating Fortas to chief justice and filling the vacant seat with Homer Thornberry, an appellate court judge, former Texas congressman, and longtime Johnson ally, all before November. The president anticipated strong conservative opposition to Fortas on two counts: his liberalism, particularly on matters related to race, and his religion. It had been easy to place Fortas in the Court's lone "Jewish seat" when LBJ had been at the height of his power. It would be another matter entirely for an outgoing president to appoint a liberal Jew to the *chief* justiceship, particularly in a climate less hospitable to Fortas's liberal outlook. Clark Clifford warned him that he would never find the votes in the Senate.

From the start, everything went wrong. Senator Robert Byrd of West Virginia, a former Klansman who filibustered the Civil Rights Act in 1964, pledged to do "everything in my power" to oppose the "leftist" Abe Fortas. Russell Long of Louisiana denounced the nominee as one of the "dirty five" who sought to expand the rights of the accused. James Eastland of Mississippi, an ardent racist and chairman of the Senate Judiciary Committee, told the president that he had "never seen so much feeling against a man as against Fortas." He might have been thinking in part of his colleague John McClellan of Arkansas, who ironically *wanted* that "SOB formally submitted to the Senate" so that he could take the fight public. Though Fortas had easily cleared the Senate confirmation process three years earlier to take his seat as an associate justice, he now served as a lightning rod for conservative Democrats and Republicans who channeled their resentment of Great Society liberalism into fervent opposition to his appointment as chief.

As a former member in good standing of the southern Democratic caucus, Johnson was firmly convinced that much of its opposition to Fortas stemmed from a toxic blend of anti-Semitism and racism. He urged the president of the American Bar Association to denounce the injection of religious bigotry into a Court nomination battle and instructed White House staff to enlist prominent rabbis to lobby senators from states with large Jewish constituencies. With prominent Republicans like Robert Griffin of Michigan also in the opposition camp, the White House activated key industrialists including Henry Ford II and Paul Austin, the president of Coca-Cola, to apply pressure where needed. Matters came to a head when Fortas appeared before the Senate Judiciary Committee for his confirmation hearings. Though a skilled litigator and no stranger to bare-knuckle politics, he was unprepared for the force of opposition that his nomination met.

Committee members relentlessly attacked Fortas for his role in shaping key Court decisions that liberalized criminal rights and public obscenity laws—proxy issues in the broader political debate over race, poverty, and counterculture. They also hammered the sitting associate justice for mixing his roles as jurist and presidential adviser and thereby eroding the Court's independence. Fortas anticipated this criticism and replied that "the history of this Republic is replete with shining examples of a close relationship between a president and a justice of the Supreme Court." In particular, he cited John Jay, who "offered George Washington the benefit of his wisdom on a variety of political problems," and Chief Justice Fred Vinson and the associate justice Sherman Minton, who the committee members knew very well had continued to serve Harry Truman as an informal adviser after each had ascended to the Court (indeed, some members had served in the House with Vinson or the Senate with Minton). To that list, Fortas might as well have added Felix Frankfurter, who, as virtually every senator understood, remained a close adviser to FDR after joining the Court, or William O. Douglas, who dabbled conspicuously with politics and even considered running for president from the bench. He also downplayed his current proximity to LBJ. Califano later admitted that "Fortas's testimony was so misleading and deceptive that those of us who were aware of his relationship with Johnson winced with each news report of his appearance before the Senate committee."

It was clear that the president's allies would struggle to secure the sixty-seven votes needed to break a filibuster. Their odds grew narrower when the committee learned that Fortas had accepted a payment of $15,000—equal to 40 percent of his government salary—to teach a seminar at American University and that the funds associated with his lectureship had been provided by a private donor. Though not an explicit ethics violation, the revelation crystallized opposition to his appointment. The Judiciary Committee ultimately sent Fortas's nomination to the full Senate by a vote of 11 to 6, but supporters failed to achieve cloture by a vote of 45 to 43. Fortas returned to the Court as an associate justice; Thornberry remained on the appellate court; and Earl Warren delayed his retirement until after Johnson's successor took office.

The Fortas nomination was just one of LBJ's many squabbles with Congress in his last months in the White House. Since 1967, when LBJ first requested a surcharge to help cover the costs of the Vietnam War, the administration had been locked in a quiet war with Wilbur Mills, the conservative Democrat who chaired the House Ways and Means Committee, which was responsible for all tax legislation. Mills refused to cooperate unless Johnson agreed to make steep cuts to domestic programs. When toward the end of the year LBJ offered to excise $2 billion from the budget in midyear—a concession that incensed liberals in his own party—Mills stiffened his position and also demanded limits to how many children in a single household could qualify for AFDC. The president patently refused this proposal, arguing in a private meeting at the White House that such limits would only hurt poor children. Unbeknownst to Mills, some of Johnson's domestic policy aides had in fact begun contemplating a shift from the "service model" (AFDC) to family income maintenance—precisely the type of massive redistribution scheme that Daniel Patrick Moynihan argued would provide the real antidote to poverty. "Nobody likes the present system: liberals, conservatives, poor, rich, white, Negroes—and welfare workers," the staff member Ben Wattenberg told Califano, Cater, and McPherson. But "opinion has not yet jelled as to an alternative program," and family income maintenance represented a sharp break with the prevailing "opportunity theory" that formed the theoretical foundation of the Great Society. In the meantime, the administration would remain firm in its position. "Basically," Wattenberg continued, "it is this: we are not talking about 'relief chiselers,' or 'promiscuous mothers,' or 'slums,' or 'Negroes.' We *are* talking about children. . . . There are 4 million American *children* living on AFDC payments today. They had no choice of their parentage. . . . The real question then is, are we prepared to help American *children* who can't help themselves?" LBJ held the line, but he could not forestall Mills forever. After his speech on March 31, in which the president renewed his call for a tax surcharge, Mills demanded $6 *billion* in spending cuts. Califano recalled that LBJ was furious and accused Mills and the Republican leader, Gerald Ford, of "courting danger" by holding up "a tax bill until you can blackmail someone into getting your own personal viewpoint on reductions." But an outgoing president had little negotiating power, and LBJ knew it. He swallowed the cuts and in turn won congressional approval of a 10 percent temporary surcharge.

On the surface, the Democratic primary results suggested an emerging antiwar consensus. But the truth was more complicated. While many of McCarthy's voters genuinely opposed the war in Vietnam, exit polls showed that a majority of his supporters in New Hampshire identified as hawks and voted against LBJ to register dissatisfaction with the slow pace of the war effort. Others were unhappy about rising inflation and urban unrest. In November, roughly 18 percent of McCarthy's primary voters would cast ballots for George Wallace, an unabashed war hawk whose running mate supported the use of nuclear weapons against North Vietnam. Lyndon Johnson's private pollster found that 55 percent of McCarthy voters supported the conventional bombing campaign against North Vietnam, while only 29 percent opposed it. Even by late fall, a majority of Americans still opposed a unilateral American bombing halt, and only 13 percent favored a complete and immediate withdrawal from Vietnam. To oppose the administration's strategy in Vietnam was not synonymous with advocating peace at any cost. The political situation was fluid as Nixon and Humphrey looked to November. Many Americans were deeply dissatisfied with the war, but there was no clear consensus about how to win or get out of Vietnam. Moreover, the country was deeply divided over hot-button issues like school desegregation and busing, urban unrest, rising crime rates, inflation, and the student movement. In such a fractured environment, the candidate who could cobble together the most votes from otherwise competing groups would prevail in November.

Complicating matters for the Democratic nominee, throughout the fall Wallace tapped into a strong reserve of voter anger, peeling away many white working-class Democrats in the North and potential white Republican voters in the South. Running on a platform of sheer rage—against African Americans, against crime, against the administration's failed Vietnam policy, against liberal intellectuals—Wallace whipped working-class audiences into a fury. He dubbed Nixon and Humphrey "Tweedledee and Tweedledum" and claimed there was not "a dime's worth of difference" between them. He slammed the "over-educated, ivory-tower folks with pointed heads looking down their noses at us" and promised that "when we get to be President and some anarchist lies down in front of our car, it'll be the *last* car he'll ever lie down in front of." Wallace thrived on his exchanges with the left-wing hecklers who attempted to disrupt his rallies, taunting them with lines like "You young people seem to know a lot of four-letter words. But I have two four-letter words you don't know: S-O-A-P and W-O-R-K," and "You just come up to the platform afterward, and I'll autograph your sandals."

Wallace made an easy target for liberals like Elizabeth Hardwick, a writer for the *New York Review of Books*, who mocked his "ill-cut suits, his greying drip-dry shirts . . . his sour, dark, unprepossessing look, carrying the scent of hurry and hair oil. . . . [His] natural home would seem to be a seedy hotel with a lot of people in the lobby, and his relaxation a cheap diner." Garry Wills similarly described Wallace's "gritty nimbus of piety, violence, sex. Picked-on and self-righteous, yet aggressive and darkly venturous, he has the dingy attractive air of a B-movie idol, the kind who plays a handsome garage attendant." But such condescension only heightened the former governor's appeal to working-class white voters who were angry at the world and needed a place to direct their rage.

Seeking to exploit the year's turmoil and to capture some of Wallace's appeal, Nixon walked a thin line between statesmanship and demagoguery, promising to speak for the "forgotten Americans . . . non-shouters, the non-demonstrators, that are not racists or sick, that are not guilty of crime that plagues the land. This I say to you tonight is the real voice of America in 1968." By focusing incessantly on racially coded issues like crime and urban unrest, Nixon signaled to white voters that he offered a respectable alternative to Wallace. Campaigning throughout the upper South, he endorsed the Supreme Court's decision in *Brown v. Board of Education*, which banned segregation in public schools, but also assured white voters that he felt it was wrong for the federal government to "force a local community to carry out what a Federal administrator or bureaucrat may think is best for that local community."

Even the conservative *Wall Street Journal* criticized Nixon's "harsh and strident efforts to capitalize on deep-seated discontent and frustration. This is the Richard Nixon who tells a whistle-stop rally in Deshler, Ohio that in the 45 minutes since his train left Lima, one murder, two rapes and 45 major crimes of violence had occurred in this country—and that 'Hubert Humphrey defends the policies under which we have seen crime rise to this point.'" It was also the same Nixon "who recalls, in Penn Square in Reading, the young girl with tears in her eyes who told him her fiancé had just been killed in Vietnam and asked, 'Mr. Nixon, can you do something about this war?'" The *Wall Street Journal* regretted that "gone almost entirely are the references of earlier days to the need for justice and action to ease the plight of Negroes and other poor people." Instead, the former vice president was peddling a brand of "extremism [that] seems not only unnecessary but self-defeating. . . . In a society already deeply divided by fear and mistrust, Mr. Nixon's hard line seems sure to deepen the divisions."

Throughout September, Nixon clung to a wide lead in the polls. Humphrey tried to campaign on "the politics of happiness, the politics of purpose, and the politics of joy," sounding traditional liberal themes and affirming that "for every jail Mr. Nixon wants to build I'd like to build a house for a family. And for every policeman he wants to hire I'd like to hire another good teacher."

But with his fortunes tied so strongly to the administration's losing policy in Vietnam, and with the country riveted by urban violence and social unrest, he made little headway.

On the right, Humphrey was bleeding blue-collar supporters to Wallace. Reports came in from across the Midwest of Wallace rallies packed "wall-to-wall [with] Steelworkers" and of union locals whose memberships were breaking three to one for the former Alabama governor. In New Jersey, 62 percent of workers at a Lincoln-Mercury plant in Middlesex County, home to Rutgers University, and 73 percent of workers at the Ternstedt division of General Motors were backing Wallace. Labor officials were so concerned that Wallace might siphon off enough votes to deliver key industrial states to Nixon that they began circulating millions of pamphlets to their members, reminding workers that Alabama was a stringently anti-union fortress with antiquated wage and hours laws. A sixteen-page fact sheet titled "The Wallace Labor Record" claimed, "If you're a carpenter it costs you more than $40 a week to work under George Wallace. If you're a bus driver it costs you more than $30 a week to work under George Wallace." For all these efforts, in late September it was still not clear that working-class white voters would come home to the Democratic Party.

Humphrey also faced trouble on the left. Wherever he went, antiwar protesters heckled him, shouting, "Stop the War," "Sieg Heil," and "Shame, Shame," and hoisting signs that read WITH HUMPHREY AND FASCIST DALEY, WHO NEEDS ENEMIES? It hardly mattered that Richard Nixon's position on Vietnam was totally inscrutable. Though he had told a New Hampshire audience, "Yes, I have a plan to end the war," and though he promised that he would "end the war and win the peace in the Pacific," Nixon stubbornly refused to reveal even the scantest details of his "plan," which, to his chagrin, reporters took to calling a "secret plan." "I don't want to pull the rug out from under our negotiations in Paris" by giving away too much detail, he explained. Unlike Humphrey, he could afford to be vague. He was not a member of the current administration and stood for change, ipso facto.

With his campaign in a rut, Humphrey's only hope was to break with Johnson and reverse course on Vietnam. On September 30, he did just that, announcing that his administration would unilaterally halt the bombing of all North Vietnamese targets and thus take a "risk for peace." It helped that Wallace had tapped the retired air force general Curtis LeMay to be his running mate. LeMay, who famously called for "bomb[ing] the Vietnamese back to the stone age" and who spoke lyrically of the salutary environmental effects of nuclear testing on the Bikini atoll, terrified many Wallace voters into taking a second look at Humphrey. (For his part, Humphrey made good political fodder of the choice, dubbing Wallace and LeMay the "bombsy twins" and emphasizing his own program for peace.) The president, in turn, was furious and contemplated withholding further support for his vice president.

It was never realistic that Johnson would disavow his longtime friend. As an unpopular president, he was of limited use to the nominee anyway, but many of his aides provided critical support. Larry O'Brien had resigned from the cabinet following LBJ's announcement on March 31 to work for Bobby Kennedy. Now he ran the Humphrey campaign's national political operation. Doug Cater also resigned his White House post to coordinate domestic policy for the campaign. From the White House, Califano supplied Humphrey with a steady flow of talking points and legislative proposals, particularly aimed at turning back Wallace's support among "lower and middle-income Americans." Many of his suggestions anticipated a continuation and expansion of the Great Society in the coming administration, though with an expanded focus on the middle class: comprehensive health care and catastrophic hospital insurance (in effect, Medicare) for children under three years old and their mothers; Head Start for all children, ages three to five ("Why shouldn't middle-class children receive the same benefits of nursery school as poor children?" Califano asked); an expansion of higher education grants to target middle-income families; an increase in ESEA funds to local schools; and a dedicated transportation construction program. Califano's memorandums effectively came full circle to the debate between Horace Busby and Bill Moyers some three years earlier. By broadening its target audience to include Middle America, Humphrey could garner wide support for measures that would also materially improve the condition of poor people. The prevailing wisdom still held: quantitative measures, not qualitative initiatives, would suffice.

LBJ's aides also believed that antiwar liberals could be won back if Humphrey drew a sharp contrast with Nixon on domestic policy. "Where would we be if Nixon had been elected in 1960?" they suggested as a talking point. "No Medicare, no Aid to Education, no War on Poverty, no Head Start, no Minimum Wage Bill, no Model Cities, no Civil Rights bills, no Social Security increases, etc." Nixon was "straddling the fence and refusing to take a stand on the war, the Non-Proliferation Treaty, jobs, aid to education, crime, older Americans, and cities." Rather than permit the GOP nominee to run as a vague change candidate, the campaign should challenge voters to consider whether they preferred a replay of the "Republican record of the fifties against the Democratic record of the sixties in the economy, jobs, education, health, housing, crime, cities, civil rights, consumer protection, quality of the environment, and agriculture." In effect, the White House urged Humphrey to meet backlash head-on by making the election a referendum on the Great Society. It was easy advice for the vice president to follow. Liberal to his core—his staff increasingly drawn from LBJ's orbit—he ran the race that Johnson had hoped to run himself. And it seemed to work.

As organized labor shifted into high gear for Humphrey, and as peace Democrats moved steadily into his column, Nixon's lead shrank to 5 percent by October 20. Then, on October 30, Nixon's advantage all but vanished as Johnson sprang a surprise, announcing to a prime-time television audience that Hanoi had agreed to a new round of four-way peace talks between North Vietnam and its ally, the National Liberation Front, and the United States and its ally, the Saigon-based Government of Vietnam. Johnson also told the nation that Hanoi had agreed to stop bombing South Vietnamese cities in return for a halt in America's bombing campaign north of the demilitarized zone. With hopes for peace running high, Humphrey surged in the polls, leading Nixon by three points on November 2.

But Nixon had an October surprise of his own. In the three weeks leading up to the election, as a newly invigorated Hubert Humphrey barnstormed the nation, touting a platform of "human equality and human opportunity," crying out for "a spirit of community," visiting black churches and tearfully celebrating America, "the only country on the face of the earth that has ever dared to try to make what we call a biracial, pluralistic society work," Nixon's campaign was using back channels to scuttle the Johnson administration's negotiations with the various parties in Vietnam. Nixon's team met secretly with Anna Chan Chennault, a wealthy supporter of Chiang Kai-shek, co-chair of Republican Women for Nixon, and confidante of the South Vietnamese president, Nguyen Van Thieu. At Nixon's behest, Chennault informed Thieu that Nixon would secure a better deal for his country than either Humphrey or Johnson and that the Democrats were effectively prepared to sell out Saigon in order to secure peace at any price. If Chennault could persuade Thieu to stay away from the negotiating table, the talks would collapse, LBJ would look foolish, and the Democrats' eleventh-hour gambit would fail.

Johnson and Humphrey were well aware of these machinations—the FBI was tapping Chennault's phone—but opted not to make them public. By one plausible, though unlikely, account, Humphrey was simply too honorable a man to reveal the GOP's shenanigans, because he feared that doing so would make it all but impossible for Nixon to govern in the event of an election victory. By another, more likely account, neither LBJ nor Humphrey wanted to acknowledge the wiretaps on Anna Chennault, for fear they would reveal other FBI taps and bugs, many of them illegal.

In the end, Nixon's surprise trumped LBJ's. On November 2, Thieu announced that "the government of South Vietnam deeply regrets not being able to participate in the [peace] talks," and as quickly as it had emerged, the euphoria over LBJ's October 31 announcement broke. Without South Vietnamese participation in the Paris talks, there was little chance of final resolution.

Even as the Nixon campaign was secretly—and quite possibly illegally—engaged in a campaign to sabotage the Paris peace talks, it allowed the vice presidential nominee Spiro T. Agnew to denounce Humphrey's call for a bombing halt. Such a promise "strengthened the hand of Hanoi," Agnew said, and undermined the Johnson administration's negotiations. It is impossible to say whether Nixon's October surprise was decisive. The election results were painfully close, with Nixon taking 43.4 percent of the popular vote to 42.7 percent for Humphrey and 13.5 percent for Wallace. In the Electoral College, Nixon's margin was wider—301 electoral votes to Humphrey's 191 and Wallace's 46. But minor swings in the popular vote in key states might have resulted in a Democratic victory.

In the election's aftermath, the *Wall Street Journal* concluded that while Nixon might have won, it was "clear that the American people have not yet settled their collective mind on what they really want." Calling Nixon's victory a "loose mandate" for change, the editors summed up America as "a people uncertain and yet searching. They do not like the kind of foreign policies that involve us in Vietnams, but they find little appeal in a new isolationism. They enjoy the new prosperity but resent having it eaten away by inflation. They see that the vast Federal social welfare programs of the past years have produced little demonstrable result, but they are by no means abandoning efforts to solve very real social problems."

Early in the afternoon of November 6, following a long night of nail-biting and poll watching, Hubert Humphrey greeted thousands of supporters at Minneapolis's Leamington hotel and announced that he had called Richard Nixon to congratulate him on a hard-fought victory. Moments later, after the crowd dispersed, Humphrey, choking back tears, told an aide, "Jesus, I think I would have done a good job in the White House."

Days later, he and his running mate, Senator Ed Muskie of Maine, came to the mansion for a prescheduled breakfast with Johnson. "Even the Vice President's natural ebullience was finally muted," recalled George Christian, "and when the three of them walked out of the Family Dining Room it appeared to me they had been attending a wake." After showing his guests to the elevator, LBJ turned to his press secretary and muttered, "Well, they almost did it."

Conclusion

January 20, 1969

I do understand power, whatever else may be said about me," Lyndon Johnson sometimes reminded his aides. "I know where to look for it and how to use it." Now, in the final weeks of his term, aides witnessed "a steady diminution of Presidential power," as Harry McPherson later recalled. "There was no point in preparing a massive legislative program for the next year since the new President would urge his own. So the lines of demand and response between the White House and the departments grew slack. There was no sense of anticipation, no fear of sanctions." Joe Califano remembered the closing days as "bleak." Bereft of clout and preparing to hand the keys of the White House to Richard Nixon—a virtuoso in the art of backlash politics who was widely expected to dismantle large parts of LBJ's domestic legacy—advisers to the outgoing president could do little but count down the hours until January 20. Many of the assistants began looking for jobs. Califano and McPherson prepared to resume the practice of law. Mike Manatos, a veteran of the Kennedy and Johnson legislative affairs office, would continue to ply his talents, but for private-sector clients. Fred Panzer, the president's research wiz, accepted an offer from the Tobacco Institute. All were "beginning to scatter, in spirit if not in body," George Christian wrote.

On his final evening in the White House, Johnson gathered his closest friends and staff in the residence for a buffet dinner. It was a "happy event," Califano recorded. "We shared a sense of relief that it was over and a sense of achievement, for despite the frightful cost of the Vietnam War in American lives and economic resources," all assembled knew that "we'd been part of a monumental social revolution. Personally, LBJ had drawn from most of us far more than we ever realized we had to give." As the evening wound down, LBJ backed Califano into the corner of the living room, just near the elevator. He spoke in a low whisper of Richard Nixon's fundamentally dishonest and vindictive nature, recalling the days when both men served together in Congress. "You're going to make some money now for the first time in your life," he advised. "First, invest it in land. This Nixon knows nothing about the economy and it's going to go to hell. Second, when you pay your income taxes, after you figure them out, pay an additional five hundred dollars. It's not enough for Nixon to win. He's going to have to put some people in jail. Third, the more you succeed, watch out for jealous people. Jealousy and sex drive people to do more damn mean and crazy things than anything else."

The next morning, shortly before the Nixons arrived for the ceremonial tea with the outgoing First Family, Johnson phoned Horace Busby, who found the president in good spirits. The moving crews, he told Buzz, were "all around," eager for LBJ and Lady Bird to leave the residence so that they could begin the frenetic process by which the Johnsons' belongings were packed and transported to awaiting trucks, crews came in to repaint and recarpet the residence, and the new president's furnishings, clothes, and personal items were installed—all by the late afternoon, when Richard and Pat Nixon would return from the inaugural parade and dress for the evening's balls. "They are watching every move I make," Johnson said with a chuckle. "If I lay a cuff link down on the dresser, a hand comes around the door and snatches it up." The two men exchanged awkward pleasantries until it was time for LBJ to greet the incoming president. "Well, see you again sometime," he muttered to Buzz.

Shortly after 10:00 a.m., the Nixons arrived for the customary tea reception, emerging at 11:05 with Lyndon and Lady Bird to climb inside the black presidential limousine for the short drive to the Capitol. The day was overcast and bitter cold. After the ceremony was over, LBJ joined some of his closest friends and former Senate colleagues for a relaxed brunch of ham and Bloody Marys at Clark Clifford's home. From there, George Christian remembered, the former president was transported to Andrews Air Force Base, where Boeing 707 No. 2600 "departed for Texas. It was difficult to believe that for this flight it was no longer Air Force One."

Among the many former staff aides who gathered at Andrews to bid the Johnsons farewell was Harry McPherson, who "thought back to that first meeting on the Senate floor—almost thirteen years ago—and how in those years Johnson had become like one of my family, not to be judged by me as others judged him, in the aesthetic terms of like and dislike, but more deeply, in love, rage, and grief."

As McPherson watched the plane disappear into the cloudy sky, he breathed a sigh of relief. He was "officially powerless, and oddly, relieved."

Johnson's aides were sure that the incoming administration would set quickly about the work of dismantling the Great Society. The new president would soon surprise them. William Safire, who served as a speechwriter in the Nixon White House, later posited a that while the president's "heart was on the right, his head was, with FDR, slightly left of center." Under his watch, Medicare, Medicaid, and aid to elementary and secondary education thrived. Indeed, spending on all three of LBJ's signature domestic programs continued to rise. Though Nixon discontinued the Community Action Program and dismantled the Office of Economic Opportunity, many of the OEO's initiatives—including popular programs like Legal Aid and Head Start—continued to operate successfully under the auspices of the cabinet departments to which they were reassigned. By far the most ambitious and potentially progressive component of Nixon's domestic agenda was a proposal to scrap the nation's complicated patchwork of welfare programs and replace it with a negative income tax that would guarantee all families a minimum annual income. Known as the Family Assistance Plan (FAP), the proposal would have streamlined the welfare state, eliminated thousands of bureaucrats and caseworkers, and substituted cash transfers in the form of a negative income tax for services. FAP included work incentives to ensure that recipients would not lose funding if they found jobs. Had Congress passed the plan, it would have covered roughly twice as many people—and three times as many children—as the principal government welfare program, Aid to Families with Dependent Children, and federal welfare spending would have increased by $4.4 billion in its first year of enactment.

But FAP proved a nonstarter. It won accolades from many people on the left, who in the final years of the Johnson administration came to doubt the underlying wisdom of opportunity theory, and from many on the right, who believed that the working poor knew how to spend their money better than social workers and public-sector bureaucrats. But a strange coalition of southern conservatives and northern liberals killed the legislation in Congress. Taking their cues from the National Welfare Rights Organization, liberals argued that the plan would not provide poor families with enough money to keep them afloat. At the same time, business and political elites in the South dreaded the possible ramifications of FAP. Studies estimated that the program would have covered 35 percent of Mississippi's population, thus equalizing the earnings of the state's black and white citizens. In Mississippi, two-thirds of black women worked in service industries. FAP would have boosted the earnings of a $40-per-week housekeeper to $3,408 per year—not too far off from the average wages of a male factory worker ($3,984). By raising income levels across the board, FAP threatened to destabilize race relations and increase the region's low prevailing wage.

Though the proposal reflected an emerging consensus that poor people needed cash income, not just qualitative assistance, FAP's early demise resulted in a continuation of Johnson's approach to fighting poverty. Nixon did sign into law the Supplemental Security Income program, which provided a minimum cash income for disabled adults and their dependents, as well as the first automatic cost-of-living adjustments for Social Security recipients. Together, these measures helped alleviate poverty by providing defined categories of Americans with income assistance. But on the whole, the federal government's antipoverty activities continued to focus on health care, nutritional assistance, education, and job training.

In other areas, too, Nixon built on LBJ's legacy—sometimes with enthusiasm, on other occasions with diffidence or outright derision. Nixon proclaimed in his 1970 State of the Union address that the "great question of the seventies is, shall we surrender to our surroundings, or shall we make peace with nature and begin to make reparations for the damage we have done to our air, our land and our water? . . . Clean air, clean water, open spaces—these should once again be the birthright of every American." Privately, the president was dismissive of environmentalists, telling his domestic policy aide, John Ehrlichman—the one member of his inner circle who was genuinely interested in the issue—that the entire question was pure "crap." Still, Nixon understood that public opinion was moving in the opposite direction. In the first year of his presidency, the country watched with horror as an accidental spill attributed to the Union Oil Company polluted two hundred miles of shoreline off the California coast and as the Cuyahoga River, which ran through Cleveland, Ohio, caught fire—the product of several decades of egregious industrial pollution.

By the early 1970s, between two-thirds and three-quarters of Americans were concerned about air and water pollution. Ever the politician, Nixon knew he could not afford to seem aloof from reality. What LBJ had begun, he would continue.

As president, Nixon asked Congress to pass legislation establishing the Environmental Protection Agency (EPA) and the National Oceanic and Atmospheric Administration. When the House and Senate complied, Nixon signed both agencies into existence. His pick for EPA chief, William Ruckelshaus, proved a strong proponent of clean air and water. Nixon also signed off on the 1970 Clean Air Act, which forced automobile manufacturers to cut carbon monoxide emissions to 90 percent of their 1970 levels within five years, and the 1972 Coastal Zone Management Act, which safeguarded estuaries. He transferred over eighty thousand acres of federal land to the states for the creation of public parks and set aside millions more acres for protection under the National Wilderness Preservation System.

Even on matters related to race relations, Nixon demonstrated unexpected continuity with his predecessor. He understood that once unleashed, federal efforts to desegregate schools would be difficult to stop, particularly given the heightened involvement of federal judges who enjoyed lifetime tenure and thus immunity from the whims of current politics. Nixon ordered his liberal HEW secretary, Bob Finch, to abandon Johnson's policy of threatening to withhold federal funds to coerce districts into developing desegregation strategies. Instead, Finch worked with Attorney General John Mitchell to develop a compromise strategy by which the Justice Department more aggressively sued recalcitrant school districts in the federal courts, a policy that became all the more powerful in October 1969 when the Supreme Court ruled in *Alexander v. Holmes County Board of Education* that the South had to "terminate dual school systems at once and . . . operate now and hereafter only unitary schools." This legalistic approach was in line with Nixon's personal feelings that "when funds are cut off, [the] law has failed. [You have] neither integration or education." On a more practical level, by relying on Justice Department lawsuits to effect desegregation, Nixon deflected southern backlash away from his administration and onto the courts. Nevertheless, the pace of desegregation continued to increase, in part because judges were newly emboldened to involve themselves on a district-by-district level.

Nixon's Labor Department also enforced employment provisions of the Civil Rights Act when it issued sweeping orders in at least ten cities compelling unions and private firms involved in federal contracting to establish hiring targets. Known as the "Philadelphia Plan" for its city of origin, this program built on a Johnson administration initiative aimed at increasing the number of black workers in the construction trades. For several decades, a powerful combination of private-sector discrimination and racism and nepotism within trade unions had excluded black workers from well-paying blue-collar industries.

Even more so than their Democratic predecessors, Secretary of Labor George Shultz and Assistant Secretary of Labor Arthur Fletcher demanded that federal contractors and the unions with which they did business draw up "goals and timetables" for black hiring. In addition to these actions, between 1969 and 1974 funding for the Equal Employment Opportunity Commission (EEOC), the federal agency empowered to take discriminatory employers to court, increased from $13.2 million to $43 million, and the agency's staff jumped from 359 professionals to 1,640. Nixon also signed into law the new Equal Employment Opportunity Act, which broadened the EEOC's jurisdiction to include educational institutions, state and local governments, and all private businesses with fifteen or more employees.

In effect, even as Nixon played the race card during political appearances before suburban and southern audiences, his administration maintained the government's commitment to Johnson's civil rights acts. Believing that "people who own their own homes don't burn them down," the president signed Executive Order 11458, which established the Office of Minority Business Enterprise (OMBE), under the auspices of the Commerce Department. In conjunction with the Small Business Administration, the OMBE promoted the start-up and expansion of minority-owned businesses. The Nixon administration also increased the volume of federal contracts with minority-owned businesses and increased the amount of federal and corporate deposits in black-owned banks.

Lyndon Johnson understood better than his aides that once established, benefits and protections are seldom eliminated but often enhanced. He died of chronic heart disease on January 22, 1973—just two days after Nixon took the oath of office for his second term—safe in the belief that his domestic achievements would long endure, though cognizant that his historical reputation would forever be clouded by Vietnam.

It was remarkable that Johnson's Great Society endured into the 1970s, 1980s, and beyond, even as the economic theory that underpinned it fell into doubt. LBJ's domestic policy was born of prevailing liberal conviction that experts could grow the economy in perpetuity while sustaining low unemployment and inflation. After 1973, this belief no longer seemed tenable. Owing in part to spending on the Vietnam War, as well as a series of supply shocks in the food and energy sectors, Americans absorbed over a decade of runaway inflation. Inflation was accompanied, in turn, by rising unemployment, particularly in the manufacturing sector, which for many years had formed the backbone of America's prosperous, postwar middle class. Stagflation—the combination of high unemployment and inflation—was the very antithesis of liberal economics, and it undercut the entire premise of opportunity theory. Experts had lost control of the economic levers, and increasingly it became clear that all the education and training in the world would not help poor people in urban ghettos, declining coal towns in Appalachia, or midsized cities like Youngstown, where in the coming decade empty steel mills stood as skeletal reminders of the region's bygone industrial might. Poor people needed jobs and income, not qualitative assistance to help them capture prosperity that no longer existed.

During the decade in which John Kennedy and Lyndon Johnson governed, the American economy expanded at an average rate of 7.5 percent each year. The country has not seen growth like this since. When the Republican Donald J. Trump won the presidency in 2016 on a platform of economic populism and white nationalism—some fifty years after the high-water mark of the Great Society—he promised to deliver 4 percent annual growth. An understated columnist spoke for most experts when he affirmed that it would be a "monumental task" to achieve such results. What liberal economists in the postwar era assumed would last forever—boundless economic growth and low inflation—was in fact an aberration.

To be sure, in the years since LBJ left office, America has experienced periods of sustained economic expansion. But in contrast to the postwar era, in

recent decades the blessings of limited economic growth have accrued principally to the wealthiest Americans. In the years since Lyndon Johnson left office in 1969, the poorest quintile of Americans have seen a steep decline in its
share of national income and wealth, while the richest quintile has seen its
portion grow.

Stagnant incomes are central to this story. Between World War II and
1973, real wages grew steadily at a rate of between 2 percent and 3 percent
each year, enabling millions of American workers to enjoy unprecedented up-
ward mobility. From that point forward, wage growth slowed dramatically for
many Americans. Over the next three decades, *household* wages remained
essentially flat, but principally because more women entered the workforce,
even as men's wages fell by roughly 9 percent. In the main, families with two
wage earners were able to maintain parity; families headed by single parents
fell behind.

Many of the problems that Daniel Patrick Moynihan perceived in impoverished black communities—namely, the rise of single-parent households and
a "tangle of poverty" that saw men exit the workforce permanently and sometimes across generations—gradually befell the white and Latino working class
as well. By 2011, some 67 percent of black children, 42 percent of Latino children, and 25 percent of white children resided in single-parent households.
Given the steady stagnation of wages since 1973, single-parent families are
more likely to be poor. At the same time, record-setting numbers of working-
age adults have slipped out of the workforce; they are neither employed nor
seeking employment, a trend that has alarmed conservatives and liberals alike.
For single parents bereft of well-paying jobs, or working-age Americans who
have dropped out of the economy, opportunity theory rings hollow.

The economic history of the last fifty years has armed Johnson's critics on
both the left and the right with ammunition to attack the Great Society. For
many conservatives, it was a noble but unsuccessful experiment in European-
style socialism that failed to eliminate poverty; instead, it generated a culture
of dependency that held millions of families in an intergenerational cycle of
privation. For some progressive critics, the Great Society's preference for qualitative rather than quantitative measures like a guaranteed household income
doomed the project from the start. Such detractors believe that opportunity

theory was scarcely adequate in good times; it was singularly ill-suited to the lean years that followed.

Each of these critiques has some merit.

Qualitative liberalism assumed that the American economy would continue to grow in perpetuity—that economists and social scientists finally understood how to manipulate the right levers to ensure steady growth and low inflation. In such a world, there was no need to slice the pie more equitably if everyone's slice continued to grow on its own. In their hubris, the generation of policy makers that endured the Great Depression, vanquished fascism, and saved capitalism could scarcely envision a time when Americans would not be the masters of their own destiny.

The Great Society concerned itself with poverty and quality of life, not economic inequality. Living in a prosperous age, its architects sought to equip Americans with skills and resources to lift themselves above a certain income level—the poverty line—and enjoy the blessings of an affluent society. Equitable distribution of wealth and income was of less concern to a generation of liberals who saw working-class households enjoy luxuries unimaginable to most families that lived through the Great Depression. In 2017, inequality—whether measured by household income, wealth, or retirement security—has achieved levels unseen since the 1920s. If many conservatives regard the Great Society as an exercise in unbridled liberalism, on the left there is growing consensus that the new political economy demands more—not less—state intervention.

But such criticisms also grossly understate the central role that the Great Society programs have played—and continue to play—in reducing poverty, alleviating the suffering of those who live in it, diminishing systemic racial discrimination, enriching the nation's cultural life, and enshrining consumer and environmental protections in the law. The noncash benefits associated with LBJ's domestic initiatives have cut the poverty rate by 26 percent since Johnson took office. Food stamps, school breakfasts and lunches, and Head Start programs minimize food insecurity for millions of poor children and their parents each day. Medicaid and Medicare amount to the difference between life and death for 119 million Americans—or roughly 37 percent of the country's population. Qualitative liberalism has not eradicated poverty, but it sharply reduces it. And today, most people cannot fathom a world in which African Americans are denied service at hotels, restaurants, and hospitals, explicitly excluded from the workplace or the housing market, or barred from voting or holding office strictly on the basis of their race. It is equally difficult to envision a country without laws governing clean air and water, consumer labeling standards, federal aid to public schools, or public television and radio.

Even as this book goes to print, the enduring value of the Great Society is no longer an academic question or political talking point but instead a real-world concern. At the heart of LBJ's belief system was the conviction that government should unlock potential for individuals while recognizing that individuals also owe certain core obligations to each other. In 2016, the Electoral College installed a president—and the American public chose a Congress—who rejects both LBJ's belief system and the policies that emanated from it. It remains to be seen whether Republicans will make good on their long-stated desire to repeal Medicare and replace it with a voucher system; convert Medicaid to a limited block grant program; divert ESEA funds away from public schools; gut environmental and consumer protections; sharply reduce funds for food stamps and school nutritional programs; abolish federal aid for the arts, humanities, and public broadcasting; allow broad-based religious exemptions to civil rights laws; or reimpose a modern-day form of poll taxes in the form of mandatory voter identification cards. As with so many things in life, Americans may learn to appreciate the Great Society only when it is gone.

But there is a cautionary tale for opponents of the Great Society. Franklin Roosevelt argued that the New Deal was designed to "save our system, the capitalistic system," from extremists on both the far left and the far right. Its expansion of state authority and construction of a partial safety net offended many conservatives but worked within the existing boundaries of the American political economy. It was designed to help capitalist institutions function with greater order, less risk and volatility, and more uniformity. In later years, many political observers noted that FDR's legacy was strikingly conservative, relative to the path traveled by many postwar European democracies. The same is true of the Great Society, a program of important but limited ambition that was predicated on growth liberalism, not redistribution. The Trump administration and its congressional allies may eliminate access to health care for tens of millions of poor people and senior citizens, strip away food security for impoverished children and their parents, erode civil rights for people of color, and make it possible once again to despoil America's water and air. But when the pendulum swings back, it may swing hard. The next burst of liberal reform may not be anywhere near as solicitous of capitalist institutions and private industry, and it may take a more radical approach to securing not just opportunity but also equality. Like the New Deal, the Great Society tamed capitalism and secured a modicum of political peace. In its absence, the political controls come off.

For those who value Lyndon Johnson's legacy, the early days of Donald Trump's presidency augur some hope. Staffed by a thin layer of political neophytes with little experience and even less curiosity, Trump's White House has no Harry McPherson or Joe Califano, no Bill Moyers or Douglass Cater. It is true that Jack Valenti was no more prepared to assume the awesome responsibilities of his office than were many of Trump's senior advisers. But Valenti threw himself into the role, worked punishing hours, and consumed tens of thousands of pages of briefing memorandums each week. The same cannot be said of Trump's aides. LBJ's White House also valued the collective expertise of the federal bureaucracy and worked closely with cabinet departments and agencies. The Trump administration has been slow to appoint subcabinet officials, has cast off career public servants as part of an enemy "deep state," and has demonstrated little facility for the art of administration. A staff unprepared to govern, and dismissive of administrative expertise and discipline, may well find itself hard-pressed to undo the work of a presidential staff that did.

Not three months after leaving the White House, Harry McPherson was asked by an interviewer what it was like "not to be there anymore." Did he feel a "loss of relevance"?

"Well," McPherson answered with a touch of sarcasm, "I'm without a car, which is a terrible loss. And I'm without constant telephone calls, which sort of makes you wonder whether you really count in the world anymore." But he was "glad to be away from Johnson at last, after so many years with him, because I need to develop my own maturity; that is, to be my own 'daddy,' to a considerable extent, so far as one can be one's own father. He has been an overpowering influence in my life, one whom I had to fight to keep from utterly dominating me. He is consuming to be with. His preoccupations become yours. Whatever he happens to be working on becomes the only thing that anybody works on around him, or thinks about."

Other aides exhibited more conflict about departing the West Wing. Even after leaving the White House, Jack Valenti remained a member of LBJ's inner circle. Despite his lucrative and glamorous position, he grappled with a sense of emptiness. "At this time [last year] I was helping the President decide whether to make a major international trip and whom to see," he told McPherson in 1967. "This week I spent an entire day trying to get 'The Sound of Music' into Kenya." He cautioned his former colleagues of what they, too, could expect upon leaving government: "the tremendous fall, drop, in relevance, in breadth of concern, that one experiences in returning to private life."

In the years that followed, the men who constituted LBJ's inner circle followed divergent paths. Some, like Joe Califano, returned to government: in 1977, President Jimmy Carter named the domestic policy wunderkind as his secretary of health, education, and welfare. By his own assessment, Califano used the post to expand and administer the very Great Society programs that in prior years he had helped to conceive. Well to the left of the administration politically, he angered several southern governors over the pace of school desegregation and—ironically—tangled frequently with Carter's inexperienced but headstrong White House staff. In 1979, the president fired Califano, who returned to the private practice of law. His dismissal drove a deeper wedge between the Democratic Party's liberal wing and the White House and was one in a series of precipitating events that led Edward Kennedy to challenge Carter unsuccessfully in the 1980 primary season.

A consummate party man, Larry O'Brien managed Hubert Humphrey's campaign in 1968 and subsequently served two turns as Democratic National Committee chairman between 1968 and 1972, resigning to accept the national chairmanship of George McGovern's doomed bid for the presidency. It was to be his last moment in politics. O'Brien moved to New York, built a successful public relations practice, and capped off a remarkable career by serving as commissioner of the National Basketball Association between 1975 and 1984. In that role, he helped to revive the game's declining fortunes. He died in 1990.

After Robert Kennedy's assassination, Richard Goodwin left politics altogether. He served briefly as editor of *Rolling Stone*, became a prolific contributor to other magazines and newspapers, and moved to Massachusetts with his second wife, Doris Kearns—a Harvard-educated political scientist who served as a presidential fellow in the Johnson White House before helping the ex-president to pen his memoirs and subsequently blazing a trail as one of America's foremost presidential biographers. Dick Goodwin returned briefly to the public eye in 1994 when the film *Quiz Show* featured him as its central character. The movie concerned Goodwin's role as a young House aide, not his work in the Kennedy or Johnson administrations.

After leaving the White House, George Reedy became a prolific author of books concerning American politics and political institutions. In 1971, he moved to Milwaukee, where he became dean of Marquette University's School of Journalism in 1972, a post he held until 1976, when he stepped down to accept an endowed professorship. He taught at the university until 1990 and subsequently took emeritus status. In later years, Reedy became a pointed if fair critic of the president with whom he had once been so close but from whom he gradually grew estranged. The two men did not speak to each other after 1970. George Reedy died in 1999.

Horace Busby maintained his business consultancy and newsletter well into the 1980s, advising large multinational companies, including American Airlines and Mobil Oil, and turning out a steady flow of memorandums—replete with sweeping political and economic syntheses—for which his corporate clients paid him handsomely. Busby retired to Southern California. Unbeknownst to his family, he penned a memoir of his time on LBJ's staff—tenure that spanned two pivotal decades of American history. His adult children found the unfinished manuscript boxed away in his daughter's garage several years after his death in 2000.

After leaving Hubert Humphrey's campaign staff in late 1968, Douglass Cater earned his living as a freelance writer and visiting scholar at various universities and think tanks. In 1982, he accepted the presidency of Washington College, a picturesque liberal arts college located on Maryland's Eastern

Shore. His books and articles received positive reviews, even after he retired from his college post and returned to Montgomery, Alabama, in 1990. When he died in 1995, the *New York Times* memorialized him as "a soft-spoken student and practitioner of government" who earned his "reputation as a civilizing influence" and "brought thoughtfulness to both his extensive writings and his other work."

Harry McPherson—of all the presidential aides, perhaps the most relieved to abandon the pressures of political life—built a successful law practice. His clients included multinational corporations and foreign governments, but he continued to take an active part in public affairs. He served on multiple presidential commissions, including one that Jimmy Carter impaneled to investigate the nuclear accident at Three Mile Island in Pennsylvania, and in 1998 played a role in helping forty-six states negotiate a multibillion-dollar settlement with the nation's big tobacco companies. His memoir, *A Political Education*, published in 1972, remains a classic study in the ways of Washington. "To put it bluntly," a reviewer noted, "few Americans have a realistic idea of how our government works. We have instead a series of naïve assumptions. If the message of this book were common knowledge, much of the sound and fury that currently caricatures our politics and our national image could be averted." McPherson died in 2012 at the age of eighty-two.

After parting ways with Johnson, Bill Moyers returned to his professional roots and built a storied career as a newspaper editor, television journalist, producer of public interest and investigative documentaries, and public television impresario. No less attentive to his personal brand than in his days as a White House adviser, over the years he cultivated a reputation for intellectual integrity and high-minded liberal enlightenment. But with very few exceptions, he rarely spoke or wrote about his association with Lyndon Johnson. Unlike most of his colleagues—Reedy, Valenti, Busby, McPherson, Califano, Goodwin— he has not, to date, written a memoir of his public life nor clarified for the record the circumstances surrounding his break with LBJ. "Lyndon B. Johnson owned and operated a ferocious ego," he offered in a rare moment of candor in 2015. "But he was curiously ill at ease with himself. He had an animal sense of weakness in other men—he wanted to know what you loved and what you feared and once he knew, he came after you. . . . He had a passion for power but suffered violent dissent in the ranks of his own personality. He could absolutely do the right thing at the right time—the reassuring grace, if you will, when he was thrust into the White House after Kennedy's assassination; the Civil Rights Act of 1964; the Voting Rights Act of 1965. But when he did the wrong thing—escalating the Vietnam war—the damage was irreparable."

"I'm sometimes amazed, and even appalled, at the fact that we did handle all of this with so small a staff," Jack Valenti later admitted. Presidents came and went during his four decades at the helm of one of the most formidable industry lobbies in the United States, but Valenti—who first arrived in Washington, D.C., on the wings of random circumstance—remained a fixture in the capital's power circles. "I have worked in two of life's classic fascinations, politics and movies," he later wrote, "and while there are dazzling attractions in both areas, it is the political man who most excites me." Valenti, who died in 2007, still marveled at the proximity he once enjoyed to Lyndon Johnson. "I think I knew him as well as anyone beyond his wife and family," he averred, "and I know I did not know all of him." Johnson was "an awesome engine of a man: 'terrorizing; tender; inexhaustibly energetic; ruthless'—'petty; clairvoyant; compassionate; bullying; sensitive; tough; resolute; charming; earthy; devious'—'disciplined; crafty; generous.'" The president he remembered "had one goal": to do "the greatest good in the history of the nation. He had one tragedy: a war whose commitments he could not break and whose tenacity he did not perceive." Valenti knew the value of what Lyndon Johnson left behind and could only wonder what more they might all have accomplished if not for the tragedy in Vietnam.

ACKNOWLEDGMENTS

A book like this is inevitably the product of years of collaboration. In the process of researching and writing, I've benefited greatly from assistance, counsel, and critical feedback from friends and peers. The best parts of this book come from their influence; any shortcomings are all mine.

I am deeply grateful to friends at *Politico* and *Politico Magazine*, where I serve as a contributing editor. Having left academia a decade ago, I've been fortunate to enjoy not just a home for my writing but also sharp substantive feedback from a group of talented editors who excel at the art of making big ideas accessible to a broader audience of nonspecialists. Past and current editors, including Blake Hounshell, Elizabeth Ralph, Susan Glasser, Garrett Graff, Margaret Slattery, Stephen Heuser, and Zack Stanton, have extended uncommon courtesy and encouragement. They afforded me the opportunity to road test some of my ideas and arguments in the magazine and provided critical advice that sharpened both the tone and substance of the finished manuscript.

The challenge of writing a book like this while based in New York was made easier by the help of two highly capable research assistants, Shannon Hildenbrand and Max Scheinin. They did much more than locate and digitize thousands of pages of manuscript collections in the LBJ Library; they took the time and care to familiarize themselves with the project, to pore over finding guides with me, and to help me understand which documents would be of particular use.

Doing so is no small task, especially given the seemingly bottomless bounty of primary source material in the LBJ archives. It's a model presidential library, and I am grateful to the talented staff that have made it so accessible and relevant to researchers—especially remote researchers like me. Special thanks goes to archivist Jenna De Graffenried, who was always quick to steer me in the right direction by phone or email.

At Viking, I am tremendously fortunate to work with the great Wendy Wolf, whose critical eye and proscriptive feedback are reflected in the book's best passages. She is as rigorous an editor as she is a passionate advocate of her authors. Her team, including assistant editor, Georgia Bodnar, is a pure delight to work with. Special thanks are due to copy editor Ingrid Sterner; production editor Sharon Gonzalez; book designer Francesca Belanger; jacket designer Matthew Varga; and publicist Louise Braverman. They took my words and made them into a book that people might just read!

I am also privileged to work with Andrew Wylie and Jacqueline Ko, agents extraordinaire. With the benefit of their care and attention, I've enjoyed unique opportunities to grow as an author and a historian.

Last, though certainly not least, I am indebted in so many ways to my family. My father, Carl Zeitz, a former State House reporter, sparked my initial passion for history and politics many decades ago. He remains my most faithful reader and an important sounding board. My wife, Angela Zeitz, is my closest friend, stalwart champion, and partner in raising two smart, engaged, and beautiful girls. There's not much that I can do without her love and support.

Our girls, Naomi and Lillian, inspired this book. At ages four and (almost) seven, they're too young, still, to know much about Lyndon Johnson. But they took an avid interest in the 2016 election. We shared their disappointment that they didn't get to see a woman ascend to the presidency—not this time, in any event—and their concern that the new administration would not treat every American with equal respect and dignity. I wrote these pages for them, in the hope that one day—when they are old enough to read this book—they'll feel inspired to do their part in finishing the work that Lyndon Johnson and his staff began.

NOTES

4 "may have had a negative impact": Reedy, *Twilight of the Presidency*, 167.

4 conservative criticism of the Great Society: "Reagan Blames 'Great Society' for Economic Woes," *New York Times*, May 10, 1983.

4 so sweeping a list: Bailey and Danziger, *Legacies of the War on Poverty*, 12–14.

5 in the Yellow Oval Room: Hardesty, *Johnson Years*, 65.

7 "He felt entitled": Califano, *Triumph and Tragedy of Lyndon Johnson*, 11.

Chapter 1: Put the Ball Through the Hoop

11 "Tonight, on this Thanksgiving": "Transcript of President Johnson's Thanksgiving Day Address," *New York Times*, Nov. 29, 1963.

11 "no memorial oration": "Johnson Bids Congress Enact Civil Rights Bill with Speed," *New York Times*, Nov. 28, 1963.

11 "for His divine wisdom": "Johnson's Thanksgiving Address Asks Nation to 'Banish Rancor' and Move On to 'New Greatness,'" *New York Times*, Nov. 29, 1963.

12 "the South's unending revenge": Zelizer, *Fierce Urgency of Now*, 4, 20.

12 "scandal of drift and inefficiency": Caro, *Passage of Power*, 347, 461.

12 "a vague feeling of doubt": McPherson, *Political Education*, 246.

14 asked the former Treasury secretary Robert Anderson: Telephone transcript: Johnson, Anderson, Nov. 30, 1963, 1:30 p.m., Johnson, *Presidential Recordings*.

15 "Wish you'd feel Byrd out": "Lyndon Johnson and George Smathers on 30 November 1963," tape K6311.07, PNO 1, in *Presidential Recordings Digital Edition*.

16 The president's approval ratings: Caro, *Passage of Power*, 595.

17 "strange amalgam of Austin": Roberts, *LBJ's Inner Circle*, 37.

17 "We are like a basketball team": Ibid., 81.

17 the value of staff: Caro, *Master of the Senate*, 311.

17 staff numbering 250: Roberts, *LBJ's Inner Circle*, 35.

18 "must be completely devoted to the man": Ibid., 14.

18 "*the key* staff member": Reedy OH, Dec. 20, 1968, 36.

18 "stabilizing force": Ibid., 37.

18 "the door opened": Caro, *Master of the Senate*, 129.

19 "brains, ability and political savvy": "Johnson Creating Team of Advisors," *Hartford Courant*, Nov. 29, 1963.

19 "the senior staff man": "Johnson's Men: 'Valuable Hunks of Humanity,'" *New York Times*, May 3, 1964.

19 "satirized as the man": "The President's Closest Shadow," *South China Sunday Post-Herald*, May 17, 1964.

19 "Above all, Walter Jenkins": Goldman, *Tragedy of Lyndon Johnson*, 105.

19 guests at the home of Walter: "Stroll Begins Moving Day for President," *Los Angeles Times*, Dec. 8, 1963.

19 "It is difficult for a man": Sinclair OH, Oct. 5, 1970, 28.

19 "always felt talking to Walter": Rowe OH, Sept. 16, 1969, 52.

19 "With no expression of liberal doctrine": Goldman, *Tragedy of Lyndon Johnson*, 107.

19 "I had a very sick feeling": Jenkins OH, Aug. 24, 1971, 39–42.

20 "sat in his big office": Goldman, *Tragedy of Lyndon Johnson*, 104.

20 untitled chief of staff: "LBJ's Texans Now Hold the Reins," *Boston Globe*, March 15, 1964.

20 "seeming every inch the all-American boy": Goldman, *Tragedy of Lyndon Johnson*, 122.

21 since the age of eight: Busby OH, April 23, 1981, 4–5, 12, 29.

21 "I knew those kinds of nuances": Ibid., 38–42.

22 minister without portfolio: Ibid., 21–22.

22 "several angry separations": "Two White House Aides Resigning Their Posts," *Los Angeles Times*, Sept. 16, 1965.

22 "reputation of having become": Goldman, *Tragedy of Lyndon Johnson*, 124.

23 "Kennedy's 'thinkers'": "LBJ Adviser Horace 'Buzz' Busby Jr., 76, Dies," *Washington Post*, June 1, 2000.

23 "remained open and freewheeling": Goldman, *Tragedy of Lyndon Johnson*, 124.

23 Gettysburg National Cemetery: Caro, *Passage of Power*, 255–66.

23 "one hell of a nice guy": Goldman, *Tragedy of Lyndon Johnson*, 122.

24 Bill Don Moyers: "Johnson's Men: 'Valuable Hunks of Humanity.'"

25 "John Connally is a really tough man": "Bill Moyers, a Gentle Gale," *Austin American*, July 12, 1964.

25 "an authentic Johnson man": "Johnson's Men: 'Valuable Hunks of Humanity.'"

25 "a slight, bespectacled": Roberts, *LBJ's Inner Circle*, 53.

25 "he began building an empire": Goldman, *Tragedy of Lyndon Johnson*, 111.

25 "get your Bible": Johnson and Moyers, April 28, 1964, WH6404.14, no. 3171.

26 "tended to lull people": Valenti OH, July 12, 1972, 14.

26 back channel to Shriver: Telephone transcript: Whitney Young to LBJ, Nov. 24, 1963, 6:23 p.m., Johnson, *Presidential Recordings*.

26 "As molder of the President's legislative program": Roberts, *LBJ's Inner Circle*, 53.

26 "exciting, interesting, mysterious person": "A White House Adviser," *New York Times*, Nov. 30, 1963.

27 "Six feet two inches tall": Goldman, *Tragedy of Lyndon Johnson*, 118–19.

27 "George lived a life": McPherson OH, Sept. 19, 1985, 10–11.

27 "George was a mirror": Rowe OH, Sept. 16, 1969, 2.

27 "I remember one time standing": McPherson OH, Sept. 19, 1985, 12.

27 Such abuse was typical: Reedy OH, Dec. 19, 1968, 27–28.

28 lavished expensive gifts: Reedy OH, Dec. 20, 1969, 25–26.

28 "grey hair *en brosse*": "They've Never Had It So Hard," *Observer*, Jan. 26, 1964.

28 "large, rumpled man": "Johnson's Men: 'Valuable Hunks of Humanity.'"

28 "You ask him what that tree": Ibid.

28 "Both Walter and I took the position": Reedy OH, Dec. 19, 1968, 24–25.

28 Kennedy's core White House aides: Caro, *Passage of Power*, 334; O'Brien OH, Feb. 11, 1986, 50.

29 O'Brien, who directed: Robert Dallek, *Camelot's Court*, 212–14.

29 pulled out all the stops: O'Brien OH, Dec. 5, 1985, 42.

30 "He would be interested": O'Brien OH, Feb. 11, 1986, 7.

30 Johnson was a careful student: Ibid., 10.

30 a more natural rapport with LBJ: Ibid., 10-11.

30 "very much a New Dealer": O'Brien OH, April 8, 1986, 43.

30 Jim Rowe: Rowe OH, Sept. 9, 1969, 1-16.

31 "I can't afford it": Caro, *Master of the Senate*, 656-57.

32 "My God, Mr. President": McPherson OH, Dec. 5, 1968, tape 2, 20-21.

32 "touching all his old bases": Rowe OH, Sept. 16, 1969, 29.

33 "this curly-haired fellow, Clifford": Busby OH, July 2, 1982, 3.

33 after he left government service: Clifford OH, Mar. 17, 1969, 3-4, 8-9, 19.

34 committed advocate of liberal reform: Kalman, *Abe Fortas*, 133-50.

35 *Gideon v. Wainwright*: Ibid., 180-83.

35 Days after Kennedy's assassination: "Lyndon Johnson and Katharine Graham on 2 December 1963," tape K6312.01, PNO 19, in Johnson and Shreve, *Presidential Recordings Digital Edition*, vol. 2, *Kennedy Assassination and the Transfer of Power*.

35 Johnson repeatedly pressed him: Kalman, *Abe Fortas*, 228-29.

36 LBJ telephoned Larry O'Brien: Telephone transcript: LBJ to O'Brien, Nov. 25, 1963, 4:04 p.m., Johnson, *Presidential Recordings*.

36 "grim, cryptic wit": Salinger, *With Kennedy*, 64.

36 "bleary-eyed and unshaven": Jenkins OH, Aug. 24, 1971, 44.

37 "There is nothing more dangerous": Schlesinger, *Journals*, 225.

37 "For all his striped shirts": Caro, *Passage of Power*, 591.

37 "declared war, I guess": Schlesinger, *Journals*, 210.

38 Katharine Graham: Telephone transcript: LBJ, Graham, Dec. 2, 1963, 11:10 a.m., Johnson, *Presidential Recordings*.

38 LBJ reluctantly accepted: Caro, *Passage of Power*, 590.

38 "the mingling of Boston Brahmins": "Johnson Herd Blends Two," *Newsday*, Aug. 22, 1964.

38 "We all have one common goal": Roberts, *LBJ's Inner Circle*, 81.

Chapter 2: Participation in Prosperity

39 "The five of us had a long, long seminar": Heller OH, Feb. 20, 1970, 13-15.

39 Heller was arguably: Lemann, *Promised Land*, 129-30.

40 three days before the assassination: Heller OH, Feb. 20, 1970, 17-20.

40 "the President gently pushed": Lemann, *Promised Land*, 141.

41 "my kind of program": Gillette, *Launching the War on Poverty*, 15.

41 Median family income: Patterson, *Grand Expectations*, 312, 451. This growth was felt across the board, with the bottom two quintiles increasing their share of national income

by 4 percent. See *Historical Statistics of the United States*, **table Be 39-46, table Be 1-18.**

41 **renter to homeowner:** Patterson, *Grand Expectations*, 312. Between 1936 and 1972, the portion of families living in owner-occupied homes increased from 44 percent to 63 percent. See Jackson, *Crabgrass Frontier*, 205.

41 **blue-collar to white-collar:** Between 1950 and 1970, the portion of the workforce engaged in what qualified as white-collar work increased from 30.5 percent to 41 percent. See Janowitz, *Last Half-Century*, 127.

41 **average American family:** Zeitz, "Back to the Barricades," 70–75.

41 **consumer luxuries:** Patterson, *Grand Expectations*, 10.

41 **In 1950, only 3 percent:** Marty, *Daily Life in the United States*, 9.

42 **"sick recoveries which die":** Hansen, "Economic Progress and Declining Population Growth," 4.

42 **"full production, full employment":** "Reuther Challenges 'Our Fear of Abundance,'" *New York Times*, Sept. 16, 1945.

42 **capitalism "works":** Davies, *From Opportunity to Entitlement*, 20.

43 **"many frustrated economists":** Collins, *More*, 17–18.

43 **"a large part of the New Deal public":** Hofstadter, *Paranoid Style in American Politics*, 42.

43 **Over 7.8 million Americans:** Patterson, *Grand Expectations*, 68.

44 **David Riesman and Nathan Glazer:** Matusow, *Unraveling of America*, 7.

44 **liberal writers in the 1950s:** Patterson, *Grand Expectations*, 337, 345.

45 **"buys the right car":** Gillon, *Boomer Nation*, 141.

45 **"production, distribution, and consumption":** Unger, *Best of Intentions*, 18.

45 **liberal intellectuals and policy makers:** Matusow, *Unraveling of America*, 391.

46 **"With the supermarket as our temple":** "The National Purpose," *Time*, May 30, 1960.

46 **"not all the roots of American life":** Norman Mailer, "Superman Comes to the Supermart," *Esquire*, Nov. 1960.

46 **"cornucopias":** Collins, *More*, 41.

47 **Galbraith wrote:** Patterson, *America's Struggle Against Poverty*, 95–96.

47 **"system designed to be impervious":** Harrington, *Other America*, 10.

47 **It shocked the liberal conscience:** Patterson, *America's Struggle Against Poverty*, 129.

48 **"Some people would say poverty":** Gillette, *Launching the War on Poverty*, 6.

49 **"full employment at a time":** Unger, *Best of Intentions*, 28.

49 **"warmed-over revisions":** Gillette, *Launching the War on Poverty*, 12.

49 **"misfit":** Hackett OH, July 22, 1970, 3.

50 **"a very hard-driving, effective, caring person":** Gillette, *Launching the War on Poverty*, 16.

50 **"The good society":** Patterson, *America's Struggle Against Poverty*, 138.

50 **summons to brief Walter Heller:** Gillette, *Launching the War on Poverty*, 16.

50 **Lampman cautioned his boss:** Lemann, *Promised Land*, 131.

51 **"An attack on ignorance":** Ibid., 132.

51 **Wilbur Cohen:** Patterson, *America's Struggle Against Poverty*, 136–37.

51 **ad hoc committee:** Unger, *Best of Intentions*, 92–93.

51 **"leave the roots of poverty":** Ibid., 87.

51 **"a generation ago":** Robert Dallek, *Flawed Giant*, 75.

52 **"hard, bedrock content":** Caro, *Passage of Power*, 541.

52 **Buzz spent the evening of December 30:** Memorandum, Busby to LBJ, Dec. 30, 1963, WHCF FG 1, LBJ Library.

53 **Elizabeth Wickenden:** Lemann, *Promised Land*, 144; Robert Dallek, *Flawed Giant*, 62.

53 **"forces of learning and light":** Caro, *Passage of Power*, 543–44; Lemann, *Promised Land*, 144; Stossel, *Sarge*, 343–45.

53 **"sound like something President Kennedy":** Caro, *Passage of Power*, 544.

53 **campaign speech at Hyde Park:** "The Office of Economic Opportunity During the Administration of Lyndon Johnson: Administrative History," 7, LBJ Library.

54 **"very often a lack of jobs":** Lyndon Johnson, Annual Message to Congress on the State of the Union, Jan. 8, 1964, Digital Collections, LBJ Library.

54 **the term "poverty" had been entirely absent:** Sundquist, *Politics and Policy*, 112.

54 **first economic report to Congress:** "Office of Economic Opportunity During the Administration of Lyndon Johnson," 22–24; Andrew, *Lyndon Johnson and the Great Society*, 61–62.

55 **"a better phrase":** Sidney M. Milkis, "Lyndon Johnson, the Great Society, and the 'Twilight' of the Modern Presidency," in Milkis and Mileur, *Great Society and the High Tide of American Liberalism*, 10–11.

55 **"widening participation in prosperity":** "Office of Economic Opportunity During the Administration of Lyndon Johnson," 16–17.

56 **pace of growth had slowed:** Council of Economic Advisers OH, Aug. 1, 1964, 219.

57 **The results were almost instantaneous:** Matusow, *Unraveling of America*, 51–57.

57 **federal revenue increased:** Unger, *Best of Intentions*, 74–75.

Chapter 3: Second Day

58 **"two-shift" day:** "Johnson Herd Blends Two," *Newsday*, Aug. 22, 1964.

58 **"night reading":** "How the President Lives," *Baltimore Sun*, Oct. 4, 1964.

58 **Valenti's steadfastness:** "Boss Reports Valenti Late for the First Time," *Washington Post*, Sept. 6, 1964.

58 **"He called me at midnight":** Busby OH, April 23, 1981, 30.

58 **After working from bed:** Roberts, *LBJ's Inner Circle*, 42–43.

59 **Valenti read *more* than 200,000 words:** Goldman, *Tragedy of Lyndon Johnson*, 108.

59 **"freedom from the white telephone":** McPherson OH, Dec. 19, 1968, 12.

59 **"It's real Orwellian":** Roberts, *LBJ's Inner Circle*, 42–43.

59 **"Where do they get the stories":** Ibid., 44–45.

59 **"fear-bent sharecroppers":** "It's Open Season on LBJ," *Newsday*, July 17, 1965.

59 "the head of the duchy": Goldman, *Tragedy of Lyndon Johnson*, 102.

60 "heavy demands": "The Men Who Wear the LBJ Brand," *Toronto Globe and Mail*, June 16, 1965.

60 "Frankly, the people around Kennedy": Roberts, *LBJ's Inner Circle*, 45.

60 Lillian Reedy: Reedy OH, Feb. 14, 1972, 43.

60 conflicts began to surface: Cater OH, May 8, 1969, 13.

60 "Court politics in the White House": Reedy OH, Dec. 20, 1968, 7.

60 "interplay of egos": Valenti OH, July 12, 1972, 17.

61 "Neither Kennedy nor Johnson": Valenti, *This Time, This Place*, 173.

61 This dynamic led to duplication: Cater OH, May 8, 1969, 13-14.

61 "deliberately chaotic": "Johnson's Men: 'Valuable Hunks of Humanity.'"

61 appointments secretary: Valenti OH, Oct. 18, 1969, 27.

61 "[He] believed it important": Goldman, *Tragedy of Lyndon Johnson*, 117.

61 "the most accessible President": Roberts, *LBJ's Inner Circle*, 83.

62 "been raising the eyebrows": Ibid., 100.

62 "Kennedyite of the Kennedyites": Goldman, *Tragedy of Lyndon Johnson*, 112.

63 in the White House pool: Goodwin, *Remembering America*.

63 "Instead of the quantitative liberalism": Woods, *Prisoners of Hope*, 54.

64 "Why not enlarge the theme": Valenti, *Very Human President*, 85.

64 While the White House tested the phrase: Bornet, *Presidency of Lyndon B. Johnson*, 101.

64 "the phrase bothered me": Milkis, "Lyndon Johnson, the Great Society, and the 'Twilight' of the Modern Presidency," 39n19.

64 Busby, for his part: Horace Busby, "The Great Society: A New American Dream," Statements of LBJ, box 106, "5/22/64 Remarks of the President at the University of Michigan," LBJ Library.

65 In a tart memo: Memorandum, Moyers to Valenti, May 18, 1964, WHCF/SP, box 161, LBJ Library.

65 "This is a political year": Memorandum, Moyers and Goodwin to LBJ, May 18, 1964, WHCF/SP, box 161, LBJ Library.

65 Riding back to Washington: Miller, *Lyndon*, 377.

66 "never really liked the term": Robert Dallek, *Flawed Giant*, 83.

67 identified a divide: Reedy OH, June 7, 1975, 63-64.

67 "militant conscience": "The President's Closest Shadow," *South China Sunday Post-Herald*, May 17, 1964.

67 "Mr. Busby would not seem conservative": "Men Who Wear the LBJ Brand."

67 "clashed very early": Valenti OH, July 12, 1972, 15-16.

67 "I am not the praying type": Memorandum, Busby to Liz Carpenter, Jan. 12, 1965, "Memos for Liz Carpenter," box 18, Office Files of Busby.

67 displays of "evangelistic fervor": Memorandum, Busby to LBJ, n.d. [ca. May 1964], "Memos to the President, May 1964," box 52, Office Files of Busby.

67 "a bully good pulpit": Memorandum ("The President's Speech on the Great Society"), May 21, 1964, WHCF/SP, box 161.

68 "we are enjoying abundance": Memorandum Outline: Suggested Theme of Remarks for Use at Proposed News Conference, Saturday, May 16, 1964, "Memos to the President, May 1964," box 52, Office Files of Busby.

68 "while comfort has come to us": Horace Busby, "The Great Society: A New American Dream," Statements of LBJ, box 106, "5/22/64 Remarks of the President at the University of Michigan," LBJ Library.

68 "Great Society rests on abundance": Memorandum, Busby to LBJ ("Image Assessment and Suggested Activities"), n.d. [ca. May 1964], box 52, Office Files of Busby.

69 "economic well-being": Memorandum, Cater to LBJ, Aug. 3, 1965, "Memos to the President: 5/64–8/64," box 13B, Office Files of Cater.

70 "rejecting efforts to label": Memorandum, Busby to LBJ, May 19, 1964, "Memos to the President, May 1964," box 52, Office Files of Busby.

70 "Dick, I love you": Risen, Bill of the Century, 138.

70 "one of the least prejudiced": Reedy OH, Dec. 19, 1968, 28.

71 "Kennedy had made an intellectual appeal": Risen, Bill of the Century, 62.

71 "If I were you, Charlie": Telephone transcript: Johnson, Halleck, Dec. 24, 1963, time unknown, Johnson, Presidential Recordings.

71 "I've been around a long time": Risen, Bill of the Century, 155.

72 "You're with me!": Telephone transcript: Johnson, Byrd, April 10, 1964, 4:55 p.m., Johnson, Presidential Recordings.

72 "had been able to hold the line": Risen, Bill of the Century, 5.

73 "You couldn't turn around": Ibid., 148–49; Zelizer, Fierce Urgency of Now, 112–14.

73 speech at the College of the Holy Cross: Zelizer, Fierce Urgency of Now, 127–28.

73 "Desegregation was absolutely": Sokol, There Goes My Everything, 8.

73 "How can I destroy the lingering faces": Ibid., 99.

73 "racism permeated every aspect": Ibid., 6.

73 "You have not lived": Ibid., 7.

73 "This thing here is a revolution": Ibid., 8.

74 "As law-abiding Americans": Ibid., 191.

74 Julius Manger: Risen, Bill of the Century, 192.

75 only 10 percent: Keyssar, Right to Vote, 212.

75 readying federal departments to issue sweeping rules: Memorandum, Douglass Cater to LBJ, May 26, 1964, "Memos to the President: 5/64–8/64," box 13B, Office Files of Cater.

75 Moyers found Johnson in a glum mood: Moyers, "Second Thoughts."

Chapter 4: Revolutionary Activity

76 "That's a decent thing to do": "How Kennedy Won the Black Vote," Los Angeles Times, Dec. 15, 1988.

76 "He was just enormously impressive": Redmon, Come as You Are, 83.

77 "Shriver had the kind of charisma": Peters, Tilting at Windmills, 134.

77 "Bill Moyers and I have been living on the Hill": Stossel, Sarge, 215, 242.

78 "Sarge was no close pal brother-in-law": Shesol, *Mutual Contempt*, 169.

79 "The glands": Stossel, *Sarge*, 347-351.

79 "Through all of this period": Mankiewicz OH, April 18, 1969, 9.

80 "like he's got a bomb": Stossel, *Sarge*, 386.

81 Johnson would later salute: Ibid., 363.

81 "Shriver's own temperament": Sundquist OH, April 7, 1969, 16, 36.

81 "the notion of organizing people": Mankiewicz OH, April 18, 1969, 11-12.

81 "One of the choices": Gillette, *Launching the War on Poverty*, 107.

82 salon-style dinners at Timberlawn: Ibid., 192.

82 "crazy about these ideas": Stossel, *Sarge*, 247.

82 "any radical shift of authority": Gillette, *Launching the War on Poverty*, 91.

82 "an essentially revolutionary activity": Mankiewicz OH, April 18, 1969, 12.

83 "He's got heads of departments": "Lyndon Johnson and Bill Moyers on 7 August 1964," Conversation WH6408-12-4815, 4816, 4817, 4818.

84 "Sarge's idea of administration": "The Poverty Non-war," *Washington Post*, Nov. 26, 1964.

84 "Sarge . . . and many others in the Congress": Gillette, *Launching the War on Poverty*, 241.

84 elected officials from across the country: Stossel, *Sarge*, 411; Andrew, *Lyndon Johnson and the Great Society*, 73.

85 "using public funds to *instruct*": Stossel, *Sarge*, 408.

85 "We are experiencing a class struggle": Lemann, *Promised Land*, 165-67; Andrew, *Lyndon Johnson and the Great Society*, 73.

85 "Both of the agencies I'm running": Gillette, *Launching the War on Poverty*, 247.

86 "What in the hell": Lemann, *Promised Land*, 167.

86 "Mayors all over the United States": Ibid., 165.

87 "the program got off the ground": Gillette, *Launching the War on Poverty*, 103.

87 "I think it is a Liberal view": Horace Busby, "Memorandum Outline: Suggested Themes of Remarks for Use at Proposed News Conference, Saturday, May 16, 1964," "Memos to the President, May 1964," box 52, Office Files of Busby.

87 In 1977, a survey: Blakeslee, "Community Action Program"; Piven and Cloward, *Regulating the Poor*, 273-74.

87 "vast network of sergeants": Moynihan, *Maximum Feasible Misunderstanding*, 130.

88 government employment helped lift: Thernstrom and Thernstrom, *America in Black and White*, 188-89.

88 Job Corps, a program modeled: Unger, *Best of Intentions*, 174-75.

88 George Foreman: Stossel, *Sarge*, 398-401.

89 generated ample cause for concern: Unger, *Best of Intentions*, 174-78.

90 Joe Alsop: Stossel, *Sarge*, 418-19.

90 prepare and launch a summer pilot program: Sugarman OH, March 14, 1969, 12-16.

91 To train the summer staff: Ibid., 17-19.

92 criticisms miss the mark: Ibid., 14–15; Andrew, *Lyndon Johnson and the Great Society,* 76–77.

93 "I don't know of many other instances": Gillette, *Launching the War on Poverty,* 279–80.

Chapter 5: Frontlash

94 **Lou Harris described for readers:** Darman, *Landslide,* 175–76.

94 **the term "white backlash":** White, *Making of the President, 1964,* 245.

94 **"spoke of the practice known as 'bussing'":** Johnson, *All the Way with LBJ,* 85–86.

95 **"If we aren't careful":** Darman, *Landslide,* 176.

95 **After launching his campaign:** Perlstein, *Before the Storm,* 317–21; Carter, *Politics of Rage,* 202–3.

96 **initial polling had Wallace:** Perlstein, *Before the Storm,* 321, 342–44; White, *Making of the President, 1964,* 245.

96 **laced with crude appeals to fear:** Perlstein, *Before the Storm,* 326.

97 **Between 1910 and 1970:** Lemann, *Promised Land,* 6.

97 **Racially restrictive housing laws:** See Jackson, *Crabgrass Frontier,* chap. 11; Connolly, *Ghetto Grows in Brooklyn;* Wilder, *Covenant with Color,* chap. 9.

98 **"They are mostly Catholic":** Memorandum, Valenti to LBJ, Aug. 4, 1964, Handwriting File, box 3.

98 **Richard Scammon:** Memorandum, Scammon to Bill Moyers, July 21, 1964, box 3, Office Files of Moyers.

100 **Buzz believed that there was ample room:** Memorandum, Busby to LBJ, July 13, 1964, box 52, Office Files of Busby.

100 **"The hour is late":** Zeitz, "Craziest Conventions in U.S. History."

101 **What one historian later dubbed:** Kabaservice, *Rule and Ruin,* 97–123.

102 **"likes to think of itself":** Johnson, *All the Way with LBJ,* 31.

102 **"Goldwater has a basic appeal":** Memorandum, Moyers to LBJ, Aug. 11, 1964, box 10, Office Files of Moyers.

102 **Goldwater deplored the New Deal:** Goldberg, *Barry Goldwater,* 23, 28, 47, 55, 75–76, 84.

102 **Teddy White observed:** White, *Making of the President, 1964,* 108–10.

102 **"We've got superpatriots":** Ibid., 125.

103 **an obscure congressman:** "Man in the News," *New York Times,* July 17, 1964.

103 **"complete zero":** Johnson, *All the Way with LBJ,* 221.

103 **"just nutty as a fruitcake":** Ibid., 69.

103 **Buzz urged the president:** Memorandum, Busby to LBJ, July 19, 1964, box 52, Office Files of Busby.

103 **"the attack should be broadened":** Memorandum, Horace Busby to LBJ, Sept. 28, 1964, box 52, Office Files of Busby.

104 **Teddy White later:** *Making of the President, 1964,* 367–370.

105 **"We're selling the President":** Perlstein, *Before the Storm,* 433.

105 The spots that DDB created: Ibid., 432–34.

105 "Daisy Girl": Ibid., 413–14; White, *Making of the President, 1964,* 339.

106 "soundest national approach": Memorandum, Scammon to Moyers, July 31, 1964, box 3, Office Files of Moyers.

106 "frontlash": Johnson, *All the Way with LBJ,* 190–92.

107 pursued their opponent without mercy: Perlstein, *Before the Storm,* 435; Johnson, *All the Way with LBJ,* 204.

107 central message of the president's campaign: Darman, *Landslide,* 197.

107 Rowland Evans and Robert Novak observed: Johnson, *All the Way with LBJ,* 137.

107 "Right now, the biggest asset": Perlstein, *Before the Storm,* 436.

107 an operation almost unprecedented: Memorandum, Moyers to LBJ, Aug. 15, 1964, box 10, Office Files of Moyers.

108 Jim Rowe took leave: Memorandum, Moyers to LBJ, Aug. 11, 1964, box 10, Office Files of Moyers.

108 "Not since the 1920s": Johnson, *All the Way,* 206.

109 "a hymn-singing group": Branch, *Pillar of Fire,* 456–57.

109 "all dressed up": Joshua Zeitz, "Democratic Debacle," *American Heritage,* June/July 2004.

111 "I always had the feeling": Ibid.

111 "if you value your party": Kotz, *Judgment Days,* 205.

112 "They're Democrats!": Ibid, 218.

112 concentrate more effort on the South: Memorandum, Busby to LBJ, May 22, 1964, box 52, Office Files of Busby.

113 Lady Bird Johnson insisted: Perlstein, *Before the Storm,* 463–65.

114 the speech left reporters "gasping": Leuchtenburg, *White House Looks South,* 321.

114 "respect and admiration": Branch, *Pillar of Fire,* 515.

115 Earlier in the year: Updegrove, "When LBJ and Goldwater Agreed to Keep Race out of the Campaign."

115 a wider constellation of grievances: *New Republic,* Oct. 31, 1964.

116 Walter Jenkins had been detained: Beschloss, *Reaching for Glory,* 72–80.

116 In a striking conversation: LBJ and Lady Bird Johnson, 9:12 a.m., tape WH6410.11, no. 5895, LBJ Recordings.

117 "a case of combat fatigue": Perlstein, *Before the Storm,* 489–90.

117 Miller asked rhetorically: Johnson, *All the Way with LBJ,* 263.

117 "likely to become Democratic converts": Ibid., 246.

117 "not a normal American politician": Darman, *Landslide,* 172.

Chapter 6: A Frustrating Paradox

121 Joe Califano later recalled: Califano, *Triumph and Tragedy of Lyndon Johnson,* 17–24.

123 Teddy White remembered: White, *Making of the President, 1964,* 54.

123 **Horace Busby remarked:** Memorandum, Busby to Carpenter, Feb. 2, 1965, "Memos for Liz Carpenter," box 18, Office Files of Busby.

124 **The Oval Office:** Valenti OH, March 3, 1971, 9.

125 **Walton transformed:** "Their Home Away from Home," *Washington Post,* July 18, 1965.

125 **"a frustrating paradox":** Roberts, *LBJ's Inner Circle,* 112.

126 **stumbled across Bill Moyers:** Reedy OH, Dec. 19, 1968, 28-29.

126 **When Reedy entered the hospital:** Roberts, *LBJ's Inner Circle,* 113.

126 **"Poor George":** Ibid., 114.

126 **"more erudite":** Ibid.

127 **"tended to view reporters":** Goldman, *Tragedy of Lyndon Johnson,* 120.

127 **regularly savaged Barry Goldwater:** "Goldwater Ready to Meet Johnson on Race Tensions," *New York Times,* July 21, 1964; Johnson, *All the Way with LBJ,* 140.

127 **the president faulted Reedy:** Reedy OH, Dec. 19, 1968, 33, 40.

128 **"The White House press corps":** Roberts, *LBJ's Inner Circle,* 112.

128 **"press was growing increasingly suspicious":** "Presidency: Press Criticism Overflows," *Los Angeles Times,* July 11, 1965.

128 **"an inquiry of Mr. Valenti":** "Johnson's Men: 'Valuable Hunks of Humanity.'"

128 **"George Reedy was a Press Secretary":** Goldman, *Tragedy of Lyndon Johnson,* 122.

129 **Asked in later years:** Reedy OH, Dec. 19, 1968, 33.

129 **out of step with Moyers and Valenti:** Robert Dallek, *Camelot's Court,* 115-17.

130 **"$600,000":** Reedy OH, Dec. 19, 1968, 37.

130 **Alan Otten:** "The President's Problems," *Wall Street Journal,* Nov. 6, 1964.

131 **Merriman Smith of UPI:** "It's Open Season on LBJ."

131 **"relaxed demeanor":** Memorandum, Busby to LBJ, April 16, 1964, "Press Conference Memos to the President," box 14, Office Files of Busby.

131 **cultivate their favor:** Memorandum, Busby to LBJ, April 4, 1964, "Memos to the President, 4/64," box 53, Office Files of Busby.

132 **"the newsmen, almost universally":** Memorandum, Busby to LBJ, May 30, 1965, "Memos to the President, 6/65," box 51, Office Files of Busby.

132 **ill at ease with the medium:** Memorandum, Douglass Cater to LBJ, Nov. 27, 1964, "Memos to the President: 11/64-3/65," box 13B, Office Files of Cater.

132 **"He was an old UPI fellow":** McPherson OH, Sept. 19, 1985, 11.

133 **Moyers would replace Reedy:** Reedy OH, Dec. 20, 1968, 8-9.

133 **Publicly, the White House maintained:** "Presidency: Press Criticism Overflows."

133 **Harry McPherson:** Roberts, *LBJ's Inner Circle,* 109.

134 **"bomb-throwing ally":** McPherson OH, Dec. 5., 1968, 3.

135 **McPherson was in Japan:** McPherson OH, Dec. 5, 1985, 18-20.

136 **"In 1965 one could still feel":** McPherson, *Political Education,* 246.

136 **Douglass Cater:** "Douglass Cater Is Dead at 72; Educator and Presidential Aide," *New York Times,* Dec. 16, 1995.

136 **He arrived at the White House:** "Cater Goes by the Book, His Own, as Johnson Aide," *Baltimore Sun,* May 28, 1966.

137 "a well-stocked mind": Goldman, *Tragedy of Lyndon Johnson*, 266-67.

137 The warm sentiment was not mutual: Cater OH, May 8, 1969, 13.

138 "It was a failure of men": Memorandum, Cater to LBJ, May 4, 1964, "Memos to the President: 5/64-8/64," box 13B, Office Files of Cater.

138 "You have the power to speak": McPherson OH, Dec. 19, 1968, 22-26.

138 never did cut off Cater's water: Cater OH, April 24, 1981, 17.

138 At the time of his appointment: Roberts, *LBJ's Inner Circle*, 91-93.

138 "He was a natty dresser": Goldman, *Tragedy of Lyndon Johnson*, 268.

138 Two qualities: "Watson Wields Increasing Influence," *Washington Post*, Dec. 6, 1965.

139 "the totalitarian days": Busby OH, Dec. 21, 1988, 10.

139 "buy a postal stamp": "Watson Wields Increasing Influence."

139 "they were excellent": Keppel OH, April 21, 1969, 27.

139 "by no means a Bircher": McPherson OH, Dec. 19, 1968, 22-26.

139 "was not abrasive": Valenti OH, July 12, 1972, 16-18.

140 "Cater, Califano, Goodwin and McPherson": Goldman, *Tragedy of Lyndon Johnson*, 275.

140 "in a place where you're sitting": Valenti OH, July 12, 1972, 14.

140 "Nothing in Joe Califano's original writ": McPherson OH, Dec. 19, 1968, 24-25.

140 "as long as I was kept informed": Cater OH, May 8, 1969, 13.

141 "interplay of egos": Valenti OH, July 12, 1972, 17.

141 "he works you like a dog": "He Demands a Lot: Johnson Hard to Work For," *Boston Globe*, Nov. 11, 1964.

141 "The President isn't a flow-chart man": Roberts, *LBJ's Inner Circle*, 38.

141 movie script: "The President's Closest Shadow," *Boston Globe*, May 17, 1964.

141 "an overpowering man": Rowe OH, Sept. 16, 1969, 51.

142 "humor or his anecdotes": Cater OH, May 8, 1969, 18-19.

142 Not everyone agreed: Califano, *Triumph and Tragedy of Lyndon Johnson*, 188.

142 "relaxed in ways that would tire me": Schultze OH, April 10, 1969, 54.

142 "It isn't that Johnson abuses people": White, *Making of the President, 1964*, 59.

143 "there is no real privacy": "Working for Johnson Is Hard but Rewarding," *New York Times*, May 1, 1966.

Chapter 7: Completing the Fair Deal

144 Truman told Congress: Harry S. Truman, Annual Message to the Congress on the State of the Union, Jan. 5, 1949; Hamby, *Beyond the New Deal*, 293.

144 "We have helped the states": Sundquist, *Politics and Policy*, 155.

144 most GOP leaders agreed: Ibid., 178, 187; Zelizer, *Fierce Urgency of Now*, 181.

145 many white ethnic communities: Zeitz, *White Ethnic New York*, 11-38; Woods, *Prisoners of Hope*, 137.

145 "lawful that public funds": Sundquist, *Politics and Policy*, 189.

145 dire need of additional education funding: Zelizer, *Fierce Urgency of Now*, 175; Sundquist, *Politics and Policy*, 159-60.

146 **student achievement reflected:** Elizabeth Cascio and Sarah Reber, "The K-12 Education Battle," in Bailey and Danziger, *Legacies of the War on Poverty*, 68.

146 **"Federal policy should be to improve":** Memorandum, Cater to LBJ, Dec. 26, 1964, "Memos to the President: 11/64-2/65," box 13B, Office Files of Cater.

146 **Yet behind closed doors:** Memorandum, Cater to LBJ, Dec. 19, 1964, "Memos to the President: 11/64-2/65," box 13B, Office Files of Cater.

147 **John Hay Whitney:** Memorandum, Cater to LBJ, Dec. 3, 1964, "Memos to the President: 11/64-2/65," box 13B, Office Files of Cater.

147 **"religious and philosophical antagonisms":** Sundquist, *Politics and Policy*, 205.

147 **Now the door seemed to budge:** Graham, *Uncertain Triumph*, 72-73.

147 **The idea was not new:** Ibid., 72-73, 77; Berkowitz, *Mr. Social Security*, 202-5.

148 **"we've got to do this in a hurry":** Keppel OH, April 21, 1969, 17-19, 26-27.

148 **Elementary and Secondary Education Act:** Woods, *Prisoners of Hope*, 138.

149 **Critics would later dismiss:** Matusow, *Unraveling of America*, 223-26.

149 **"income correlates highly":** Ibid., 221.

150 **"In 1965, the issue was not good education policy":** Patrick McGuinn and Frederick Hess, "Freedom from Ignorance? The Great Society and the Evolution of the Elementary and Secondary Education Act of 1965," in Milkis and Mileur, *Great Society and the High Tide of American Liberalism*, 297.

150 **federal assistance proved critical:** Andrew, *Lyndon Johnson and the Great Society*, 119-20.

150 **federal spending on primary and secondary education:** Cascio and Reber, "K-12 Education Battle," 73.

151 **number of independent school districts:** McGuinn and Hess, "Freedom from Ignorance?," 302-3.

151 **"where President Kennedy used to use":** Roberts, *LBJ's Inner Circle*, 49.

152 **"His choir-like directions":** "The Transition Over, The White House Staff Is Strictly Johnson in Outlook," *New York Times*, June 13, 1965.

152 **In 1964, the office of the secretary of HEW:** "Department of Health, Education, and Welfare—Statistical Summary," "Background on HEW Programs," box 32, Office Files of Califano.

152 **"a holding company":** Graham, *Uncertain Triumph*, 107.

152 **"utterly ridiculous to be trying":** Ibid., 101.

152 **"not well equipped":** Ibid., 94.

153 **"dedicated to servicing local":** Orfield, *Reconstruction of Southern Education*, 49.

153 **"What's all this about this fellow":** Graham, *Uncertain Triumph*, 42-43.

153 **a major overhaul of the office:** Memorandum, Keppel to Califano, Nov. 29, 1965, "HEW Report on Education," box 36, Office Files of Califano.

153 **"The anguish can only be imagined":** Graham, *Uncertain Triumph*, 99.

154 **personnel grew by an astonishing 50 percent:** Bernstein, *Guns or Butter*, 201.

154 **It went nowhere:** Berkowitz, *Mr. Social Security*, 167.

154 **powerful opposition:** Sundquist, *Politics and Policy*, 290, 298.

155 **Treaty of Detroit:** Lichtenstein, *State of the Union*, 123.

155 100 million Americans: Unger, *Best of Intentions*, 35.

155 At a hearing in 1959: Sundquist, *Politics and Policy*, 288–89.

156 "problem of aging amounts": Woods, *Prisoners of Hope*, 146.

156 angry opposition: Ibid., 148; Sundquist, *Politics and Policy*, 309–10; Unger, *Best of Intentions*, 41.

157 "We do not, by profession, compromise": Sundquist, *Politics and Policy*, 318.

157 labyrinthine negotiations: Woods, *Prisoners of Hope*, 153–54.

157 Busby was particularly concerned: Memorandum, Busby to LBJ, July 22, 1965, "Memos to Douglass Cater," box 18, Office Files of Busby; Zelizer, *Fierce Urgency of Now*, 201; Bernstein, *Guns or Butter*, 179.

158 "George, have you ever fed chickens?": Woods, *Prisoners of Hope*, 152–53.

159 "If you're wrong": Ibid. 154.

159 "collapse under its own weight": Robert Dallek, *Flawed Giant*, 209.

159 daunting challenges: M. G. Gluck and V. Reno, *Reflections on Implementing Medicare*, 39.

160 Postal Service hung: Ibid., 33–34.

160 "if ever in history": Ibid., 49.

161 "no strong advocacy groups": Ibid., 16.

161 medical inflation began outstripping: Andrew, *Lyndon Johnson and the Great Society*, 106.

161 "unquestionable capability to administer": Edward Berkowitz, "Medicare: The Great Society's Enduring National Health Insurance Program," in Milkis and Mileur, *Great Society and the High Tide of American Liberalism*, 339.

161 "accepted the going system": Ibid., 323.

161 "wasn't possible in 1965": Andrew, *Lyndon Johnson and the Great Society*, 105.

162 "Medicare . . . began with an apparent paradox": Stevens and Stevens, *Welfare Medicine in America*, 50.

162 learned to love it: Andrew, *Lyndon Johnson and the Great Society*, 102.

Chapter 8: Get 'Em! Get the Last Ones!

165 surge of optimism: Patterson, *Brown v. Board of Education*, 70.

165 In 1960, less than 1 percent: Orfield and Yun, *Resegregation in American Schools*, 29.

165 Alabama, Mississippi, and Louisiana: Halpern, *On the Limits of the Law*, 43.

165 Dorothy Counts: Patterson, *Brown v. Board of Education*, 105–7.

166 Ruby Bridges: Patterson, *Brown v. Board of Education*, 107.

166 "she showed a lot of courage": "Ruby Bridges, Made Famous in Iconic Painting, Goes to White House," *Colorlines*, July 15, 2011.

167 "It is as if no taxpayer sent in a return": Marshall, *Federalism and Civil Rights*, 7.

167 "abnormal, superstitious respect": Reedy OH, Feb. 14, 1972, 30.

167 "Those little brown bodies": Caro, *Master of the Senate*, 721–22.

167 Federal funding now amounted: Patterson, *Brown v. Board of Education*, 139.

167 "golden opportunity": Halpern, *On the Limits of the Law*, 44.

168 bumped up against local resistance: Memorandum, Douglass Cater to LBJ, March 12, 1965, "Memos to the President: 3/65–4/65," box 13B, Office Files of Cater.

168 gave his aides free rein: Memorandum, Cater to LBJ, March 24, 1965, "Memos to the President: 3/65–4/65," box 13B, Office Files of Cater.

168 "The problem was simply this": Memorandum, Cater to LBJ, April 23, 1965, "Memos to the President: 3/65–4/65," box 13B, Office Files of Cater.

169 "'Get 'em'": Keppel OH, April 21, 1969, 17–19, 26.

169 "anxious to put all the states": Transcript, n.d., "School Desegregation," box 8, Office Files of Califano.

170 "never had any doubts": Keppel OH, Aug. 17, 1972, 4.

170 "resignation": Memorandum, Cater to LBJ, May 14, 1965, "Memos to the President: 5/65," box 13B, Office Files of Cater.

171 "was not stringent enough": Halpern, *On the Limits of the Law*, 48–49.

171 State Councils on Human Relations: Memorandum, "School Desegregation in the Southern States," May 1966, "Material on Title VI, Civil Rights Bill," box 52, Office Files of Cater.

172 "We think time is running out": Marion S. Barry and Betty Garman to John Gardner, Feb. 16, 1966, "Material on Title VI, Civil Rights Bill," box 52, Office Files of Cater.

172 HEW prepared revised guidelines: Memorandum, F. Peter Libassi to Douglass Cater and Lee White, Feb. 2, 1966, "Material on Title VI, Civil Rights Bill," box 52, Office Files of Cater; Memorandum, Alanson W. Willcox to Harold Howe II, March 7, 1966, "Material on Title VI, Civil Rights Bill," box 52, Office Files of Cater.

173 "nothing in Title VI": Halpern, *On the Limits of the Law*, 55.

173 "speaks in terms of *exclusion*": "Statement to the United States Commissioner of Education Harold Howe II by Charles F. Carroll, Superintendent of Public Instruction, State of North Carolina," April 14, 1966, "Material on Title VI, Civil Rights Bill," box 52, Office Files of Cater.

173 "guidelines are not designed": LBJ to Richard B. Russell, May 16, 1966, "Material on Title VI, Civil Rights Bill," box 52, Office Files of Cater.

174 "It will be impossible to avoid": Memorandum, Cater to LBJ, Aug. 4, 1966, "Material on Title VI, Civil Rights Bill," box 52, Office Files of Cater.

174 Writing for the appellate panel: *Derek Jerome Singleton, Minor, by Mrs. Edna Marie Singleton, His Mother and Next Friend, et al., Appellants, v. Jackson Municipal Separate School District et al., Appellees*, No. 22527, U.S. Court of Appeals Fifth Circuit, June 22, 1965.

174 administrative and judicial firepower worked: J. Michael Ross, "Trends in Black Student Racial Isolation, 1968-1992," Office of Educational Research and Improvement, U.S. Department of Education, 1995.

175 That scrutiny became more standard: Graham, *Civil Rights Era*, 372–75; Patterson, *Brown v. Board of Education*, 144–46.

176 "While we are investigating complaints": Memorandum, Libassi to Cater, "Civil Rights Bill: Proposed Guidelines and Summary, Title VI," box 52, Office Files of Cater.

176 **Chicago's de facto segregation:** Coordinating Council of Community Organizations to Francis Keppel, July 4, 1965; and Albert A. Raby to Francis Keppel, Oct. 19, 1965, "Material on Title VI, Civil Rights Bill," box 52, Office Files of Cater.

177 **"The Elementary and Secondary Education Act":** Albert A. Raby to Cater, Oct. 19, 1965, "Material on Title VI, Civil Rights Bill," box 52, Office Files of Cater.

177 **Keppel's office instructed Willis:** Alvin G. Cohen to Willis, Sept. 23, 1965, "Material on Title VI, Civil Rights Bill," box 52, Office Files of Cater.

178 **defer the delivery of federal funds:** Keppel to Willis, Sept. 30, 1965; Keppel to Ray Page, Sept. 30, 1965; Memorandum, Cater to LBJ, Oct. 1, 1965, "Memos to the President: 10/65," box 13B, Office Files of Cater.

178 **"northern school districts were practicing":** Keppel OH, April 21, 1969, 19–20.

178 **Daley was in town:** Ibid., 24–25.

178 **the city's schools were out of compliance:** Memorandum, Howe to John Gardner, Dec. 16, 1966, "School Desegregation," box 8, Office Files of Califano.

179 **"the reversal of the withholding action":** Seeley to Joe Frantz, March 20, 1972, amended to Keppel OH, April 21, 1969, 27.

180 **HEW dispatched more than a thousand inspectors:** Memorandum, F. Peter Libassi to Cater, Califano, and Nicholas Katzenbach, May 13, 1966, "Material on Title VI, Civil Rights Bill," box 52, Office Files of Cater.

180 **The guidelines were sweeping:** "Guidelines for Compliance with Title VI of the Civil Rights Act of 1964," n.d., "Material on Title VI, Civil Rights Bill," box 52, Office Files of Cater.

181 **"transition has not been as difficult":** "Dear Hospital Administrator," n.d. [ca. May 1966], "Material on Title VI, Civil Rights Bill," box 52, Office Files of Cater.

181 **The administration dispatched Stewart:** Memorandum, F. Peter Libassi to Douglass Cater, Joseph Califano, and Nicholas Katzenbach, June 1, 1966, "Material on Title VI, Civil Rights Bill," box 52, Office Files of Cater.

181 **15 percent of all hospital beds:** Berkowitz, "Medicare: The Great Society's Enduring National Health Insurance Program," 326.

182 **memorable visit to a southern hospital:** Ibid., 327.

182 **The pressure worked:** Andrew, *Lyndon Johnson and the Great Society*, 105.

182 **"most of the hospital discrimination":** Memorandum, Libassi to Cater, Califano, and Nicholas Katzenbach, July 15, 1966, "Material on Title VI, Civil Rights Bill," box 52, Office Files of Cater.

182 **"the day before Medicare":** Andrew, *Lyndon Johnson and the Great Society*, 105.

183 **"And they won't [comply] Lyndon":** Woods, *LBJ*, 573.

Chapter 9: The Fabulous Eighty-Ninth

184 **task forces:** Woods, *Prisoners of Hope*, 127–28.

185 **abridged twelve-hundred-page version:** Memorandum, Cater to LBJ, Nov. 3, 1964, "Memos to the President: 9/64–11/64," box 13B, Office Files of Cater.

185 **LBJ had instructed Bill Moyers:** LBJ and Moyers, Nov. 5, 1964, WH6411-05-6198.

185 **In the Senate:** Woods, *Prisoners of Hope*, 130; Zelizer, *Fierce Urgency of Now*, 169–72.

186 **Under O'Brien's leadership:** O'Brien OH, Sept. 18, 1985, 21–30; April 8, 1986, 39.

187 **"the kind of seniority":** O'Brien OH, Sept. 18, 1985, 39.

187 **"I would be very, very careful":** O'Brien OH, Oct. 29, 1985, 9.

187 **"Why didn't you call me?":** Ibid., 10.

187 **"would devote an inordinate amount of time":** Ibid., 13.

188 **"Selma has succeeded in limiting":** Stanton, *From Selma to Sorrow*, 34.

189 **"find[ing] the worst condition":** Beschloss, *Reaching for Glory*, 159.

189 **"take that one illustration":** Beschloss, *Reaching for Glory, 162.*

189 **King's own notes:** Garrow, *Protest at Selma*, 225.

190 **"disgraceful exercise":** Kotz, *Judgment Days*, 290.

190 **Inside the White House:** Zelizer, *Fierce Urgency of Now*, 213.

190 **"America didn't like what it saw":** Goodwin, *Remembering America*, 319.

190 **"This time, on this issue":** "When LBJ Said, 'We Shall Overcome,'" *New York Times*, Aug. 28, 2008.

191 **"was an instant of silence":** Goodwin, *Remembering America*, 334.

191 **"immediately mounted an all-fronts attack":** Califano, *Triumph and Tragedy of Lyndon Johnson*, 58.

191 **federal examiners descended:** Keyssar, *The Right to Vote*, 264; Califano, *The Triumph and Tragedy of Lyndon Johnson*, 47.

192 **"never shook hands":** Sokol, *There Goes My Everything*, 109.

192 **roughly thirty-seven million European immigrants:** For background, see John Bodnar, *The Transplanted: A History of Immigrants in Urban America* (Bloomington: Indiana University Press, 1987).

193 **"free white persons":** For background on race and immigration, see Matthew Frye Jacobson, *Whiteness of a Different Color: European Immigrants and the Alchemy of Race* (Cambridge, Mass.: Harvard University Press, 1999); Noel Ignatiev, *How the Irish Became White* (London: Routledge, 1995); David R. Roediger, *The Wages of Whiteness: Race and the Making of the American Working Class* (New York: Verso, 1991); Eric L. Goldstein, *The Price of Whiteness: Jews, Race, and American Identity* (Princeton, N.J.: Princeton University Press, 2006).

193 **In 1911, a government commission:** Jacobson, *Whiteness of a Different Color*, 78–82.

194 **"The welfare of the United States":** Gillon, *"That's Not What We Meant to Do,"* 163–64.

194 **Immigration Act of 1924:** Jacobson, *Whiteness of a Different Color*, 82–84.

194 **Nazi race policy:** Ibid., 101.

195 **"a policy of deliberate discrimination":** Roger Daniels, *Guarding the Golden Door: American Immigration Policy and Immigrants Since 1882* (New York: Hill and Wang, 2004), 129.

195 **The new law:** Gillon, *"That's Not What We Meant to Do."*

195 **In signing the law:** Ibid., 168–69, 173.

196 **By 1972:** Ibid., 182.

198 **Model Cities program:** Robert Dallek, *Flawed Giant*, 317-22.

198 **higher education:** Bridget Terry Long, "Supporting Higher Education," in Bailey and Danziger, *Legacies of the War on Poverty*, 97.

199 **spending on postsecondary student expenses:** Ibid., 95.

199 **"The important role":** Ibid., 101.

199 **more middle-income students:** Ibid., 95, 103-4.

199 **federal grants account:** Weissman, "Here's Exactly How Much the Government Would Have to Spend to Make Public College Tuition-Free."

200 **"children whose nutritional":** Jane Waldfogel, "The Safety Net for Families with Children," in Bailey and Danziger, *Legacies of the War on Poverty*, 154-55.

200 **subsidized food stamp program:** Ibid., 155-58.

201 **Child Nutrition Act:** Ibid., 158-59; Child poverty rates based on American Community Survey Briefs (U. S. Census Bureau), November 2011.

202 **roughly three hundred such measures:** Woods, *Prisoners of Hope*, 231-34.

202 **"No longer is peripheral action":** Ibid., 235.

203 **"Considering that the thrust":** Bornet, *Presidency of Lyndon B. Johnson*, 128-29.

203 **Children's Television Workshop:** Stark, *Glued to the Set*, 150-51.

203 **advertising techniques:** Ibid., 152.

204 **Not everyone shared the enthusiasm:** Ibid., 153-54.

204 **"dreamy vague proposals":** Woods, *Prisoners of Hope*, 57.

204 **"living intellectually off":** Schlesinger, *Journals*, 232-36.

205 **"Mr. President, this has been a remarkable":** Leuchtenburg, "Visit with LBJ."

Chapter 10: Guns and Butter

209 **"I don't want to be known":** Herring, *From Colony to Superpower*, 736.

209 **had heard of Vietnam:** See Herring, *America's Longest War*.

211 **"If I don't go in now":** Zelizer, *Arsenal of Democracy*, 193-94.

211 **In World War II:** Appy, *Working-Class War*, 27.

211 **"all painted in their designer colors":** Baker, *Nam*, 33.

211 **"you could cut the fear":** Appy, *Working-Class War*, 123.

211 **a grim battleground:** Engelhardt, *End of Victory Culture*, 177-78.

212 **"I went to Vietnam":** Terry, *Bloods*, 243, 251, 255-56.

212 **American war crimes:** *New York Times*, April 6, 1971, 18; *New York Times*, April 12, 1971, 5; *New York Times*, April 11, 1971, E1; *New York Times*, April 9, 1971, 10.

213 **"out there, lacking restraints":** Appy, *Working-Class War*, 252.

213 **"I gave them a good boy":** Andrew Huebner, "The Embattled Americans: A Cultural History of Soldiers and Veterans, 1941-1982" (Ph.D. diss., Brown University, 2004), 329.

213 **"I was shivering":** Leroy V. Quintana, "Old Geezers . . . Playing Taps on a Tape Recorder," in Appy, *Patriots*, 538-39.

213 "it was never easy to guess": Michael Herr, *Dispatches* (New York: Alfred A. Knopf, 1977), 88.

213 They also turned to drugs: Appy, *Working-Class War*, 283–85.

214 over thirty thousand servicemen: U.S. Department of Commerce, Bureau of the Census, "Vietnam Conflict—U.S. Military Forces in Vietnam and Casualties Incurred: 1961 to 1972," table 590, 369.

214 trap of their own making: VanDeMark, *Into the Quagmire*, 154–55.

215 "credibility gap": Unger, *Best of Intentions*, 240.

215 "The old C&O canal": VanDeMark, *Into the Quagmire*, 155.

215 "simply not believed": Unger, *Best of Intentions*, 202, 240–41.

215 playing hardball: "Is Ill Will Behind Piece '60 Minutes' Plans to Do on PBS' Bill Moyers?," *Baltimore Sun*, May 29, 1992.

216 "The credibility gap was purely": Jacobsen OH, May 27, 1969, 36.

216 "less and less successful": McPherson OH, Jan. 16, 1969, 1.

216 "You just tell these reporters": Califano, *Triumph and Tragedy of Lyndon Johnson*, 165.

216 atmosphere of diminishing trust: Memorandum, McPherson to LBJ, Nov. 30, 1965; Memorandum, Carol Welch to Secretaries to the Special Assistants, June 21, 1966, "Press Talks," box 32, Office Files of McPherson.

217 thinly camouflaged contempt: "White House Curbs on Newsmen Slowly Mount," *Los Angeles Times*, Jan. 16, 1966; "White House Drops Recording of Calls," *Los Angles Times*, Jan. 20, 1966.

217 "I did," Califano told him: Califano, *Triumph and Tragedy of Lyndon Johnson*, 172.

217 "it was still the general economic opinion": Schultze OH, April 10, 1969, 3–5.

217 "myth that education": Woods, *Prisoners of Hope*, 241.

217 McNamara informed the president: Ibid., 240; Matusow, *Unraveling of America*, 160; Schultze OH, April 10, 1969, 10–11.

218 role of budget director: Schultze OH, April 10, 1969, 49.

218 thankless task: Ibid., 12.

219 "He had no stomach for it": Robert Dallek, *Flawed Giant*, 249.

219 "Johnson pushed me": Califano, *Triumph and Tragedy of Lyndon Johnson*, 131.

219 jawboned labor and business: Robert Dallek, *Flawed Giant*, 305.

220 "within the administration": Davies, *From Opportunity to Entitlement*, 133.

220 "complicated and difficult problem": Robert Dallek, *Flawed Giant*, 307.

220 "nickel-and-dime": Schultze OH, April 10, 1969, 24.

221 "great expectations": Davies, *From Opportunity to Entitlement*, 108–9.

221 sharp memorandum: Graham, *Uncertain Triumph*, 129, 139.

222 "not closing the door": Memorandum, McPherson to Moyers, Dec. 13, 1965, "Bill Moyers," box 51, Office Files of McPherson.

222 pressure from powerful liberals: Califano, *Triumph and Tragedy of Lyndon Johnson*, 111–12.

222 Johnson snapped: Ibid., 142.

222 **the unemployment rate:** "Consumer Price Index, 1913–," Federal Reserve Bank of Minneapolis; "Labor Force Statistics from the Current Population Survey," Bureau of Labor Statistics, Department of Labor.

222 **"was taking a toll on his credibility":** Califano, *Triumph and Tragedy of Lyndon Johnson*, 143.

222 **many stalwart defenders:** Cater OH, May 26, 1974.

223 **"tired and disheartened":** Telegraph, Moyers to LBJ, Dec. 1965, "Poverty," box 7, Office Files of Califano.

223 **"take a rather sizeable":** Memorandum, Shriver to LBJ, Dec. 22, 1967, "Memos to the President, 12/22–12/31/1967," box 8, Office Files of Califano.

223 **implored the president:** Gillette, *Launching the War on Poverty*, 206.

224 **"a lot of the Congressional dissatisfaction":** Memorandum, McPherson to Moyers, July 22, 1966, "Press Talks," box 32, Office Files of McPherson.

224 **"massive school building program":** Memorandum, McPherson to Moyers, June 29, 1966, "Press Talks," box 32, Office Files of McPherson.

224 **"there was no reason to believe":** Memorandum, McPherson to George Christian, Dec. 28, 1966, "Press Talks," box 32, Office Files of McPherson.

225 **"move in liberal circles":** Memorandum, Califano to Busby, June 22, 1965, "Joe Califano," box 18, Office Files of Busby.

225 **stony resistance:** Lemann, *Promised Land*, 187.

225 **"How nice it is to have":** Unger, *Best of Intentions*, 202.

225 **"neurotic and demagogic":** Memorandum, McPherson to Moyers, Oct. 10, 1965, "Bill Moyers," box 51, Office Files of McPherson.

225 **"a beautiful and creative":** Memorandum, McPherson to Moyers, July 18, 1966, "Press Talks," box 32, Office Files of McPherson.

225 **"Stable, rapid, noncyclical, noninflationary":** Collins, *More*, 59–60.

226 **"Let no one doubt":** Ibid., 55–57, 58.

226 **"snot-nosed little son-of-a-bitch":** Shesol, *Mutual Contempt*, 66.

226 **"sonny boy":** Ibid., 34.

226 **"you've got to learn to handle":** Evan Thomas, *Robert Kennedy: His Life* (New York: Simon & Schuster, 2000), 96.

227 **"Lyndon Johnson has compared":** Caro, *Passage of Power*, 106.

227 **"just awful . . . inexcusable":** Ibid., 247.

227 **"we just insulted":** Shesol, *Mutual Contempt*, 104–5.

228 **"Bobby symbolized everything":** Caro, *Passage of Power*, 249.

228 **"When this fellow looks":** Ibid., 228.

228 **"I don't understand you":** Ibid., 229.

229 **"Our President was a gentleman":** Ibid., 243.

229 **"always afraid of Bobby":** Ibid., 246.

229 **"What does [Johnson] know":** Shesol, *Mutual Contempt*, 176.

229 **"It's too little":** Lemann, *Promised Land*, 187.

230 **The empathy was real:** Shesol, *Mutual Contempt*, 130–31.

230 **"not want to upset the entire program":** Ibid., 300.

230 attempted to find middle ground: Ibid., 265–67, 289–90.

231 his seeming dual loyalty: Ibid., 291–92.

231 KENNEDY: HAWK, DOVE, OR CHICKEN: Schlesinger, *Robert Kennedy and His Times*, 2:836.

232 It did not escape LBJ: Shesol, *Mutual Contempt*, 296–99.

232 "interesting parallels": "No. 2 Texan in the White House," *New York Times*, April 3, 1966.

232 urged Johnson essentially to ignore RFK: Memorandum, McPherson to LBJ, June 24, 1965, "RFK," box 21, Office Files of McPherson.

233 the president's obsession with Kennedy: Shesol, *Mutual Contempt*, 357–61.

234 official visit to Paris: "Kennedy 'Signal' Echoes in Capitol," *New York Times*, Feb. 12, 1967.

234 "your State Department": Shesol, *Mutual Contempt*, 366–67.

Chapter 11: Backlash

236 evening of August 11: Califano, *Triumph and Tragedy of Lyndon Johnson*, 61–63.

237 ghetto conditions: Zeitz, *White Ethnic New York*, 148–52; Jackson, *Crabgrass Frontier*, 203–18; Patterson, *Grand Expectations*, 30–31.

239 "I would just like to say": Davies, *From Opportunity to Entitlement*, 149.

239 George Meany: Kotlowski, *Nixon's Civil Rights*, 90–93.

239 liberal bastions like New York City: Wilder, *Covenant with Color*, 169, 173; Freeman, *Working-Class New York*, 180–81; Glazer and Moynihan, *Beyond the Melting Pot*, 30–31.

239 "commodity riots": Cohen, *Consumers' Republic*, 376–80.

240 They saw minority neighborhoods: Jonathan Rieder, *Canarsie: The Jews and Italians of Brooklyn Against Liberalism* (Cambridge, Mass.: Harvard University Press, 1985), 24, 83.

240 national crime rate increased: Walsh, "Stretching His Arms Out to Either Side," 7.

240 annual murder rate: Mason, *Richard Nixon and the Quest for a New Majority*, 21.

241 rights of the accused: Lewis, *Gideon's Trumpet*.

241 Other rulings: Jenkins, *Decade of Nightmares*, 42–44.

241 Aid to Families with Dependent Children: Davies, *From Opportunity to Entitlement*, 25.

241 rolls almost doubled: Patterson, *Grand Expectations*, 672–73; Piven and Cloward, *Regulating the Poor*, 321–38; Jackson and Johnson, *Protest by the Poor*, 75–207; Patterson, *Freedom Is Not Enough*, 96.

242 "We've got to end this": Califano, *Triumph and Tragedy of Lyndon Johnson*, 51.

243 constituent mail: Perlstein, *Nixonland*, 107.

243 Douglas's home state was ground zero: Ibid., 117–20.

244 "We mostly talked about civil rights": Memorandum, McPherson to Moyers, Aug. 15, 1966, "Press Talks," box 32, Office Files of McPherson.

244 a correspondent for *Time:* Memorandum, McPherson to Moyers, Sept. 20, 1966, "Press Talks," box 32, Office Files of McPherson.

245 "Who is responsible for the breakdown": "If Mob Rule Takes Hold," *U.S. News & World Report,* Aug. 15, 1966.

245 "Last summer I went to Mississippi": Anderson, *The Movement and the Sixties,* 87.

246 Prior to World War II: Ibid., 95.

246 "They always seem to be wanting": Ibid., 97.

246 *in loco parentis:* Ibid., 99.

247 feeling of oppression: Ibid., 101.

247 2.5 million men served: Appy, *Working-Class War,* 17–18.

247 Roughly 25 percent: Ibid., 24–26.

248 "When I was in high school": Baker, *Nam,* 13.

248 Among enlisted men who fought: Appy, *Working-Class War,* 28.

248 Unemployment rates for young men: Ibid., 45.

248 "You try to get a job": *New York Times,* July 12, 1967, 4.

248 "I was in school": Appy, *Working-Class War,* 46–47.

248 "Most poor and working-class kids": James Lafferty, "No Draft Board Ever Failed to Meet Its Quota," in Appy, *Patriots,* 165.

249 Because of the built-in bias: For a more positive view of the Selective Service System, see Flynn, *Draft,* 188–223.

249 Where a man lived: Appy, *Working-Class War,* 12–14.

249 compulsory national service: Memorandum, McPherson to Califano, Nov. 12, 1965, "Califano," box 50, Office Files of McPherson.

249 ended the deferment system: U.S. Department of Commerce, Bureau of the Census, "Vietnam Conflict—U.S. Military Forces in Vietnam and Casualties Incurred: 1961 to 1972," table 590, 369.

249 "most people in the middle": Memorandum, McPherson to George Christian, May 12, 1967, "Press Talks," box 32, Office Files of McPherson.

249 "Here were these kids": Rieder, *Canarsie,* 157.

249 "I'm bitter": Coles, *Middle Americans,* 131–34.

250 "You won't have Nixon to kick around": Small, *Presidency of Richard Nixon,* 22.

250 During his eight years in office: Perlstein, *Nixonland,* 72.

251 "I don't know, I've never played": Darman, *Landslide,* 133.

251 Yet Reagan had been an avid student of politics: Ibid., 137.

251 "If you and I don't do this": Ibid., 143.

252 "How much are they paying you": Evans, *Education of Ronald Reagan,* 63.

252 "California is the most populous state": Darman, *Landslide,* 311.

252 "We've just got to go after him": Ibid.

252 "If anyone chooses to vote": Perlstein, *Nixonland,* 113.

252 He avoided Goldwater's angry dogmatism: Darman, *Landslide,* 295, 312.

253 "I disagree with almost everything": Perlstein, *Nixonland,* 113.

253 adroit at channeling backlash: Ibid., 71, 83, 113.

253 "one of the great victories": Matthew Dallek, *Right Moment,* 51.

254 **Proposition 14:** Perlstein, *Nixonland*, 91–92.

254 **On September 14:** Matusow, *Unraveling of America*, 207.

254 **"Go . . . into any home":** Ibid., 214.

255 **"Now the wraps are off ":** Darman, *Landslide*, 289.

255 **By 1966, a small but influential group:** Steinfels, *Neoconservatives*.

255 **Daniel Patrick Moynihan:** Patterson, *Freedom Is Not Enough*, 11–13, 15.

256 **critical of Aid to Families with Dependent Children:** Ibid., 11–13, 15–17.

257 **Of equal inspiration:** Ibid., 28–35.

257 **controversial and flawed report:** Ibid., 54–55.

258 **equality of outcome:** McPherson, *Political Education*, 343.

259 **how to handle the report:** Patterson, *Freedom Is Not Enough*, 47–63.

259 **took great umbrage:** McPherson, *Political Education*, 342–43.

260 **growing skepticism:** Unger, *Best of Intentions*, 195; Davies, *From Opportunity to Entitlement*, 97–102.

261 **challenge to the intellectual foundation:** Andrew, *Lyndon Johnson and the Great Society*, 124–28.

263 **a multifront war:** Unger, *Best of Intentions*, 157–58.

263 **Shriver's handwritten resignation:** Stossel, *Sarge*, 452–67.

Chapter 12: You Aren't a Man in Your Own Right

265 **"extremely demanding":** "Working for Johnson Is Hard but Rewarding."

265 **"more important than a valet":** Roberts, *LBJ's Inner Circle*, 82.

265 **"You didn't take work home":** Valenti OH, March 3, 1971, 32.

266 **"the most stereotyped image":** "The Transition Over," *New York Times*, June 13, 1965.

266 **"When the crunches came":** Valenti OH, July 12, 1972, 32.

266 **"What the hell did you say":** Valenti, *Very Human President*, 94–97.

267 **"love-that-boss":** "It's Open Season on LBJ."

267 **Motion Picture Association of America:** "How Valenti Hit the Jackpot," *Boston Globe*, May 8, 1966.

267 **summoning him to Manila:** Valenti, *Very Human President*, 252–57.

268 **"admired Lyndon Johnson":** Goldman, *Tragedy of Lyndon Johnson*, 122–23.

268 **"probably the single greatest influence":** Kalman, *Abe Fortas*, 224.

269 **"provide our people":** Ibid., 215.

269 **"It seems to me I'm on opposite sides":** McPherson OH, Jan. 16, 1969, 29.

269 **persuaded Fortas to accept:** Kalman, *Abe Fortas*, 243–45.

270 **"The President has got too much respect":** McPherson OH, Jan. 16, 1969, 29–30.

271 **extraordinary even by contemporary standards:** Califano, *Triumph and Tragedy of Lyndon Johnson*, 160–63.

271 **stringent anticrime bill:** Ibid., 153–54.

272 **"I was intimidated by the stature":** McPherson OH, April 9, 1969, 15–16.

272 **"We on the White House staff":** "No. 2 Texan in the White House."

272 modern-day "Elmer Gantry": Goldman, *Tragedy of Lyndon Johnson*, 109.

272 "a rather unfortunate predilection to flattery": Reedy OH, Dec. 20, 1968, 32.

272 "They made it appear": McPherson OH, Jan. 16, 1969.

273 "developed a relationship": "No. 2 Texan in the White House."

273 "Moyers was always undercutting somebody": Jacobsen OH, May 27, 1969, 33-36.

273 "He's way out in front": "No. 2 Texan in the White House."

273 "ideal press secretary": Ibid.

274 "by far the best man": "Bill Moyers: President Johnson's Strong 'Right Hand' Draws High Praise—Harsh Criticism," *Austin American-Statesman*, Feb. 13, 1966.

274 "would sometimes be better advised": "The President and the Press," *New York Times*, Feb. 28, 1966.

274 "convenience of the President": "Moyers Explains the News Parley," *New York Times*, Jan. 1, 1966.

275 replacement as press secretary: "Press Aide Moyers Seeking Replacement," *Boston Globe*, Jan. 26, 1966.

275 reshuffle was maddening: "LBJ Names Rostow, Kintner Special Assistants," *Chicago Tribune*, April 1, 1966; "Moyers on the Way Up," *Los Angeles Times*, April 5, 1966.

275 With clear ambition: "Moyers to Give Up His Press Duties," *Los Angeles Times*, April 2, 1966; "Moyers Back in Office as Press Secretary," *Los Angeles Times*, Sept. 11, 1966.

275 served to poison further his relationship: Valenti, *Very Human President*, 250-51.

275 At a dinner party: Ibid., 358-59.

276 "intelligent social conscience": "The Dozen Faces of LBJ," *Washington Reporter*, Jan. 24, 1965.

276 "fairly near a snapping point": McPherson OH, Jan. 16, 1969, 2.

276 In late September, his older brother: "Moyers' Death Laid to Drugs," *Austin Statesman*, Sept. 21, 1966.

276 "once-close personal relationship": Christian, *President Steps Down*, 12.

276 "His ambition": Jacobsen OH, May 27, 1969, 35.

276 "I don't think the President cried": Ibid., 36.

277 "it is always a mistake". Kalman, *Abe Fortas*, 224.

277 "inhaling other secretaries": Jacobsen OH, May 27, 1969, 35.

277 a crack staff: Graham, *Uncertain Triumph*, 132-33; Christian, *President Steps Down*, 13.

278 "rational concept": McPherson, *Political Education*, 254.

278 It required skillful negotiations: Graham, *Uncertain Triumph*, 148-49.

278 compromise set of amendments: Andrew, *Lyndon Johnson and the Great Society*, 109-11.

278 administration was even less successful: Perlstein, *Nixonland*, 197-98.

279 "the great Detroit-style wars": Fred Panzer, "Draft," May 4, 1967, "Politics Folder," box 30, Office Files of McPherson.

279 Califano left a considerable mark: Robert Dallek, *Flawed Giant*, 313-14.

280 "Unzip your fly": Califano, *Triumph and Tragedy of Lyndon Johnson*, 122-26.

280 a singular accomplishment: Robert Dallek, *Flawed Giant*, 314–17.

281 "operated a very extensive network": McPherson OH, April 9, 1969, 2.

281 "desultory way of getting information": McPherson, *Political Education*, 375.

282 "My job was to make staying with it": Ibid., 327.

282 "steady hand on an erratic wheel": McPherson OH, Jan. 16, 1969, 4–5.

282 "peace of mind": Christian, *President Steps Down*, 14.

282 "matter what kind of a majority": McPherson, *Political Education*, 268.

Chapter 13: The Thirty-first of March

283 500,000 American troops: U.S. Department of Commerce, Bureau of the Census, "Vietnam Conflict—U.S. Military Forces in Vietnam and Casualties Incurred: 1961 to 1972," table 590, 369.

283 "all people talked about": Sandbrook, *Eugene McCarthy*, 163.

283 Johnson's approval rating plummeted: Ibid., 164.

283 accelerated his political activities: Small, *Presidency of Richard Nixon*, 23.

283 emerged as a leading contender: Ambrose, *Nixon*, 84–87, 100.

283 "a born loser": Memorandum, Cater, Ben Wattenberg, and Ervin Duggan to LBJ, Aug. 19, 1967, "Memos to the President, 8/67," box 17, Office Files of Cater.

284 "I believe we are going to have": White, *Making of the President, 1968*, 121–22.

285 "New forces were changing the country": Ibid., 123.

285 Allard K. Lowenstein: Ibid., 83–85.

286 lazy and diffident candidate: Sandbrook, *Eugene McCarthy*, 176–77, 194.

287 Tet Offensive: Matusow, *Unraveling of America*, 391.

287 his young staff and volunteers: White, *Making of the President, 1968*, 95–99.

288 stunning near upset: Matusow, *Unraveling of America*, 392.

288 "I think I can get the nomination": White, *Making of the President, 1968*, 102.

289 "We woke up": Ibid., 103, 183–89.

289 McPherson outlined his understanding: Memorandum, McPherson to LBJ, March 18, 1968, "Memos for the President 1968," box 53, Office Files of McPherson.

290 The president's other aides: White, *Making of the President, 1968*, 128–37.

291 "I was jubilant": Busby, *Thirty-first of March*, 9.

292 "I want out of this cage": Ibid., 194, 214, 225.

293 "The world has never been": Small, *Presidency of Richard Nixon*, 31.

293 over two-thirds of primary voters: Sandbrook, *Eugene McCarthy*, 212.

293 only fifteen states: Edsall and Edsall, *Chain Reaction*, 92.

293 Humphrey did not need: *New York Times*, June 2, 1968, E3.

293 fight and fracture: Patterson, *Grand Expectations*, 694.

293 several organized groups: Chester, Hodgson, and Page, *American Melodrama*, 579–80.

294 "I wasn't sentenced": Matusow, *Unraveling of America*, 416.

294 "left Vice President Humphrey": *New York Times*, Aug. 28, 1968, 32.

295 **"Fuck you"**: Matusow, *Unraveling of America*, 421.

295 **trailed Richard Nixon**: *Washington Post*, Sept. 28, 1969, G1. A poll taken between September 3 and September 7 gave Nixon 43 percent of the vote to 31 percent for Humphrey and 19 percent for Wallace.

295 **"Johnson saw the Court"**: Robert Dallek, *Flawed Giant*, 556.

295 **everything went wrong**: Ibid., 557–62.

297 **"Fortas's testimony was so misleading"**: Ibid., 562.

298 **"Nobody likes the present system"**: Memorandum, Wattenberg to Califano, Cater, and McPherson, Oct. 26, 1967, "Income Plans," box 30, Office Files of McPherson; Memorandum, Wattenberg to Califano, Feb. 9, 1967, "Califano," box 50, Office Files of McPherson.

298 **"courting danger"**: Joseph Califano, "Balancing the Budget, L.B.J. Style," *New York Times*, Dec. 31, 1995.

298 **exit polls showed**: Matusow, *Unraveling of America*, 392; Sandbrook, *Eugene McCarthy*, 184, 202.

299 **only 13 percent favored**: *New York Times*, Oct. 8, 1968, 36.

299 **"Tweedledee and Tweedledum"**: Kazin, *Populist Persuasion*, 240.

299 **"over-educated, ivory-tower folks"**: Matusow, *Unraveling of America*, 425.

299 **"You young people seem to know"**: Kazin, *Populist Persuasion*, 240.

299 **"ill-cut suits"**: Ibid., 235.

299 **"gritty nimbus of piety"**: Ibid., 240.

300 **"forgotten Americans"**: *Wall Street Journal*, Sept. 5, 1968, 12.

300 **respectable alternative**: *Washington Post*, Sept. 12, 1968, A2.

300 **"force a local community"**: Matusow, *Unraveling of America*, 428.

300 **"harsh and strident efforts"**: *Wall Street Journal*, Oct. 29, 1968, 20.

300 **"politics of happiness"**: Matusow, *Unraveling of America*, 405.

300 **"for every jail"**: Ambrose, *Nixon*, 184.

301 **"wall-to-wall"**: *Wall Street Journal*, Sept. 19, 1968, 1.

301 **In New Jersey**: *New York Times*, Sept. 13, 1968, 50.

301 **"The Wallace Labor Record"**: *New York Times*, Sept. 14, 1968, 14.

301 **trouble on the left**: *New York Times*, Sept. 2, 1968, 20; Matusow, *Unraveling of America*, 430.

301 **Nixon's position on Vietnam**: Ambrose, *Nixon*, 197.

301 **could afford to be vague**: Small, *Presidency of Richard Nixon*, 28.

301 **"risk for peace"**: Ambrose, *Nixon*, 197.

302 **"bombsy twins"**: Matusow, *Unraveling of America*, 434.

302 **"lower and middle-income Americans"**: Memorandum, Califano to Humphrey, Sept. 25, 1968, "Politics," box 30, Office Files of McPherson.

302 **"Where would we be if Nixon"**: Ibid.

303 **Nixon's lead shrank**: Ambrose, *Nixon*, 205.

303 **Johnson sprang a surprise**: Ibid., 211.

303 **Humphrey surged**: Ibid., 211–12.

303 "human equality": Matusow, *Unraveling of America*, 432.

303 Nixon's team met secretly: Ambrose, *Nixon*, 207–17.

304 "strengthened the hand": *New York Times*, Oct. 2, 1968, 24.

304 "clear that the American people": *Wall Street Journal*, Nov. 7, 1968, 20.

305 "Jesus, I think I would have": Sandbrook, *Eugene McCarthy*, 225.

305 "Even the Vice President's natural ebullience": Christian, *President Steps Down*, 181.

Conclusion

306 "I do understand power": McPherson, *Political Education*, 449–50.

306 assistants began looking for jobs: Christian, *President Steps Down*, 256–57.

306 "We shared a sense of relief": Califano, *Triumph and Tragedy*, 335.

307 "You're going to make some money": Ibid., 337–38.

308 "officially powerless": "Harry McPherson," *Washington Post*, Feb. 17, 2012.

308 "heart was on the right": Small, *Presidency of Richard Nixon*, 154.

308 Family Assistance Plan: Patterson, *America's Struggle Against Poverty*, 192–94; Hoff, *Nixon Reconsidered*, 115–19; Sandbrook, *Eugene McCarthy*, 233.

308 FAP proved a nonstarter: Sandbrook, *Eugene McCarthy*, 233–38.

309 business and political elites: Quadagno, "Race, Class, and Gender in the U.S. Welfare State"; Waddan, "Liberal in Wolf's Clothing."

309 poor people needed cash: Patterson, *America's Struggle Against Poverty*, 198–200.

309 "great question of the seventies": Train, "Environmental Record of the Nixon Administration," 185.

309 country watched with horror: Small, *Presidency of Richard Nixon*, 196–97.

310 Nixon asked Congress: Ibid., 196–200.

310 eighty thousand acres: Flippen, "Nixon Administration, Timber, and the Call of the Wild."

310 unexpected continuity: Hoff, *Nixon Reconsidered*, 84–88. See also McAndrews, "Politics of Principle."

310 worked with Attorney General John Mitchell: Kotlowski, *Nixon's Civil Rights*, 23–36.

310 "when funds are cut off": Kotlowski, "Nixon's Southern Strategy Revisited," 216.

311 "Philadelphia Plan": Kotlowski, *Nixon's Civil Rights*, 99; Hoff, *Nixon Reconsidered*, 90–93.

311 "goals and timetables": Hoff, *Nixon Reconsidered*, 90–94.

311 Equal Employment Opportunity Act: Thernstrom and Thernstrom, *America in Black and White*, 431–33.

311 "people who own their own homes": Kotlowski, *Nixon's Civil Rights*, 131.

311 Executive Order 11458: Dean Kotlowski, "Black Power—Nixon Style," 423.

312 "monumental task": Bryan, "Trump Is Officially Making an Economic Promise That Will Be Nearly Impossible to Keep."

313 the poorest quintile: Center on Budget Policy and Priorities, "A Guide to Statistics on Historical Trends in Income Inequality," Nov. 7, 2016.

313 *household* wages: Levy, *New Dollars and Dreams*, 1-8.

313 single-parent families: "How Poor Single Moms Survive," *Atlantic*, Dec. 1, 2015.

313 slipped out of the workforce: "More and More Americans Are Outside the Labor Force Entirely. Who Are They?," Pew Research Center, Nov. 14, 2014.

314 levels unseen since the 1920s: "A Guide to Statistics on Historical Trends in Income Inequality."

314 cut the poverty rate by 26 percent: U.S. Department of Health and Human Services, "2014 CMS Statistics," 1.

315 In later years, many political observers: Katznelson, *Fear Itself.*

316 "I'm without a car": McPherson OH, April 9, 1969, tape 3, 7.

317 "At this time [last year]": McPherson OH, Jan. 16, 1969, 3-4.

317 the president fired Califano: "Califano, Blumenthal Are Fired from Cabinet," *Washington Post*, July 20, 1979.

318 Busby retired to Southern California: "LBJ Adviser Horace 'Buzz' Busby Jr., 76, Dies."

319 Douglass Cater: "Douglass Cater Is Dead at 72; Educator and Presidential Aide."

319 Harry McPherson: "Harry C. McPherson, a Presidential Counsel, Dies at 82," *New York Times*, Feb. 17, 2012.

319 "Lyndon B. Johnson owned and operated": "Bill Moyers on LBJ and 'Selma,'" *Moyers & Company*, Jan. 15, 2015.

320 "sometimes amazed": Valenti OH, Mar. 3, 1971, 22.

320 "two of life's classic fascinations": Cowger and Markman, *Lyndon Johnson Remembered*, 34-35.

BIBLIOGRAPHY

Newspapers and Magazines

Atlanta Constitution
Atlantic
Austin American
Austin American-Statesman
Austin Statesman
Baltimore Sun
Boston Globe
Chicago Tribune
Christian Science Monitor
Esquire
Hartford Courant
Long Island Newsday
Los Angeles Times
Newsweek
New York Times
New York Times Magazine
Observer
South China Sunday Post-Herald
Time
Toronto Globe and Mail
U.S. News & World Report
Wall Street Journal
Washington Post
Washington Reporter

JFK Library

ORAL HISTORIES (OH)

Council of Economic Advisers, Aug. 1, 1964
David Hackett, July 22, 1970

LBJ Library

ORAL HISTORIES (OH)

Gardner Ackley
Horace Busby
Douglass Cater
Anthony Celebrezze
Clark Clifford
Abe Fortas
James Gaither
John Gardner
Kermit Gordon
Walter Heller
Jake Jacobsen
Walter Jenkins
Francis Keppel
Harry McPherson
Frank Mankiewicz
Lawrence O'Brien
Arthur Okun
George Reedy
Juanita Roberts
James Roche
James Rowe
Charles Schultze
Ivan Sinclair
Otis Singletary
Cecil Stoughton
Jule Sugarman
James Sundquist
Jack Valenti
Adam Yarmolinsky

MANUSCRIPT COLLECTIONS

Handwriting File
Office Files of Fred Bohen
Office Files of Horace Busby
Office Files of Joseph Califano
Office Files of Douglass Cater
Office Files of James Gaither
Office Files of Richard Goodwin
Office Files of Bertrand Harding
Office Files of Harry McPherson
Office Files of Bill D. Moyers

Office Files of Frederick Panzer
Office Files of George Reedy
Office Files of Ben Wattenberg
Statements of Lyndon B. Johnson
White House Central File, Speeches

Selected Works

Ambrose, Stephen E. *Nixon: The Triumph of a Politician, 1962–1972*. New York: Simon & Schuster, 1989.

Anderson, Terry H. *The Movement and the Sixties: Protest in America from Greensboro to Wounded Knee*. New York: Oxford University Press, 1996.

Andrew, John, III. *Lyndon Johnson and the Great Society*. Chicago: Ivan R. Dee, 1998.

Appy, Christian G. *Working-Class War: American Combat Soldiers in Vietnam*. Chapel Hill: University of North Carolina Press, 1993.

——, ed. *Patriots: The Vietnam War Remembered from All Sides*. New York: Viking, 2003.

Bailey, Martha J., and Sheldon Danziger, eds. *Legacies of the War on Poverty*. New York: Russell Sage Foundation, 2013.

Baker, Mark. *Nam: The Vietnam War in the Words of the Men and Women Who Fought There*. London: Abacus, 1982.

Berkowitz, Edward D. *Mr. Social Security: The Life of Wilbur J. Cohen*. Lawrence: University Press of Kansas, 1995.

Bernstein, Irving. *Guns or Butter: The Presidency of Lyndon Johnson*. New York: Oxford University Press, 1996.

Beschloss, Michael, ed. *Reaching for Glory: Lyndon Johnson's Secret White House Tapes, 1964–1965*. New York: Simon & Schuster, 2001.

Blakeslee, Jan. "The Community Action Program: A Stimulus to Black Political Leadership." Institute for Research on Poverty, Discussion Paper no. 493-78.

Bornet, Vaughn Davis. *The Presidency of Lyndon B. Johnson*. Lawrence: University Press of Kansas, 1983.

Branch, Taylor. *At Canaan's Edge: America in the King Years, 1965–1968*. New York: Simon & Schuster, 2006.

——. *Pillar of Fire: America in the King Years, 1963–1965*. New York: Simon & Schuster, 1998.

Bryan, Bob. "Trump Is Officially Making an Economic Promise That Will Be Nearly Impossible to Keep." *Business Insider*, Jan. 22, 2017.

Busby, Horace. *The Thirty-first of March: An Intimate Portrait of Lyndon Johnson's Final Days in Office*. New York: Farrar, Straus and Giroux, 2005.

Califano, Joseph A., Jr. *The Triumph and Tragedy of Lyndon Johnson: The White House Years*. New York: Simon & Schuster, 1991.

Caro, Robert A. *Master of the Senate*. New York: Knopf, 2002.

——. *Means of Ascent*. New York: Knopf, 1990.

——. *The Passage of Power*. New York: Vintage Books, 2012.

Carter, Dan T. *The Politics of Rage: George Wallace, the Origins of the New Conservatism, and the Transformation of American Politics*. New York: Simon & Schuster, 1995.

Chester, Lewis, Godfrey Hodgson, and Bruce Page. *An American Melodrama: The Presidential Campaign of 1968*. New York: Dell, 1969.

Christian, George. *The President Steps Down: A Personal Memoir of the Transfer of Power*. New York: Macmillan, 1970.

Cohen, Lizabeth. *A Consumers' Republic: The Politics of Mass Consumption in Postwar America*. New York: Knopf, 2003.

Coles, Robert. *The Middle Americans*. Boston: Little, Brown, 1971.

Collins, Robert M. *More: The Politics of Economic Growth in Postwar America*. New York: Oxford University Press, 2000.

Connolly, Harold X. *A Ghetto Grows in Brooklyn*. New York: New York University Press, 1977.

Cowger, Thomas W., and Markman, Sherwin, eds. *Lyndon Johnson Remembered: An Intimate Portrait of a Presidency*. New York: Rowman and Littlefield Publishers, 2003.

Dallek, Matthew. *The Right Moment: Ronald Reagan's First Victory and the Decisive Turning Point in American Politics*. New York: Oxford University Press, 2004.

Dallek, Robert. *Camelot's Court: Inside the Kennedy White House*. New York: Harper, 2013.

———. *Flawed Giant: Lyndon Johnson and His Times, 1961-1973*. New York: Oxford University Press, 1998.

Darman, Jonathan. *Landslide: LBJ and Ronald Reagan at the Dawn of a New America*. New York: Random House, 2015.

Davies, Gareth. *From Opportunity to Entitlement: The Transformation and Decline of Great Society Liberalism*. Lawrence: University Press of Kansas, 1996.

Edsall, Thomas Byrne, and Mary Edsall. *Chain Reaction: The Impact of Race, Rights, and Taxes on American Politics*. New York: W. W. Norton, 1991.

Engelhardt, Tom. *The End of Victory Culture: Cold War America and the Disillusioning of a Generation*. New York: Basic Books, 1995.

Evans, Thomas W. *The Education of Ronald Reagan: The General Electric Years and the Untold Story of His Conversion to Conservatism*. New York: Columbia University Press, 2007.

Flippen, John Brooks. "The Nixon Administration, Timber, and the Call of the Wild." *Environmental History Review* 19, no. 2 (Summer 1995): 37-54.

Flynn, George Q. *The Draft, 1940-1973*. Lawrence: University Press of Kansas, 1993.

Freeman, Joshua. *Working-Class New York: Life and Labor Since World War II*. New York: New Press, 2000.

Garrow, David. *Protest at Selma: Martin Luther King, Jr., and the Voting Rights Act of 1965*. New Haven, Conn.: Yale University Press, 1978.

Gillette, Michael L., ed. *Launching the War on Poverty: An Oral History*. New York: Oxford University Press, 2010.

Gillon, Steven M. *Boomer Nation: The Largest and Richest Generation Ever, and How It Changed America*. New York: Free Press, 2004.

———. *"That's Not What We Meant to Do": Reform and Its Unintended Consequences in Twentieth-Century America*. New York: W. W. Norton, 2000.

Glazer, Nathan, and Daniel Patrick Moynihan. *Beyond the Melting Pot: The Negroes, Puerto Ricans, Jews, Italians, and Irish of New York City*. Cambridge, Mass.: MIT Press, 1963.

Gluck, M. G., and Reno, V., eds., *Reflections on Implementing Medicare*. Washington, D.C.: National Academy of Social Insurance, January 2001.

Goldberg, Robert Alan. *Barry Goldwater*. New Haven, Conn.: Yale University Press, 1995.

Goldman, Eric. *The Tragedy of Lyndon Johnson*. New York: Alfred A. Knopf, 1969.

Goodwin, Richard N. *Remembering America: A Voice from the Sixties*. Boston: Little, Brown, 1988.

Graham, Hugh Davis. *The Civil Rights Era: Origins and Development of National Policy, 1960–1972*. New York: Oxford University Press, 1990.

———. *The Uncertain Triumph: Federal Education Policy in the Kennedy and Johnson Years*. Chapel Hill: University of North Carolina Press, 1984.

Halpern, Stephen. *On the Limits of the Law: The Ironic Legacy of Title VI of the Civil Rights Act of 1964*. Baltimore: Johns Hopkins University Press, 1995.

Hamby, Alonzo. *Beyond the New Deal: Harry S. Truman and American Liberalism*. New York: Columbia University Press, 1976.

Hansen, Alvin. "Economic Progress and Declining Population Growth." *American Economic Review* 29, no. 1 (March 1939).

Hardesty, Robert, ed. *The Johnson Years: The Difference He Made*. Austin, Tex.: Lyndon B. Johnson School of Public Affairs, 1993.

Harrington, Michael. *The Other America*. New York: Macmillan, 1962.

Herring, George C. *America's Longest War: The United States and Vietnam, 1950–1975*. Rev. ed. New York: McGraw-Hill, 1996.

———. *From Colony to Superpower: U.S. Foreign Relations Since 1776*. New York: Oxford University Press, 2008.

Historical Statistics of the United States, Colonial Times to 1970. New York: Cambridge University Press, 1997.

Hoff, Joan. *Nixon Reconsidered*. New York: Basic Books, 1994.

Hofstadter, Richard. *The Paranoid Style in American Politics, and Other Essays*. Cambridge, Mass.: Harvard University Press, 1996.

Jackson, Kenneth. *Crabgrass Frontier: The Suburbanization of the United States*. New York: Oxford University Press, 1987.

Jackson, Larry R., and William A. Johnson. *Protest by the Poor: The Welfare Rights Movement in New York City*. New York: New York City Rand Institute, 1973.

Janowitz, Morris. *The Last Half-Century: Societal Change and Politics in America*. Chicago: University of Chicago Press, 1978.

Jenkins, Philip. *Decade of Nightmares: The End of the Sixties and the Making of Eighties America*. New York: Oxford University Press, 2006.

Johnson, Lyndon. *Presidential Recordings*. 6 vols. Edited by Philip Zelikow, Ernest May, and Timothy Naftali. New York: W.W. Norton, 2006–2007.

Johnson, Robert David. *All the Way with LBJ: The 1964 Presidential Election*. New York: Cambridge University Press, 2009.

Johnson, Robert David, and David Shreve, eds. *Presidential Recordings Digital Edition: The Kennedy Assassination and the Transfer of Power*. Charlottesville: University of Virginia Press, 2014–.

Kabaservice, Geoffrey. *Rule and Ruin: The Downfall of Moderation and the Destruction of the Republican Party, from Eisenhower to the Tea Party.* New York: Oxford University Press, 2013.

Kalman, Laura. *Abe Fortas: A Biography.* New Haven, Conn.: Yale University Press, 1990.

Katznelson, Ira. *Fear Itself: The New Deal and the Origins of Our Time.* New York: Liveright, 2014.

Kazin, Michael. *The Populist Persuasion: An American History.* New York: Basic Books, 1995.

Keyssar, Alexander. *The Right to Vote: The Contested History of Democracy in the United States.* Rev. ed. New York: Basic Books, 2009.

Kotlowski, Dean J. *Nixon's Civil Rights: Politics, Principle, and Policy.* Cambridge, Mass.: Harvard University Press, 2001.

——. "Nixon's Southern Strategy Revisited." *Journal of Policy History* 10, no. 2 (1998).

——. "Black Power—Nixon Style: The Nixon Administration and Minority Business Enterprise," *Business History Review* 72, no. 3 (1998).

Kotz, Nick. *Judgment Days: Lyndon Baines Johnson, Martin Luther King Jr., and the Laws That Changed America.* Boston: Houghton Mifflin, 2005.

Kruse, Kevin M. *White Flight: Atlanta and the Making of Modern Conservatism.* Princeton, N.J.: Princeton University Press, 2005.

Lassiter, Matthew D. *The Silent Majority: Suburban Politics in the Sunbelt South.* Princeton, N.J.: Princeton University Press, 2006.

Lemann, Nicholas. *The Promised Land: The Great Black Migration and How It Changed America.* New York: Vintage, 1999.

Leuchtenburg, William. "A Visit with LBJ." *American Heritage,* May/June 1990.

——. *The White House Looks South: Franklin D. Roosevelt, Harry S. Truman, Lyndon B. Johnson.* Baton Rouge: Louisiana State University Press, 2007.

Levy, Frank. *The New Dollars and Dreams: American Incomes in the Late 1990s.* New York: Russell Sage Foundation, 1998.

Lewis, Anthony. *Gideon's Trumpet.* New York: Random House, 1964.

Lichtenstein, Nelson. *State of the Union: A Century of American Labor.* Princeton, N.J.: Princeton University Press, 2003.

McAndrews, Lawrence J. "The Politics of Principle: Richard Nixon and School Desegregation." *Journal of Negro History* 83, no. 3 (Summer 1998): 187–200.

McPherson, Harry. *A Political Education.* Austin: University of Texas Press, 1972.

Manchester, William. *The Death of a President: November 20–November 25, 1963.* New York: Harper & Row, 1967.

Mann, Robert. *The Walls of Jericho: Lyndon Johnson, Hubert Humphrey, Richard Russell, and the Struggle for Civil Rights.* New York: Harcourt Brace, 1996.

Marshall, Burke. *Federalism and Civil Rights.* New York: Columbia University Press, 1964.

Marty, Myron A. *Daily Life in the United States, 1960–1990: Decades of Discord.* Westport, Conn.: Greenwood Press, 1997.

Mason, Robert. *Richard Nixon and the Quest for a New Majority.* Chapel Hill: University of North Carolina Press, 2004.

Matusow, Allen J. *The Unraveling of America: A History of Liberalism in the 1960s.* New York: Harper & Row, 1984.

Milkis, Sidney M., and Jerome M. Mileur, eds. *The Great Society and the High Tide of American Liberalism.* Amherst: University of Massachusetts Press, 2005.

Miller, Merle. *Lyndon: An Oral Biography.* New York: G. P. Putnam's Sons, 1980.

Moyers, Bill D. "Second Thoughts: Reflections on the Great Society." *New Perspectives Quarterly* 4, no. 1 (Winter 1987).

Moynihan, Daniel P. *Maximum Feasible Misunderstanding: Community Action in the War on Poverty.* New York: Free Press, 1969.

Orfield, Gary. *The Reconstruction of Southern Education: The Schools and the 1964 Civil Rights Act.* New York: John Wiley & Sons, 1969.

Orfield, Gary, and John T. Yun. *Resegregation in American Schools.* Cambridge, Mass.: Harvard Civil Rights Project, 1999.

Orleck, Annelise, and Lisa Hazirjian, eds. *The War on Poverty: A New Grassroots History, 1964-1980.* Athens: University of Georgia Press, 2011.

Patterson, James T. *America's Struggle Against Poverty, 1900-1994.* Cambridge, Mass.: Harvard University Press, 1994.

——. *Brown v. Board of Education: A Civil Rights Milestone and Its Troubled Legacy.* New York: Oxford University Press, 2002.

——. *Freedom Is Not Enough: The Moynihan Report and America's Struggle over Black Family Life from LBJ to Obama.* New York: Basic Books, 2010.

——. *Grand Expectations: The United States, 1945-1974.* New York: Oxford University Press, 1996.

Pells, Richard. *The Liberal Mind in a Conservative Age.* Middletown, Conn.: Wesleyan University Press, 1989.

Perlstein, Rick. *Before the Storm: Barry Goldwater and the Unmaking of the American Consensus.* New York: Simon & Schuster, 2001.

——. *Nixonland: The Rise of a President and the Fracturing of America.* New York: Scribner, 2008.

Peters, Charles. *Tilting at Windmills: An Autobiography.* Boston: Addison-Wesley, 1990.

Piven, Frances Fox, and Richard Cloward. *Regulating the Poor: The Functions of Public Welfare.* New York: Vintage, 1971.

Quadagno, Jill. "Race, Class, and Gender in the U.S. Welfare Stare: Nixon's Failed Family Assistance Plan." *American Sociological Review* 55, no. 1 (Feb. 1990): 11-28.

Redmon, Coates. *Come as You Are: The Peace Corps Story.* New York: Harcourt, 1986.

Reedy, George. *The Twilight of the Presidency: From Johnson to Reagan.* Rev. ed. New York: New American Library, 1987.

Risen, Clay. *The Bill of the Century: The Epic Battle for the Civil Rights Act.* New York: Bloomsbury Press, 2014.

Roberts, Charles. *LBJ's Inner Circle.* New York: Delacorte Press, 1965.

Salinger, Pierre. *With Kennedy.* Garden City, N.Y.: Doubleday, 1966.

Samuelson, Robert J. "How Our American Dream Unraveled." *Newsweek,* March 1, 1992.

Sandbrook, Dominic. *Eugene McCarthy and the Rise and Fall of Postwar American Liberalism.* New York: Random House, 2004.

Schlesinger, Arthur M., Jr. *Journals, 1952-2000.* New York: Penguin Books, 2008.

——. *Robert Kennedy and His Times.* 2 vols. New York: Houghton Mifflin, 1978.

Self, Robert O. *American Babylon: Race and the Struggle for Postwar Oakland.* Princeton, N.J.: Princeton University Press, 2003.

Shesol, Jeff. *Mutual Contempt: Lyndon Johnson, Robert Kennedy, and the Feud That Defined a Decade.* New York: W. W. Norton, 1997.

Small, Melvin. *The Presidency of Richard Nixon.* Lawrence: University Press of Kansas, 1999.

Sokol, Jason. *There Goes My Everything: White Southerners in the Age of Civil Rights, 1945–1975.* New York: Random House, 2006.

Stanton, Mary, *From Selma to Sorrow: The Life and Death of Viola Liuzzo.* Athens: University of Georgia Press, 1998.

Stark, Steven D. *Glued to the Set: The 60 Television Shows and Events That Made Us Who We Are Today.* New York: Free Press, 1997.

Steinfels, Peter. *The Neoconservatives: The Men Who Are Changing America's Politics.* New York: Simon & Schuster, 1979.

Stevens, Robert, and Rosemary Stevens. *Welfare Medicine in America: A Case Study of Medicaid.* New York: Free Press, 1974.

Stossel, Scott. *Sarge: The Life and Times of Sargent Shriver.* New York: Other Press, 2011.

Sugrue, Thomas J. *The Origins of the Urban Crisis: Race and Inequality in Postwar Detroit.* Princeton, N.J.: Princeton University Press, 1996.

Sundquist, James L. *Politics and Policy: The Eisenhower, Kennedy, and Johnson Years.* Washington, D.C.: Brookings Institution, 1968.

Terry, Wallace. *Bloods: An Oral History of the Vietnam War by Black Veterans.* New York: Random House, 1984.

Thernstrom, Stephan, and Abigail Thernstrom. *America in Black and White: One Nation, Indivisible.* New York: Simon & Schuster, 1999.

Train, Russell E. "The Environmental Record of the Nixon Administration." *Presidential Studies Quarterly* 26, no. 1 (1996).

Unger, Irwin. *The Best of Intentions.* New York: Doubleday, 1996.

Updegrove, Mark K. *Indomitable Will: LBJ in the Presidency.* New York: Skyhorse, 2014.

———. "When LBJ and Goldwater Agreed to Keep Race out of the Campaign." *Politico,* Aug. 28, 2016.

U.S. Department of Commerce, Bureau of the Census. "Vietnam Conflict—U.S. Military Forces in Vietnam and Casualties Incurred: 1961 to 1972," table 590. In *Statistical Abstract of the United States, 1977.* Washington, D.C.: U.S. Department of Commerce, Bureau of the Census, 1980.

Valenti, Jack. *This Time, This Place: My Life in War, the White House, and Hollywood.* New York: Three Rivers Press, 2007.

———. *A Very Human President.* New York: W. W. Norton, 1975.

VanDeMark, Brian. *Into the Quagmire: Lyndon Johnson and the Escalation of the Vietnam War.* New York: Oxford University Press, 1995.

Waddan, Alex. "A Liberal in Wolf's Clothing: Nixon's Family Assistance Plan in the Light of 1990s Welfare Reform." *Journal of American Studies* 32, no. 2 (1998): 203–18.

Walsh, Elizabeth G. "Stretching His Arms Out to Either Side: Politics, Race, and the Rockefeller Drug Laws of 1973." Bachelor's thesis, Brown University, 2003.

Weissman, Jordan. "Here's Exactly How Much the Government Would Have to Spend to Make Public College Tuition-Free." *Atlantic,* Jan. 3, 2014.

White, Theodore H. *The Making of the President, 1968*. New York: Atheneum, 1969.

——. *The Making of the President, 1964*. New York: Atheneum, 1965.

Wilder, Craig Steven. *A Covenant with Color: Race and Social Power in Brooklyn*. New York: Columbia University Press, 2000.

Woods, Randall B. *LBJ: Architect of American Ambition*. Cambridge, Mass.: Harvard University Press, 2007.

——. *Prisoners of Hope: Lyndon Johnson, the Great Society, and the Limits of Liberalism*. New York: Basic Books, 2016.

Zeitz, Joshua. "Back to the Barricades." *American Heritage*, Oct. 2001.

——. "The Craziest Conventions in U.S. History." *Politico*, March 12, 2016.

——. *White Ethnic New York: Jews, Catholics, and the Shaping of Postwar Politics*. Chapel Hill: University of North Carolina Press, 2007.

Zelizer, Julian E. *Arsenal of Democracy: The Politics of National Security—from World War II to the War on Terrorism*. New York: Basic Books, 2012.

——. *The Fierce Urgency of Now: Lyndon Johnson, Congress, and the Battle for the Great Society*. New York: Penguin Press, 2015.

INDEX